PRODUCTION TECHNOLOGY
Industry Today and Tomorrow

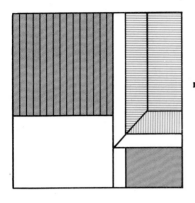

PRODUCTION TECHNOLOGY
Industry Today and Tomorrow

John L. Feirer
Distinguished Faculty Scholar
Western Michigan University

John R. Lindbeck
Professor
Engineering Technology Department
Western Michigan University

BENNETT & McKNIGHT PUBLISHING COMPANY
Peoria, Illinois

Bennett & McKnight Publishing Company
809 West Detweiller Drive
Peoria, Illinois 61615

86 87 88 89 90 RRD 5 4 3 2 1

ISBN 0-02-667590-0

Library of Congress catalog card number: 84-71308

Printed in the United States of America

Preface

Production Technology has been designed to help you learn more about modern industry. This book explains the important processes used to make the products you use every day. The book also discusses recent changes in industry. For example, motorcycles and television sets once were made mostly by hand. Today, they are designed and made using computers and robots.

Basic hand and tool skills are discussed in *Production Technology.* They are stressed because computer-aided manufacturing involves basic machining operations. The computer controls the machines. However, people with basic skills are needed to plan the work for the computer.

In this book, you will learn drafting and design skills. You will also learn some of the skills needed to work wood, metals, and plastics. You also will learn the rules of safety in the shop. You will learn to plan mass production operations. A section on construction also is included.

This book also includes several Key Ideas. They offer more information on important topics.

You may already be thinking about a career. In considering any career, remember that education is the key to obtaining a good job. Certain qualities are common to every career. To do any job well, you must develop good job skills. The development of such skills depends on three things: knowledge of the job being done, safe work habits, and the practice of economy. Economy means that there is little waste of time or material.

The job skills taught in *Production Technology* will help you develop good work habits. These work habits will be important to you in any career you many choose.

Acknowledgments

Many companies have aided the authors in their work on this book. The authors are especially grateful to the following for their assistance.

American Concrete Institute
American Iron and Steel Institute
American Plywood Association
Bell System News Features
Caterpillar Tractor Company
GBH-Way Homes, Inc.
Gulf Oil Company
International Nickel Company, Inc.
Miller-Davis Construction Company
Phillips Petroleum Company
Portland Cement Association
United States Steel Corporation
Western Electric News Features
Western Wood Products Association
Zinc Institute, Inc.

Developmental Editor: H. Wesley Coulter
Manuscript Editor: Ed Zempel
Production Manager: Gordon Guderjan
Layout: Carol Owen
Art: James Kasprzyk, Linda Verkler
Design: Ed Frank

TRW, Inc.

Table of Contents

Potlatch

Exxon

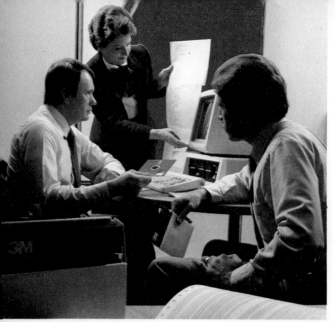

3M

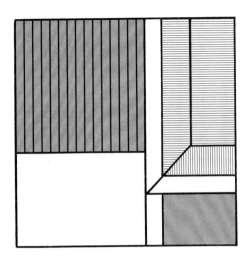

TECHNOLOGY AND OUR CHANGING WORLD

High Technology

You have probably heard the word *technology*. Today, the word is more commonly used than ever before. Technology is the use of science to achieve a practical purpose. A plow, for instance, is one example of technology. A plow is an example of the use of the lever and the wedge. The lever and the wedge are simple machines.

A machine is a tool. A tool makes good use of technology. By using tools, human beings have been able to improve their world. Tools have helped people change their world. At times, by changing their world, people have been able to make their lives easier.

The plow is one example of a valuable tool. There are several parts to a plow. The plowshare is that part of the plow that cuts into the soil. Basically, the plowshare is a wedge. The plow is an ancient tool. Over the centuries, the design of the plow has changed greatly. One particular change in plow design had an important effect on American life. It made possible the farming of the rich soil of the Midwestern prairie.

When pioneers first entered the Midwest, they found open prairie. The land was covered with tall grass. The sod was thick and tough. It was very hard for a horse or ox to pull a plow through this tough sod. In fact, the sod was so hard that it broke many plows.

The plow needed to be redesigned to break the tough sod of the prairie. An American inventor, John Deere, was responsible for the new plow design. Deere also introduced the first all-steel plow. This new plow design enabled farmers to work the rich black soil of the Midwest.

In the beginning of human history, all technology was simple. As we do, early humans needed food, shelter, and clothing. To obtain these, they changed the raw materials in their *environment*. The environment is all of the things around you. To make useful items from raw materials, early humans needed tools. The first tools were simply sticks and stones. After some time, humans learned to make rough tools from stones. You may have seen flint arrowheads and stone ax heads. These arrowheads and ax heads are examples of tools made from stones.

Technology is changing the entire world. In some countries, complex technology is already in common use. In other nations, complex technology has just been introduced. In developing nations, the use of such technology will become more important. In some instances, it will enable those countries to increase their production of goods.

Tools have been important in human history. In fact, some early periods of human history have been named for the materials used to make the tools of that period. Thus, there has been the Stone Age, the Bronze Age, and the Iron Age. This does not mean that stone tools were not made during the Bronze Age. Neither does it mean that bronze tools were not made during the Iron Age. The names mean that during that time humans learned to make tools from a particular material.

In each of these ages, technology advanced. In the Bronze Age, humans learned to make tools from bronze. Bronze is a mixture of copper and tin. A bronze tool is usually stronger than a stone tool. In the Iron Age, humans learned to smelt iron from iron ore. (Ore is rock with metal in it.) In *smelting*, ore is heated to release the pure metal. Thus, iron ore is heated to obtain iron. The iron was then used to make tools. As stronger tools were developed, humans gained more control of their environment.

In the centuries since, technology has developed rapidly. In the eighteenth-century, technology was used to build factories. In our own time, these factories have used technology to mass-produce products. In producing any product, industry changes raw materials into usable goods. To change a raw material into a usable product, technology is usually needed.

Look around the classroom at the various items in the room. All of the objects you see have been made from materials taken from the earth. Those items made of wood have been made from trees. Those items made of metal have been made from the metal obtained from metal ore. Trees and metal ore are two examples of *natural resources*. Natural resources are the raw materials of industry.

Courtesy Shopsmith, Inc.

Woods, metals, and plastics are used in the manufacture of most of the items we now use. The items shown here may seem simple. The design and manufacture of each of them, however, requires several steps. Each of these steps must be carefully planned. In the making of any object, large or small, attention to detail is important.

3M Company

Our age might be called the "Age of the Computer." Because it can store information easily, the computer can replace bulky storage cabinets. It also can organize information. It can, for example, alphabetize a list of several thousand names. The increasing use of the computer as a valuable tool in business and industry has created many new jobs. There are, for example, computer programmers. These people set up a computer to provide the services the user will need. There also are computer operators. As shown here, these people are responsible for the day-to-day operations of the computer.

You can easily see that natural resources must be changed before we can use them. The wood from a tree, for example, must be cut and smoothed before it can be used to make a table. To release its metal, ore must be heated to a high temperature. The metal that is obtained can then be used to make the various metal items you use every day.

Both of these examples are quite simple. The wood in trees and the metal in metal ore must be processed before they can be used.

Xerox

The computer is perhaps the most obvious example of high technology. It has been perfected in just the last few years. Already, it is finding valuable uses in the high-technology industries. The photo here shows the final assembly of word processor printers.

When a material is processed, it is changed. For example, there are many steps in making a table from a tree. The steps needed to make a metal item from the metal in metal ore are more difficult. In each case, though, technology is used to change a raw material into a useful product.

We often think of technology as being complicated. Some technologies are complicated. The technology used to shape metal is somewhat complicated, for example. However, the technology used to shape wood using hand tools is somewhat simple. In the beginning of human history, there were only simple technologies. Today there are simple technologies and complex technologies. Some of the complex technologies are used in certain industries. We have come to call some of these industries high-technology (or "high-tech") industries. They are called "high-tech" industries because they use complex technologies. The computer industry, for example, is a high-tech industry.

High technology uses advanced machines and materials. High technology is used in the mass-production of goods. For example, computer-driven machines can turn out large quantities of high-quality goods. Robots are used to make some of these products. Robots can do complex welding operations. They can maintain an almost perfect level of quality.

High technology uses raw materials. For example, we may soon have a lightweight plastic automobile engine. Parts of other engines will have ceramic parts to withstand high temperatures.

Today we are surrounded by inventions of modern industry and technology. These are changing the way we live, work, and play. On the following pages you will see several examples of this high technology. You also will learn something about the various careers in high technology.

Technology Literacy

A person who is literate is one who is able to read and write. Every country of the world has, then, a literacy rate. This rate is the

3M Company

Not all of us will work with the new high technology. For many of us, our knowledge of high technology will depend on our jobs. The designers shown here are discussing the color variations in the images shown on the color monitors. The maintenance of such equipment requires skilled workers.

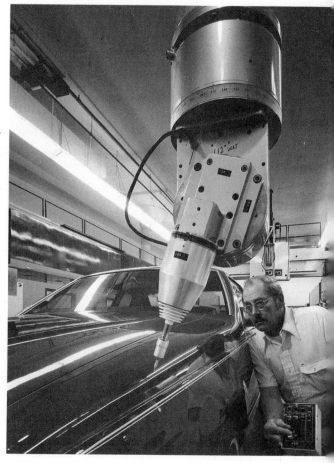

Ford Motor Company

In industry, high technology is used in product design. The car shown here is not an actual car. Rather, it is a clay model of a new design. The scanner to the right of the car traces the shape of the clay model. The information gathered is stored in computers. Later, this information can be used to make engineering drawings. The information can also be used to make the many tools that will be needed to mass-produce the car. The scanner is operated by the technician shown here. A set of electronic controls enables him to guide the probe carefully over the surface of the clay model.

number of people in the country who can read and write. Recently, the word *literacy* has been applied to areas other than reading and writing. For example, you may have heard of the term *computer literacy*. You may also have heard of *technology literacy*. Here, the word *literacy* refers to the knowledge that a person has of a particular subject. In this case, the subjects are computers and technology.

Our society is a technological society. This means that it depends heavily on technology. To understand technology, you must have *technology literacy*. Technology literacy means that a person understands the principles of how mechanical things work. The person also may understand how to fix them when they don't work. This ability to repair mechanical objects is often called *mechanical aptitude*. You may have used your mechanical aptitude when you repaired a bicycle or fixed a lawnmower. You also develop mechanical aptitude when you work on certain crafts or hobbies.

The skills needed in today's industry are often not simply mechanical skills. Because technology is now more complex, different

In industry, high technology is used in manufacturing. Here, a complex machining system is shown. This system is controlled by a computer program. This program tells the machine exactly what to do. The computer program ensures that the tool operations will be done quickly and accurately. The technician responsible for the machine's operation is shown in the foreground.

skills are needed. Many of us may not need to learn the skills needed to operate the various complex machines of our age. Most of us, for example, will never work with robots or lasers. Many of us, however, will work with computers. A few of you may already have a computer in your home. Regardless, modern technology will affect the way we live and work. An understanding of how computers work can help us become technologically literate. There are several reasons for developing sound basic knowledge of computers and the other complex tools of our time. Technological literacy will help us:

- To participate in the growth of technology.
- To measure the value of present and future technology. This will help us determine how effective it is.
- To control technology. This will help us prevent serious accidents.
- To evaluate decisions made by industry and government about technology.
- To apply technology to our jobs. Properly used, technology can make a job safer and more satisfying.
- To adapt to our changing world.

Not all of you will find jobs in which you work directly with new technologies. All of us, though, will feel the effect of such technologies. The more we know of recent inventions, the better we will be able to understand our world.

The Computer

At several points in human history, a single invention has changed the life of the people of that age. The wheel, the steam engine, the automobile, and the airplane are examples of such inventions. The invention that has had the greatest impact on life in our time has been the computer.

A computer can be used for many different jobs. Because of this, it is used in all areas of business. The computer is used by cashiers in the check-out lanes of our supermarkets. It is used by pilots to guide their airplanes. Technicians use computers to control robots in factories. Bankers use computers to keep track of your savings account. Librarians use computers to find books. You may use a computer in your classes in school. At home, you may use a computer to play games of skill. The computer is used by engineers and scientists to solve complicated problems.

The first computers were large, slow, and expensive. As computer technology developed, computers became smaller. They also became faster and more powerful. They became less expensive. Already, some have predicted that the computer will soon be as common as the television in the American homes. While this may not happen, it shows the effect the computer has had on our way of life.

Most of the products shown in the photos on these pages were made with the help of a

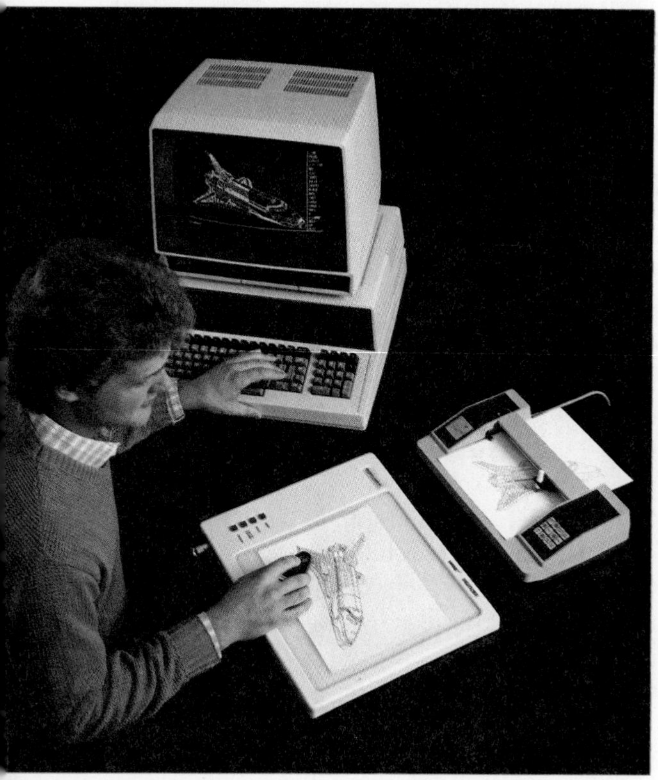

Heathkit/Zenith

The use of the computer has introduced new techniques to drafting. Computer-aided design (CAD) systems are used to design a wide range of products. The student shown here is analyzing the design of the Space Shuttle.

computer. As you can see, there is a broad range of products. The variety of products shows the many ways in which the computer can be used.

Computer Graphics

The computer is being used as a drafting and design tool. Computer-aided design (or CAD) systems allow drafters and engineers to design and dimension parts. This allows mechanical drawings of these parts to be made. This same computer graphics technology makes it possible to produce computer simulations of aircraft in flight. Airport runways can also be simulated. This allows pilots to practice night landings. Such scenes are accurate and very realistic. They permit the design and testing of systems without having to build them first. The CAD system also can be applied to the design and layout of factory

Ford Motor Company

Not only can the computer design parts—it also can test them. The engineer shown here programs the stresses that will affect the finished part. The weak places on the part will show in bright colors. The part will then be redesigned for added strength. The computer will be used to redesign the part.

Xerox
This color plotter can produce drawing-size prints rapidly and economically. These prints are a great aid to product designers. The plotter can produce prints up to 50 feet long.

equipment. It also can be used to analyze automobile traffic patterns.

Laser Technology

Laser technology is important today. It will become even more important in the future. The word *laser* is an acronym. (An acronym is a word made up of the first letter of each of several words.) For example, *laser* stands for *L*ight *A*mplification by *S*timulated *E*mission of *R*adiation.

A laser is a machine that strengthens a beam of light. Very simply, the laser produces narrow beams of intense light. It controls this light to do a variety of tasks. Lasers can weld, cut, heat-treat metal, and drill holes. They also can be used in sensitive eye-surgery. They can measure distances and transmit messages.

A laser can be carefully controlled. This is the feature that makes it so useful. For exam-

ple, one problem with welding is that the high heat can affect the metal workpieces being welded. This causes the workpieces to soften or become brittle. A laser can weld quickly. It can be directed to the joint so accurately that the character of the metal is not changed.

The laser is important in mass production. Laser tools can be used in an automated manufacturing system. They can be attached to robot arms. For example, a laser can cut intricate wooden furniture parts rapidly and accurately. Such parts could be sawn or stamped out using sharp cutting dies. Then, however, the cuts would not be clean. The parts would require further processing.

Racing Car Design

The design of today's automobiles would be impossible without technology. Most of us have ridden only in ordinary passenger cars. Few of us have ever ridden in a race car. Most

In pilot training, flight simulation is important. Flight simulation presents a pilot with the problems of an actual flight. In fact, sitting in the cockpit, the pilot has the feeling that he or she is in a real plane. Through the use of the computer an actual scene can be simulated just outside the window of the cockpit. Here, the pilots are shown in the flight simulator (above). Through the cockpit window, they see a lighted runway. (The runway is shown near the center of the window.) Another view of the runway is shown below. This view shows the runway as it would appear to the pilots as the plane is about to land. The dotted lines leading to the runway show the planned approach of the plane onto the runway.

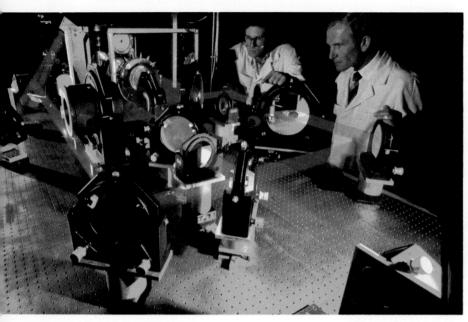

TRW
Advanced technology has developed high-energy lasers. These lasers have many uses. Here, a laser beam (shown in red) is being tested by two technicians.

of us, however, have seen such cars. It is easy to tell a race car from a passenger car. They have a shape different from that of a passenger car. Also, they are usually lower to the ground. They have bigger tires. They always have smoother lines.

Smooth lines are important on a racing car. Without a smooth body surface, the body of the car would resist the force of the air. The force of the air increases as the car goes faster.

Of course, if the car is to travel fast, it needs a smooth body. The racing car's body must not have surfaces that resist the flow of air over the car. Remember, racing cars travel at very high speeds, often close to 200 miles per hour. At these speeds, the force of the air is greatly increased. A body design that can smooth the flow of air over the car will increase the car's speed. Many high-speed auto races are very close. Often, the winning car is just seconds

Ford Motor Company
The design of any car requires careful work. A racing car travels at high speeds. Thus, it must have a smoother body than other cars. It also must have a stronger engine and a more effective braking system.

ahead of the second-place car. In some cases, the design of the car's body makes the difference between a winning car and one that loses.

Today, the bodies of racing cars are aerodynamically designed. Simply, this means that the car is designed to ease the flow of air over it.

A Mustang GTP racing car is shown here. This car was designed and built by Ford. Both automotive and aerospace engineers worked on the project. An aerodynamic body design was important for this racing car. To obtain this design, a computer-aided design system was used. This system helped the engineers find the body shape that would offer the least resistance to the air.

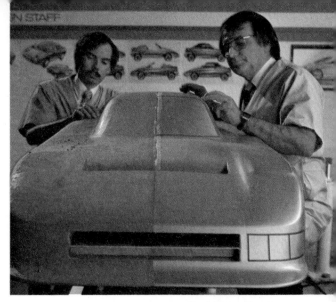

Ford Motor Company

The computer helps car designers in their work. Here, a clay model of a car is being prepared. This model will be tested to make sure that air will flow smoothly over its surface.

Here, the shape of the car appears to be outlined with wires. This is a drawing of the car. A model of the car was measured by an electronic scanner similar to the one shown on page 16. The measurements were then stored in a computer. The computer directs the pen over the drawing board. The car shown here is not the racing car shown on page 22. Nonetheless, the technique shown here can be used in the design of any type of car.

Ford Motor Company

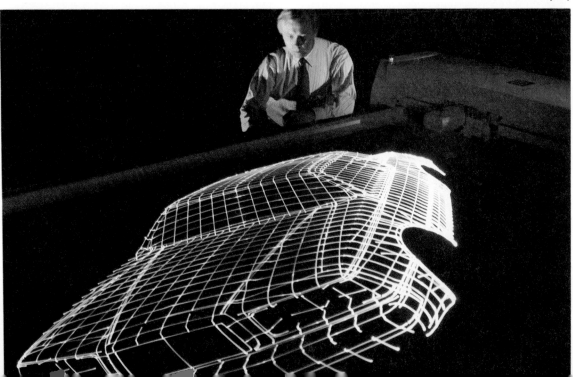

This car may never be placed in production. However, the design of such cars helps engineers in their work. By designing racing cars and cars such as the one shown here, engineers can learn much. They can gain new knowledge of materials. They can also learn more about airflow and the importance of smooth design.

The commercial aircraft industry has grown enormously. This growth has been aided by new discoveries regarding aircraft materials.

The body of the Mustang GTP is made of plastic and carbon-fiber materials. Both of these are lightweight. The car has a 1.7-liter turbocharged four-cylinder engine. This engine is in the front. The car has a rear-wheel drive. The Mustang GTP has an estimated top speed of 210 mph.

The car's design creates a vacuum beneath the car at high speeds. A vacuum is the absence of air. This vacuum helps to hold the car to the track. This is especially important. In fact, this feature allows the car to remain firmly on the track at very high speeds. This feature also helps the driver keep control of the car at high speeds.

Aerospace Technology

In our time, we have seen the birth of aerospace technology. This is the technology concerned with the design and manufacture of objects that are sent into outer space. Such objects travel in an environment different from that of the earth's atmosphere. Therefore, they must be designed to withstand unusual forces. In designing space vehicles and satellites, engineers have developed many new materials. Some of these materials are now used in the manufacture of airplanes. Many of the devices now found on the car were introduced in a similar way. They were first used in special situations and then adapted for regular use.

The automobile rear-view mirror is one example. We now think of a rear-view mirror as essential on a car. In fact, it is. However, it was developed for use in a special situation— the automobile raceway. The rear-view mirror was introduced years ago at the Indianapolis 500 race. Many of the advances in aircraft design and construction have come about in

RCA

There are many weather satellites orbiting our planet. Designed and built for years of use, these satellites are tested before launch. Here, a weather satellite is prepared for pre-launch testing. The satellite will be tested in a special test chamber. In this chamber, the satellite will be subjected to extremes of pressure. These temperatures and pressures will simulate those of Space.

the same way. They have resulted because materials were developed for use in special situations. Some of the new materials were developed for use in outer space.

The aerospace industry has developed several strong lightweight materials. Materials with these two qualities are desirable for use in space vehicles. In developing such materials, aerospace engineers have developed new materials for use on regular aircraft. They also have developed new aircraft construction techniques.

Modern commercial airplanes, for example, have many parts made of tough plastic. Various parts of the wing, rudder, and elevator are made of plastic. These plastic parts have replaced parts that were formerly made of metal. The plastic used is not ordinary plastic. Instead, it is a honeycomb sandwich made of graphite epoxy composite material. This provides a tough, stiff panel. The plastic is as strong as steel, but has only one-fourth the weight. This plastic is similar to that used in tennis rackets and skis.

Technology has improved aircraft design as well. Much has been learned about the way air flows over different shapes. This knowledge has been used to create new designs for wings and propellers. These new designs provide greater lift, more stability, and smoother flights.

Aircraft engines have also been improved. They are more quiet and more fuel-efficient. Their communications and guidance systems reflect the latest technologies. For example, modern airplanes have electronic controls, on-board computers, and radar guidance systems. All of these improvements have made flying safer and more enjoyable.

The Space Shuttle

In our time, the Space Shuttle has been perhaps the most dramatic evidence of the new technologies. It joined in one project several different sciences. Every system used in the Shuttle needed to be carefully de-

NASA
The Space Shuttle has been a triumph of technology. The construction of such a vehicle has called on the talents and abilities of many men and women. Here, the Space Shuttle is shown being readied for launch.

Robots are used in many manufacturing plants. Here, a battery of welding robots is shown in an automobile assembly plant. These robots are being used to make spot welds. When made by a robot, such welds are precisely placed and of consistently high quality.

signed. The purpose of the Shuttle required that its materials should be tough and lightweight. The engines were built to deliver tremendous thrust. The guidance system was the most complex ever built. Of course, the safe return of the Shuttle depended on the smooth operation of all its systems.

Many of the devices used on the Space Shuttle have been adapted for use in everyday life. There were, for example, miniature computers and communications devices. There were also space foods. These led to a broad range of new consumer products. As a result of the flight of the Space Shuttle, new photographic techniques also were developed.

Robotics

Robotics is the use of *robots* in industry. Robots are computerized devices that can be programmed to do many tasks. Often, these tasks are too boring for human beings to do again and again. Other times, the jobs may be too difficult or dangerous for humans to do. Robots are used in hot foundries and in smoky environments. Generally, they do jobs that human beings should not have to do. This is important to remember as more and more robots are used in industry.

Robots don't usually look like the cute little metal creatures seen in the movies. Instead, they are machines that have arms and hands. A robot can grip a nut, drill a hole, weld a seam, or turn a wrench. In the future, we will find even more uses for robots. They might, for example, be used for mining on the Moon or building structures in space.

For example, a robot can search for the starting point of a weld that will be made to join two workpieces. The robot can be programmed, or directed, to follow a certain weld path. The robot will do this again and again. Each time, it will produce a high-quality weld. A robot also can do hundreds of other industrial jobs. A robot, for example, can be used to spray-paint automobile bodies. Robots are used to place metal parts in heat-treating furnaces. Robots remove these same parts when the heat-treatment is completed.

The use of robots by industry has helped assure high quality in manufactured products. It has also reduced the risk to the human worker.

Superplastics

The use of plastic by industry has increased the number of consumer products available. Less expensive than wood or metal, plastic is also more lightweight. Generally, it is tougher than most metals. It is more easily shaped and formed than wood. Usually, it is less expensive. The increased use of plastic for consumer goods has made available a broad range of items.

Superplastics are used in a variety of consumer products. These new plastics are excellent for use in products that must be tough and lightweight. For example, the new plastics are used in football helmets and small boats. Toughness and light weight are needed in each of these products. A small boat, for example, must be able to withstand the pounding of the surf and waves. It also must be watertight. Plastic offers such protection. A football helmet must be strong to protect the head. For comfort, it also must be lightweight.

Besides being tough and lightweight, plastic has other advantages. Plastic is easily cleaned. It is colorful, waterproof, and shock resistant. It is easily adapted to automatic production.

The increased use of plastic has, however, created some problems. Plastic is cheap, lightweight, and tough. It does not rot as wood will. Neither does it rust or tarnish, as metal will. Its toughness is the quality that makes plastic so desirable for use in consumer products.

This toughness also prevents plastic from disintegrating. If buried in the ground, items made of wood or metal eventually will rot. This is not true of most plastic items. Certain plastics take hundreds of years to disintegrate. We have all seen plastic bottles discarded along our streets and highways. Millions more of these bottles are buried in dumps and trash heaps across the country. The use of plastic has certainly enabled us to create many new and useful products. However, as with many advances in technology, it has also created some problems.

Industry is continually searching for new uses for plastic. As the industry grows, it will need more people. For example, designers of plastic products will be required. The industry will also need those who are able to design the molds used to make plastic products. Plastic is a material of our century. As the

Fiber-optic systems are used in communication systems. Vast amounts of information can be sent over glass fibers thinner than a human hair.

TRW

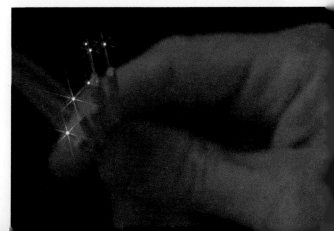

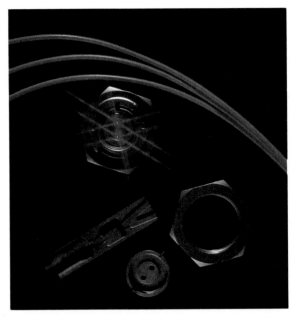

TRW

Work on fiber-optic systems has developed new connectors. Several fiber-optic connectors are shown here. These connectors are made of new lightweight materials. They will replace older, heavier connectors.

plastics industry continues to expand, career opportunities in the field will continue to grow.

Fiber Optics

The development of fiber optics is another example of the use of a new technology. You probably have heard of *optics*. This term relates to the passage of light through prisms. It also relates to the reflection of light by mirrors. Optical principles are used to design many scientific instruments, such as microscopes. Eyeglasses are perhaps the most common example of the use of optical principles.

Fiber optics is a new development in optics.

In fiber optics, glass or plastic fibers are used to transmit light. The use of these fibers enables light to be "bent." This "bending" of light has several advantages. Light can be directed around corners. For this reason, fiber optics are used in medical instruments. Some of these are used to examine the lining of the stomach. Without fiber optics, such medical examinations would be difficult, if not impossible. The principles of fiber optics also are used in designing communications systems.

Careers in Technology

On the past few pages, you have read of many new inventions. Perhaps you have become interested in the people who work with these inventions. Who are these people? What are their backgrounds? What type of training have they had for their careers?

One advantage of fiber-optic systems is their light weight and small size. A special core, here shown held between the finger and thumb, aligns the optical fibers. It also registers the signal transmitted between the fibers.

Polaroid

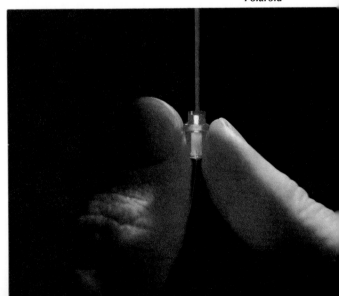

Xerox

Any job requires good communication skills. Through communication you are able to share your own knowledge with others. Careful listening and the asking of questions will help you draw on the experience of others. Thus, you can share in their knowledge. In high-tech fields, communication skills are especially important. The machines in use today are accurate and effective only when carefully controlled. In any job, a careful listener can gain valuable information from his or her co-workers.

The people working with these new technologies are educated and highly-skilled. They are aware of new developments in their field. They have good problem-solving skills. All of these qualities are needed to do a good job.

As you might imagine, there are many types of jobs in the new technologies. The photos you see on the next few pages show people at work in just a few of these jobs. One person is working in forestry science. A group of students are learning to program an industrial robot. Another person is editing the manuscript of a book on a word processor. These are only three of the job opportunities available. In any industry there will be a range of jobs available. For example, skilled people are needed to design a product. Product manufacture requires special training. The repair of a high-tech product is also important. Repairpersons must be able to work quickly and effectively.

The point of all this is that modern industry requires some people with high technology skills. It also requires people with "traditional" job skills. For example, not all printers will work in automated printing plants. Many will also be needed in smaller shops. Carpenters, machinists, drafters, electricians, and mechanics will always be in demand. Homes, cars, and appliances will always be in need of repair. Obviously, most jobs now and in the future *will not be* in high technology.

Technology has changed the way in which many jobs are now being done. Even the study of forestry has changed. Here, a forestry student is taking a core sample from a tree. This is not a new technique. However, forestry technicians now have more knowledge of growth cycles in trees. They also know more about soil and water conditions. This information helps them "read" the core sample more accurately. For example, by a careful examination of this sample, forestry technicians can know the age of a tree. They can also identify those years in which the winters were extremely cold. They can identify those years when the tree did not receive enough water.

ITT

Most of those seeking technical jobs will need special training. These students are enrolled at a technical school. There, they learn to program and operate industrial robots. The arm of one of these robots is shown here. As you can see, it is holding a light bulb. Properly controlled, industrial robots can handle even the most delicate objects.

Many people who work with the new technologies need not be technicians. This editor is working with a word processor. This tool enables her to edit the manuscript of a book on a computer screen. She can make changes in the manuscript by operating the keyboard of the word processor. In editing certain types of books, a tool such as the one shown here can save time.

As you begin to think of a career, remember that most jobs in high technology require some special training. As well as having special training, to maintain a career in high technology, you may have to change your job. You must recognize that your job might change several times throughout your career. Success in your career may depend on your willingness to change your job.

33

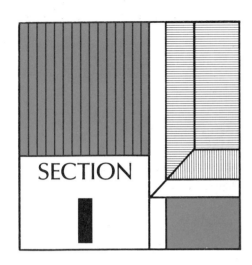

SECTION

Drafting

U.S. Department of Labor

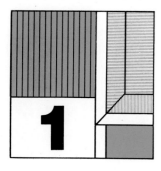

Basic Production

What Is an Industry?

An *industry* may be defined as an organization that produces goods or services. Goods are material things such as clothes and tools. Services are non-material items. For example, television and radio programs are services provided by the entertainment industry.

Think of the working men and women you know. How many of them have jobs related to one of the industries shown in Table 1-A? Many of them probably do. Most workers in the United States are employed in the production of goods and services.

We have not always had an industrial society. In past centuries most people worked at providing food. In some developing nations this is still true today. However, as farm machinery and methods have improved, fewer people are needed to work on farms. Many have given up farming to take jobs in industry.

The growth of industry has changed our society greatly. Not all of the changes have been good, however. Crowded cities and smog, for example, are problems related to industry. Still, most would agree that industry does far more good than harm to our society. Who would want to do without electricity,

automobiles, and modern plumbing? Today, because of industry, many people have the highest standard of living they have ever known.

Some of the problems connected with an industrial society are solved by industry. Con-

Table 1-A. Some Important Industries in the United States

Goods Producing		Services
Manufacturing	*Construction*	Advertising
Chemicals	Homes	Appliance
Raw materials	Commercial	repair
Food	buildings	Banking and
Transportation	Structures	finance
equipment	(Bridges,	Education
Communica-	TV towers,	Entertainment
tion equip-	etc.)	Food distri-
ment		bution
Power		Health
Consumer		Importing
products		Insurance
(non-food		Publishing
items, such		Sanitation
as clothing,		Shipping
furniture)		
Heavy ma-		
chinery		

1-1. The printed circuit board is one development of our time. Here, an electronic technician is correcting such a board. For many uses, though, such boards are outdated. In many cases, they have been replaced by the computer chip.

sider the example of air pollution. This is partly a result of factory smoke and automobile exhaust. Air pollution, though, is being relieved by air-purifying systems and automobile emissions controls developed by industry.

Throughout the centuries, people have tried to find better ways of producing goods and services. The resulting progress can be called industrial-technological advancement. This has resulted in progress toward the kind of life most people want. For example, many

dangerous factory jobs now are done by robots.

Historically, nations and societies have ceased to progress when they have been unable to provide the products that their people need and want. Thus the industrial efficiency reached today is important for keeping our society strong and healthy. Another name for this efficiency is *productivity*. This term refers to the ability to turn out a maximum of high-quality goods and services with a minimum of effort. Fig. 1-1. Skill and better tools and machinery make people more productive. For example, it takes much time and effort to dig a ditch using a hand shovel and a pick. With a power shovel, and the skill to use it, a person can dig a ditch faster, with far less effort. The same holds true for people working in factories. Better equipment, and the skill to use it, makes better workers. This is why productivity has increased over the years.

A nation may have great natural resources. Only when the resources are made useful to people do they add to a nation's prosperity. Thus, a nation's wealth can be measured by the productivity of it workers. The total value of goods and services produced by a nation's workers is its *gross national product*, or *GNP*. Generally, nations with the largest GNPs are those with the highest standards of living.

The Essentials of Industry

As mentioned, productivity has increased because skilled workers have been able to turn raw materials into useful products more efficiently. This points out the three basic resources that are necessary to every industry. They are:

● Material resources—timber and iron ore, for example.

Table 1-B. Production Processes

Process	Examples	
	Cutting is the process of removing or separating pieces of material from a base material.	Sawing, shearing, abrading, shaping, drilling, milling, turning, and electrochemical.
	Forming is giving shape to a material without adding to or removing any of the material.	Bending, casting, forging, pressing, drawing, extruding, rolling.
	Fastening is joining materials together permanently or non-permanently.	Mechanical, adhesive, cohesive.
	Finishing is treating the surface of a material for protection or appearance.	Coating, remove finishing, displacement finishing, coloring.

● Human resources—people, everyone from top management to typing clerks, whose work helps produce goods and services.
● Capital resources—factories, equipment, and money.

Without these resources, industry could not exist. That is why these three basic resources are called the *essentials* of industry.

Goods are produced by changing materials. For example, the basic processes used to change metal are cutting, forming, fastening, and finishing. Table 1-B. Industry must use these processes to meet the demands people have for their goods.

For industry to do this most efficiently, it must have modern equipment and skilled

U.S. Department of Labor

1-2. Use of the computer speeds the processing of information. Capable of being used for many different jobs, the computer is the most useful electronic tool we now have.

workers. Today we hear much about robots, computer-aided design (CAD), lasers, computer-aided manufacturing (CAM) and automatic factories. All of these are part of high technology. High technology is revolutionizing industry. It helps industry make goods faster, better, and at less cost. But this can happen only if people are trained to use high technology equipment. Fig. 1-2.

In this book you must learn the basic processes in order to make projects. You will be learning new skills, reading about new tools, and studying different materials. You will learn about the ways industry produces goods, while producing projects of your own.

REVIEW QUESTIONS

1. How would you define "industry"?
2. What is another word for industrial efficiency?
3. What are the three essentials of industry?
4. Define "Gross National Product."
5. What is high technology?

|||||||||||||||||||||||||||||||||||||||||||| **KEY IDEA** ||||||||||||||||||||||||||||||||||||||||||||

HOW TECHNOLOGY AFFECTS US

Our basic needs are the same as those of the early humans. Like them, we need food, clothing, and shelter. However, we do not need to provide for these needs directly. We can hire others to provide us with these needs. We do this when we buy food and clothing. When people buy houses or rent apartments, they are paying others to provide them with shelter.

Because we buy our needs in this way, we have more free time. It is, for example, easier to turn on an electric light than it is to make a candle. It is not hard to see that free time has been one benefit of technology. You can see this easily in your own life. Imagine that you had lived on a farm in Illinois in 1850. Almost every part of your life would have been different. Most of your day would have been spent working. You would have had little free time.

You would have to have risen before dawn to do chores on the farm. There would have been no electric lights. Instead, candles would have been used. There would have been no furnace. Rather, a fire would have to have been built. This fire would have been used for cooking, as well as heat. Your food would have been different. There were no refrigerators. Most fruits and vegetables needed to be eaten soon after they were picked. Meat would need to be eaten soon after the animal was killed. Of course, some meat was salted. Other meat (such as hams) was smoked. This meat could be kept for a time.

You probably would have to walk several miles to school—if there was a school at all!

You can see that there would have been little free time. In the free time that you did have, there would have been none of the amusements we have today.

Most of the free time that we have is due to technology. Technology is the use of science to achieve a practical purpose. Technology has been used to develop electric lights and gas and electric stoves. Because of these, we do not need to make candles, light lanterns, or build fires. Technology has also been used to preserve food. We can now buy food that has been shipped in refrigerated trucks. We also can buy canned and frozen foods. This frees us from the need to raise our own crops and animals.

Technology is also used to make the many items we use today. Making even the simplest item demands skill. On your desk, you probably have a pencil. If you look carefully at it, you will see that several operations would have been needed to make it. Even if you had all of the materials, you probably would be able to make only a crude pencil. To make a

WORK IN THE UNITED STATES
Percentage done by machines, people, and animals

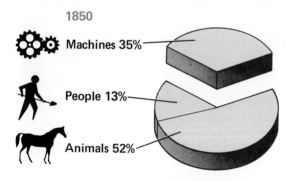

1850

Machines 35%

People 13%

Animals 52%

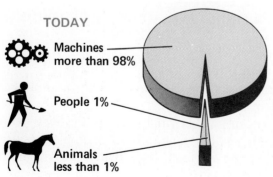

TODAY

Machines more than 98%

People 1%

Animals less than 1%

Fig. A. Look carefully at these two charts. You can see that machines now do more work in the United States. Animals were once widely used for work. Now, though, they are used hardly at all.

Source: U.S. Bureau of Labor Statistics.

Fig. B. In the 1800s, one farmer could produce enough food for only four people. The use of a horse-drawn plow (above) limited the amount of land a farmer could plow and plant. Today, one farmer can produce enough food for eighty people. Technology has increased the production of farm crops. Notice how much land the tractor (below) is able to plow. Compare this with the narrow strip of land plowed by the horse-drawn plow.

pencil as good as the one you are holding would take skill and practice. Others can make for us better pencils than we can make ourselves. Thus, we chose to buy our pencils, rather than make them. This gives us more time. (It takes less time to work to pay for a pencil than it does to make the pencil itself.)

Today, more work is being done by machines. The charts in Fig. A show the percentage of work done by animals, people, and machines. There are two charts, one for 1850 and one for today. You can see that machines are now doing more work, while people and animals are doing less work.

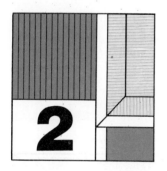

Drafting: A Way to Communicate

Drafting is the drawing of a plan or sketch. It is a way to communicate through pictures, rather than words. Such communication is called *visual communication*. One common example of visual communication is a traffic sign. Look at the traffic signs in Fig. 2-1. Here, symbols, rather than words, are used to give information. When you are riding a bicycle, you may not have time to read the words on a traffic sign. However, you can understand most symbols instantly.

Have you ever tried to describe something to a friend? Often you will say, "Just a minute

2-1. New traffic signs (on the right) use fewer words and more symbols.

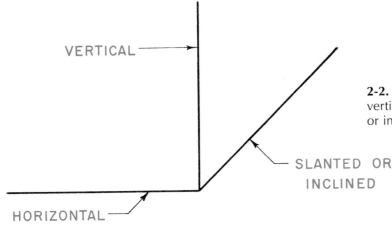

VERTICAL

SLANTED OR INCLINED

HORIZONTAL

2-2. Most drawings include these vertical, horizontal, and slanted or inclined lines.

and I'll show you!" Then, with a pencil, you make a sketch of the object. You draw it. A famous designer of cars said, "Drawing is what you put on paper after you have done a lot of thinking." That is true. Drawing is a way of telling someone else your ideas.

Drawings are of two kinds. *Illustrative drawings* show how an object looks. *Construction drawings* show how to make the object. Sometimes, one drawing does both of these jobs. Here, we are interested mainly in drawings that show how to make something.

What's in a Drawing?

You have used drawings many times. For example, you may have used a drawing to build a craft project.

Three basic *elements* make up all drawings. These are lines, dimensions or sizes, and symbols. The shape of an object is shown with *lines*. These lines are vertical (up and down), horizontal (right and left), slanted or inclined, and curved or circular (round). Figure 2-2 shows the vertical, horizontal, and slanted lines found in the eraser drawing in Fig. 2-3. Curved or circular lines show the shape of such things as a baseball. Fig. 2-4. Lines can

also be used for other purposes. This will be shown later.

Dimensions tell the size of an object. Dimensions are the numbers you see on a drawing. Without these it would be impossible to build objects correctly. See Fig. 2-3.

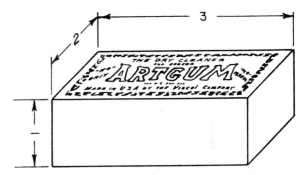

2-3. The numbers on the drawing give the size (dimensions) of the eraser.

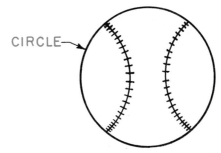

CIRCLE

2-4. A circle shows the shape of this baseball.

2-5. A photograph of a copy machine.

The Four Basic Types of Drawings

The third basic element in drawing is the *symbol*. A symbol is a very simple drawing of an object. Most objects are too difficult to draw exactly as they are. Therefore, symbols are used instead. Figure 2-1 showed some examples of the ways symbols are used.

Figures 2-5 to 2-9 show a photo of a print machine and four different drawings of it. Note that three of these look much like the photograph. Fig. 2-5. These drawings are called *pictorial drawings*. The drawing that is most like the photograph, Fig. 2-6, is called a *perspective drawing*. The other two pictorial drawings are called *cabinet drawings*, Fig. 2-7, and *isometric drawings*, Fig. 2-8. The

2-6. A perspective drawing of the copy machine.

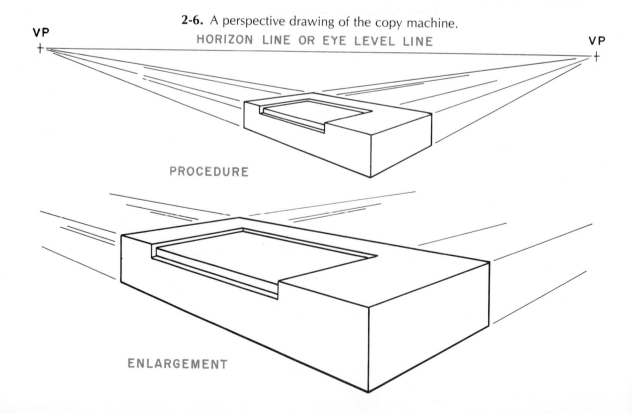

VP

HORIZON LINE OR EYE LEVEL LINE

VP

PROCEDURE

ENLARGEMENT

fourth drawing, Fig. 2-9, looks the least like the photograph. It is, however, the most useful. It is often called a *working drawing*, since it has dimensions and is often used by builders. Some call it a *multiview* (many view) *drawing*. (It usually shows two or three views of the object.) A working drawing also is called an *orthographic* (or-tho-GRAF-ic) *projection*.

Careers in Drafting

Thousands of men and women have jobs that require drawing and designing. Millions of others must know how to use and to read drawings. Fig. 2-10. Remember, almost everything that is made or built must first be drawn. There are many job opportunities in drafting and design. Some of them are described below.

Training, practice, patience, and attention to detail are important in drafting. Each job in drafting requires a certain level of skill.

Junior detailers are beginners, with little or no drafting experience. They have, though, the ability and willingness to learn. The junior detailer must know how to do simple detail and assembly drawings.

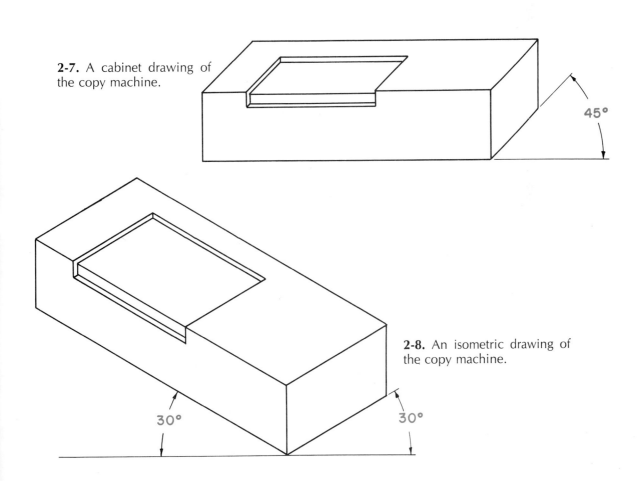

2-7. A cabinet drawing of the copy machine.

45°

2-8. An isometric drawing of the copy machine.

30°

30°

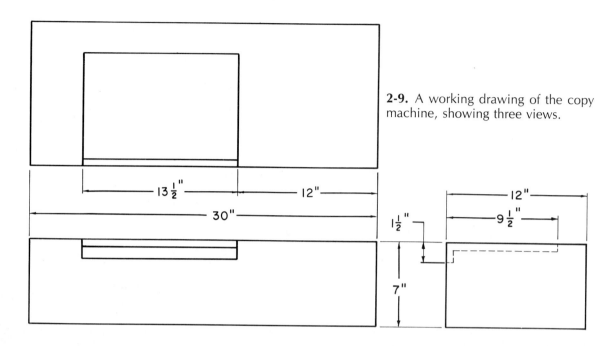

2-9. A working drawing of the copy machine, showing three views.

Detailers draw more difficult detail and assembly drawings and make changes in these drawings. The detailer usually works from sketches, other drawings, outlines, or notes.

Senior detailers must be able to make design drawings. He or she draws detail, assembly, and installation drawings to exact scale.

Junior designers work from notes and specifications. There is some similarity between the work of the junior designer and senior detailer. However, the junior designer is involved in more design work.

Layout drafters prepare drawings from specifications. They also work from written

Government of Puerto Rico

2-10. These technicians are testing a computer circuit by checking it against an electronic drawing.

Jervis B. Webb Co.

2-11. Computer-aided drafting (CAD) is a new skill that every modern drafter must have.

descriptions of details not shown on drawings and from sketches and notes furnished by others.

Designers work closely with technicians, engineers, and scientists. The operating principles help determine the details of any machine design. Graphics designers specialize in layouts for advertising and packaging.

Technical illustrators make pictorial drawings or retouch photographs. The illustrations may be used in manufacturing, in repair manuals, and in books and magazines.

Tool designers work from the drawings made by the industrial designer and engineer. First, they sketch the designs for the tools, dies, jigs, and fixtures needed to make the parts of a product. These sketches are then made into working drawings. They are checked for accuracy and given to the tool and die makers. They use the drawings to build the tools and fixtures needed to make the parts.

Architects design new homes and buildings. A degree in architecture requires four to five years of study.

Industrial designers create the new car models, refrigerators, and many other things we use. The industrial designer usually works for a large company or for an independent designing firm. Usually, the designs are shown in pictorial drawings or as scale models.

Engineers design, build, test, and operate the objects we use. They often specialize in one field, such as mechanical, electrical, chemical, or civil engineering.

Teachers instruct others in drawing. Thousands of industrial arts and technical teachers teach drawing either part-time or full-time. If you like to work with other people, you might consider teaching. It offers the chance to be of service to others.

COMPUTER-AIDED DRAFTING (CAD)

Computer-aided drafting (CAD) brings high technology to the drafting board. Many drafters must be able to use the computer in drafting and design work. Products can be designed and drawn on the computer display screen. Fig. 2-11. They can then be drawn pictorially, rotated, matched with another part, and dimensioned. This is done by using light pencils, menu boards, input keyboards, and other equipment. A *hard copy* (paper print-out) can be made at the push of a button.

BECOMING A DRAFTER

There are at least two ways of becoming a drafter. You can take all of the drafting courses possible in high school. You can then go to a trade, vocational, or technical school. There, you can take a one- to two-year program in drafting. You also could go to college. There, you could take a four-year program in drafting and design. In these schools, in addition to drafting, you will study mathematics, computers, science, English, and basic manufacturing processes.

A second way to become a drafter is to work for three or four years as a drafting apprentice. In doing this, you sign a contract to work with experienced drafters until you have learned the trade.

Most drafters specialize in some area of drafting. There are architectural, structural, mechanical, aeronautical, electrical, marine, and map drafters. They usually work for private drafting companies, manufacturers, or the government.

SELF-TEST

To do a job well, you need ability and interest. Following are six questions. They might help you find out if you are interested in becoming a drafter, teacher, or designer.

1. Do you like to work on mechanical things?

2. Do you like to build things—such as models?

3. Are you neat and accurate?

4. Can you stay with a job until you finish it?

5. Are you good in mathematics and science?

6. By looking at a drawing, can you imagine how the object really looks?

If your answer is Yes to all of these questions, you might consider an occupation in drawing or designing.

REVIEW QUESTIONS

1. What are the three basic elements of a drawing?
2. What are the four basic kinds of drawings?
3. List five different drafting jobs.

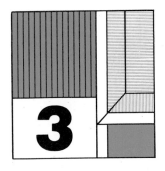

Measurement

How tall are you? Are you 5' 6" or 1.35 metres?* Are you taller or shorter than the student next to you? Your exact height can be found only by measuring. There are two kinds of measuring systems: the customary (inch) system and the metric system.

In all the activities in this book, you must be able to measure. This means you have to know how to read a rule. It is surprising that few people learn to read a rule in the inch system. Now many people must be able to read a metric rule, as well.

How People Learned to Measure

People have always needed to know the size of things. Hundreds of years ago this was difficult. There was then no standard of measurement. According to history, the Romans invented the inch. They decided that an inch was the width of a grown man's thumb. Fig. 3-1. There is a story that King Alfred of England decided the length of the foot. He said that a foot would be the distance from the heel to the toe of his own foot. He ordered a

piece of iron cut to a length of three feet. It was to serve as a master yardstick, a standard for the whole kingdom. From "standards" like

3-1. In ancient times people used parts of the body as standards for measuring.

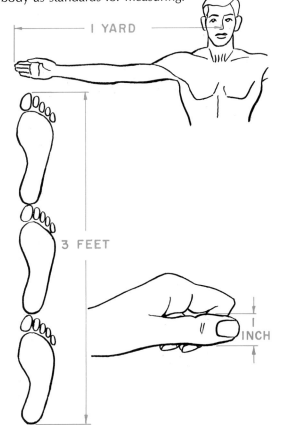

---

*Metre is also spelled "meter." Either spelling is correct.

these, the English, or customary, system of measurement developed.

The Metric System

In 1791, the French government adopted a standard of measurement called the metric system. This was based on a unit called the *metre*.

Today, the United States still uses the customary, or English, system of measurement. It is the only major country that does so. Even the English have adopted metrics. However, the United States is now on its way toward using metrics. In doing so, we will adopt the SI Metric System. The abbreviation SI stands for "International System of Units," the modern metric system of measurement.

There are seven base metric units. In beginning drawing you will need to know only about the metre.

Because we still use the customary system, many of the dimensions in this book are in inches or fractions of an inch. However, the metric system is also used by many companies. Thus, a system called "dual dimensioning" is sometimes used. This means that both the English and metric measurements are given. You should learn to read a rule in both systems accurately.

The metric system is not difficult. All that you need to know is that *milli* means one one-thousandth; *centi* means one one-hundredth; and *kilo* means one thousand. Because it is a decimal system, it is quite easy to learn. One inch equals 25.4 millimetres, or 2.4 centimetres. One metre equals 39.4 inches.

Reading a Rule

Most rules used in drawing are one foot, or twelve inches, long in the customary system. The measurements are usually given in feet, inches, and parts of an inch. You should not find it hard to measure feet in exact inches. You already know that there are twelve inches in a foot and three feet, or thirty-six inches, in a yard. In the metric system, measurement is even easier. There are ten millimetres in one centimetre, a hundred centimetres in one metre, and a thousand metres in one kilometre.

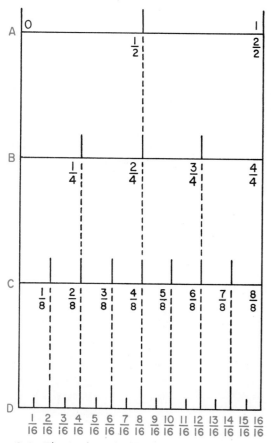

3-2. The inch is divided into smaller units.

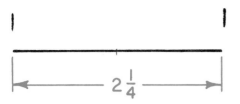

3-3. Use a rule to measure this line. (It is 2¼″ long.)

Figure 3-2 shows how the inch is divided into smaller units. The distance between 0 and 1 is one inch. At line A the inch is divided into two equal parts. Each half is one-half inch (½″). On a rule, this half-inch division line is the longest line between the inch marks. At line B the inch is divided into four equal parts. The first line is ¼″; the second line is 2/4″, or ½″; the third line is ¾″. At line C, you will notice that the inch is divided into eight equal parts so that each small division is ⅛″. Two of these divisions make 2/8″, or ¼″ (as shown on line B). Four of these divisions make 4/8″, or 2/4″, or ½″. At line D, the inch is divided into sixteen parts. Each part is 1/16″. This is usually the smallest division found on rules used in drawing. Notice again that 4/16″ is equal to 2/8″, or ¼″. One line past ¼″ is equal to 5/16″. You will see on your rule that between each one-inch mark, the half-inch mark is the longest one. The quarter-inch mark is the next longest and the eighth-inch mark the next. The sixteenth-inch mark is the shortest.

To read a part or fraction of an inch, count the number of small divisions beyond the last inch mark. For example, when measuring the line in Fig. 3-3, you will find that it is 2″ plus four small divisions. This is 4/16″, which is the same as 2/8″ or ¼″. The line measures 2¼″. One small division past ½″ would be 9/16″ (8/16″ + 1/16″).

Now let's look at a metric rule. Fig. 3-4. Here you see that the rule is divided into millimetres. Ten millimetres equal one centimetre. Most shop measurements are in millimetres.

Figure 3-5 is a sample metric measuring problem. Measure the line with a metric rule. The line is 47 millimetres long. For more practice, measure the lines in Fig. 3-6.

3-5. Use a metric rule to measure this line. You will find that it is 47 mm long.

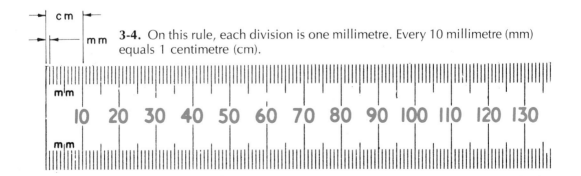

3-4. On this rule, each division is one millimetre. Every 10 millimetre (mm) equals 1 centimetre (cm).

3-6. Measure these lines with customary and metric scales.

1. Name two measuring systems used in this country.
2. How many base units are there in the metric system?
3. How many millimetres are there in a metre?

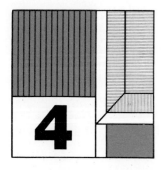

Making a Shop Sketch

In your workshop you will need a simple drawing of each project you are going to build. These simple drawings, sometimes called *shop sketches*, are made on squared grid paper.

You will need squared grid paper to make a shop sketch. This paper is lined in squares, usually four or eight to the inch. These squares help you to find the size of the object. They also help you keep your lines straight. Isometric grid paper is used to make pictorial sketches.

A medium-soft H or HB pencil, an eraser, a 12″ rule or straightedge, and a pencil compass

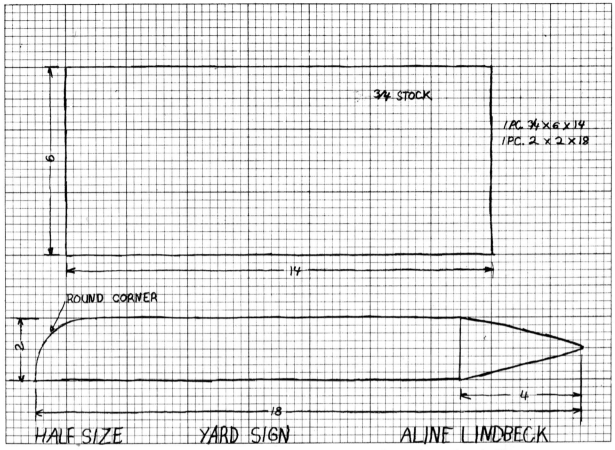

3/4 STOCK

1 PC. 3/4 × 6 × 14
1 PC. 2 × 2 × 18

6

14

ROUND CORNER

2

4

18

HALF SIZE   YARD SIGN   ALINE LINDBECK

4-1. A simple shop sketch of a yard sign. As shown here, the scale is half size.

are used. The compass may be used for drawing circles and arcs. These also can be sketched freehand, however.

Making a Shop Sketch

1. Get a piece of grid paper.
2. Decide on the views you will need to build the project. Often only one view of each part is needed.
3. Decide if you will make the drawing full size, half size, or to some other scale. If there

are eight squares to the inch, each square can represent ⅛″, ¼″, ½″, or any other fraction. For example, suppose you want to make a shop sketch of a yard sign. Fig. 4-1. Note that the post is 18″ long and the board is 14″. If it is drawn half size, both parts of the sign will fit easily on 8½″ × 11″ paper. On paper with eight squares to the inch, four squares will equal one inch. Each square will represent ¼″.

4. Draw the post. The post is 2″ square and 18″ long. Start about 1½″ from the bottom of the page and 1″ in from the left edge. Mark a

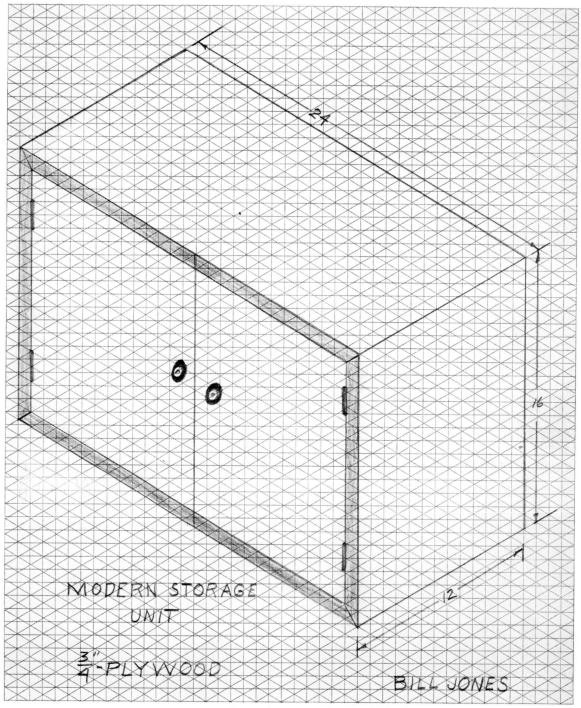

4-2. A storage unit drawn in isometric.

point. Draw a light horizontal line that represents the overall length of the post, or 9″. Draw a light vertical line for the thickness, 1″. Complete the rectangle. Measure in 2½″ from the right and measure up ½″ from the lower right corner. Draw the point at the end of the post. Round off the opposite corner either freehand or with a compass. Darken in the outline. Draw the extension and dimension lines, as shown in Fig. 4-1.

5. Make a one-view drawing of the board in the same general way.

6. Add the dimensions and notes. Note that the lines and lettering aren't as perfect as you would make them in mechanical drawings. They are good enough for your own use, however. Remember—to be useful the drawing or sketch must be correct. It's a good drawing if you can build the project with it.

Making an Isometric Shop Drawing

Isometric grid paper has lines drawn at angles of 30° and 60°.

Note that the length of the sides of the isometric square is the same as that of the square formed by vertical and horizontal lines. This makes it possible to count the correct number of units along a vertical, horizontal, or slanted line, knowing that all will be equal. You should, therefore, start the isometric drawing at a point on the paper where the corners of both squares intersect.

Suppose you want to make an isometric drawing of the storage cabinet shown in Fig. 4-2. It is 16″ high, 12″ wide and 24″ long. It is necessary to use a scale of one-fourth size (3″ = 1′). Begin the drawing about two-thirds of the distance over on the page. Draw a vertical line that is 4″ long (height). Draw a line at 30

degrees to the right that is 3″ long (width). Draw a line at 30 degrees to the left that is 6″ long (length).

Freehand Sketching

Grid paper makes it easy to sketch straight lines. However, you can make shop sketches on plain paper. This is called *freehand sketching*. You should practice sketching lines, freehand, using a soft pencil. Fig. 4-3. Hold your pencil easily, and sketch short, "squiggly" lines.

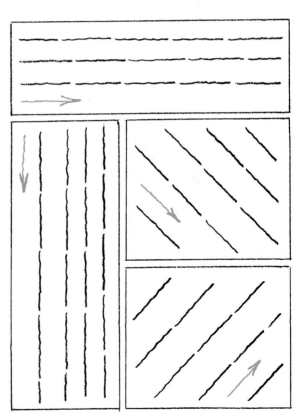

4-3. The way to sketch lines. The arrow shows the direction your pencil should follow.

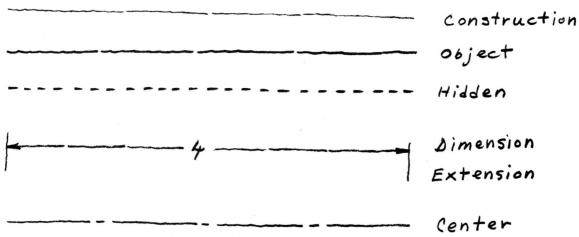

4-4. The types of lines used in sketching and drawing.

The lines for freehand sketching are the same as those for mechanical drawing. See Unit 6. *Construction* lines are used to "block in" an object. They show the location and length of the *object* lines. The *object* lines outline the shape of the part. *Hidden* lines show edges and contours that are not visible. *Dimension* lines and *extension* lines show the sizes of the object. The *center* line indicates the middle. Fig. 4-4. The outline and hidden lines are quite dark. The other lines are lighter. Make the constuction lines so light that they do not need to be erased.

Follow these directions when sketching squares, triangles, and circles.

1. Draw light vertical and horizontal construction lines that intersect in the center. Fig 4-5.

2. Mark points on these lines to show the approximate width, length, or radius. You may measure from the intersecting lines an equal number of spaces for drawing a square. In sketching, use your pencil as a measuring tool. For example, suppose the rectangle is twice as long as it is wide. Place your fingers on your pencil at a distance from the point that is equal to the width of the rectangle. Turn the pencil sideways and twice that amount is the length.

Draw light vertical and horizontal lines to form the square or rectangle. Go over the lines to darken them. Do not erase the construction lines.

Follow similar steps to sketch triangles and circles.

When you have practiced sketching lines and shapes, sketch a project. With practice, you will learn to sketch quickly and accurately.

REVIEW QUESTIONS
1. Explain what freehand sketching is.
2. Why is grid paper often used when making sketches?

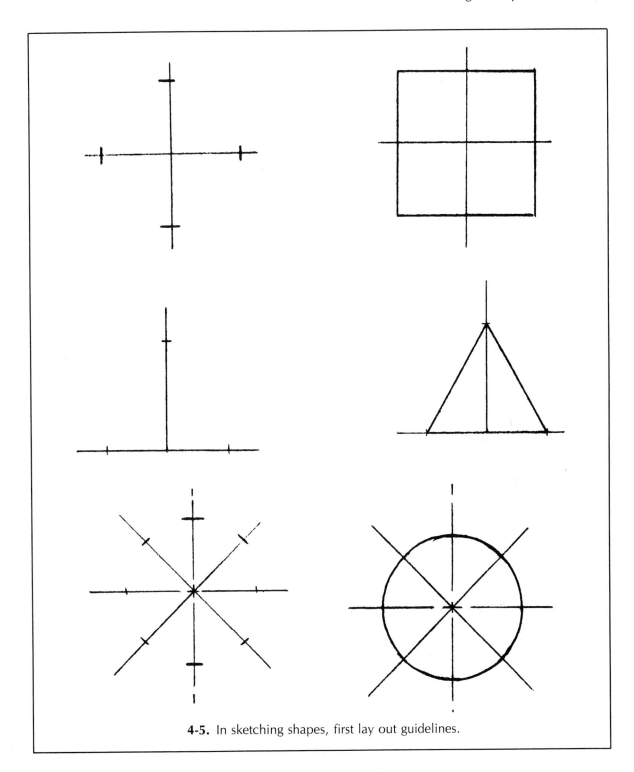

4-5. In sketching shapes, first lay out guidelines.

|||||||||||||||||||||||||||||||||||||||| **KEY IDEA** ||||||||||||||||||||||||||||||||||||||||||||||||

NATURAL RESOURCES AND TECHNOLOGY

Look around the classroom at the various items in the room. All of the items in the room have been made from materials taken from the earth. Those items made of wood have been made from trees. Those items made of metal have been made from the metal obtained from metal ore. (This is rock with metal in it.) Such ore is mined from the earth. Trees and metal ore are two examples of *natural resources*. Those materials that we take from the earth for our own use are called natural resources.

You can easily see that natural resources must be changed before we can use them. The wood from a tree, for example, must be cut and smoothed before it can be used to make a table. To obtain metal, the ore must be heated to a high temperature. The metal that is obtained can then be used to make the various metal items you use every day.

Both of these examples are quite simple. The wood in trees and the metal in metal ore must be processed before they can be used. When a material is processed, it is changed. For example, there are many steps in making a table from a tree. The steps needed to make a metal item from the metal in metal ore are more difficult.

Wood is fairly easy to work. For example, a small tree can be cut down with an ax. The wood can then be cut with a saw and smoothed out with several tools. Wood is a *raw material* that is fairly easy to process. A raw material is a natural resource as it exists in nature. Thus, wood is a raw material found in trees.

As mentioned, a raw material must be changed before it can be used. To change a

Texas Highways

Fig. A. Technology can be used to draw energy from natural resources. Early in this century, few farms were without a windmill. These windmills were used to pump water from wells. On the flat prairie, the wind was often the only source of energy that could be easily harnessed.

USDA

Fig. B. Every second, the sun releases an enormous amount of energy. Before the development of solar panels, there was no effective way to store the sun's energy. The house shown here has solar panels above the greenhouse. These solar panels are positioned to catch the maximum amount of sunlight. The energy stored in the panels will help heat the house. The attached greenhouse is an important part of such a system. The air heated there rises to the top of the house. Then, as it cools, it flows down into the greenhouse. There, the cold air is heated and rises again.

raw material, *technology* usually is necessary. Technology is the use of science to achieve a practical purpose. An ax, for example, is an example of technology. It is an example of the use of the lever and the wedge. The lever and the wedge are both simple machines.

The ax head is a sharpened *wedge*. The force of this wedge is increased by the ax handle. The ax handle is a *lever*. A lever extends the arm of the person using the tool. It allows the person to increase the force of the tool. If you held the ax head in your hand it would be hard for you to chop down a tree. If you hold the ax by the ax handle, your strength is greatly increased. You would then find it much easier to chop down a tree. You may never have used an ax. However, you probably have used a hammer. The handle of the hammer also is a lever. If you held the head of the hammer in your hand, you would have a hard time driving a nail. If you hold the hammer by the handle, the job is much easier.

The ax and the hammer can be thought of as *inventions*. Our age has become one of the most inventive in human history. Now, in the United States, many new inventions are patented each year. They are registered with the U.S. Patent Office. Each year, the U.S. Patent Office receives more than 100,000 applications for patents. Of course, some of the inventions are worthless. Others, however, are quite valuable. Television, the laser, and the computer are all inventions of this century.

58

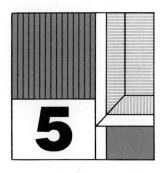

Drafting Instruments and Scales

5

You have seen that simple sketches can be made with a pencil on a sheet of paper. However, to make more accurate mechanical drawings, you need special instruments. Some of these are shown and discussed in this unit.

The *drawing board* provides a smooth, flat wooden surface for drawing. Sometimes a drafting bench with a slanted top for drawing is also used.

The *T-square* is used on the drawing board to draw lines and to hold triangles. Fig. 5-1.

Triangles are used to draw vertical and slanted lines. There are 30°, 60°, and 45° triangles. Fig. 5-2. These can be used sepa-

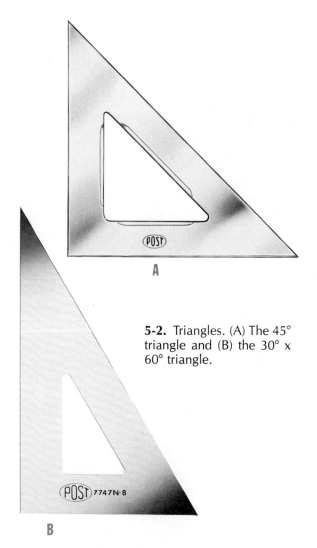

A

5-2. Triangles. (A) The 45° triangle and (B) the 30° x 60° triangle.

B

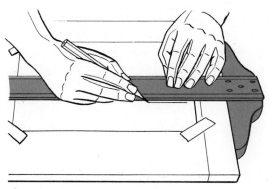

5-1. A drawing board and a T-square. The paper is fastened to the board with drafting tape.

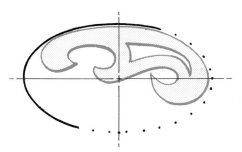

5-3. Using the irregular curve to draw a curved shape.

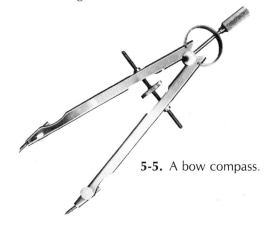

5-5. A bow compass.

rately or in combination to draw lines at specific angles.

Irregular curves, or French curves, are used to draw curved shapes that cannot be drawn with instruments. Fig. 5-3.

All drawing is done with wooden or mechanical *pencils.* These should be kept sharp for clean linework. Pencils and pencil leads are graded according to hardness from 5B (softest) to 9H (hardest). A 2H pencil generally is used for drawing object lines and for lettering. A softer pencil, such as an HB, is used for sketching.

Drafting instruments generally come in a set. Fig. 5-4. These are precision tools. You must treat them carefully if they are to work properly. The pencil, bow compass, and dividers are the tools used most often. The bow compass is used to draw arcs and circles. The dividers are used to lay out equal spaces and transfer measurements from one part of the drawing to another. Fig. 5-5 and 5-6. As you

5-4. A typical set of drafting instruments. (A) Small ink compass; (B) small dividers; (C) small drawing compass; (D) lead pointer; (E) extension bar adapter; (F) bow compass; (G) pencil; (H) extension bar adapter; (I) large dividers; (J) pen point; (K) ruling pen.

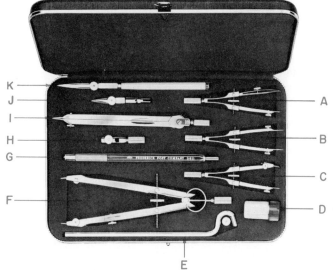

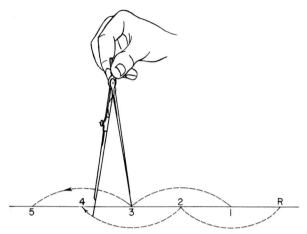

5-6. Using dividers to lay off equal spaces. Notice how the dividers are rotated from one point to the next.

practice your drawing skills, you will learn to use the other instruments in your set.

Drafting scales are the measuring tools for drafting. They are used in drawing objects full size, as well as larger or smaller than full size. There are several kinds, most of them 12″ long. One edge of the *architect's scale* is a rule with inches divided into sixteenths of an inch. Fig. 5-7. This edge is stamped "16" at one end. To draw an object full size or half size, this scale must be used. For example, you may be drawing an object half size (6″ = 1′). Then every one of the smallest divisions on the rule represents ⅛″ (instead of ¹⁄₁₆″) and each inch mark represents 2″.

If the object must be drawn smaller than half size, the architect's scale has other scales you can use. Remember—in using any scale, you must think in terms of full-size dimensions. They are always given that way on the completed drawing. For example, if you wish to draw an object one-fourth full size (3″ = 1′), turn to the scale that has "3" stamped on its end. Note that from 0 to the end stamped "3", there are many small divisions. This distance between 0 and 3 represents 12″, or 1′. There are twelve larger divisions, each representing 1″. Every third inch mark is stamped 3, 6, and 9. Fig. 5-8.

The *mechanical engineer's scale* is divided into measuring units similar to those on the architect's scale. It can be used for objects that will be drawn one-eighth, one-quarter, one-half, and full size. The *civil engineer's scale* has graduations of ten, twenty, thirty, forty, fifty, and sixty parts to the inch. In making a full-size drawing, you would use the scale marked 10. Fig. 5-9. On this scale the distance between 0 and 1 is 1″. This distance is divided into ten equal parts (instead of sixteen as on an ordinary rule). Thus, each part represents 0.100″.

The *metric scales* are used like the other scales. There are several scales. Three of the more common ones are shown in Fig. 5-10. The 1:1 scale (1 mm = 1 mm) is used for full-size drawings. For plans, elevations, and sections, use the 1:25, 1:50, or 1:100 scales. Detail drawings are made with the 1:10 scale.

5-7. The architect's scale.

Drawn one-fourth size, this 10½" bar would be the size of the small bar.

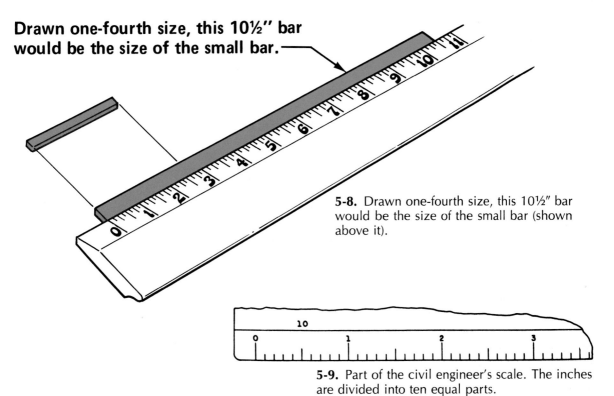

5-8. Drawn one-fourth size, this 10½" bar would be the size of the small bar (shown above it).

5-9. Part of the civil engineer's scale. The inches are divided into ten equal parts.

REVIEW QUESTIONS

1. Explain the use of the triangle, scale, curve, and T-square.
2. Name the two kinds of triangles.
3. What four types of drafting scales are described in this unit?

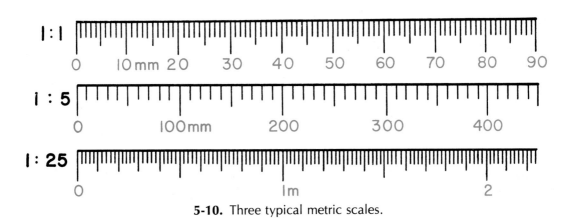

5-10. Three typical metric scales.

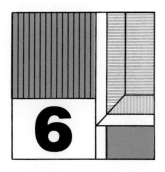

Orthographic Projection and Working Drawings

6

Working drawings are a guide or plan to follow when making a project. The drawing must show the exact shape and size of the object. This can best be done by making a drawing with two, three, or more views. This is called a *working drawing* because it is used to "work from" when making an object. It also is called a *multiview drawing* because it shows several views. Another name for it is *orthographic projection*. This means "right-writing" (the views are at right angles to each other).

Understanding Working Drawings

There are two ways to understand how a working drawing is made. One method is the *natural way* of looking at the different views. Suppose you want to make a drawing of a house. First, look at the front of the house. What do you see? You see the outline of the front view showing the *height* and *length*. Fig. 6-1. When you look down on the house, you see the top view, which shows the *width* and *length*. Fig. 6-2. When you look at the right side, you see the right side, or end, view. You see the *height* and *width*. Fig. 6-3. Each view shows the true size, shape, and other details of that part of the house. When drawn on a

single sheet of paper, the three views show how the object looks. The drawing is known as a *working drawing*. Fig. 6-4.

A second way to understand working drawings is to imagine the object in a clear plastic box. Figs. 6-5 and 6-6. Notice that the box is hinged at the top and the right side of the

6-1. This front view of a model house shows the height and length. It also shows details of the front, such as the door and windows.

6-2. The top view of the house shows the width and length. It also shows details of the ridge, chimney, and gutters.

6-3. The right-side view (or end view) shows the height and width. It also shows side details, such as windows.

6-4. Three views of a house can be drawn on a single sheet of paper. The paper can then be folded to show how the views are drawn.

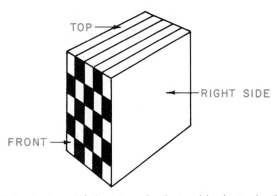

6-5. A pictorial drawing of a design block. Each of the three surfaces can be easily seen.

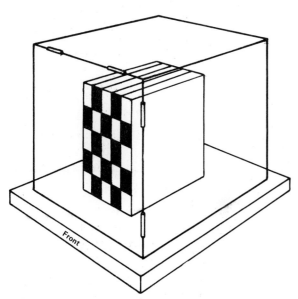

6-6. The design block inside a clear plastic box. Note that the top and side of the box are hinged to the front.

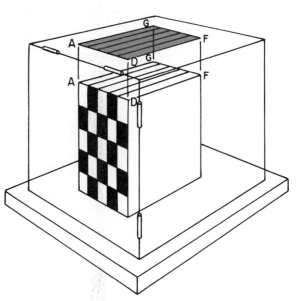

6-8. Drawing the top view on the top of the box. Edge AD is the same as edge AD on the front view.

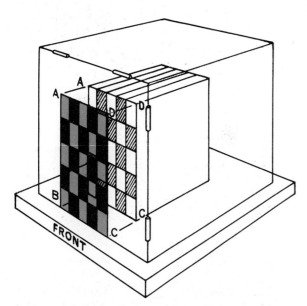

6-7. Drawing the front view of the block on the front of the plastic box. The corners are marked A, B, C, and D.

front surface. This allows it to be opened. Sketch the front view on the front surface of the box. Fig. 6-7. Sketch the top view on its top surface. Fig. 6-8. Finally, sketch the right-side view of the object on the right side of the box. Fig. 6-9. When you open out the sides of the box, you will see the three views in their proper positions. Fig. 6-10. If you now remove the lines of the box itself, the working drawing will look like Fig. 6-11.

Most objects have six sides: front, top, right side, left side, bottom, and rear (back). For most drawings, only the front, top, and right sides are shown.

In making a working drawing the views can be completed in part by *projection*. Projection is the "making" of one view by using the width, height, or length of a complete view. In Fig. 6-12, the height of the front view can be "projected" to form the height of the side

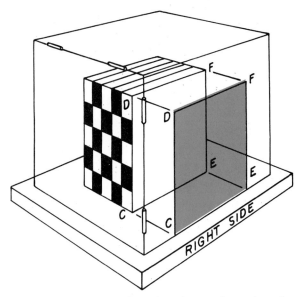

6-9. Drawing the right-side view on the right side of the box. Edge DC is the same as edge DC on the front view.

view. It is possible also to complete the side view by projection. First draw the front and top views. Then draw a light line at an angle of 45° at the upper right-hand corner. Now project the *height* from the front view and the *width* from the top view, as shown. Notice also that the width can be projected with a compass by drawing light arcs from the top view to the side view. The distances can also be measured and transferred by using the dividers.

Views in Working Drawings

In making working drawings, remember the following.

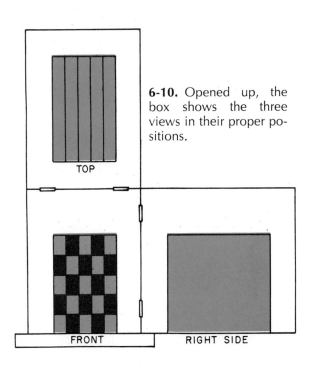

6-10. Opened up, the box shows the three views in their proper positions.

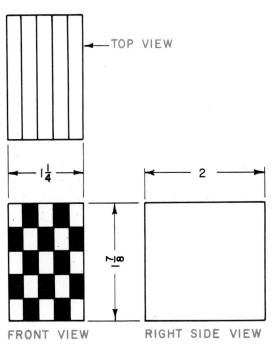

6-11. The plastic box is removed. You can now see the three-view drawing of the block.

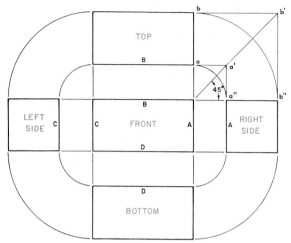

6-12. Notice the location of the five views and how the views can be projected one to the other. The height of the front view can be projected to the height of the right-side view and left-side view. The length can be projected from the front view to the top view and bottom view. The width can be projected from the top view to the right- or left-side view by drawing arcs a-a", b-b". The width can be projected from the top to the right side by drawing a line at 45° degrees and then projecting a line from a to a' to a" and b to b' to b".

1. The front view should show the best shape of the object.

2. Arrange the front view so that the other views will have the fewest number of hidden lines. See below.

3. Show only the number of views that you need. Sometimes you will need two, most often three and, rarely, four or more.

4. The *front view* is placed in the lower left-hand corner of the paper.

5. The *top view* is always placed in line with and directly above the front view.

6. The *right-side view* (*end view*) is in line with and directly to the right of the front view.

7. The height (sometimes called thickness) and the length of the object are shown in the *front view.*

8. The width (sometimes called the depth) and length of the object are shown in the *top view.*

9. The height (or thickness) and width (or depth) of the object are shown in the *right-side view.*

10. Center the whole drawing on the page.

11. Allow about ½" to 1" between views.

Making a Three-View Drawing

Let's try to make a three-view drawing of an oilstone, or sharpening stone. Fig. 6-13.

1. Lay out the drawing on an 8½" × 11" piece of drawing paper so that it is well balanced. Place it widthwise on the drawing board. See Fig. 6-14. First determine the length (6") and the width (2") of the object. Allow space between the views (1"). More than 1" may be left between views if many dimensions are needed. Remember, howev-

6-13. An oilstone has a rectangular shape. The arrow shows the side selected for the front view.

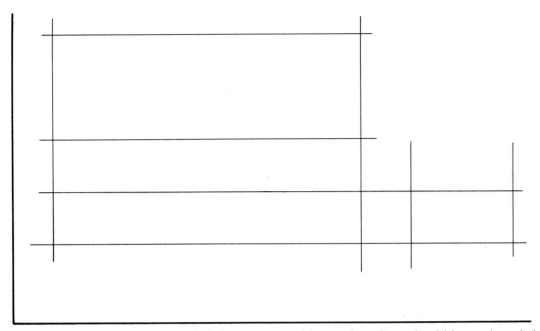

6-14. Blocking in the three views with light construction lines. These lines should be made as light as possible. Do not worry about lines crossing at corners. These can be erased after the drawing is completed.

er, that the distance between views must be equal. The total distance, then, horizontally, is 9″ (6″ + 2″ + 1″). This means that you should start 1″ in from the left edge of the paper. The thickness of the oilstone is 1″, and the width 2″. The distance you should start up from the bottom edge of the paper is 2¼″.

2. With your rule held against the triangle, make a short dash that will locate the horizontal lines of the views of the object.

3. With your rule held against the upper edge of the T-square, make a short dash to locate the vertical lines.

4. Draw light horizontal and vertical lines to "block in" the object as shown in Fig. 6-14.

5. Retrace the outline of each view of the object with an H or 2H pencil. Erase the construction lines.

6. Draw in the dimension lines and extension lines.

7. Add the dimensions and notes. Fig. 6-15.

Hidden Lines

If you removed the lead from the pencil you are using, there would be a hole through the pencil. From the side of the pencil you couldn't see this hole, but you'd know it was there. In a working drawing, this hole is shown with *hidden* lines. These lines are used on all view drawings. Hidden lines are used to show edges, holes, corners, and surfaces that cannot be seen from that view but are a part of the object.

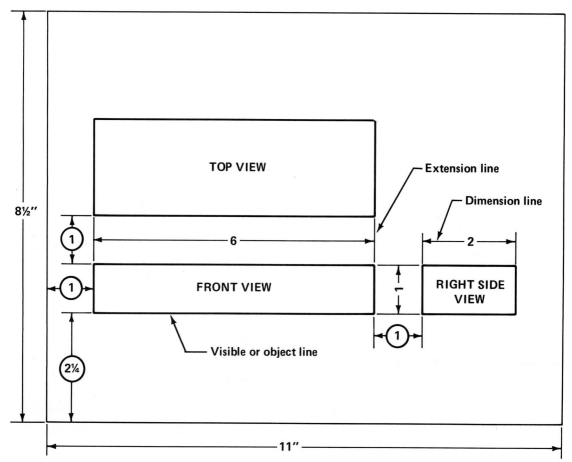

6-15. The three-view drawing of the oilstone. The circled dimensions are for your convenience. If you make the drawing, do not include them.

USING HIDDEN LINES

The turned wooden bowl in Fig. 6-16 is shown in a pictorial sketch and a two-view working drawing. Hidden lines are needed in both views. Can you tell what part of the bowl each of these lines represents?

Many industrial machines have hidden surfaces. The drafter must draw hidden lines carefully to show all parts. In making hidden lines, remember the following.

1. Make the dashes of equal length (about ⅛″) with an equal amount of white space (about ¹⁄₃₂″) between.

2. If two hidden lines are parallel to one another, see that the dashes are "staggered."

3. Hidden lines should always start and stop with one of the object lines. Never start with a white space, except when it is a continuation of a solid line.

4. When hidden lines join in a corner or cross each other, always cross or join the dashes, not the white space. Fig. 6-16.

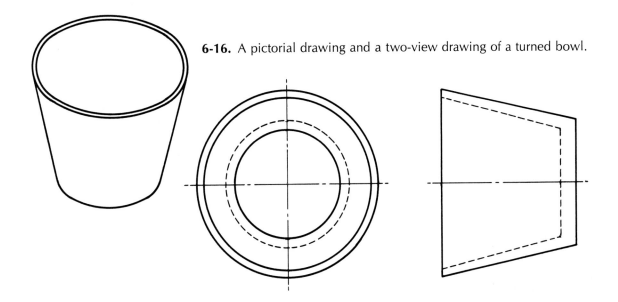

6-16. A pictorial drawing and a two-view drawing of a turned bowl.

5. The weight of the hidden line should be somewhat lighter than the object lines.

Two-View Drawings

What would a working drawing of a rolling pin look like? Fig. 6-17. If you used three views what would you see? Yes, the front view and the top view would be exactly alike. Often it is not necessary to have three views for a good working drawing. This is almost always true of cylindrical shapes. Many other objects can be drawn to show all needed information with only two views.

Points to Remember

1. Always make the most descriptive view the front view. For example, suppose you are making a working drawing of the top of a footstool or small table. Fig. 6-18. You need only two views—one to show its shape and one to show its thickness. Fig. 6-19. Since the circular shape is more important, this should be made the front view.

2. Draw a top or side view, whichever is best, as the second view. Fig. 6-19.

3. Whenever possible use only two views, even though three could be drawn. It is often

6-17. The top and side views of this rolling pin are alike. A two-view drawing, then, is all that is needed.

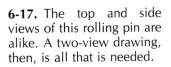

ALIKE

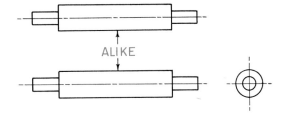

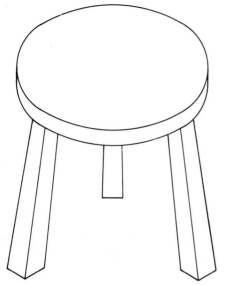

6-18. The top of a footstool would require only two views.

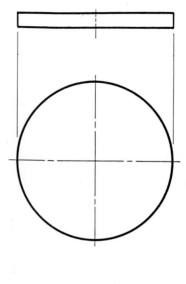

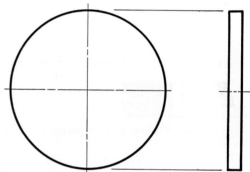

6-19. Two methods of drawing the top of a table or stool.

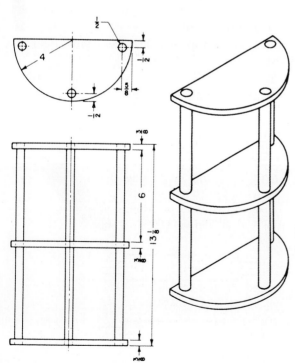

6-20. The front and top views of a wall shelf. A side view would give no new information.

a waste of effort and space to show the third view. This is especially true of woodworking drawings. For example, nothing new could be learned by making a side view of the small wall shelf in Fig. 6-20. All the information you need for making it is shown on the front and top views.

1. What are two other names for working drawings?
2. Most objects have six sides or views. What are they?
3. What three views generally are used in a three-view drawing?

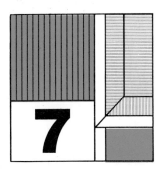

Lettering and Dimensioning

Lettering

Lettering is the forming of numbers and letters with a pen or pencil. Good lettering requires only patience and practice. The lettering alphabet discussed here is *single stroke Gothic*. Its letters are easily formed with *single strokes* of the pen or pencil.

Look at an alphabet of capital letters. Notice that all letters are not the same width. Also, some are made only with straight lines, while others have curves. Fig. 7-1. A simple way to learn to letter is to make all the letters the same width except three. The J is a little narrower than the others. The I is just one line wide, and the W is a little wider than most.

Now let's look at the alphabet to see how the letters are drawn. Notice that E, F, H, I, L, and T combine vertical and horizontal lines only. The A, K, M, N, V, W, X, Y, and Z use vertical, horizontal, and/or inclined lines. The remaining letters combine all these, plus the curve. Figure 7-1 shows arrows and numbers beside each letter. These show how to make each stroke that forms the letter.

LETTERING PRACTICE

Now let's do some lettering. First, always use guidelines to keep the lettering straight. You should use guidelines even when you add a single dimension to a drawing so that the numbers look uniform in size. On most draw-

• LETTERING WITH THE RIGHT HAND •

7-1. The correct way to form the letters if you are right-handed.

ings letters are about ⅛″ to ³⁄₁₆″ high. The size, of course, varies with the overall size of the drawing. It's easier to form smaller letters than larger ones. Lay out light, horizontal guidelines on your paper. You also can draw guidelines for slanted lettering. Fig. 7-2. These can remain on the drawing. Use an H or 2H pencil for lettering. Be sure it is sharp. Sit or stand in a relaxed position. Hold the pencil lightly but firmly in your hand.

Many people never learn to letter well because they are tense as they letter. Relax and take it easy. Rest your elbow on the drawing bench for firm, easy support.

Practice vertical, horizontal, slanted, and curved strokes. See Fig. 7-1. Practice making straight lines of the same length. Practice making curved lines. The curves should be smooth. Each should have the same arc. Are the lines straight, the curves smooth and always the same angle? After you have done this for a while, begin to form the letters. The A has a horizontal line about one-third of the way up. All the rest of the letters are divided about (but slightly above) center. The bottom of the letter should be a little larger than the top so it looks stable. Form all letters of the same shape at one time—the vertical and horizontal letters. Then go on to form the others.

Making the O. Many of you will find that your poorest letters are those with curved lines. These are more difficult to make free-hand. The O is the basic letter in this group. Make several of them until you get a feel for the circular motion. Don't be discouraged

with your early lettering. It may not be as even as you'd like it to be. Lettering improves with practice.

Numbers. After forming letters, try numbers. These are made in the same general way. When lettering fractions, make the overall fraction about two times the height of a whole number.

Words and Phrases. If spaced an equal distance apart, some letters appear farther apart than others. For example, an I following an L will appear farther away than a D that follows an M. This is because the first I and L have a lot of white space around them. Thus, they are called *open* letters. The D and M have little or no space around them. They are called *closed* letters. Therefore, in forming words, place the open letters closer together than the closed letters. This will make the words appear to be uniformly spaced.

When lettering a sentence, leave a space between words equal to the width of the average letter. The space between sentences should equal twice the height of the letters. The space between lines of words should be

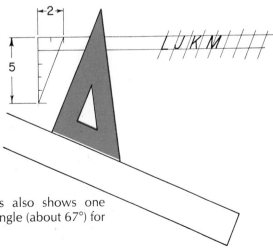

7-2. Drawing guidelines. This also shows one method of getting the correct angle (about 67°) for inclined lettering.

about equal to the height of the letters. Fig. 7-3.

Dimensioning

To be completely useful, a drawing must show the shape of the object, its size, and the other information needed to construct it. Even the simplest dimensions help to describe an object. The shape is shown by lines. Fig. 7-4. Dimensions tell the size or the measurements. Other information, such as the material to use and the number of pieces is added in the *title block* or *record strip* or as a *note*.

GENERAL RULES FOR DIMENSIONING

1. Place the dimensions so they are easy to read.

2. Show *only* the dimensions needed to build the object, nothing more. Rules 1 and 2 are the most important rules in drawing.

3. Do not repeat dimensions.

4. Use detail, location, and overall dimensions. (Some drafters call the over-all dimension the size dimension.) Fig. 7-5.

(a) Over-all (size) dimensions show the total height, width, and length of the object.

(b) Detail (size) dimensions show the measurement of important details.

(c) Location, or position, dimensions show where the details are.

5. Place the dimensions on the drawing in one of the two ways shown in Fig. 7-6. Both methods are correct. However, be uniform in each drawing.

6. Letter the dimensions correctly. Most dimensions on beginning drawings are given in *inches* and *fractions* of an inch. On many drawings used in industry, the dimensions are

MORE OR LESS THAN HEIGHT OF LETTERS
WIDTH OF AVERAGE LETTER

SELF CHECK YOUR LETTERING

AND LINE WORK. PRACTICE IS

$\frac{1}{4}$ WIDTH OF AVERAGE LETTER — TWICE HEIGHT OF LETTERS

7-3. The correct spacing of words in sentences.

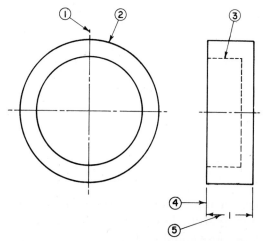

7-4. Lines used in drafting. (1) Center line; (2) object line; (3) hidden line; (4) extension line; (5) dimension line.

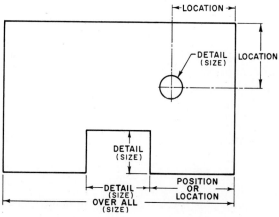

7-5. The three dimensions used in drafting: detail, location, and overall.

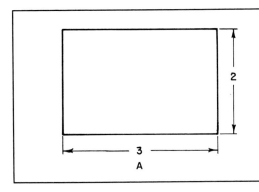

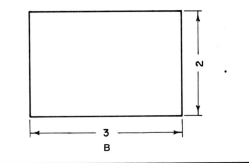

7-6. The two methods of placing dimensions. (A) The one-direction (undirectional) method of dimensioning. All figures are made straight up and down. (B) The two-direction (aligned) system of dimensioning. The dimensions are read from the bottom and right-hand edge of the paper.

given in *decimals*. For example, instead of 1¼″, the dimension is shown as 1.250″. Metric dimensions are also used.

WHERE AND HOW TO DIMENSION

1. Place all dimensions *outside* the views rather than inside the drawing. If possible place all dimensions between the views. If easier to read, however, certain dimensions can be placed inside the views.

2. Place the dimensions on the view that shows the shape most clearly. Do not place dimensions on views where they are not needed. Fig. 7-7. Usually the height and length are shown on the front view.

3. The *extension lines* should be light, sharp lines starting about ¹⁄₁₆″ from the outline

or object. They should extend only slightly beyond the arrowheads of the outside dimension lines. See Fig. 7-7.

4. The dimension lines should start about ⅜″ to ½″ from the outline or object. If there are several parallel dimension lines, they should be ¼″ to ⅜″ apart.

5. If there are several parallel dimension lines, do not place dimension *figures* above one another. "Staggering" them makes them easier to read. See Fig. 7-7.

6. Always place the detail and location dimensions inside the overall dimensions. Fig. 7-8.

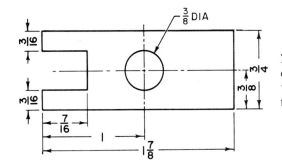

7-7. Dimensions placed on a drawing where they can be easily read. Notice that the dimensions are "staggered." Also, the extension lines do not cross the dimension lines.

7-8. The detail dimensions are placed inside the over-all dimension. *This dimension is usually omitted on machine drawings where great accuracy is required. It can, however, be added and marked REF (Reference). This dimension is included on house plans and other drawings where great accuracy is not required.

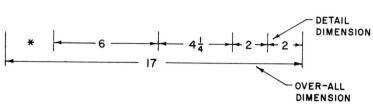

7. Always show each overall (long size) dimension only once on the drawing. Don't repeat dimensions.

8. Never allow dimension lines to cross extension lines.

9. Never use a center line as a dimension line. (Center lines may cross all other lines because they are lighter and are "broken" lines.)

10. Use inches to and including 72, and feet and inches above this amount. Use the mark " for inches and use ' for feet. *If all dimensions are in inches, the inch mark can be omitted.*

11. Avoid bringing an extension line from an invisible or hidden line (which shows a part of an object behind the surface). Sometimes, especially on the side view, it may be necessary.

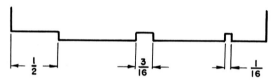

7-9. The two spaces on the right are small. They are too small to hold the dimension and the arrowheads.

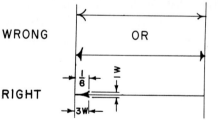

7-10. Correctly and incorrectly drawn arrowheads.

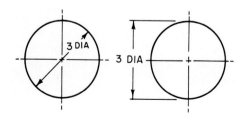

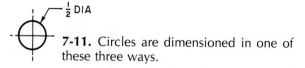

7-11. Circles are dimensioned in one of these three ways.

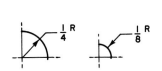

7-12. To dimension an arc, use one of these three methods.

12. If the space for dimensioning is small, place the arrowheads *outside* the extension lines, pointing in, as shown in Fig. 7-9.

DRAWING ARROWHEADS

Arrowheads are drawn on one or both ends of most dimension lines. Only one arrowhead is used on the dimension line for the *radius*. The length of the arrowhead should be about three times its width. On the average drawing it should be about ⅛" long. Examples of correctly and incorrectly drawn arrowheads are shown in Fig. 7-10.

DIMENSIONING CIRCLES, ARCS, AND ANGLES

1. Always dimension the *diameter* of circles, cylinders, and holes. Fig. 7-11. There are three common ways to do this.

   a. The dimension may be placed *inside* the circle.

   b. The dimension can be placed *outside* the circle.

   c. *Leaders* can be used. These are fine lines drawn at a 45° or 60° angle to the center, just touching the circumference. An arrowhead is drawn on one end and a short horizontal line

on the other. Leaders can also be used to add notes to a drawing.

2. Place DIA after the dimension if it is not clear that it refers to a circle or hole. DIA means "diameter." The symbol ∅ is also used. It should be placed before the dimension.

3. Give the *radius* of an arc. Place an R after the dimension. Follow one of the methods shown in Fig. 7-12. The method will depend on the size of the space you have for the dimension.

4. Place dimensions for angles so they can be read without turning the paper. Fig. 7-13.

ADDING NOTES TO DRAWINGS

Notes are placed on the drawing to give the worker information not shown by the dimensions. An example is shown in Fig. 7-14.

REVIEW QUESTIONS

1. What two grades of pencils are used for lettering?
2. How long is the typical arrowhead?
3. Why are notes used on some drawings?

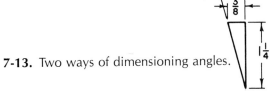

7-13. Two ways of dimensioning angles.

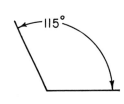

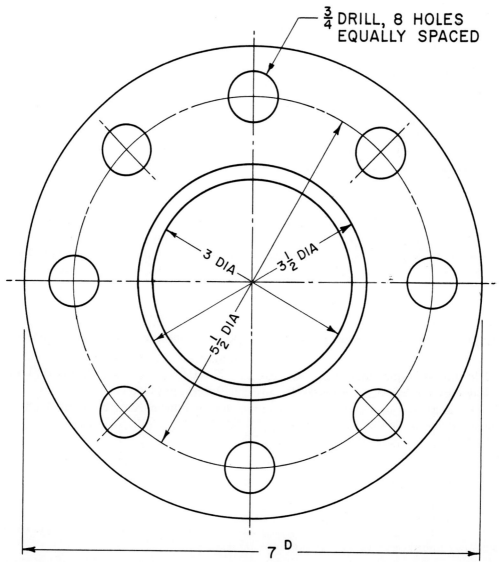

7-14. The note at the top of this front view gives information on drilling equally-spaced holes.

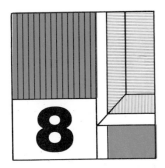

Pictorial Drawings

A pictorial drawing looks very much like a photograph of an object. Two types of pictorial drawings are commonly used. They are the isometric and the oblique. Each is described in this unit.

Isometric Pictorial Drawings

Isometric means "equal measure." An isometric drawing is a picture drawing. In an isometric drawing, one corner of the object appears closest to you. The lines that form the sides are 120° apart. Fig. 8-1.

An isometric drawing is used primarily for rectangular objects. In a single view it provides both a picture of the object and a place to dimension it. Fig. 8-2. Let's make a simple drawing of a rectangular object such as a basketball bankboard. Fig. 8-3.

1. Draw a light horizontal line. Fig. 8-4. Draw a vertical line to represent one edge of the object (width AB). Fig. 8-3.

2. (A) Draw lines to the right and left at an angle of 30° to the horizontal. (B) Mark off AC to represent the length of the bankboard. Mark AD to represent its thickness.

3. Draw vertical lines CE and DF.

4. Now, with the 30°-60° triangle, complete the outline. Draw lines BF, BE, FG, and EG. Notice that these lines are given their true length since they are isometric lines.

5. Hidden lines are not usually shown on isometric drawings.

NON-ISOMETRIC LINES

Many objects are not true rectangles. For example, the tapered block in Fig. 8-5 has a

8-1. The three lines used as a base for constructing an isometric. Notice that they are 120° apart. Two lines are drawn at an angle of 30° to the horizontal.

8-2. An isometric drawing of a knife rack. The overall dimensions are ½" x 6½" x 11¾". The top and bottom are ⅜" thick. The back is ¼" thick.

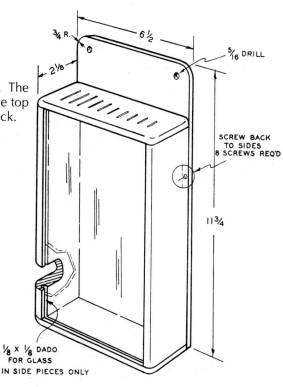

8-3. An isometric drawing of a basketball backboard.

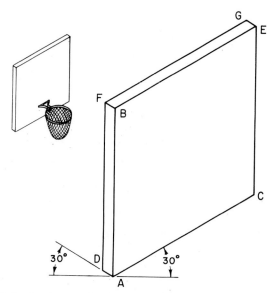

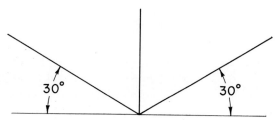

8-4. The first step in making an isometric drawing.

slanted top. To make a drawing of such an object, it is necessary to enclose the object in an "isometric box." Fig. 8-5. Measure from corners A and B. Mark the location of the slanted lines (F and C). Connect points FC, CD, FE, and ED. Lines CD and FE will not be their true length. They are called *non-isometric lines*. Non-isometric lines must be drawn by locating their ends on isometric lines and connecting the points with a straightedge.

DRAWING CIRCLES IN ISOMETRIC

A circle in isometric is really an ellipse. For this reason the isometric drawing is not the

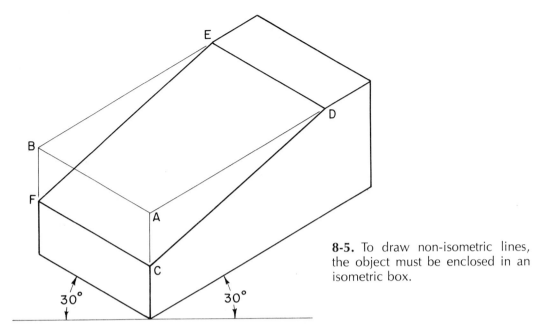

8-5. To draw non-isometric lines, the object must be enclosed in an isometric box.

best one for circular objects. However, to draw a circle in isometric, proceed as follows. Fig. 8-6.

1. Draw a square in isometric, ABCD.

2. Divide the sides in half. Mark these points E, F, G, and H.

3. Draw light construction lines AE, AF, CG, and CH. Mark the points of intersection I and J.

4. Adjust a compass to a radius equal to JF. Place the point of the compass at J and draw the arc FH. Place the point of the compass at I and draw the arc EG.

5. Adjust the compass to a radius of AE. Place the point of the compass at C and draw the arc HG. Place the point of the compass at A and draw the arc EF. This will complete the isometric circle.

Special templates or plastic guides are also used to draw isometric circles.

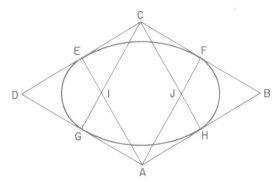

8-6. Drawing a circle in isometric.

Oblique Pictorial Drawings

The oblique drawing is another type of picture drawing. Oblique means "slanting" or "inclined." One side of the object appears closest to you. The top and right or left side slant away from you.

The two kinds of oblique drawings are *cavalier* and *cabinet*. In a cavalier drawing the true lengths of the side and top are measured off along the inclined lines. Look at Fig. 8-7. It looks as if the top and side are longer than they really are. For this reason the cavalier drawing is seldom used.

In the cabinet drawing this is corrected. Fig. 8-7. If an object is a true rectangle, the front side is drawn exactly as in a working drawing. This surface is shown by vertical and horizontal lines of true length. The other surfaces are formed by drawing inclined lines at an angle of 30° to 45° (usually 45 degrees) to the right or left. Half the true length is measured off on the inclined lines to complete the drawing. The correct dimension, however, is always given.

The cabinet drawing was so named because it is the favorite of cabinetmakers. It is an excellent picture drawing for rectangular cabinets, chests, and tables.

Points to Remember

1. If a cabinet drawing contains circular parts, always draw the circle on the surface that appears nearest you. It will then be a true circle in size and shape. For example, to draw the head of a croquet mallet, make the circle a part of the side nearest you as shown in Fig. 8-8. Circles on the top or right or left surface would be ellipses, as in isometric drawings.

2. If a long object is drawn in a cabinet drawing, always place the long side as part of the surface nearest you. Never place the short side nearest you. Fig. 8-9. Notice that rules 1 and 2 sometimes clash. If they do, the first rule is the more important. The croquet mallet is an example.

To make a cabinet drawing, proceed as follows:

1. Select the side that will give the best front view.

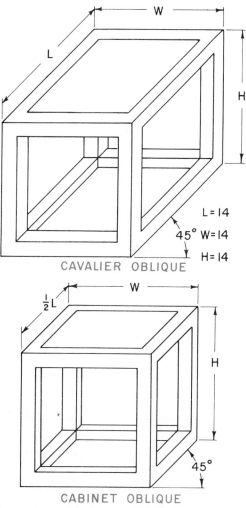

CAVALIER OBLIQUE

L = 14
45° W = 14
H = 14

CABINET OBLIQUE

8-7. A cube drawn as a cavalier oblique drawing and as a cabinet oblique drawing. Which looks more like a cube? The cabinet oblique drawing looks like a cube. However, it is not a good illustration of optical illusion.

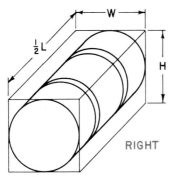 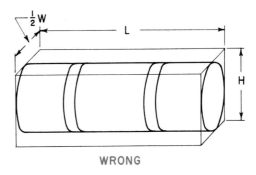

8-8. The right and wrong way to draw the head of a croquet mallet.

2. Draw this front view as you would draw the front view of a working drawing.

3. Draw inclined lines from the front view at an angle of 45° to the right or left to form the top and side.

4. Lay off only *half* the true length on these inclined lines.

5. Draw the horizontal and vertical lines from these points to complete the outline of the object.

REVIEW QUESTIONS

1. What are the two types of pictorial drawings described in this unit?
2. What is the difference between the cavalier and cabinet oblique drawings?

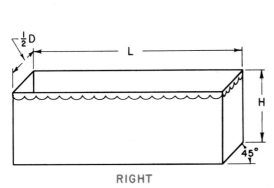 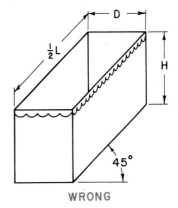

8-9. The right and wrong way to draw a long flower box. Notice that the long side is a part of the surface nearest you.

Thinking about a Career

THE ENTREPRENEUR

In your town or city, there are many businesses—some large, others small. You may be very familiar with some of them. Perhaps you walk past them on your way to school. Perhaps you or your parents buy goods and services from the businesses you pass. Some of the small businesses may be owned and managed by one person. Others may be medium-sized, employing several people. There may also be large businesses in your town or city. For example, there may be a large manufacturing plant. Or, the headquarters of a large company may be in your town. Either of these could employ hundreds—or even thousands—of people.

Most large businesses started as small businesses. This is true of some of the largest corporations. The building of a business requires skill and hard work. It can be difficult to imagine the energy needed to start a business. Anyone starting a small business faces a variety of tasks. He or she first must have the money needed. (This money may have to be borrowed.) He or she also must have a product or service that can be sold at a profit. He or she must have a way of distributing the product or service to the public. The smaller the business, the more of these jobs the owner-operator may have to do. In some small businesses, the owner-operator has all of these responsibilities. In larger businesses, such duties are divided. For example, one person (or one department) may be in charge of making the product. Another may be in charge of advertising it. A third may be in charge of delivering the item. Usually, the larger the business, the greater the number of people needed for each of these duties.

The person who starts a business is usually an *entrepreneur* (ahn-tray-prah-NWUR). This term may be unfamiliar to you. However, you certainly know some entrepreneurs. An entrepreneur is anyone who organizes and manages a business. This person also assumes the risks of the business. This means that the entrepreneur is responsible for paying the business expenses. All responsibility for the success of the business rests with the entrepreneur.

A person who is self-employed, or in business for himself or herself, is an entrepreneur. Perhaps you have been an entrepreneur. If you set up a summertime lawn-mowing business, you were an entrepreneur. Of course, there is a difference between setting up a small business for the summer and setting up a business from which you hope to make a living. But even in setting up a small summer business, you face some of the concerns faced by those who are self-employed.

All entrepreneurs face four similar problems. These problems are:
- Identifying a *need.*
- Finding a *product* to satisfy the need.
- *Financing* the business.
- *Selling* the product.

Let's look at each of these concerns.

All successful businesses have one thing in common. They were started because someone noticed that people needed or wanted an item or service. Once an entrepreneur has noticed a need, he or she can then find a product to fill the need. This product might be an item (such

Did you ever set up a soft drink stand? If you did, you faced some of the problems faced by those who are in business for themselves. You would quickly have learned that an eye-catching sign, low prices, and good service were needed. Perhaps there was another such stand on your street at the same time. You would then have learned about the need to make your product more desirable. Perhaps you did this by lowering your price. You may have increased the size of the glass. Or, you may have made a larger sign. You might also have chosen another location for your stand. Though your business was small, you would have practiced some of the basic skills needed to operate a larger business.

as a kitchen gadget). It might also be a service (such as a lawn-mowing service). Let's consider one example to see how an entrepreneur can provide a product to satisfy a need.

Last summer, you may have noticed that the grass on neighborhood lawns was growing quickly. This might have suggested to you the need for a lawn-mowing service in your neighborhood.

Let's assume that you plan to set up a lawn-mowing service this coming summer. By identifying a need, you are on your way to starting your own business. First, though, you must have the necessary money. You must finance your business. You may need money to buy a lawn-mower. If your family already has a lawn-mower, you would not need to buy one. Let's assume, however, that you need to buy a mower. You might be able to do this by withdrawing money from your savings account. If you have no money, you would need to borrow the money. You might, for example, borrow the money from your parents. You

could then repay the loan from the profits of your lawn-mowing service.

After you have financed your business, you need to sell your product. You might do this in a number of ways. You might advertise your service door-to-door. You would ask each person if he or she would like to have their lawn mowed. You might also place notices on the bulletin boards of neighborhood stores.

In selling your service, you will need to set a price that will make it attractive. If the price is high, the customer may not want your service. If the price is low, you may not make a profit. (Profit is the money left over after your expenses have been subtracted.) In setting the price, you should consider what the competition is charging. The competition would be anyone else in your neighborhood who is offering the same service.

Starting a business is not easy. Succeeding in business is ever harder. Anyone who starts a business is an entrepreneur. But not all entrepreneurs are successful. For an entrepreneur to be successful, his or her business must be successful.

There are five success stories in this book. Titled *Thinking about a Career,* these stories appear after each section of the book except the last. As you read about people who have started their own business, you might want to think about your own career plans. You might want to consider various career possibilities. The stories of the five entrepreneurs might help you decide whether you would like to be self-employed.

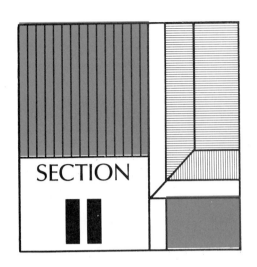

SECTION II

Woodworking Technology

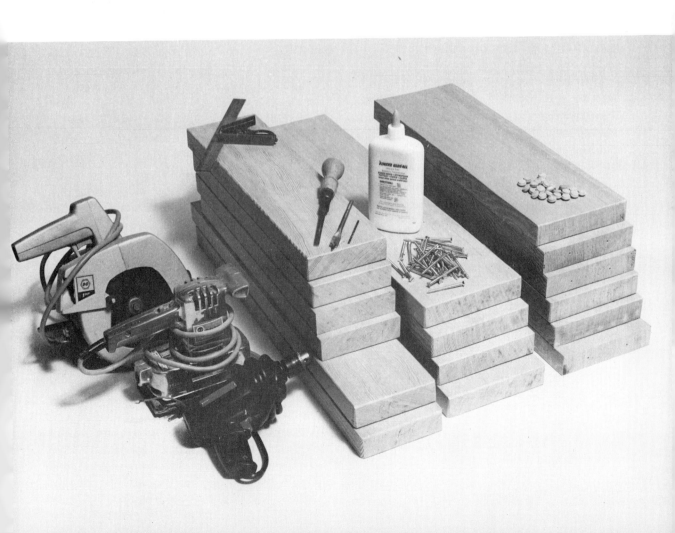

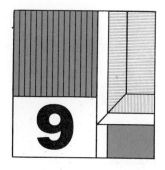

Safety

9

Do you have a friend who has had a serious accident? Perhaps this person broke an arm or leg while riding a bicycle or playing football. Maybe you have heard of someone who has lost an arm or a leg. If you ask why the accident happened, the victim will probably have to admit, "I took a chance," or, "I was careless."

Most accidents can be avoided by developing safe work habits. *Safety is a way of living.* It is learning to be careful. In the shop this means learning to handle tools, machines, and materials with care. It also means learning to follow instructions, and never taking chances. Always read and follow the directions in this book. Then watch your instructor as he or she demonstrates the correct way of using tools and machines.

Learn the hazards of the shop and avoid them. For example, when soldering, the danger is in getting burned. When grinding metal, you must be careful not to injure your eyes. When cutting a piece of wood, the hazard is in cutting yourself.

Six Safety Rules

Here are six major rules you should observe in the shop. You will find other safety suggestions throughout the book.

1. *Always dress correctly for the job.*

Roll up your sleeves. Never wear loose-fitting clothes. Fig. 9-1. Standard dress in the shop is a protective apron or coat. Wear one. Remove your watch and rings. Always wear an eye shield or goggles when grinding, drilling, cutting, or machining. Fig. 9-2. Wear special protective clothing when welding or in the foundry. For example, goggles are needed in welding or when using acids.

2. *Follow directions.*

The correct way is the safe way. That is the way shown in this book. Your instructor will show you how to do things correctly and safely. Never work in the shop when your instructor is not in the room. Do not use any tools, machines, or materials until you have been taught how to use them. Make sure you receive permission from your instructor before using any machine. Never try to get by "just this once." That's usually the time an accident happens. A good slogan to follow is, "It is better to be safe than sorry." The ABC's of safety are *Always Be Careful.*

3. *Do your share in good shop housekeeping.*

Keep the top of your bench and the floor around it clean and neat. Don't leave scraps or wood and other materials on the floor where they can cause someone to slip or fall. Wipe up oil and grease spots. Keep rags in a metal

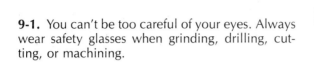

9-1. You can't be too careful of your eyes. Always wear safety glasses when grinding, drilling, cutting, or machining.

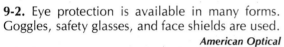

9-2. Eye protection is available in many forms. Goggles, safety glasses, and face shields are used.

American Optical

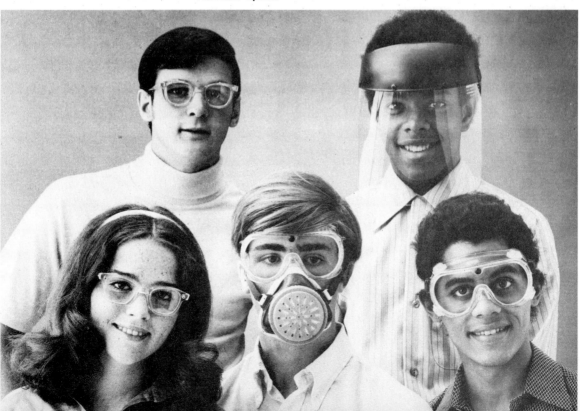

container. Report all hazards, such as a loose guard on a machine, to your instructor immediately. A clean shop is a safe shop.

4. *Learn to use tools and machines correctly.*

A cutting tool must be sharp, not only for easier use, but also for safety. A dull tool is more likely to slip and cut you than a sharp one. Be sure you understand a tool or a machine before you try to use it. Learn by watching and listening to your instructor, and by asking questions, not by making dangerous mistakes. Check to see that the tool or machine is in good condition. Never try to use a tool that is broken. Use the correct tool for every job. For example, don't use a file as a crowbar. The body of the file is very brittle and will break easily. When carrying tools, always keep the *pointed ends down* and away from you. Never carry any sharp-edged tools in a way that would cause injury to yourself or others. When passing another student who is working, be careful of sharp edges, points, and other hazards.

5. *Avoid horseplay.*

Fooling around in the shop is dangerous. Practical jokes aren't funny, especially when they cause an accident, as they often do. Your instructor can't allow it, and you can't afford it. You may hurt not only yourself, but other students as well.

6. *Report every injury, no matter how small, to your instructor.*

Get first aid for every cut or scratch. Remember, an infection can start from the smallest cut. A wood or metal sliver can cause blood poisoning if not treated right away. This can result in the loss of a finger or hand. To remove something from your eye, get help from an expert.

As a final thought, remember that the shop can be as safe as any place in the school. It will be as safe as you make it.

OSHA Safety Standards

In April, 1971, the congress of the United States passed the Federal Occupational Safety and Health Act (OSHA). Its purpose is "to assure so far as possible every working man and woman in the nation safe and healthful working conditions and to preserve our human resources." This law affects most employees working in industry. As a student in a shop class, it is important for you to develop the safe work attitudes and habits outlined by this law. Your instructor will inform you of these standards as they apply to your work situation. Employers are looking for people who work safely.

REVIEW QUESTIONS
1. What are the six safety rules listed in this unit?
2. What do the letters O-S-H-A stand for?
3. What are the ABC's of safety?

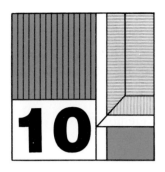

Exploring Woodworking

There's so much to do and learn in woodworking. You can make a project of wood. You can learn to use hand tools and machines safely. You can find out how a house is built. You can be part of a manufacturing company. In this book you will find ideas about things to make, tools to use, machines to run, and materials to try.

The Many Uses of Wood

You will learn how important wood is to the way we live. The average person in the United States uses more wood products than the average person in other countries. Almost 90 percent of us live in homes made of wood. Every day we use paper, furniture, and many other things made from wood. Most manufactured items are first made of wood. For example, even a jet airplane is first made of wood. A small model and/or full-size mock-up is made. These are studied and tested before the real product is built.

Wood comes in many colors, textures, strengths, weights, and costs. The wood to use depends on the item being made. For a baseball bat, the wood used might be hickory or ash. For fine furniture, it might be walnut, cherry, or mahogany. Most of the woods used in building construction are pine, fir, or cedar.

Wood is one of our most important renewable resources. Trees provide wood for houses, furniture, sporting goods, musical instruments, and fuel. Wood is plentiful and easy to work. Thus, it is a favorite material for many things we use in the home, school, and workplace. It is also the most popular material for hobby activities.

You will find woodworking interesting and useful. Here are some of the things you will learn:
• Where wood and other products of trees come from.
• How lumbering is done.
• How plywood and similar products are made.
• Common kinds of woods and their uses.
• How to buy lumber and other wood supplies.
• How to buy woodworking tools and machines.
• How to work safely with hand tools and simple power tools. Fig. 10-1.
• How to work with others. Fig. 10-2.
• How to design, plan, and construct useful and attractive projects. Fig. 10-3.
• How to apply a finish.

10-1. Knowing how tools work allows you to use them more effectively.

- How people earn a living in woodworking. Fig. 10-4.
- How to begin a lifelong hobby in woods.
- How to keep the shop or work area clean and neat.
- How houses and other living units are built.
- How wood products are manufactured.

All of these skills and information will come as you make projects with tools and machines.

Let's take a look at what you will do when you make a project:

1. *Selecting or designing the project.* What to make is a big question. Will it be something for yourself? Will it be a gift for your mother or father or someone else in your family? Maybe you'd like to make a game or build a piece of sports equipment. Or perhaps you'd like an out-of-doors project for birds or a pet. You, your instructor, and the other students

10-2. Working together in the shop is a good way to learn how to get along with other people.

10-3. It is interesting to make things of wood. Here a group is listening while the instructor evaluates their work.

10-4. This woman works in a manufacturing plant. She is cutting boards to size.

10-5. Suppose you decide to make a message center. Would you know how to begin?

will all help you decide what to make. You may find a drawing of a project in a book or magazine. Maybe you would like to design your own project. Fig. 10-5. Your instructor may want you to build the first project from a design he or she has chosen. The students in the class may decide to vote on what will be the mass production project. Fig. 10-6. After learning the basic skills, you will probably select and design your own project.

2. *Reading a drawing and making a sketch.* You must be able to read a drawing to find the answers to these questions:

- What is the overall size of the project?
- How big are the pieces?
- What shape are the pieces?

Sometimes it will be necessary to make a *shop sketch.* A shop sketch is a simple drawing made on squared paper. You always need one when you design your own project. You also need a shop sketch if the project is in a library book or a magazine that you can't keep.

3. *Selecting the materials.* What materials will you use to make the project? For example, will you use pine, cedar, or poplar? Could plywood be used? How would you buy it if you had to go to a lumberyard yourself?

4. *Planning your work.* What is the size of each part? How many parts are alike? How

10-6. These students decided to make house numbers for their manufacturing project.

will you make the project? What steps will you follow? What tools will you need?

5. *Building the project.* Now you are ready to follow the steps for building the project.

6. *Rating the project.* After the project is finished, ask yourself these questions:
- Am I satisfied with it?
- What have I done well?
- What could I have done better?
- How can I improve on the next project?

REVIEW QUESTIONS

1. Name at least four products that are made from wood.
2. List some of the things you expect to learn in woodworking.
3. How is a first project in woodworking usually chosen?
4. Why must you be able to read a drawing?
5. Why should you rate a project after building it?

IIIIIIIIIIIIIIIIIIIIIIIIIIIIIIIIIIIIIIIIII **KEY IDEA** IIIIIIIIIIIIIIIIIIIIIIIIIIIIIIIIIIIIIIIIII

PRESERVING NATURAL RESOURCES

Those materials that we take from the earth for our use are known as *natural resources.* Wood, coal, metal ore, and water are examples of natural resources. Humans have always depended on natural resources to survive. In ancient times, for example, wood was burned to give heat or light. Later, humans learned to make charcoal from wood.

As a fuel, charcoal has advantages over wood. Since it is lighter than wood, it can be more easily carried. It also gives out a high heat for a longer period than does wood. The heat given out by charcoal is also more even.

When a natural resource, such as wood, is used, the environment is affected. The effect on the environment may be small. It may be so small that it is not noticed. Consider the example of wood being burned to make charcoal. To obtain the wood, a tree would need to be cut down. If much charcoal was needed, whole forests might be cut down. (In fact, this happened in seventeenth-century Europe.

Texas Highways

Fig. A. The preservation of natural resources is important in every society. When natural resources are destroyed, they should be replaced, if possible. Several large trees once grew on the land shown here. The trees were cut down to allow the growing of crops. In this case, the cutting of the trees allowed the land to be put to a more valuable use. In many cases, however, natural resources are destroyed needlessly.

The forests near some French cities were cut down to make charcoal. The charcoal was needed to fire the furnaces that smelted metals from metal ore.)

In the past, there were fewer people than there are today. There also were more natural resources on Earth. In the last few centuries we have been using large amounts of our natural resources. The use of these natural resources has been especially heavy in the last twenty years.

In earlier centuries, there was little concern that the Earth's natural resources might be used up. However, people were certainly aware of the consequences of using up natural resources. For example, in those French cities where most of the charcoal was used to smelt metal ore, charcoal for cooking became expensive. This points out one lesson: we often are not aware of a change until it affects us directly. The French people in that city did not know what effect the large demand for charcoal would have on its price. Of course, the demand for charcoal by the smelters raised its price. Cutting down the trees would have had other effects. Without trees, the land could be eroded, or worn away by wind and rain. Large gullies and ravines could be formed. Topsoil could be washed away. These changes would make the land unfit for crops.

The demand for charcoal in that one French town shows the following:
- The use of a natural resource usually requires that it be changed. For example, if a piece of wood is to provide heat, it must be burned.
- If used in certain ways, some natural resources are destroyed. (The trees were burned for charcoal. The charcoal was burned in the smelting furnace. The charcoal was reduced to ashes there.)
- The use of a natural resource can cause a change in the landscape. (In this case, the cutting of the trees caused the land to erode.)
- The scarcity of a natural resource can cause human hardship. There was a heavy demand

for charcoal for the smelting furnaces. Thus, those who needed charcoal to heat their homes and cook their food paid more for it.

In using any natural resource, it is important to remember that not all natural resources can be replaced. A seedling can be planted to replace a mature tree that has been cut down.

It may take, however, thirty years for the seedling to grow to maturity. A tree is an example of a natural resource that can be replaced rather quickly. It can take much longer to replace some natural resources. For example, it took millions of years to form the coal and oil reserves we are using today.

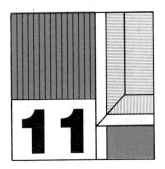

Ordering Materials

You don't have to be an expert to start making something in the shop. As you work with woods, you'll learn more about them. You also will learn how to buy materials from a lumberyard. Materials are expensive. You won't want to waste them by buying too much or buying the wrong thing. In this unit, you will learn how to order lumber.

Lumber

Lumber is wood that comes from trees. Fig. 11-1. *Wood* is the hard substance under the bark of trees and shrubs. Fig. 11-2. If you could look at a piece of wood through a microscope, you would see long, narrow tubes. Each tube is as small as a hair on your head. These tubes, or wood fibers, usually grow straight up and down. This makes wood straight-grained. Look at Fig. 11-3. You can see that it is easier to cut it with the grain than across it. When you cut across the grain, you must cut through the packed fibers.

The tree trunk is cut lengthwise into lumber. Some of the fibers are cut off at an angle. This makes the grain surface look something like the wood shown in Fig. 11-4.

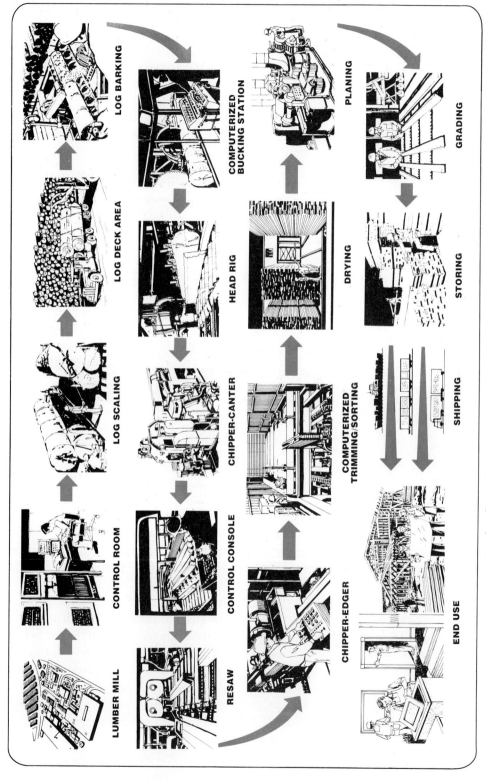

11-1. This flow chart shows how lumber is manufactured.

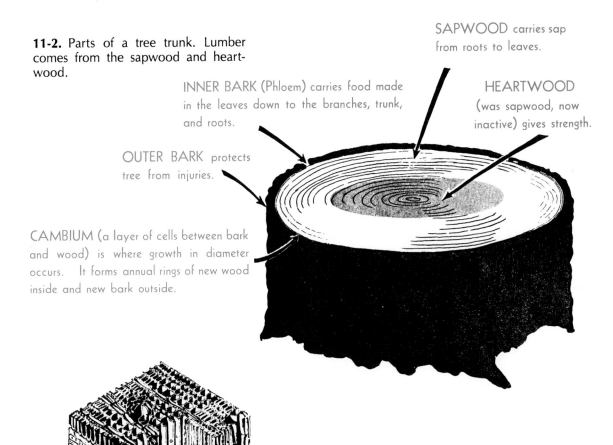

11-2. Parts of a tree trunk. Lumber comes from the sapwood and heartwood.

SAPWOOD carries sap from roots to leaves.

INNER BARK (Phloem) carries food made in the leaves down to the branches, trunk, and roots.

HEARTWOOD (was sapwood, now inactive) gives strength.

OUTER BARK protects tree from injuries.

CAMBIUM (a layer of cells between bark and wood) is where growth in diameter occurs.   It forms annual rings of new wood inside and new bark outside.

11-3. This drawing shows the tube structure of wood. It is easy to see why wood can be cut with the grain more easily than across it.

HOW LUMBER IS CLASSIFIED

Lumber is classified as either softwood or hardwood. *Softwoods* come from evergreen, or needle-bearing, trees. Fig. 11-5. Common softwoods are pine, cedar, fir, and redwood. *Hardwoods* come from broad-leaved trees that shed their leaves in the fall. Fig. 11-6. Some of these are birch, maple, oak, walnut, cherry, poplar, and mahogany.

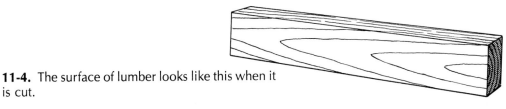

11-4. The surface of lumber looks like this when it is cut.

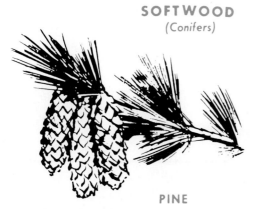

11-5. Softwoods come from evergreen trees such as pine.

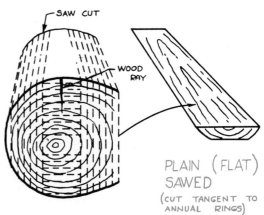

11-7. Plainsawed, or flat-grained, lumber.

11-6. Hardwoods come from broad-leaved trees such as maple.

You will soon find that these terms do not tell how hard the wood really is. Some softwoods are actually harder than some hardwoods! Hardwoods usually cost more than softwoods.

HOW BOARDS ARE CUT FROM LOGS

Boards are cut from logs in two major ways. The cheapest and most economical way is called *plainsawed* (when it is a hardwood tree) or *flat-grained* (when is is a softwood tree). The log is squared and sawed lengthwise from one side to the other. Fig. 11-7. *Quartersawed* (for hardwood) or *edge-grained* (for softwood) is a more expensive method of cutting. It shows a better grain pattern, especially in oak and other hardwoods. Fig. 11-8.

HOW LUMBER IS WORKED

Some lumber is purchased just as it comes from the sawmill. The surface of the lumber is rough ("Rgh"). It must be smoothed by running it through a machine called a *surfacer*, or *planer*, before it can be used in the shop.

Most lumber comes from the lumberyard already smoothed (surfaced, or dressed). Lumber can be purchased surfaced on two sides (S2S) or surfaced on four sides (S4S). You would purchase surfaced, or dressed, lumber if you wanted to build something at home.

HOW LUMBER IS DRIED

When a tree is first cut down, the wood contains much moisture. Most lumber is dried before it is used. *Softwood* lumber is cut into logs and dried in the open air. Lumber made this way is called air-dried lumber (AD). If this lumber is sold with a moisture content of more than 19 percent, it is called green lumber. If the lumber has a moisture content of 19 percent or less, it is classified as dry lumber. Most *hardwoods* are dried in special drying rooms called *kilns* (often pronounced "kills"). Hardwood lumber used for furniture and interiors is kiln-dried (KD) to about 6 to 12 percent moisture. This is the only kind to buy for furniture and other fine projects.

LUMBER SIZES

The nominal, or stock, size of lumber is always larger than its actual size. The actual size is smaller because the lumber is seasoned (dried). It also is surfaced (run through a machine to smooth it). The actual size of softwood is determined by whether it is green or dry. For example, a 2 × 4 (2″ × 4″) will actually measure only 1½″ × 3½″ if dry or 1⁹⁄₁₆″ × 3⁹⁄₁₆″ if green. The actual size of 1″

hardwood that has been surfaced on two sides (S2S) is 1³⁄₁₆″.

LUMBER GRADES

The *select*, or best, grades of softwood lumber are *Grade A* and *Grade B*. These are often sold as "B and better." B-and-better lumber is used for trim on the inside of a house and for projects you make in the school shop. The *C* and *D* grades of lumber are less expensive but can be used for the same things as Grades A and B. *Common lumber* is used only for rough purposes such as in house framing.

The best grade of hardwood is FAS. This means "first and seconds." It is the best grade for making furniture. Number 1 and Number 2 have some defects and are of poorer quality than FAS.

HOW LUMBER IS SOLD

Lumber is sold by the board foot. A *board foot* of lumber is a piece 1″ thick, 12″ wide, and 12″ long. The board foot is the standard unit of measurement used in lumberyards. Lumber less than 1″ thick is figured as 1″. Here is one way to figure board feet: multiply the thickness in inches by the width in feet by the length in feet.

$$BF = T(in.) \times W(ft.) \times L(ft.)$$

For example, a 2″ × 4″ piece that is 12′ long would be 8 board feet:

$$2 \times \tfrac{4}{12} \times 12 = 8$$

The width (4″) is divided by 12 to change it to feet.

A simpler way to figure board feet for small projects is as follows: Board feet equals the thickness in inches times the width in inches time the length in feet, all divided by 12.

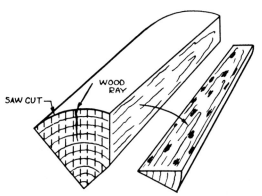

11-8. Quartersawed or edge-grained lumber.

$$BF = \frac{T \ (in.) \times W \ (in.) \times L \ (ft.)}{12}$$

For example, how many board feet are there in a piece of white pine $1'' \times 7'' \times 6'$?

$$BF = \frac{1 \times 7 \times 6}{12}, \text{ or } 3\frac{1}{2}$$

For very small pieces found in many smaller projects, you can figure board feet this way: Board feet equals the thickness in inches times the width in inches times the length in inches divided by 144. There are 144 cubic inches in one board foot.

$$BF = \frac{T \times W \times L \ (all \ in \ inches)}{144}$$

For example: How many board feet are there in a piece of walnut $\frac{1}{2}''$ thick, $9''$ wide, and $28''$ long? (Remember that stock less than $1''$ thick is figured as $1''$.)

$$BF = \frac{1 \times 9 \times 28}{144}, \text{ or } 1\frac{3}{4}$$

Lumber is sold by the board foot, by the hundred board feet, or by the thousand board feet (M). For example, if lumber sells for $600.00 per M, it would cost $60.00 for 100 board feet and 60 cents for one board foot. If you purchased one board foot, the piece would be about $\frac{3}{4}''$ to $1\frac{3}{16}''$ thick, $11\frac{1}{2}''$ to $11\frac{5}{8}''$ wide, and $12''$ long.

In the metric system lumber is always dimensioned in millimetres for thickness and width and in metres for length. Lumber is sold in bulk by the cubic metre—a very large amount of about 424 board feet. Panel stock is dimensioned in millimetres for thickness, width, and length. The metric equivalents given in Tables 11-A, 11-B, and 11-C are *soft* conversions. They are merely a change in the measuring language, not in the real size of the material. In a *hard* conversion, all building construction would be based on a module of 100 millimetres. The preferred sizes would be multiples of 300 (600, 900, etc.). This would mean an actual change in the size of materials. For example, panel stock that is $4' \times 8'$ measures 1220×2440 mm. This size would be reduced to 1200×2400 mm in hard conversion.

HOW TO ORDER LUMBER

To order lumber you must specify:
- The number of pieces you want.
- The size of the pieces.
- The kind of wood.
- The grade of lumber.
- The surface (whether it is to be rough or surfaced).
- Whether it is to be air-dried or kiln-dried. Table 11-D.

Plywood

Plywood is a panel made by gluing layers of wood together. The outside layers are single plies (thin sheets) of wood. They are called *faces* or *face* and *back*. The center layer, or *core*, may be one or more plies of wood. It may also be glued-up lumber or particle board. The plies between the faces and the core are called *cross-bands*.

The layers are placed so that the grain of one runs at right angles to the grain of the

Table 11-A
Common Lumber
Thicknesses

in.	mm
¼	6
½	12 or 13
¾	19
1	25

Table 11-B.
Common Lumber
Lengths

ft.	m
6	1.8
8	2.4
10	3.0
12	3.6
14	4.2
16	4.8

next. When the core consists of more than one ply, these plies may be glued with their grains parallel. The entire core is considered one layer. It is glued with the grain at right angles to the adjoining layers. There are usually three, five, or seven layers.

Softwood plywoods are also called "construction and industrial" plywoods. They are divided into exterior (waterproof) and interior (not waterproof) types. For projects that are to be painted or enameled, interior plywood should be used. The more common grades of softwood plywood are A-A (both sides with a smooth surface), A-B (the face side smooth

Table 11-C. Common Lumber Sizes
for Home Construction

Nominal size (in.)	Actual Dry Size (in.)	Dry Size (mm)
1 × 2	¾ × 1½	19 × 38
1 × 4	¾ × 3½	19 × 89
1 × 6	¾ × 5½	19 × 140
1 × 10	¾ × 9¼	19 × 235
1 × 12	¾ × 11¼	19 × 285
2 × 4	1½ × 3½	38 × 89
2 × 6	1½ × 5½	38 × 140
2 × 10	1½ × 9¼	38 × 235
2 × 12	1½ × 11¼	38 × 285
3 × 6	2½ × 5½	75 × 140
4 × 4	3½ × 3½	89 × 89
4 × 6	3½ × 5½	89 × 140

and the back side with a solid surface), and A-C (the back side of poor quality).

On hardwood plywoods, the outside ply is a good hardwood. Birch, mahogany, walnut, cherry, or gum might be used. The grade of the entire panel is determined by the quality of the face and back. In order of quality, the grades are: (1) premium, (2) good, (3) sound, and (4) utility.

Plywood comes in standard thicknesses such as ¼", ⅜", ½", etc. The most common size plywood sheet is 4' × 8'. Plywood is sold by the square foot. A piece 2' wide and 4' long has 8 square feet. Table 11-E.

Hardboard

Hardboard is made by "exploding" wood chips into wood fibers and then forming them into panels under heat and pressure. There are two types: standard, or untreated, and tempered, or treated. In tempering, the board is dipped in drying oils and baked.

On some hardboard, one face is smooth and the other is rough. The rough face looks like screening. Other hardboard has two smooth surfaces.

Tempered hardboard can be purchased already drilled with evenly spaced holes. This type of board is used for hanging tools, and other items.

The standard sizes of hardboard are 4' × 6' (⅛" thick) and 2' × 12' (¼" thick).

Particle Board

Particle board is a type of composition board made from wood chips. The chips are joined under heat and pressure with an adhesive or other binder. This material is some-

Table 11-D. Guidelines for Selecting Lumber

Standard Sizes of Softwood

Nominal or Stock Size	Actual Size	
	Green	**Dry**
1"	25/32"	3/4"
2"	1 9/16"	1 1/2"
3"	2 9/16"	2 1/2"
4"	3 9/16"	3 1/2"
5"	4 5/8"	4 1/2"
6"	5 5/8"	5 1/2"
7"	6 5/8"	6 1/2"
8"	7 1/2"	7 1/4"
9"	8 1/2"	8 1/4"
10"	9 1/2"	9 1/4"

Standard Thickness of Hardwoods

Rough	S2S
3/8"	3/16"
1/2"	5/16"
5/8"	7/16"
3/4"	9/16"
1"	13/16"
1 1/4"	1 1/16"

Grade

Softwood

1. Yard Lumber
   Select—Good appearance and finishing quality. Includes:
   Grade A—Clear.
   Grade B—High Quality.
   Grade C—For best paint finishes.
   Grade D—Lowest select

   Common—General utility. Not of finishing quality. Includes:
   Construction or No. 1—Best Grade.
   Standard or No. 2—Good Grade.
   Utility or No. 3—Fair Grade.
   Economy or No. 4—Poor.
   No. 5—Lowest.

2. Shop Lumber—For manufacturing purposes. Equal to Grade B Select or better of Yard Lumber. Includes:
   No. 1—Average 8" wide.
   No. 2—Average 7" wide.

3. Structural Lumber.

Hardwood

FAS—Firsts and seconds. Highest Grade.

No. 1 Common and Select. Some Defects.

No. 2 Common. For small cuttings.

Surface	Method of Drying	Method of Cutting
Rgh. or Rough—as it comes from the sawmill	AD—Air dried.	Plainsawed or Flat-grained
S2S—surfaced on two sides.	KD—Kiln dried.	Quartersawed or Edge-grained
S4S—surfaced all four sides.		

Table 11-E. Guidelines for Selecting Plywood

Hardwoods		Construction and Industrial (Softwoods)	
Grade	Uses	Grade	Uses
Premium Grade	Best quality for very high-grade natural finish. Too expensive except for best cabinet work or paneling.	A–A	Best grade for all uses where both sides will show. Exterior or interior.
Good Grade (1)	For good natural finish. Excellent for cabinets, built-ins, paneling and furniture.	A–B	An alternate for A–A grade for high-quality uses where only one side will show. Exterior or interior. The back side is less important.
Sound Grade (2)	For simple natural finishes and high-grade painted surfaces.	A–D	A good all-purpose "good-one-side" panel for lesser quality interior work.
Utility Grade (3)	Not used for project work.	B–D	Utility grade. Used for backing, cabinet sides, etc.
Reject Grade (4)	Not used for project work.		
Widths from 24″ to 48″ in 6″ multiples. Lengths from 36″ to 96″. Veneer-core panels in plies of 3, 5, 7, and 9 are available as follows: 3 ply—⅛″, 3/16″, ¼″; 5 ply—5/16″, ⅜″, ½″; 5 and 7 ply—⅝″; 7 and 9 ply—¾″. There are three types: Type 1 is fully waterproof, Type II is water resistant, and Type III is dry bond.		Many other grades for special uses in home construction are available in thicknesses of ½″, ⅜″, ⅝″, and ¾″; both exterior and interior; 1″ is also available in exterior grades. Common widths 3′ 4″, or 4′; common length is 8′. Be sure to specify exterior grade for outside work (including boats) and interior grade for interior construction.	

thing like hardboard. However, it is thicker and whole chips are used in making it. Shavings from lumber planing mills are a cheap source of the wood chips used in particle board.

Particle board is available in common thicknesses of ⅜″, ½″, and ¾″ and in sheets of 4′ × 8′. Both particle board and hardboard can be worked with regular woodworking tools and machines.

Choosing Lumber for Projects

Which wood to choose for a project depends on three things:

• The type of project. For example, for outdoor furniture, you would want a wood that resists decay.
• The price of the wood.
• The appearance of the wood.

This section describes some of the woods that can be used for beginning, intermediate, and advanced projects. It is important to choose the correct wood for the project.

BEGINNING PROJECTS

For beginning projects, the wood should be easy to work with hand tools. The grain should not become ragged when hand planed. The wood should not be expensive. Some good woods for beginning projects include:

Willow, which is the best wood for beginning projects. It is low-priced, lightweight, strong, and tough. Willow is easy to work, glue, and finish. It has interesting grain patterns. If care is used in finishing, willow is a very handsome wood. It can be stained to resemble walnut. It is also pleasing in its natural colors. There is a wide color range in willow. Thus, pieces should be sorted for color harmony. A filler may be used for the best work, but it isn't necessary as a rule. Willow grows in the eastern United States.

Basswood, which is soft and easy to work. It sands smoothly and is easy to glue. Basswood holds its shape well. It will not twist or warp if properly seasoned (dried). The texture is fine and even. Though lightweight, basswood is strong enough for most projects. Simple finishes are suggested. Strong stains should not be used because basswood is porous and does not stain evenly. It does take paint well and is often used in place of pine for shop projects. Basswood grows in the eastern United States.

Poplar grows in the northeastern part of the United States from Rhode Island to Michigan and as far south as Georgia and Arkansas. It is sometimes called the tulip tree because it bears tuliplike flowers. Poplar is classified as a hardwood but is rather soft and easy to work. However, tools should be sharp. Poplar has a very straight grain and uniform texture. It is light in weight. It tends to be slightly fuzzy when sanded. Poplar takes a very good finish and is used in house building for both inside and outside trim. In commercial furniture making, parts are sometimes made of poplar. They are then stained to look like mahogany.

Pine is a common wood. There are many trees in the pine family. Some of the most common are ponderosa, red, sugar, white, and Idaho. These are similar in general appearance, but they vary in color, texture, hardness, and working qualities. Most are medium-soft and easy to work. They have a light color and a fairly straight grain. Pine is used in building construction for making doors, frames, siding, paneling, and many other things. It is also used for interior woodwork. You will probably use white or ponderosa pine for simple projects. The western soft pines—sugar pine and ponderosa pine—do not take a finish as well as some of the other woods and are often painted. Pine forests are found in many areas of the United States.

INTERMEDIATE PROJECTS

For intermediate projects the wood should be fairly easy to work with hand tools and simple power tools. It should be reasonable in price. The wood should take a good finish. Recommended woods include poplar, willow, and western soft pines (already described) plus the following.

Northern soft elm has a prominent grain and light color. It is a good wood for natural finishes. The coloring is generally even, with some mineral spots or streaks. Elm can be an economical substitute for more expensive hardwoods in some projects. However, it is not always available, so make sure you can get it before designing your project. Elm is harvested in the eastern United States and southeastern Canada.

Philippine mahogany (lauan) comes from the Philippine Islands. It is reasonable in price and not too hard to work. It can be used for almost anything you would choose to build. It machines well and finishes well. Philippine mahogany runs from very light red to deep red in color. The color and grain pattern often vary a great deal from board to board.

ADVANCED PROJECTS

The following woods have fine decorative and finishing qualities. They are valued as cabinet woods.

Genuine mahoganies include Honduras (American) and African mahogany. Honduras mahogany is found in Mexico and Central America. African mahogany comes from Western Africa. Genuine mahogany is the ideal cabinet wood. It is tough, strong, easy to work, and takes a good polish. It is also quite expensive. Genuine mahogany has a deep reddish-brown color that darkens with age.

Black walnut is the most valuable cabinet wood that grows in the United States. Most black walnut comes from the central states of Missouri, Kansas, Iowa, Illinois, Indiana, Ohio, Kentucky, and Tennessee. Although fairly hard and dense, walnut works well with both hand tools and machines. This wood takes a beautiful polish. It varies in color from rich chocolate brown in the heartwood to creamy white in the sapwood. It has a very attractive grain that takes almost any kind of finish. Besides fine furniture, walnut is used for veneer, interior finish, and cabinets. The upper grades are expensive. Thus, you might consider using a lower grade of walnut for your project.

Cherry is very good for furniture because, once dried, it doesn't warp. This hardwood machines well and takes a beautiful finish. It is strong, stiff, and relatively hard. It varies in color from reddish brown in the heartwood to yellow in the sapwood. Cherry has a fairly uniform texture. The cherry used for woodworking does *not* come from the cultivated fruit tree. It grows wild in the forests of the eastern United States.

White ash is one of the finest hardwoods. It has a beautiful grain and a firm texture. White ash turns well on a lathe. Therefore, it is popular for woodworking and furniture making. It is found in the northern and eastern United States.

Hard maple is excellent for many advanced projects. It is a hard, dense, and beautiful wood that resists shock and wear. Be sure to buy "selected white" hard maple. "Selected white" is not a grade but refers only to color. Maple lumber comes mostly from the Middle Atlantic and Lake states. It is a hard, strong wood that resists shock and wear.

Oak is an open-grained wood that has been widely used in furniture and interiors. It is quarter-sawed to show its broad rays, which add to its beauty. Oak is somewhat hard on machinery blades and knives, but it finishes well. Red oak has a slightly reddish tinge and a rather coarse grain. It is used in furniture, paneling, moldings, and flooring. Most red oak lumber comes from the southern states and Atlantic coastal plain. White oak has a better color, finer texture, and more interesting grain pattern than red oak. It is considered the better choice for fine furniture. White oak is also more resistant to rot, moisture, and weathering. The heartwood is grayish brown. The sapwood is nearly white. White oak grows throughout the eastern half of the United States and Canada.

REVIEW QUESTIONS

1. What is lumber?
2. What is the difference between softwood and hardwood?
3. Are all softwoods softer than hardwoods? Explain.
4. What does the expression "dressed lumber" mean?
5. How many board feet are there in a piece of lumber $1'' \times 10'' \times 8'$?

6. Why is the actual size of lumber always smaller than the nominal size?
7. What is the best grade of hardwood lumber?
8. What information should be included to order lumber correctly?

9. What is plywood?
10. Name three good woods for a beginning project. Explain why each is good.

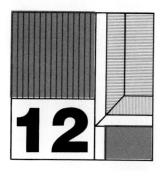

Measuring and Marking

You must learn to measure accurately in both systems of measurement. Remember the motto, "Measure twice; cut once." No project will turn out well if you measure incorrectly.

Tools for Measuring

RULES

A *bench rule* is a wood rule with brass tips on the ends. The brass tips protect the ends from damage. A damaged rule will not measure accurately. One side is graduated (divided) into eighths of an inch along both edges. The other side is graduated in sixteenths of an inch. Bench rules are made in 1' (12"), 2' (24"), and 3' (36") lengths. Sometimes the 3' rule is

called a yardstick. Metric bench rules are also available. Fig. 12-1.

The *zigzag rule*, or *folding rule*, is used to measure longer stock when very exact measurements are not too important. Fig. 12-2.

12-1. One side of this 12" bench rule is a 300-mm metric rule.

12-2. A zigzag rule with inch measurements.

12-3. This tape rule has metric measurements on the upper edge. It has customary measurements on the lower edge.

12-4. Using a steel tape to check the width of material.

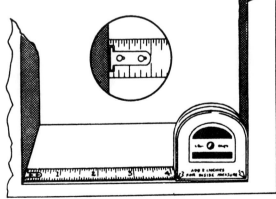

12-5. Checking an inside measurement with a steel tape. You must add 2″ to the amount shown on the tape to allow for the size of the tape's case.

The *push-pull, steel tape,* or *tape rule* is a metal rule that rolls up into a case. Fig. 12-3. There is a hook at the end to slip over the edge of the board. Fig. 12-4. Since it is flexible (bends easily) it can measure curved surfaces. It is also very good for measuring the inside diameter of things. Fig. 12-5.

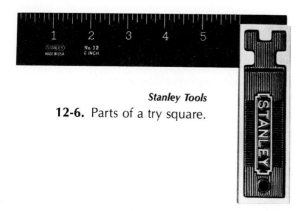

Stanley Tools

12-6. Parts of a try square.

SQUARES

The *try square* is used for squaring, measuring, and testing. Fig. 12-6. The blade and handle are at right angles (90°) to each other. The try square is used:

● To test whether a surface is flat.

● To check a face and edge surface for squareness.

● To mark lines across the face or edge of stock. Fig. 12-7. There are graduations along the edge for measuring. *Never use this tool for pounding or hammering.*

The *combination square* can do many things. This tool has a blade and a head. The blade has a groove cut along its length so that it can slide into the head. One side of the head makes a 90° angle with the blade and the other side a 45° angle. There is a *level* (a tool for testing for a flat, horizontal surface) in the head. Fig. 12-8. The combination square can be used as:

● A try square.

● A miter square to lay out 45° angles and check them.

● A depth gauge.

● A level.

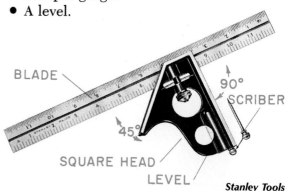

BLADE   90°   SCRIBER   45°   SQUARE HEAD   LEVEL

Stanley Tools

12-8. Parts of a combination square.

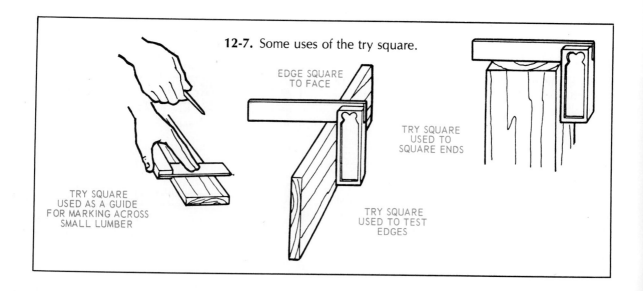

12-7. Some uses of the try square.

EDGE SQUARE TO FACE

TRY SQUARE USED TO SQUARE ENDS

TRY SQUARE USED AS A GUIDE FOR MARKING ACROSS SMALL LUMBER

TRY SQUARE USED TO TEST EDGES

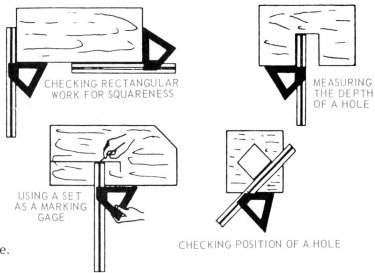

CHECKING RECTANGULAR WORK FOR SQUARENESS

MEASURING THE DEPTH OF A HOLE

USING A SET AS A MARKING GAGE

CHECKING POSITION OF A HOLE

12-9. Using a combination square.

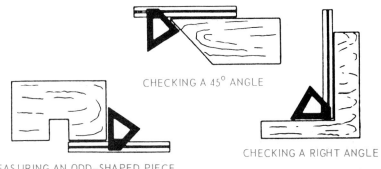

CHECKING A 45° ANGLE

CHECKING A RIGHT ANGLE

MEASURING AN ODD—SHAPED PIECE

- A marking gauge. Fig. 12-9.

The *steel square* is L-shaped like the try square but larger. It has a body (the longer part) and a tongue (the shorter part). The steel square is used for measuring and checking. Fig. 12-10.

The *carpenter's square* is also called a *framing square*. It is a large steel square used for measuring and laying out. The body is 2″ × 24″ and the tongue is 1½″ × 16″. The tables of figures on this square are useful to the carpenter.

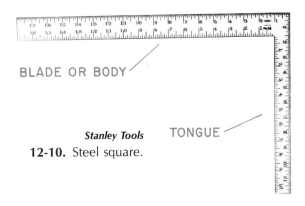

BLADE OR BODY

TONGUE

Stanley Tools
12-10. Steel square.

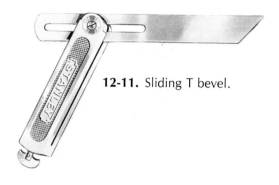

12-11. Sliding T bevel.

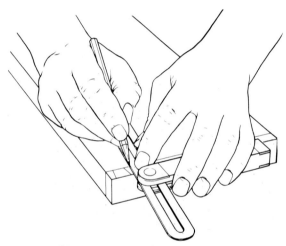

12-12. Using a sliding T bevel.

OTHER COMMON MEASURING TOOLS

The *T bevel (sliding T bevel)* consists of a handle and an adjustable blade. It is used to lay out and check all angles other than those of 45° and 90°. Figs. 12-11 and 12-12.

Outside calipers have two curved legs hinged at the end. Thus, the distance between them is adjustable. Outside calipers are used to measure the outside diameter of round pieces. Fig. 12-13.

The *all-purpose measuring tool* has many uses. It can serve as a square, marking gauge, protractor, depth gauge, dowel gauge, nail gauge, and other types of measuring tools. Fig. 12-14.

Tools for Marking

An ordinary *lead pencil* is the most common marking tool. A pencil mark is easy to see and can be quickly removed. Use a hard lead (such as No. 2) and mark lightly. When working with dark woods like walnut, a white or yellow artist's pencil will show up better. *Never sand off pencil lines.* Doing so forces the lead (actually graphite) into the wood grain. The

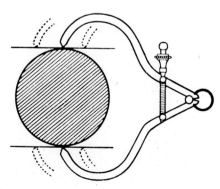

12-13. Using calipers to measure the outside diameter of a cylinder.

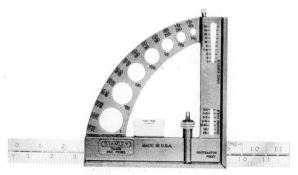

12-14. The all-purpose measuring tool can be used in many ways.

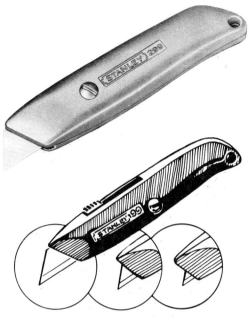

12-15. Utility knife.

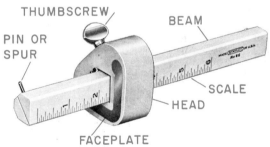

marks will show after the finish has been applied. Either plane or scrape off the lines.

A short-bladed *knife* (like the *sloyd knife*) is used for very accurate marking. It is used also for cutting and whittling. It should be used only when sawing to (on) the line. Then the saw will remove the mark.

The *utility knife* has a sharp blade that extends from a handle. Use it only when you know the mark will disappear as the wood is cut, formed, or shaped. Fig. 12-15.

The *marking gauge* is used for marking a line parallel with the edge or face. It is used especially when the distance is less than 6″. Fig. 12-16.

The *combination square* is used often for marking as well as for measuring. Fig. 12-9.

A *scratch awl* is used for marking the center of holes to be drilled or bored. It can also serve as a punch to make a small dent for

starting nails and screws. It is handy for scribing (drawing) lines on wood to show where it will be cut. Fig. 12-17.

Measuring Stock

LENGTH

To check length, place the left end of the rule directly over one end of the stock, with the rule on edge. At the other end of the stock, read the measurement on the rule. For longer lengths, use a zigzag rule or a steel tape. This will avoid measuring errors that come from moving a short rule several times.

WIDTH

Measure the width by holding the left end of the rule on one edge of the stock. Slide your right thumb along the rule until you can read the correct width. Fig. 12-18.

THUMBSCREW

PIN OR SPUR

BEAM

SCALE

HEAD

FACEPLATE

12-16. Parts of a marking gauge.

Stanley Tools
12-17. Scratch awl.

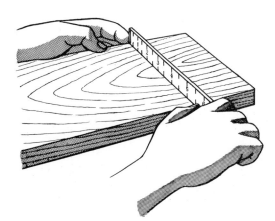

12-18. Checking the width of stock. One finger holds the end of the rule even with the edge of stock. Slide the other finger along until you can read the correct width. '

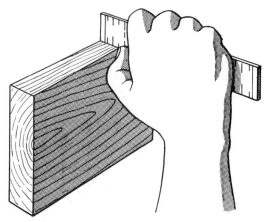

12-19. Checking the thickness of stock. Notice that one end of the rule is held over one edge of the board. Slide your thumb until you can read the thickness.

THICKNESS

To check thickness, hold the rule as shown in Fig. 12-19. Read the thickness by looking at the graduation mark directly over the corner.

Marking Stock

LENGTH

1. Look at the end of the board. Make sure it is square and doesn't have a split, check (slight separation), or other flaw. If it is not square, trim the end. (Find out from the drawing how long the board must be. Then add about ½″ for trimming and squaring up. Use the try square to test for squareness.)

2. Hold the rule on edge and parallel with the edge of the board. Place the end of the rule exactly even with the end of the board. The rule must not be at an angle. It is held on edge so that the graduation marks are right next to the surface of the wood. Fig. 12-20.

3. Mark the wood at the correct length with a sharp pencil or knife. Make a small point right at the mark on the rule.

4. Place a try square so that the handle is against the edge of the board. Slide the blade along until the pencil mark just barely shows.

5. Rule a line along the board. If it is a wide board, use a steel or carpenter's square instead. Fig. 12-21. Tilt the blade slightly and

12-20. Marking to length. Note that the rule is held on edge for more accurate measurement.

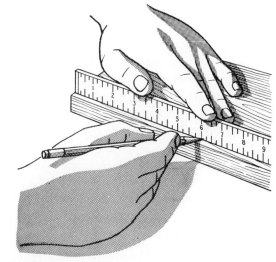

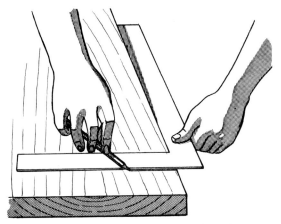

12-21. Drawing a line across the board using a steel, or carpenter's, square.

12-23. Drawing a line with a try square before cutting to width.

then hold it firmly against the edge. For long boards, use a zigzag rule or tape rule.

WIDTH

1. Find out from the drawing how wide the board must be. Allow about ¼" to ⅜" extra for squaring up.

2. Hold a rule at right angles to the edge and mark this width at several points. Fig. 12-22.

12-22. Marking for width. Several marks should be made at various points along the board.

3. Hold a try square or carpenter's square along these points and draw the line. Fig. 12-23.

USING A MARKING GAUGE

1. Check the marking gauge to make sure the spur, or pin, is a sharp wedge shape. If dull, this must be sharpened. Some types have a wheel at the end of the beam.

2. Adjust to the correct length. Notice the rule on the side of the beam. This can be used to set the distance. It will not be accurate, however, after you have sharpened the pin, or spur. To adjust again:

● Adjust to the distance as shown on the beam, and tighten the thumbscrew lightly.

● Hold the gauge in your left hand with the spur up.

● Hold a rule on edge in your right hand. Place the end of the rule against the head of the gauge. Fig. 12-24.

● Check the distance. A slight movement of the head in either direction will adjust it to the correct amount. Tighten the thumbscrew.

3. Try the gauge on a piece of scrap stock. Get the "feel" of the tool. It is better to push the tool than to pull it.

12-24. Setting a marking gauge.

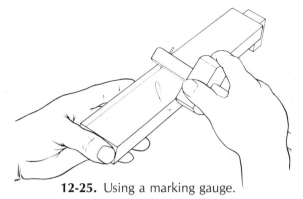

12-25. Using a marking gauge.

4. Tilt the gauge at a slight angle. Hold the head gently, but firmly, against the surface or edge. Fig. 12-25. Push the tool away from you. Make a shallow groove. If you push too hard, the point may jump out of place and scratch the surface.

5. Never mark across the grain. Do not use the gauge to mark for a bevel or chamfer (slanted cut).

MARKING WITH A COMBINATION SQUARE

1. Adjust the blade to the correct length measured from the right-angle side of the head.

2. Hold the head against the work and a pencil against the end of the blade. Fig. 12-26.

3. Slide both along the board to mark the line.

You can also use a rule and pencil for gauge-marking. This is a little more difficult because you must keep the rule square with the edge as you slide it along.

12-26. Using a combination square and pencil for marking. This is one of the simplest ways of marking to width.

REVIEW QUESTIONS

1. Name three common kinds of rules.
2. What kind of rule is good for measuring curved surfaces?
3. Name four kinds of squares found in the wood shop.
4. Name three things that can be done with a try square.
5. Which kind of square has a blade that can be removed from the handle or head?
6. What is the purpose of outside calipers?
7. About how much material must be allowed for squaring up stock?

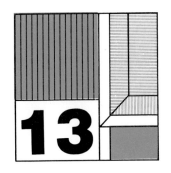

Planning and Making a Layout

Before you can begin to build a project, you must plan your work. When the plans are completed, the next step is to make the layouts.

Planning is important when you are going to use tools and materials to make things. In fact, the job is already half done when it is well planned. A good slogan to follow is *"Plan your work; then work your plan."* Sure, you can start right out "butchering wood." But, if you do, you'll waste a lot of material. You will also do poor work.

What You Will Need for Planning

How do you plan in wood? Suppose the class and your instructor have decided on the first project. Fig. 13-1. In making your plans, you will need the following items:
• Drawing of the Project.
• Bill of Materials.
• Procedures List.
• List of Tools and Machines.

DRAWING OF THE PROJECT

You will need a drawing of the project or a shop sketch that you have made yourself. This drawing or sketch must have the dimensions on it. Fig. 13-1.

BILL OF MATERIALS

This is the list of all the things you will need to build a project. Fig. 13-2. Always make out the bill of materials before you start because:
• It tells you exactly what size and kind of lumber and other materials you will need.
• It helps you find out the cost of the project.
• You can take the list with you if you must buy your own materials.
• It is a good check list when you are getting the materials together.

A complete bill of materials includes *everything* you need to build the project. The list includes:
• Number of pieces needed.
• Thickness, width, and length of each piece.
• Name of each part.
• Kind of lumber or other building material.
• Cost.

The size of each part listed in the bill of materials is the exact, final dimension. Before you get out your materials, you can make a *stock-cutting list*. This list gives the size of each piece that you cut from the lumber, before the finished size. To the sizes in the bill of materials you must add the following:
• 1/16" to 1/8" for thickness.
• 1/8" to 1/4" for width.
• 1/2" for length.

Of course, plywood is cut from the exact

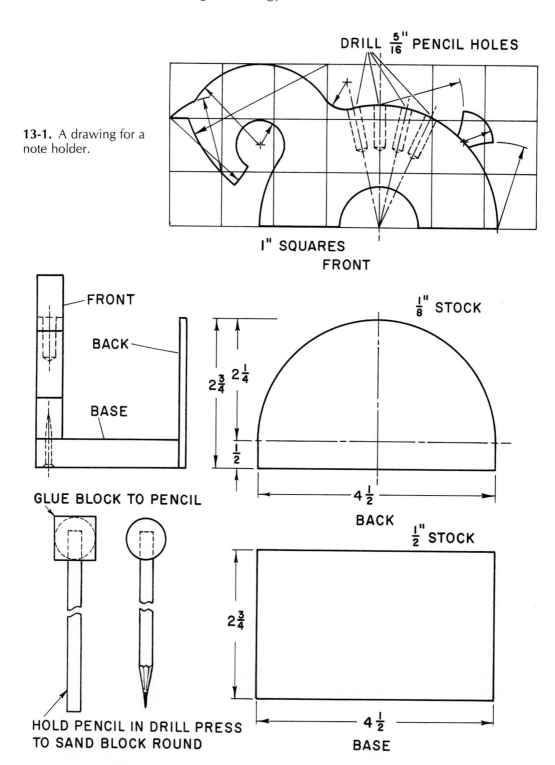

DRILL $\frac{5"}{16}$ PENCIL HOLES

13-1. A drawing for a note holder.

1" SQUARES
FRONT

FRONT

BACK

BASE

GLUE BLOCK TO PENCIL

HOLD PENCIL IN DRILL PRESS
TO SAND BLOCK ROUND

$\frac{1}{8}$" STOCK

$2\frac{3}{4}$ $2\frac{1}{4}$ $\frac{1}{2}$

$4\frac{1}{2}$

BACK $\frac{1}{2}$" STOCK

$2\frac{3}{4}$

$4\frac{1}{2}$

BASE

thickness and as close to finished size as possible.

PROCEDURES LIST

This is a list of the steps to follow in making each part, putting the project together, and applying a finish. Drawing up a procedures list is an important part of a project.

LIST OF TOOLS AND MACHINES

You should make a list of the tools and power machines you will need. Then you can make sure that the tools are available. You should also be sure you will be allowed to operate the machines. Fig. 13-2.

Planning Sheet

To help with your planning, use a form like the one shown in Fig. 13-2. Fill out the form as carefully as you can. Check it. Did you forget anything? When your plan is approved, you can begin to draw the project. Check off each step as you do it.

In your planning, follow the examples shown in Figs. 13-1 and 13-2. Notice that:
- There is a clear, easy-to-read drawing.
- The bill of materials lists exactly what you need.
- The steps in making the project are clear and easy to follow.

PLANNING SHEET

Name _____ Grade _____

Note Holder

Name of the Project   Date Started   Date Completed

Bill of Materials:

No.	T	W	L	Name of Part	Material	Unit Cost	Total Cost
1	½″	3″	7″	Front	Pine		
1	⅛″	2¾″	4½″	Back	Pine		
1	½″	2¾″	4½″	Base	Pine		
1	⅝″	⅝″	⅝″	Pencil top	Pine		

TOOLS AND MACHINES:
Crosscut saw, coping saw or jigsaw, backsaw, rule, try square, pencil, jack plane, twist drill, hand drill, sandpaper, drill press, hammer, screwdriver.

PROCEDURES OR STEPS:
1. Make a stock-cutting list.
2. Lay out and cut all pieces to size.
3. Complete the front:
   - Enlarge the design.
   - Transfer the design to the wood.
   - Cut out design with coping saw or jigsaw.
   - Smooth the edges.
   - Drill the holes for the pencils.
4. Square up the base.
5. Lay out and cut the back to shape.
6. Assemble the parts with screws and nails.
7. Make the ball for the end of the pencil.
8. Apply the finish.

13-2. The planning sheet contains the bill of materials.

• The list of tools includes only those really needed.

Making a Layout

A *layout* is a guide, or pattern, that can be drawn or traced directly on the wood for each part. The layout shows shape and size, location of holes and other openings, and all the things to be worked. For irregular shapes and designs, a *template* is often used.

On some parts, the layout may be made one step at a time as you work the wood.

Points to Consider in Making a Layout

LUMBER DEFECTS

Most lumber has some defects. Lumber with bad defects such as a crack or a hole must be avoided. Get the most out of the lumber by first checking the sizes of each part of the project. Then lay out the pieces around these defects. Defects such as knots are sometimes left in the pieces. They can add interest. For example, most knotty pine furniture has some exposed but tight knots.

ALLOWANCE FOR CUTTING, PLANING, AND SHAPING

Make sure you allow some extra material for working the wood to size. However, keep this waste to a minimum. If rough lumber is used, allow ⅛" in thickness, ¼" in width, and ½" in length for cutting, planing, and shaping to size.

GRAIN

Grain direction is the way in which the pores of the wood are arranged. Wood is

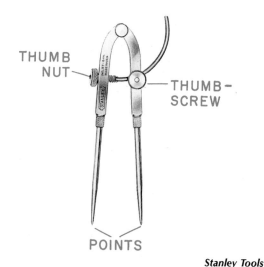

THUMB NUT

THUMB-SCREW

POINTS

Stanley Tools

13-3. Dividers.

stronger when pressure is applied "with the grain"; that is, in the same direction as the grain. Wood is weaker when the force is across the grain. Therefore, make the layout for legs and other support parts so that their length is *with* the grain.

USING SHEET STOCK

Plywood, particle board, and hardboard are sheet materials. These are accurately cut to a rectangular shape during manufacturing. Always start a layout at the corners since these first two edges will not have to be reworked.

Layout Tools

All the tools used for measuring and marking are used in making a layout. Thus, you will need rules, a marking gauge, squares, a pencil, and a knife. In addition, you will need dividers or a pencil compass.

A *dividers* is a tool with two pointed metal legs. Fig. 13-3. It is used to lay out circles and

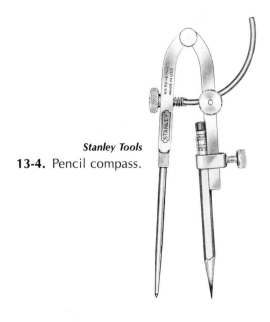

Stanley Tools
13-4. Pencil compass.

arcs and for stepping off equal distances. To set a dividers, place one leg over an inch mark of the rule. Open the other leg to the measurement you want. To use a dividers, place one leg over the starting point and tilt the dividers slightly. Turn it clockwise (the direction clock hands move). Be careful not to change the setting of the dividers.

A *pencil compass* can be used in place of a dividers in the wood shop. Fig. 13-4. It has one metal leg and one pencil leg.

Drawing a Circle

Draw a circle as follows.
1. Locate the center of the circle.
2. Adjust the dividers or compass to equal the radius of the circle. The *radius* is half the diameter. The *diameter* is the distance across the middle of the circle. The circumference of a circle is the distance completely around it. It is equal to the diameter times 3.1416.

3. Place one leg at the center mark. Tilt the compass or dividers slightly. Swing it clockwise to draw the line or sharp groove. An *arc* (a part of a circle) is drawn the same way. Fig. 13-5.

4. To keep from scratching the wood surface at the center, place a small rubber eraser over the sharp point of the dividers or compass. A piece of masking tape can also be placed at the center.

Drawing a Rounded Corner

Rounded corners can improve the appearance of a project.
1. Find the radius of the corner.
2. Mark this distance from the corner on one side and end.

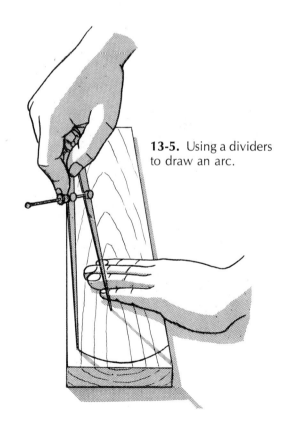

13-5. Using a dividers to draw an arc.

3. Hold a try square against the side and end and draw two lines to mark the center. Fig. 13-6.

4. Set the dividers to the correct radius.

5. Swing the dividers from the left to the right, clockwise, to mark the rounded corner.

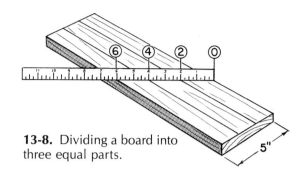

13-8. Dividing a board into three equal parts.

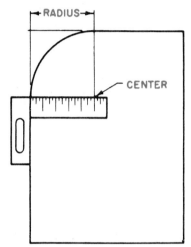

13-6. Finding the center for drawing a rounded corner.

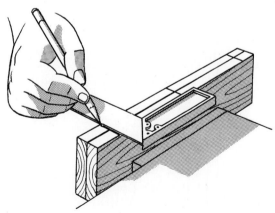

13-7. Laying out duplicate parts. Mark all pieces at the same time.

Layout of Duplicate Parts

Many items have parts that are exactly alike. Lay out these duplicate parts together. This will save time.

1. Place the pieces on edge and side by side on a bench top.

2. To make sure the working ends are even, hold a try square over them. Hold the pieces together firmly in a vise or with a clamp.

3. Measure the correct length along one edge.

4. Mark a line across all the pieces at the same time. Fig. 13-7.

Dividing a Board into Equal Parts

A board may have an odd width. You can divide it into any number of equal parts as follows.

1. Hold a rule at an angle across the face of the board until the inch marks divide the space evenly. For example, the board may be 5" wide. If you want to divide it into three equal parts, hold the rule at an angle with the 6" mark on one edge. Then make a mark at the 2", 4", and 6" marks. Fig. 13-8.

2. Draw lines through these marks. The lines should be parallel with the edge of the board.

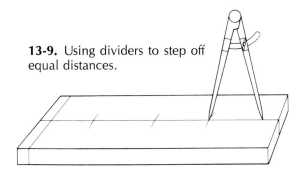

13-9. Using dividers to step off equal distances.

amount. This is usually a small, even part of the total distance.

2. Place one leg on the starting point. Then turn the dividers from side to side as shown in Fig. 13-9.

Enlarging a Design and Using a Template

Often you will find the plan for a project you like in a book or magazine. The plan may be less than full size. You must enlarge this pattern before transferring it to the wood. This is something you'll be doing often in woodworking. The steps are simple. However, you must follow them carefully.

Suppose you saw the design in Fig. 13-10 in a book. In most books and magazines the

Stepping Off Equal Distances

To step off equal distances or to divide a space into equal parts, the dividers or compass can be used. This is especially good for dividing a curved line.

1. Adjust the dividers to the correct

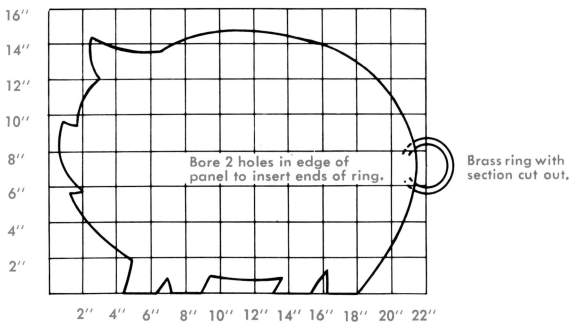

Bore 2 holes in edge of panel to insert ends of ring.

Brass ring with section cut out.

13-10. Pattern for cutting board to be made from 1" thick lumber.

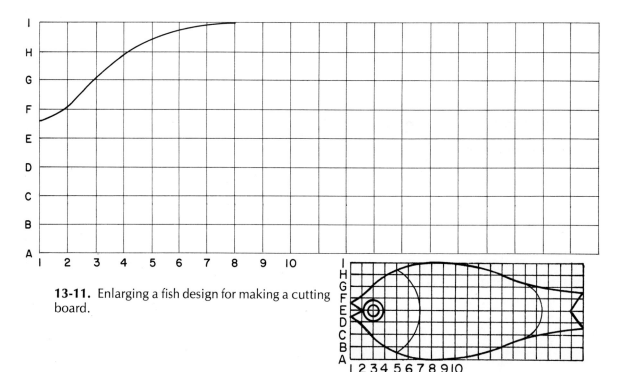

13-11. Enlarging a fish design for making a cutting board.

drawing is laid out in squares. A note tells you what size the full-size squares must be. Sometimes, however, a drawing or photograph has no squares. If the design is about ¼ the size you would like to have it, first cover it with ¼-inch squares. If the design is in a book, draw the squares on transparent paper. (You can see through it.) Then clip the paper over the page. Now proceed as follows:

1. On a large piece of paper, draw squares the full size. (You can also use cross-sectioned paper.) For example, if the drawing says, "one-inch squares," make your squares that size. Start in the lower left-hand corner of both the original drawing and the full-size sheet. Letter up the left side A, B, C, etc. Number across the bottom, 1, 2, 3, etc. Fig. 13-11.

2. Locate points on the drawing. Transfer them to the full-size pattern. Locate enough points to make the outline take shape.

3. After enough points are located, use a French curve (also called an irregular curve) to trace the outline. You can also bend a piece of soft wire (such as solder) to follow the points. Trace the line.

4. If the design is the same on both sides the plan is *symmetrical*. Then you need to trace only half the pattern. Fig. 13-12. Then fold the paper down the center. Cut out or trace the full pattern. To trace, place carbon paper between the folds, carbon side facing toward the blank half.

5. A design can be made smaller by using smaller squares. If the original is on ¼" squares, you can make the design half-size by drawing it on ⅛" squares.

6. You can use the full-size plan in one of several ways:

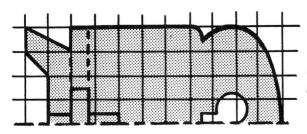

EACH SQUARE = ½-INCH

13-12. In this drawing of a bookrack, only half the design is shown.

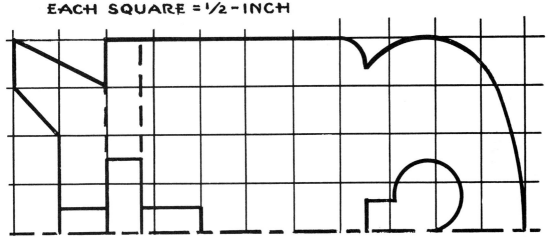

● Cut out the plan with scissors. Fasten corners with transparent tape. Trace around the plan on the wood. Then remove the plan.

● Cut out the pattern with scissors. Paste or glue it on the wood. It stays on while the wood is trimmed to size.

● Place carbon paper between the pattern and the wood and trace the design. Then remove.

7. If the drawing shows only half the plan, you can transfer the pattern to the wood as shown in Fig. 13-13.

8. When many parts of the same design are to be made, a *template* is made of thin wood or

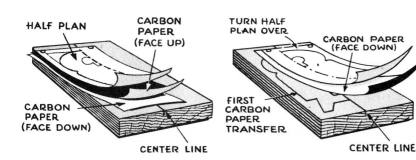

HALF PLAN

CARBON PAPER (FACE UP)

CARBON PAPER (FACE DOWN)

CENTER LINE

TURN HALF PLAN OVER

CARBON PAPER (FACE DOWN)

FIRST CARBON PAPER TRANSFER

CENTER LINE

13-13. Transferring the pattern to the wood when only half the plane is drawn.

metal. (A template is a pattern that can be used many times.) Hold the template firmly on the wood and trace around it.

REVIEW QUESTIONS

1. Name the four important parts of a plan. Describe each one.
2. Is a stock-cutting list the same as a bill of materials? Explain.
3. What is a layout?
4. What is a dividers?
5. Describe the way to adjust dividers to draw a circle that is 3″ in diameter.
6. List the steps necessary for making the layout for a rounded corner.
7. Tell how to lay out duplicate parts.
8. How can you divide a 9″ board into four equal parts?
9. If the plan is one-third as large as you want it and it is covered with ¼-inch squares, how large must the full-size squares be?
10. Tell three ways to use a pattern in making a layout on wood.
11. What is a template?

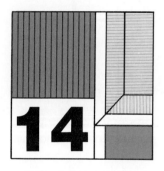

Machines in Woodworking

You probably know that complicated devices such as the drill press and jigsaw are machines. However, you might be surprised to learn that the hand tools used in the shop are also machines. Chisels, hammers—even things like a nail or screw—are machines. They are, however, operated with hand power. Each of these simple items is just as truly a machine as the more complicated ones. As a matter of fact, machines such as the jigsaw are made up of several very simple machines that work together.

What Is a Machine?

A *machine* is a device used to make work easier. As you use hand tools, materials, and machines in woodwork, you will be doing work. What do we mean by work? *Work* is

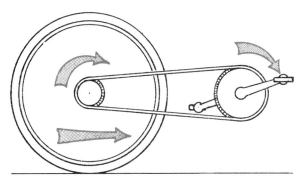

14-1. Force applied to the pedals of a bicycle is changed from rotary motion to forward motion.

done when a force moves through a distance to make something move or stop moving. You are "working" when you strike a ball with a bat or when you ride a bicycle. You are also doing work when you pound a nail or saw a board.

Force is the push or pull that can do work. A machine helps you work by multiplying the force you use. Such a gain of force is obtained by "trading" distance. Work accomplished over a short distance requires more force than the same work done over a long distance. For example, try turning a screw into wood with your fingers. Can you do it? Now use a screwdriver. How can such a simple machine help you do work? Easy. You apply force to the handle. The outside of the handle moves a *greater distance* with less force so that the tip of the blade moves a *shorter distance* with more force.

By exerting a force on a machine in one place, the machine can exert a force at another place and, in some cases, in another direction. Consider the bicycle. You apply an up-and-down force with your thighs while your feet go around in a circle. The force applied to the pedals turns the large gear wheel. The large gear wheel is connected to the small gear

wheel with a chain. The small gear wheel turns the rear wheel to move the bicycle forward. The bicycle gears change the direction of the force that you apply with your legs to a forward motion. Fig. 14-1.

Some force is lost through the friction of the machine itself. *Friction* is the resistance caused by the rubbing together of machine parts. No machine can increase both force and distance at the same time. The screwdriver tip has the greater force but moves through less distance than the handle. The rear wheel of the bicycle moves through a greater distance but has less force than that applied to the pedals.

The Six Simple Machines

There are six simple machines. All complicated woodworking machines are made up of a combination of these.

1. The *inclined plane* makes work easier, since a smaller effort (the force exerted) can lift a heavy weight. However, the effort must move farther (along the incline) than when a weight is lifted directly. Inclined planes are found, for example, on a woodworking plane. Fig. 14-2.

2. A *wedge* has one or two sloping sides. All

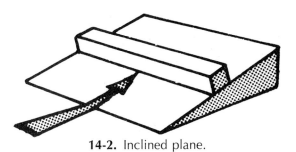

14-2. Inclined plane.

14-3. Wedge. You will find the wedge shape on the cutting edge of a chisel, knife, or gouge, on the teeth of a saw or file, and on a nail.

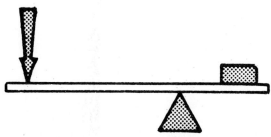

14-5. Lever. Hammers, pliers, hinges, and paintbrushes make use of the lever.

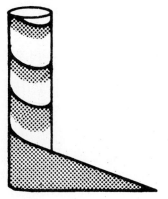

14-4. Screw. This simple machine is found in tools such as the wood screw, vise, hand clamp, C-clamp, and bar clamp.

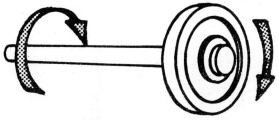

14-6. Wheel and axle. This is found in braces, screwdrivers, and hand drills.

knives, chisels, saws, and axes have wedges. Fig. 14-3.

3. A *screw* is actually a spiral-shaped inclined plane. A wood screw clamp or vise is a good example of the screw. Fig. 14-4.

4. A *lever* is a long, rigid bar supported at one point. The support point is called the fulcrum. The hammer and axe are levers. Fig. 14-5.

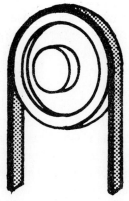

14-7. Pulley. The pulley can be seen on a band saw, belt sander, or jigsaw.

5. The *wheel and axle* has a wheel connected firmly to an axle. When one turns, the other turns too. A screwdriver, a door handle, and a brace are examples of the wheel and axle. Fig. 14-6.

6. A *pulley* is a wheel that turns around an axle. Fig. 14-7.

Remember these six simple machines. As you study this book, you'll see how woodworking tools are based on them.

REVIEW QUESTIONS

1. What is a machine?
2. What is friction?
3. Name the six simple machines.

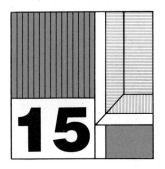

Sawing to a Line

15

A *saw* is a woodcutting tool that has a thin steel blade with small sharp teeth along the edge. Saws are hand tools used to cut wood to different sizes and shapes. They are also used for making the joints that hold parts together. Your skill in using saws is important because it shows in the final appearance of the project. Fig. 15-1.

Tools and Equipment for Sawing

The *crosscut saw* is used to saw across grain. Its parts are shown in Fig. 15-2. The teeth of the crosscut saw are knife-shaped. They are bent alternately to the right and left. This is called *set*. It makes the saw cut wider than the blade. The saw cut is called the *kerf*.

15-1. Sawing a board. The teeth of a handsaw are wedges. The saw itself is a lever in your hand. Notice that the wedges are shaped to cut mostly on the down, or forward, stroke. Here again the force applied to the handle is divided into smaller forces. These forces make each tooth (wedge) do the cutting.

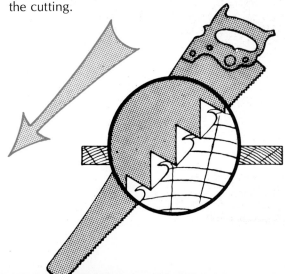

POINTS TO THE INCH

"Points to the inch" is the term used to designate the size of the teeth in a saw. The smaller the number of teeth to the inch the rougher the cut; the greater the number of teeth, the smoother the cut.

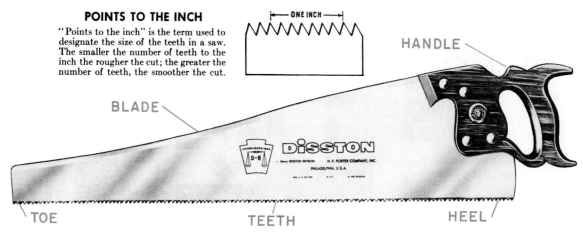

← ONE INCH →

HANDLE

BLADE

DiSSTON
D-8
Henry DISSTON DIVISION   H. K. PORTER COMPANY, INC.
PHILADELPHIA, U.S.A.

TOE   TEETH   HEEL

15-2. Parts of a handsaw.

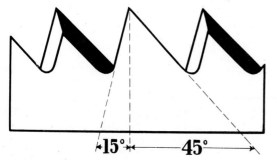

15°   45°

15-3(a). This enlarged view of a crosscut saw blade section shows the knifelike teeth.

Since the kerf is wider than the blade, the blade will not bind (stick) as the sawing is done. Fig. 15-3. The saw teeth may be coarse (with only six or eight teeth per inch). It can be fine (with as many as ten or twelve per inch). A saw for general-purpose cutting should have about eight or nine *points* per inch. There is always one more point than

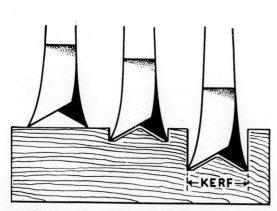

←KERF→

15-3(b). Here you see how the teeth of the saw blade form a kerf. One tooth is bent to the left, the next is bent to the right, the next to the left, and so on.

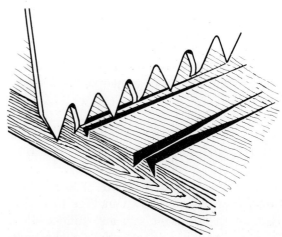

15-3(c). An example of how a crosscut saw cuts. The beginning cut makes two grooves if drawn lightly over the surface.

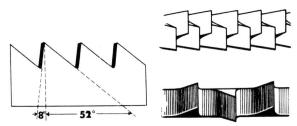

15-4(a). The teeth of the ripsaw are shaped like small chisels. They are designed to cut with the grain.

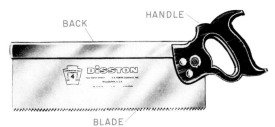

15-5. Parts of a backsaw.

teeth per inch. The length of the saw should be about 20″ to 26″.

The *ripsaw* is used for sawing with the grain. Its teeth are chisel-shaped and set alternately to the right and left. Fig. 15-4. A 26″ 5½-point saw is good for most work.

The *backsaw* is a fine-tooth crosscut saw. It has a heavy metal band along the back that supports the thin blade. Fig. 15-5.

A *workbench* is needed to do all kinds of operations. Some benches are designed to be used by one or two people. Others have room for four workers. Fig. 15-6.

A *bench hook* is a wooden board. It has a cleat slightly shorter than the width of the board across the ends. There is one cleat on each side. It is used on the bench top for cutting and chiseling. It supports the work and protects the bench. Fig. 15-7.

A *miter box*, can be used for cutting 45° and 90° angles. Fig. 15-8.

A *wood vise* is a clamping device. It holds wood to the workbench for sawing and other work. The metal vise is lined with wood to protect the work. Fig. 15-6. One type of vise has movable jaws on a continuous thread. Thus, the jaws can be opened or closed by turning the handle. A quick-action vise has movable jaws that can be pushed closed on the work. A short turn of the handle tightens the jaws. There is a dog (section) in the movable jaw that can be raised. A bench stop can be

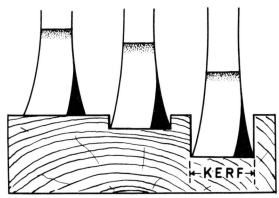

15-4(b). This drawing shows the cutting action of the ripsaw teeth.

15-4(c). The ripsaw cuts with many small chisels. First a tooth on one side cuts a small piece free. Then the tooth on the other side cuts a similar piece.

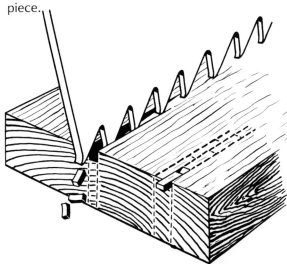

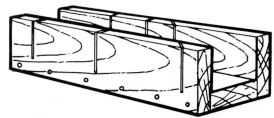

15-8. This miter box has slots to guide the backsaw in cutting 45° and 90° angles.

15-6. A wood vise made of metal is used to hold the stock when cutting short pieces. The vise is mounted on a sturdy bench.

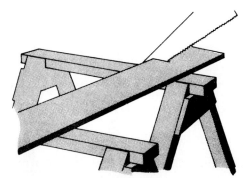

15-9. When cutting large pieces, place the lumber over one or two sawhorses.

USE THIS CLEAT, AS SHOWN, WHEN
SAWING WITH RIGHT HAND

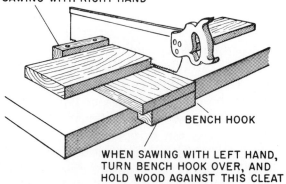

BENCH HOOK

WHEN SAWING WITH LEFT HAND,
TURN BENCH HOOK OVER, AND
HOLD WOOD AGAINST THIS CLEAT

BOTH CLEATS ARE SHORTER THAN WIDTH OF THE
HOOK, & ARE SET TO RIGHT OR LEFT OF CENTER

15-7. A bench hook in use.

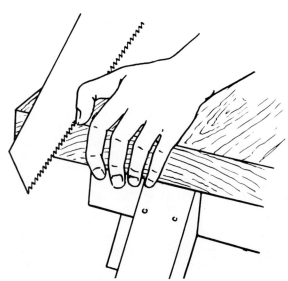

15-10. Use your thumb as a guide to get the saw started.

15-11(a). Saw just outside the layout line. The kerf must be in the waste stock.

inserted in holes along the top of the bench. The work is held between the dog and the bench stop when cutting or planing.

A *sawhorse* supports the lumber for cutting. One or two are needed. Fig. 15-9.

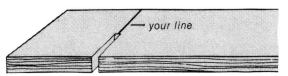

15-11(b). Do not saw directly on the layout line.

Cutting Stock to Length with a Crosscut Saw

1. Lay out the cutoff line across the board with a pencil. Unit 12 explains how to do this.

2. Place the board in a vise or over sawhorses. The cutoff line must be outside the supports, never between them.

3. Hold the saw handle in your right hand with your index finger extended to support it. If left-handed, reverse.

4. Place your free hand on the board, using your thumb as a guide to start the cut. Fig. 15-10. Remember: The kerf must be in the waste stock. Don't try to saw on the line or "saw out" the line. If you do, the piece may be too short. Fig. 15-11.

5. Start the cut by pulling back on the saw once or twice. Be careful that the saw doesn't jump and cut your thumb.

6. After the kerf is started, hold the saw at an angle of 45° to the surface. Fig. 15-12. Move your hand away from the blade. Take long, even strokes. Sawing is easier, truer, and faster when full-length strokes are made. Unlike the ripsaw, the crosscut saw cuts both on the forward and back strokes.

7. Sight along the saw or check with the try

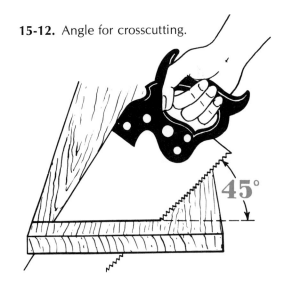

15-12. Angle for crosscutting.

45°

square to make sure you are making a square cut. Fig. 15-13.

8. As you cut, watch the layout line, not the saw. Blow the sawdust away.

9. If the saw is moving into or away from the line, twist the handle slightly to bring it back.

10. As the final strokes are made, hold the end to be cut off. If you don't do this, the corner will split out as the piece drops. Never twist off thin strips of wood with the saw blade.

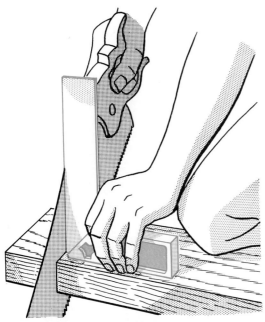

15-13. A way to keep the saw cut square with the face of the board. Place the handle of the try square firmly on the face of the wood. Then slide it until the blade of the try square contacts the saw blade. By doing this, you can check for squareness.

Cutting Stock to Width with a Ripsaw

1. Mark the cutting line along the length of the board. Be sure to measure accurately before starting. For a very long cut you might want to use a guide board. Fasten this just outside the layout line to help keep the cut straight.

2. Place the board over two sawhorses so that your cut will be at knee height. If you are right-handed, put your right knee on the board. Place your left hand a few inches to the left of the cutting line. If you are left-handed, do the opposite. Start by taking short strokes, backward only. Use the teeth at the heel of the

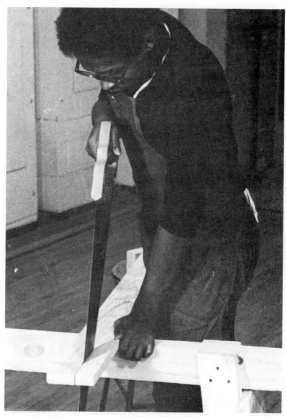

15-14. Sight along the saw to keep it cutting straight.

blade. Don't put pressure on the saw until the kerf is well started.

3. As you saw, watch the layout line so that you keep the saw cut straight. Fig. 15-14. Hold the saw at an angle of 60°. Fig. 15-15.

4. On a long cut, the kerf may close enough to cause the saw to bind. To avoid this, insert a wooden wedge into the kerf to keep it open. Fig. 15-16.

5. Fasten shorter boards in the vise with the layout line vertical (up and down) and slightly left of the vise jaw. If the board is quite long, clamp it near the top at first. Move it up as you cut. Fig. 15-17.

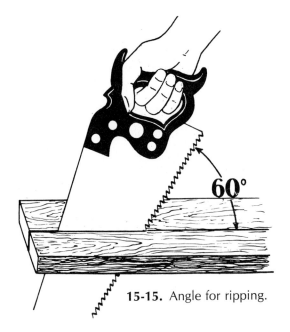

15-15. Angle for ripping.

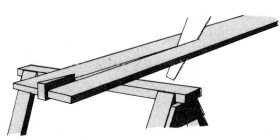

15-16. You can use a wedge of wood to hold the kerf open during sawing.

15-17. Ripping with the stock held in a vise.

6. When cutting plywood to width, use a crosscut saw. Keep the saw at an angle of about 30°.

Cutting with a Backsaw

1. Carefully mark the location of the cut.
2. Place the bench hook over the top of the bench.
3. Hold the saw in your right hand. Hold the work against the bench hook with the layout line to the right. If left-handed, reverse. Make sure the kerf will be in the waste stock. Fig. 15-18.
4. Use your thumb as a guide. Start the cut with the handle held high.
5. As the cut is started, lower the blade a little at a time until the saw is parallel with the surface.
6. Continue to cut until the correct depth is reached or the waste stock is cut off.
7. To help the saw make an accurate cut, clamp a smooth piece of scrap stock right next to the layout line. Fig. 15-19. Then you can hold the saw with both hands to start the cut. Don't start with the handle held high. Keep the blade flat against the guide board. Then the cut will be in the correct location and square with the surface.

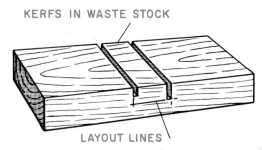

15-18. Make the cuts at the layout line but in the waste stock.

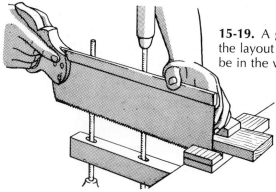

15-19. A guide board has been clamped next to the layout line. Remember that the saw kerf must be in the waste stock.

REVIEW QUESTIONS

1. What kind of saw must be used to cut across the grain? With the grain?
2. What do you call the groove cut by a saw?
3. Why are the teeth of the saw wider than the saw itself?
4. What is a bench hook?
5. Is the saw cut started by pushing or pulling?
6. How should you guide the saw when starting a cut?
7. At about what angle should the saw be held for cutting across grain?
8. Which should you watch when the cutting is done, the layout line or the saw?
9. At about what angle do you hold a saw when cutting with the grain?
10. Why should the handle of the backsaw be held high when starting a cut?

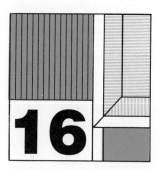

Assembling and Adjusting a Plane

A *plane* is a tool with a blade for smoothing and removing wood as shavings. The modern plane developed from the chisel. The plane is nothing more than a chisel held in a block of metal. Thus, the chisel can be controlled to take an even cut. The plane is one tool you'll use often.

It takes patience to learn to adjust and use the plane correctly. Even more skill is needed to sharpen the blade correctly. A plane works

Stanley Tools

16-1. The jack plane is the most useful, all-around tool for both rough planing and final smoothing.

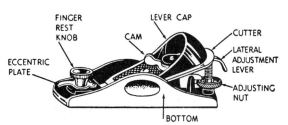

16-2. Parts of a block plane.

well only if the blade is sharp and adjusted correctly. Even then it will smooth a surface only if it is used in the right way.

Kinds of Planes

The *jack plane* ("Jack of all trades") is the most common plane. It is either 14" or 15" long, with a 2" blade. It is ideal for rough surfaces that require a heavier chip. It is also good for obtaining a smooth, flat surface. Fig. 16-1.

A slightly narrower and shorter plane is the *junior jack plane*. It is 11½" long with a 1¾" blade.

A *smooth plane* is 9¼" or 9¾" long. It is used for smaller work. It is a good plane for general use around the home.

A *fore plane* is longer (18") and has a 2¾" cutter. It is used to plane long surfaces and edges.

A *block plane* is a small plane that has a low-angle cutter. Fig. 16-2. Because the blade is held at a low angle to the surface, it works well on end grain. Because of its low angle, the cutter is set bevel up. The cutter is a single plane iron with no chip breaker. The block plane can be held with one or both hands.

Besides cutting end grain, the block plane is also useful for general-purpose planing. For example, it is a good plane for shaping a ship-model hull or for planing a chamfer.

To adjust the cutter for thickness, sight along the plane bottom. Turn the adjusting screw to push the cutter out or to pull it in. To adjust the cutter for evenness of shaving, sight along the bottom. Move the lateral adjusting lever to the right or left as necessary.

Parts of a Bench Plane

The plane is the most complicated hand tool you will use. You should learn its major parts and how to adjust it. Let's look at the hand plane in Fig. 16-3. The main part is called the *body*, or *bed*. The wide flat part is called the

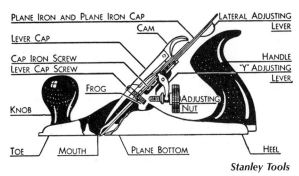

Stanley Tools

16-3. Parts of a plane.

bottom. The back of the bottom is the *heel* and the front is the *toe*. The opening across the bottom is called the *mouth*, or *throat*. The *knob* (in front) is held in one hand and the *handle* (in back) in the other hand. Lift up the *cam lever* to release the *lever cap*. Then slide the lever cap up. It will come off over the *lever cap screw*. Now carefully lift the *double plane iron* out of the plane. Notice that this is made in two parts. The top one is called the *plane iron cap*. It breaks the chips and forces the chips or shavings up and out. The lower edge of the plane iron cap is called the *chip break*. The lower part of the double plane iron is the actual cutting edge. It is called a *single plane iron*. It must be kept sharp. The part that supports the double plane iron is called the *frog*. There is an *adjusting nut* for changing the depth of the cut. A *lateral adjusting lever* can be moved to the right or left. It keeps the cutting edge straight (parallel with the bottom).

How to Put the Double Plane Iron Together

1. Hold the single plane iron in your left hand with the bevel side of the blade down.

Hold the plane iron cap crosswise. Drop the cap screw through the hole. Fig. 16-4(A).

2. Slide the plane iron cap away from the cutting edge. Fig. 16-4(B).

3. Rotate it ¼ turn so that it is straight with the plane iron. Fig. 16-4(C).

4. Carefully slide the cap forward, guiding it with your left thumb and forefinger. Fig. 16-4(D). Be careful not to slip the cap over the cutting edge, as this might nick it. The cap should be about 1/16″ from the cutting edge for most work. For very fine planing, about 1/32″ is better.

5. Hold the two parts together. Then tighten the cap screw with a screwdriver or with the lever cap. Be sure the two parts are tight. If chips get between the plane iron and the cap, you'll have trouble planing. Fig. 16-5.

Putting the Double Plane Iron in the Plane

1. Place the plane upright on the bench with a small scrap of wood under the toe to raise one end of the bottom. This is done to protect the cutting edge.

2. Hold the double plane iron with the cap up. Carefully guide the cutter into the plane

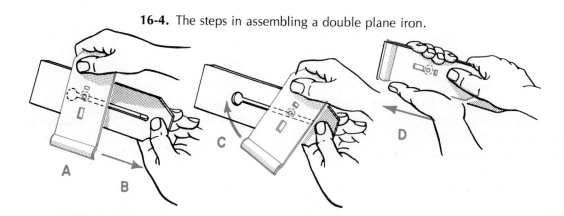

16-4. The steps in assembling a double plane iron.

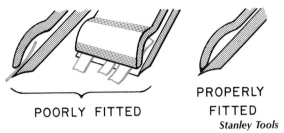

POORLY FITTED   PROPERLY
                        FITTED
                        Stanley Tools

16-5. The plane iron cap must fit the plane iron tightly. If it doesn't, chips get between the two parts and cause poor planing action.

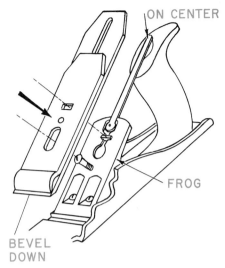

ON CENTER

BEVEL
DOWN

FROG

16-6. The assembled double plane iron is placed over the frog.

and over the lever cap screw. Be careful not to hit the cutting edge on the side of the plane. Fig. 16-6.

3. Now make sure that:

(a) The long slot in the plane iron fits over the roller of the lateral adjusting lever.

(b) The small slot in the plane iron cap fits over the depth-of-cut or Y adjusting lever.

Both must be in place before you can adjust the plane. Fig. 16-7.

4. Slip the lever cap in place and push the cam down. Fig. 16-8. The cap should hold the double plane iron snugly. If the cap is too tight, it will be hard to adjust the plane. If it is too loose, the plane won't stay in adjustment. You can tighten or loosen the lever cap screw (with a screwdriver) until the cam lever will close with a little push.

Adjusting the Plane

1. Turn the plane upside down, holding the knob in your left hand.

2. Look along the bottom. It's a good idea to face a window. Fig. 16-9.

3. Turn the adjusting nut with your right hand until the cutting edge appears. It should stick out about the thickness of a hair.

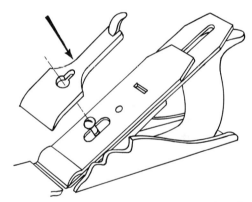

16-7. The lever cap is placed over the double plane iron.

USE ONLY THUMB
PRESSURE

16-8. Push the cam down to lock the assembly in place.

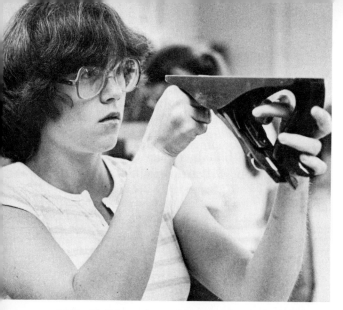

16-9. Sighting along the bottom of the plane to make sure the cutting edge is parallel with the bottom.

4. Now move the lateral adjusting lever to the left or right until the cutting edge is parallel with the bottom. Figs. 16-10 and 16-11.

5. Turn the adjusting nut again until the blade just appears above the bottom.

6. Try the plane on a piece of scrap stock. Adjust it until you are satisfied with the appearance of the shavings. They should be smooth, silky, and of uniform (even) thickness.

Points to Remember

1. Always plane with the grain to get a smooth surface. Planing against the grain roughens the wood.

2. If possible, clamp the stock to the workbench to hold it steady.

3. Check often to make sure the plane's cutting edge is sharp. A blade which is sharp will not reflect much light. A dull blade appears shiny. Test the blade by planing a piece of scrap stock.

4. Do not let the cutting edge contact metal. Scraping metal can ruin the blade.

5. When you stop planing, always rest the tool on its side, never on its bottom. Fig. 16-12. The cutting edge will be damaged if you put the tool down in an upright position. Never place it in a pile with other hand tools.

REVIEW QUESTIONS

1. Which is the most common type of plane for general work?
2. What do you do to change the depth of cut?
3. Which adjustment changes the blade so that it is straight, or parallel with the bottom?
4. When assembling a double plane iron,

16-10. Adjusting the plane.

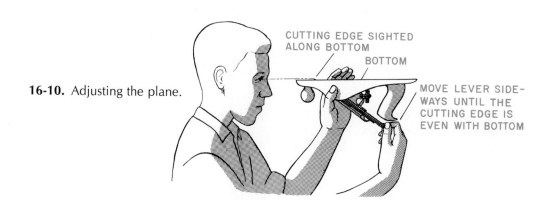

CUTTING EDGE SIGHTED ALONG BOTTOM

BOTTOM

MOVE LEVER SIDEWAYS UNTIL THE CUTTING EDGE IS EVEN WITH BOTTOM

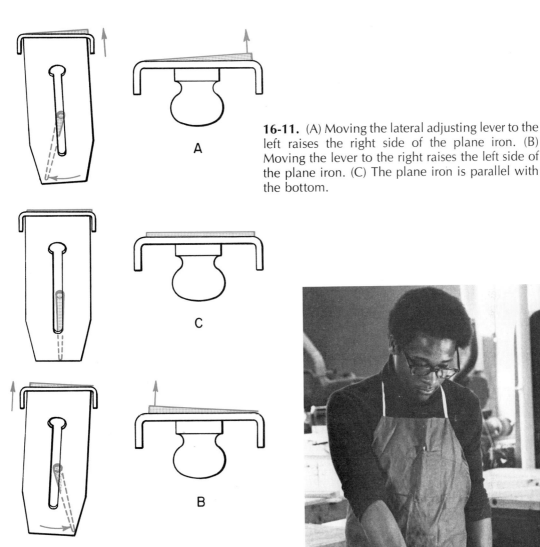

16-11. (A) Moving the lateral adjusting lever to the left raises the right side of the plane iron. (B) Moving the lever to the right raises the left side of the plane iron. (C) The plane iron is parallel with the bottom.

what must you watch for to prevent the cutting edge from becoming nicked?

5. For most work about how far should the cap be set from the cutting edge?

6. Why should one end of the bottom of a plane be kept off the bench surface when installing the double plane iron?

7. Describe the way to install the double plane iron in the plane.

16-12. Always place the plane on its side when it is not in use.

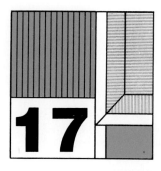

Planing Stock

Planing is done to produce a smooth, perfectly flat "plane" surface. You will use a plane to:
- Square stock.
- Cut bevels, chamfers and tapers.
- Make a joint.
- Fit and assemble a project.

Squaring up Stock

Rough lumber is sometimes used in building construction and repair work but never for small articles. Most of the lumber you use will be S2S—surfaced two sides. This lumber will have to be planed very little on the surface. At other times you might have to plane two surfaces and one edge. You may need to do this when cutting out a design. In other cases,

when the ends don't show, the surfaces and edges are planed. The ends are simply cut to length with a saw. There will be many times, however, when you must square up stock. To *square up* stock means to make all surfaces flat, all corners square, and all opposite sides parallel. Fig. 17-1.

Planing the First Surface

1. Check the stock and choose the better of the two largest surfaces. Check the board for three things:
- *Bow*. Bow (rhymes with *low*) means that one side of the board is concave (dished in). The

17-1. Steps in squaring up stock.

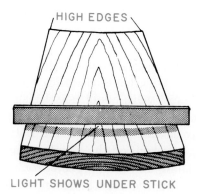

17-2. Testing a board for bow.

HIGH CORNER

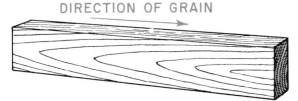

HIGH CORNER

THE STICKS DO NOT LIE LEVEL

17-3. Two sticks placed across either end of the board show wind, or twist.

DIRECTION OF GRAIN

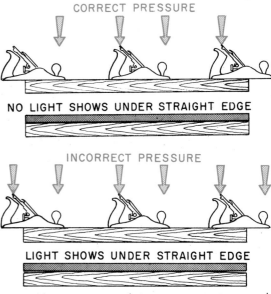

CORRECT PRESSURE

NO LIGHT SHOWS UNDER STRAIGHT EDGE

INCORRECT PRESSURE

LIGHT SHOWS UNDER STRAIGHT EDGE

17-5. The correct and incorrect way to apply pressure when planing. If the pressure is wrong, the surface will be high in the center.

17-4. Grain direction. This is the direction in which the planing should be done.

other side is convex (rounded outward). With a pencil, mark the high spots that must be planed. Fig. 17-2.

• *Wind* (rhymes with *kind*). A board has wind if it twists along its length. You can check this by placing two broad sticks on the board and sighting along them. Fig. 17-3. Another way is to place the board on a flat surface. If it has wind, it will rock on two corners.

• *Grain direction.* If possible, decide the direction of the grain. Always plane with the grain, never against it. Fig. 17-4. Planing against the grain roughens the wood. It is difficult to see grain direction on a rough board.

2. Clamp the work so that it is held securely. Two ways to do this are:

(a) Place a bench stop in a hole in the bench and place the work on the bench with the end grain against it. The work must be centered or it will slip as you begin to plane. Clamp the work between the bench stop and the vise dog.

(b) Place the work against a board fastened to the end of the bench.

3. Stand with your feet apart (left foot forward) and your right side near the bench. *Left-handed persons reverse the procedure.*

4. Hold the knob firmly in your left hand and the handle in your right.

5. Place the toe of the plane over the end of the board. Push down on the knob as you start the stroke.

6. As the whole plane comes onto the board, apply equal pressure on both the knob and handle. As the toe of the plane leaves the board, apply more pressure to the handle. This kind of stroke will keep the surface level from one end to the other. Fig. 17-5.

7. Lift the plane on the return stroke. Dragging it back will roughen the surface and dull the cutting edge.

8. After the first few strokes, you'll be able to tell for sure if you're planing with the grain.

9. Start at one edge of the board and make a series of strokes until you reach the other side. *Always place the plane on its side when not in use.*

10. Test the surface with the try square or straightedge in several directions as shown in Fig. 17-6.

11. If there are high spots, mark these with a pencil. Then make heavy cuts diagonally across the board. Reduce the depth of cut. Plane in the opposite direction until the high points are removed. Then plane straight along the board. Fig. 17-7.

12. If only the end towards you must be planed, start the stroke as before. Then, as you near the end of the area, slowly lift up on the handle to stop the shaving gradually.

13. If the end away from you must be planed, start the stroke with the toe of the plane against the surface and the heel held high. Gradually lower the plane as the stroke is made.

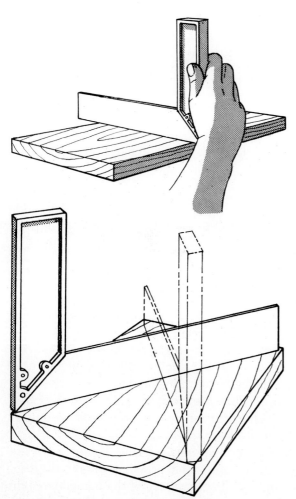

17-6. Check the surface for flatness with a try square. Check from edge to edge and diagonally across the corners.

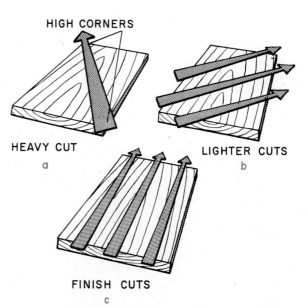

HIGH CORNERS

HEAVY CUT
a

LIGHTER CUTS
b

FINISH CUTS
c

17-7. (a) Make a heavy cut at an angle across the board to remove the high spots. (b) Reduce the depth of cut and plane in the opposite direction, taking off the other high spots. (c) Plane with the grain to smooth the surface.

17-8. Notice that the plane with the long bed will straighten out the edge.

14. Decide which edge should be planed first. Mark the face surface near this edge.

Planing the First Edge

1. Clamp the work in the vise with the edge about 2″ or 3″ above the jaw. If the piece is long, support the other end with a hand clamp. Also, use a jointer plane on long boards. Notice how a long plane bridges (reaches across) the low spots. Fig. 17-8.

2. Hold the plane at right angles to the face surface and make a long, even stroke. Fig. 17-9. It is very important to keep the plane square with the face surface. Curl your thumb around the back of the knob and place your fingers against the bottom. Take a light cut.

3. Continue to plane until a uniform shaving comes off the edge. To get the edge square and the surface smooth, remove as little stock as possible.

4. Remove the board from the vise. Hold the handle of a try square against the face surface. Use the try square to check for squareness along the entire edge. Fig. 17-10.

17-9. Hold the plane at right angles to the face surface. Here the smooth plane is being used to remove the rough surface. The fore plane will be used to smooth-plane the edge.

17-10. Testing the edge for squareness. Notice also the face mark. This is used to show which is the face surface and which is the face edge.

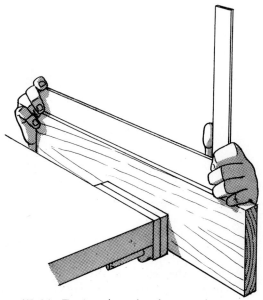

17-11. Testing the edge for straightness.

5. It is also a good idea to test for straightness. Hold a straightedge along the edge from one end to the other. Fig. 17-11.

6. Mark the *face surface* and *face edge* with a face mark as shown in Fig. 17-10. This mark will be your guide in making measurements to square up stock.

Planing the First End

1. Choose the end that needs the least amount of planing. Mark a sharp line across the face surface and edge as a guide to show how much stock is to be removed.

2. Clamp the work in the vise with about 1" of the end grain showing. Don't plane end grain with the board sticking out too far from the vise. The work will vibrate and the cutting tool will jump.

3. The plane must be very sharp and the cap set close to the cutting edge. Adjust the depth of cut as thin as possible.

4. If you plane completely across end

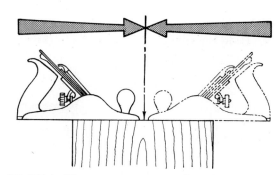

17-12(a). The correct way to plane end grain by planing halfway across the stock.

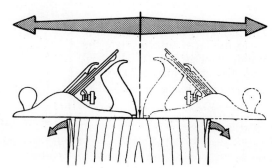

17-12(b). This is what happens if you plane toward the outer edge.

grain, the back edge will split off. There are three ways to avoid this:

(a) Plane halfway across the end. Then lift the heel. This will feather the shaving (thin it out). Then plane from the other edge. Fig. 17-12.

(b) Select a piece of waste stock the same thickness as the board. Place it behind the board. Fig. 17-13.

(c) Plane a short chamfer in the waste stock on the opposite edge. Then you can plane all the way in one direction.

5. Readjust the plane to a very light cut. Hold the plane at a slight angle and take a shearing cut. Try to plane an even surface that will look good when a finish is applied.

6. Check the end with a try square from both the face surface and edge. Fig. 17-14. Put an "X" in pencil on the end so that you know it has been planed.

Completing the Squaring Up of Stock

1. Measure the correct length and mark a line across the face surface and end. With a backsaw cut about 1/16" longer than the finished length. Plane the second end to correct length.

2. Plane to correct width. If the board is rather narrow, adjust the marking gauge to the correct width and mark a line along the face surface and the second surface. You can also use the other methods of gauging as described in Unit 12. If the board is quite wide, mark the width at several points. Then use a straightedge to draw a line showing the width. Saw to about 1/8" of the layout line. Now plane the second edge smooth, straight, and square.

3. Plane the second face. Adjust the mark-

ing gauge to correct thickness. Mark a line from the face surface along the edges and ends. Plane to correct thickness. It is easy to remember the steps—face, edge, end; then reverse: end, edge, and face. Steps can be marked on the wood.

Cutting a Chamfer, Bevel, or Taper

Three angle surfaces cut in the same way are the chamfer, bevel, and taper.

A *chamfer* is a slanted surface made by cutting off an edge, end, or corner. The

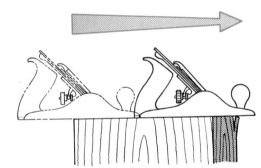

17-13. Notice the piece of waste stock. This makes it possible to plane all the way across the end from one direction.

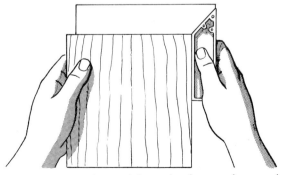

17-14. Testing the end from the face surface and face edge to make sure it is square.

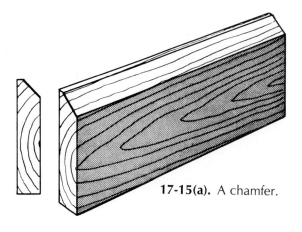

17-15(a). A chamfer.

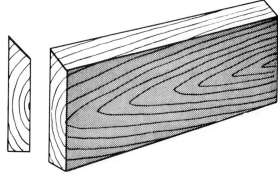

17-16. A bevel. Note that it is cut all the way across the edge.

17-15(b). Planing a chamfer. See how the plane is held at an angle of about 45°.

chamfer is cut only partway down, usually at an angle of 45°. Fig. 17-15. A chamfer is cut to remove the sharp edge and improve appearance.

A *bevel* is a sloping edge or end. Fig. 17-16. It is used, for example, to fit two pieces together to form a V shape.

A *taper* is a cut that becomes gradually smaller toward one end. Fig. 17-17. For example, tent pegs and the legs of tables, chairs, and stools are often tapered. Sometimes all four sides of a leg are tapered. At other times only the two inside sides may be tapered.

TOOLS

The sliding T bevel is used to lay out and check angles, especially those other than 45° or 90°. Fig. 17-18. It consists of a handle with an adjustable blade. A clamping screw at one end of the handle locks the blade. To set a bevel, use a protractor or carpenter's square. A protractor is used if you must set the bevel at an "odd" angle, such as 62°. Fig. 17-19. To set a sliding T bevel to a 45° angle, hold the blade of the bevel across the corner of a carpenter's square until there is equal distance on the body and tongue. To set a 30° or 60° angle, set the blade to 3″ on the tongue and 5 ³⁄₁₆″ on the body. Fig. 17-20.

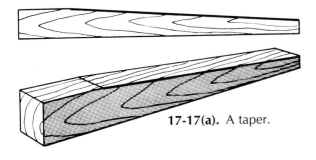

17-17(a). A taper.

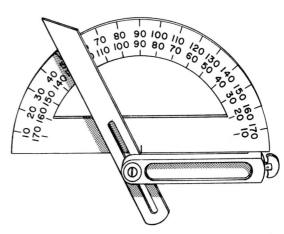

17-19. Using a metal protractor to adjust the sliding T bevel. Loosen the nut slightly, so that the blade will just move. Set the blade to the correct angle. Then retighten the nut.

FIRST TAPER MARKED

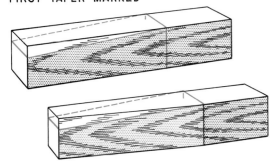

FIRST TAPER CUT, SECOND TAPER MARKED

17-17(b). Sometimes, the taper is to be cut on two adjoining surfaces. Then one side should be laid out and cut before the second layout is made.

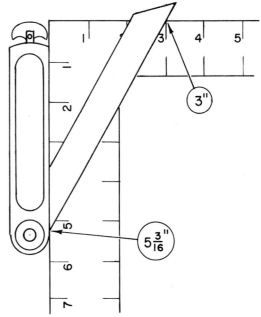

17-20. Setting the blade to 3″ on the tongue and 5 3/16″ on the blade of the carpenter's square. This setting gives angles of 30° and 60°.

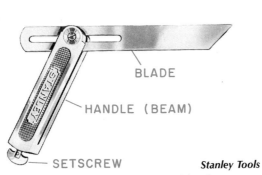

BLADE

HANDLE (BEAM)

SETSCREW   *Stanley Tools*

17-18. Parts of a sliding T bevel.

Other tools needed for making chamfers, bevels, and tapers are a plane, pencil, rule, and try square.

CUTTING A CHAMFER

1. Decide on the amount of the chamfer. For example, on ¾″ stock, the chamfer usually is made ³⁄₁₆″ to ¼″.

2. Lay out the lines for all chamfers with a pencil. *Never use a marking gauge.* The spur of the marking gauge will cut a groove that never comes out.

3. Clamp the work in a vise with the chamfer side toward you and somewhat above the top of the vise.

4. Tilt the plane at about a 45° angle and begin to plane. See Fig. 16-15(B). You may guide the plane by curling the fingers of your left hand under the bottom of the plane. Make the movements of the plane even and long.

5. After you have planed partway, check the chamfer with a try square. Fig. 17-21. Is there about an equal amount to be removed to bring it to the layout lines? If not, you might have to tilt the plane more in the direction where the most stock must be removed. You can also check the chamfer with a sliding T bevel.

6. Always plane the chamfer *with the grain* (along the edges) first.

7. To plane end grain, clamp the work rather high in a vise. Make a shearing cut to plane the chamfer. This is done by holding the plane at an angle as well as at a tilt. Fig. 17-22.

8. For small work a block plane is a good tool to use.

CUTTING A BEVEL

1. Determine the angle of the bevel and adjust the sliding T bevel to that angle.

2. Mark a line across the ends of the stock to show the bevel angle. Then draw a line

across the second surface of the board as a guide.

3. Place the bevel as you did a chamfer. Check frequently with the T bevel to be sure you are cutting it at the correct angle.

CUTTING A TAPER

1. Mark a line around the leg to show how far the taper will go.

2. If the leg is to be tapered on all four sides, first mark the two opposite sides on one end to show the amount of the taper. Draw lines along the legs to show the stock to be

17-21. Checking a chamfer to make sure it is even.

17-22. Planing an end-grain chamfer using a shearing cut.

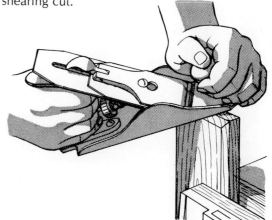

removed. If the leg is tapered only on two adjoining sides, mark the taper on one side only. See Fig. 16-17(B).

3. If it is a rather sharp taper, saw away some of the waste stock. Planing is usually enough, however.

4. Clamp the work in a vise with the taper line parallel with the top.

5. Start planing near the end of the leg. Each cut will be a little longer until you have reached the taper line.

6. After you have planed both sides (or one side if only two are to be tapered), lay out and cut the taper on the other sides (or side).

REVIEW QUESTIONS

1. Describe bow.
2. What is wind in a board?
3. Describe how to stand when planing a board.
4. How do you test the surface to make sure it is true?
5. Describe two ways of holding the front of the plane for planing an edge.
6. Describe how to check the first edge to see if it is square with the face surface.
7. Why do you mark the face surface to show that the edge has been planed?
8. Why is end grain more difficult to plane?
9. Which end should be planed first?
10. Describe three ways to avoid splitting off the back edge of the wood when planing end grain.
11. Why must a light cut be made when planing end grain?
12. How is a bevel different from a chamfer?
13. What is a taper?
14. What is the usual size of a chamfer on ¾" stock?
15. Why should a marking gauge never be used in laying out a chamfer?
16. What tool do you need to lay out a bevel?
17. Where is a taper most commonly used?

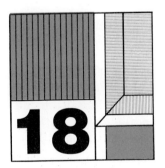

Cutting Curves and Inside Openings

Many cutout designs and projects have curved edges, very sharp corners, or angles that must be cut with a thin saw blade. Inside openings also must be cut with a narrow blade.

Tools

The *coping saw* has a U-shaped frame that holds a replaceable blade. The blade can be adjusted to any angle to the frame. For exam-

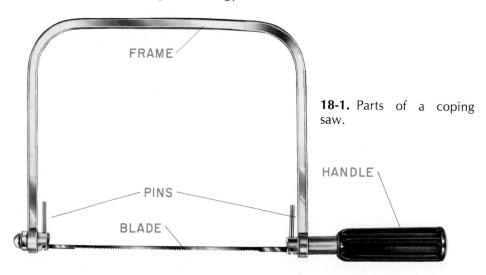

18-1. Parts of a coping saw.

ple, it can be turned so that the teeth point in, toward the frame. Fig. 18-1.

The *compass saw* has a tapered blade that fits into a handle. It is really a fine-tooth crosscut saw. Sometimes several sizes of blades are furnished with the same handle. The compass saw is used to cut curves and inside openings. Fig. 18-2.

A *keyhole saw* is much like a compass saw. However, it is smaller and has a shorter blade.

A *saw V-bracket*, or *jack*, is a wooden support used with a coping saw. One type is a rectangular piece of wood with a V cut from the end. This is clamped to the top of the table. The other type is clamped in a vise. With this type, you can stand up to do the cutting. Fig. 18-3.

Coping saw blades are made in different widths with teeth similar to a ripsaw. Blades with ten to fifteen teeth to the inch are used for wood. Those with twenty and thirty-two teeth are for cutting metal. Another type of blade has spiral-shaped teeth. These will saw up or down, right or left, or in circles.

Using a Coping Saw with the Work Held in the Vise

1. Fasten the work in the vise with the start of the layout line just above the vise jaws. Move the work away from the top of the vise a little at a time as the cutting proceeds. If the sawing is done too far away from the vise, the work vibrates. This makes the cutting difficult.

2. Install a blade in the frame with the teeth pointing *away from the handle.*

3. Hold the saw in both hands as shown in

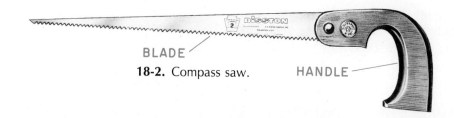

BLADE

18-2. Compass saw.

HANDLE

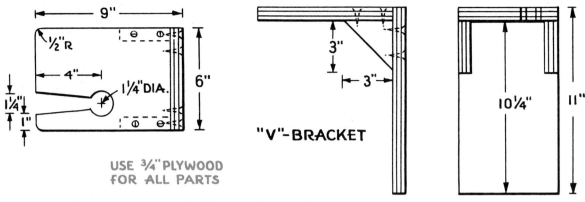

18-3. Here's how to build a saw bracket that can be used with the coping saw.

Fig. 18-4. Cut just outside the layout line, using even strokes. Apply a little pressure as you push forward. Release the pressure as you pull back.

4. Guide the saw frame so that the saw follows the line. At sharp curves, move the saw back and forth as you slowly turn the frame without applying much pressure. *Do not twist the saw.* This will break the blade.

5. The blade can be turned at any angle to the frame. Make sure both pins are turned the same amount. For example, to make a long cut, adjust the blade at a right angle to the frame.

2. Fasten a blade in the frame with the teeth pointing *toward the handle*. The cutting is done on the downstroke. Fig. 18-5.

3. Hold the work firmly on the bracket, with the area to be cut near the bottom of the V.

4. Draw down on the saw to cut. Move the work so that the cutting is always near the bottom of the V.

5. For inside cutting, drill or bore a hole in the waste stock. Fig. 18-6. Remove the blade from the frame. Then slip the blade through the hole and fasten it in the frame again. Cut

Using a Coping Saw with the Work Held Over a Saw Jack or V Bracket

1. Clamp the bracket to the bench or in the vise.

18-4. Sawing a curve with the work held in a vise. The teeth must be pointed away from the handle.

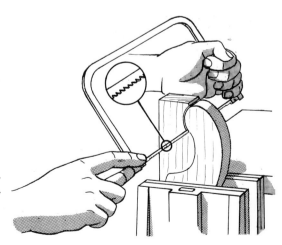

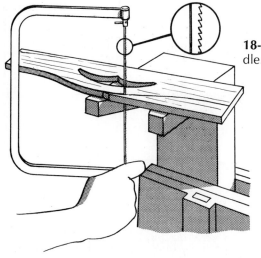

18-5. The teeth must be pointed toward the handle.

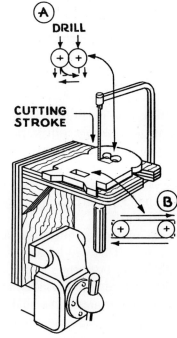

18-6. In cutting an inside opening, drill or bore holes in the waste stock. You could also make them part of the design.

up to and around the design. Then remove the blade.

Using a Compass Saw

The compass saw is best for sawing gentle curves in heavy stock.

1. For outside curves, use short strokes. Twist the handle slightly to follow the curve. Do not force the saw. It may bend or buckle.

2. For inside curves, bore a hole in the waste stock to start the cutting. Sometimes a hole is part of the design. Start the saw, using short strokes. Work slowly. For very small openings, use the keyhole saw. It is like a miniature compass saw.

REVIEW QUESTIONS

1. List three kinds of saws for cutting curves and irregular shapes.
2. What is the difference between a keyhole saw and a compass saw?
3. In using a coping saw with the work held in a vise, how should the blade be installed in the frame?
4. How should the blade be placed in a coping saw when cutting with the work held over a V bracket?
5. What must you do before you can cut an inside opening?

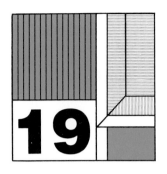

Using Chisels and Other Edged Cutting Tools

A *chisel* is a strong, steel cutting tool with a sharp bevel edge at one end. Chisels are used to shape and fit parts. Several different shaping tools are used to form irregularly shaped objects. The most common are the *spokeshave*, *files*, *rasps*, and the *multi-tooth (Surform®) tools*.

Tools

There are three types of chisels: the *pointed tang* (also called *shank*), the *solid tang*, and the *socket* type. Fig. 19-1. The pointed-tang chisel has a short point, or tang, that extends into the wood handle. Present-day solid-tang chisels have the blade and tang in one piece. The tang extends through the handle to a metal cap. The socket chisel has a socket (cup shape) at the end of the blade into which the handle fits.

Chisel size is shown by blade widths. The widths range from ⅛″ to 1″, in ⅛″ intervals, and from 1″ to 2″ in ¼″ intervals. The most common sizes are ¼″, ½″, ¾″, 1″, 1¼″, and 1½″.

A *mallet* is a short-handled hammer with a large head. The head is made of wood, rawhide, or plastic. It is used to strike a socket or solid-tang chisel for heavy cutting. Fig. 19-2.

BEVEL EDGE BLADE

CUTTING EDGE HANDLE HEAD

Stanley Tools

19-1(a). A solid tang chisel. The tank, or shank, extends all the way through the handle and is attached to a steel head.

19-1(b). A socket chisel. The handle fits into the socket. (The socket is the cup-shaped part of the blade.)

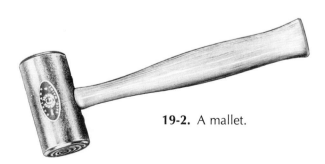

19-2. A mallet.

19-3. Parts of a spokeshave.

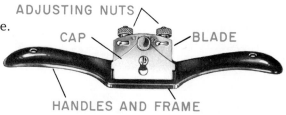

ADJUSTING NUTS

CAP   BLADE

HANDLES AND FRAME

The *spokeshave* is a small cutting tool much like a simple plane. It has a handle on each side. It was named the spokeshave because it was originally used to shape the spokes of wagon wheels. It has a frame 10″ to 12″ long, a blade, and a cap. The blade can be adjusted with two small thumb nuts. It is a very safe tool to use. Fig. 19-3.

There are many shapes of files. The most common ones for woodworking are *half-round cabinet* and *flat wood* files in lengths of 8″, 10″, or 12″. Fig. 19-4. Wood files usually have double-cut teeth. That is, there are two rows of teeth cut diagonally across the face. The file is not as rough as the wood rasp.

The *rasp* is a tool with individual cutting teeth. Fig. 19-5. It removes material faster than a file. However, it leaves a rougher surface.

A *file cleaner*, or *file card*, is needed. It keeps the teeth of the file or rasp clean and free of wood, resin, and finishing materials.

The *multi-tooth (Surform®) tool* has a hardened and tempered tool-steel cutting blade. Fig. 19-6. The blade has 45° cutting edges that easily cut wood, plastic, or soft metals. The teeth of this tool never become clogged because there are small openings between the teeth. The wood shavings go through these

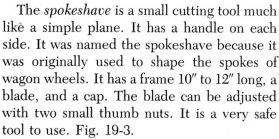

POINT   FACE   HEEL   TANG

LENGTH

19-4. Parts of a flat wood file. Make sure the tool has a handle.

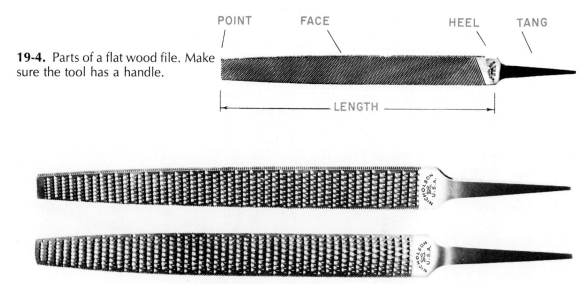

19-5. A flat and a half-round rasp. Make sure the rasp has a handle.

openings. The tool has a replaceable blade that fits into a holder.

Horizontal Chiseling Across Grain

1. Select a socket or solid-tang chisel. Make sure it is sharp and free of nicks.

2. Clamp the work in a vise or fasten it to the top of the bench. Cut across grain or with the grain, never against it. Fig. 19-7. "Against the grain" means that the chisel slopes down into the wood. When you cut against the grain, the chisel tends to dig into the wood. Then, it will split rather than cut it.

3. To remove large amounts of wood, turn the chisel with the *bevel side down*.

4. Hold the chisel in one hand. Use your other hand to strike the chisel with a mallet. Cut from both sides towards the center. Fig. 19-8. Cutting from one side will chip out the opposite edge.

5. When the cutting is within about 1/8" of the layout line, continue the cutting by hand rather than with the mallet.

6. For light trimming, turn the chisel with the *bevel up*. Guide the blade by pressing the hand that holds the chisel against the edge of the wood. Work at a slight angle to the grain.

19-6. Surform® tools: (A) File type. (B) Plane type. (C) Shaver. (D) Another file type.

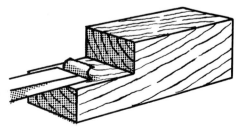

19-7. Always cut with the grain or across it. Avoid cutting against the grain.

19-8. Making rough cuts with the bevel side down. Strike the chisel with a mallet. Cut from both sides toward the center.

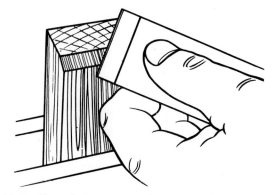

19-9. Chamfering across the grain. Chisel at 45°, producing a slicing cut.

7. Apply pressure with your other hand, cutting a little at a time. Sometimes you must swing the handle from side to side to do the cutting.

8. Be sure to hold the flat side parallel with the work but at an angle to the grain.

Horizontal Chiseling with the Grain

1. Clamp the work in a vise in such a way that you can cut with the grain.

2. For heavy cutting, hold the chisel with the bevel side down. For light paring cuts, hold the chisel with the bevel side up.

3. Grasp the blade in your left hand and the handle in your right hand. Reverse if left-handed.

4. Press forward as you push the cutting edge into the wood.

5. Guide the chisel so that the cut is not too deep.

6. Sometimes it is better to move the handle back and forth in a short arc as you push.

Vertical Chiseling Across Grain

1. Place the work over a bench hook or scrap stock.

2. Hold the chisel with the flat side against the wood.

3. Rest one hand on the wood to guide the chisel. Use your other hand to apply pressure.

4. Take a light cut. Apply pressure and move the handle in an arc from an angle to a vertical position. This makes a shearing cut.

5. To cut a chamfer across the grain, fasten the stock in a vise. Hold the chisel at an angle of 45°. Swing the handle back and forth, making a slicing cut. Fig. 19-9.

Cutting a Convex (Curved-out) Surface

1. Clamp the work in a vise so that the cutting can be done with the grain (towards the end grain).

2. Hold the chisel with the flat side down. Fig. 19-10.

3. Guide the chisel with one hand and

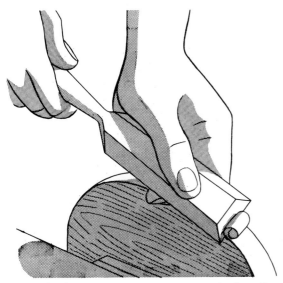

19-10. Cutting a convex curve. Raise the handle a little at a time to follow the curve.

19-11. For cutting a concave curve, hold the chisel with the bevel side down. Cut from the edge toward the end grain.

press forward with the other. Move the handle in an arc that is the same as the convex surface.

Chiseling a Concave (Curved-in) Surface

1. Hold the chisel with the bevel side down. Cut with the grain. Fig. 19-11.
2. Move the handle toward you as you press forward.

Using a Spokeshave

1. Adjust the blade (cutter) until it can just be seen through the mouth of the frame. Do not expose too much of it. If you do, the tool will chatter (jump away) as you use it. It will make small ridges in the wood.

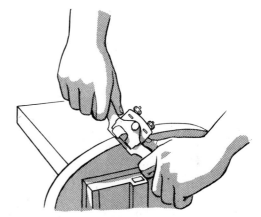

19-12. Pushing the spokeshave to shape a curved edge. Place your thumbs on each side near the blade.

2. Fasten the work in a vise so that you can push or pull the tool across the surface. Work with the grain.
3. To push the spokeshave, grasp the handles with your thumbs just behind the blade on each side of the frame. Fig. 19-12.

4. Hold the bottom of the frame firmly against the wood and push evenly. Try it a few times. You should produce a long, thin shaving. Make the tool follow the shape of the work.

5. To pull the tool, draw it toward you in long, even strokes.

Using a File or Rasp

1. Files or rasps are never to be used without handles. The tang can puncture your hand and cause a serious injury. *Always fit a handle to the tool before using it.*

2. Clamp the work in a vise.

3. Select the finest tool possible. A tool too coarse will splinter the wood.

4. Hold the handle of the tool in your right hand and the point in your left. (If left-handed, reverse this.)

5. Apply moderate (a medium amount of) pressure on the forward stroke. Make a shear-ing cut at a slight angle. Lift the file slightly on the return stroke.

6. To shape a curved edge, use the round side of the tool. Twist the tool slightly as you push.

7. Always keep the teeth clean with the file card or cleaner.

8. A piece of sandpaper of the correct grade can be wrapped around the file. This can be used to smooth the stock after a file or rasp has been used. A round file may be used to shape an inside opening.

Using a Multi-Tooth (Surform®) Tool

1. Use the multi-tooth (Surform®) tool as you would a rasp.

2. To get best results, apply light, even pressure against the wood. Fig. 19-13

3. The Surform® tool produces a smooth, even surface. As a repair tool it is excellent for

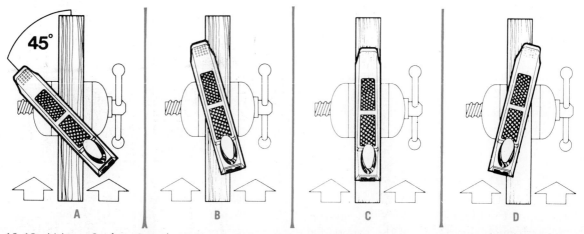

19-13. Using a Surform® tool: (A) To remove a maximum amount of material, simply hold the tool at 45° to the direction of the stroke. (B) To remove less material and obtain a smoother surface, reduce the angle. (C) To finely smooth the work surface, simply direct the tool parallel to it. (D) You can almost achieve a polishing effect by directing the tool at a slightly reversed angle.

smoothing an edge or end that has been chipped or splintered. The Surform® is ideal for shaping a canoe paddle or other odd-shaped pieces.

REVIEW QUESTIONS

1. Name the parts of a chisel.
2. Describe two types of chisels.
3. What is a mallet? How does it differ from a hammer?
4. How should you hold a chisel when doing horizontal cutting across grain?
5. Why should work be placed on a bench hook or scrap stock when doing vertical cutting?
6. What is meant by convex? Concave?
7. How should the blade of a spokeshave be adjusted?
8. Name the most common kinds of files used in woodworking.
9. How do you shape a curve or edge with a file?
10. What is used to keep the teeth of the file clean?
11. Describe the way a Surform® tool operates.

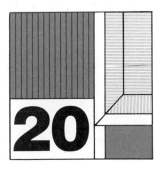

Drilling and Boring Holes

Holes are made by drilling and boring. It is usually called *drilling* when the holes are ¼" or smaller and *boring* when the holes are larger than ¼".

These drills can be used for both metal and wood. Drills ⅜" and smaller can be held in a hand drill. Larger sizes can be used in a drill press. See Unit 26.

Drilling Holes

TOOLS

Twist drills come in fractional-sized sets from ¹⁄₆₄" to ½", in steps of ¹⁄₆₄". Fig. 20-1.

20-1. Parts of a twist drill. The size is stamped on the shank.

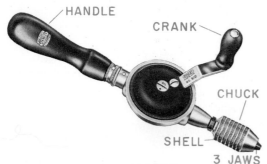

20-2. Parts of a hand drill.

The parts of a *hand drill* are shown in Fig. 20-2. Most hand drills are made to hold twist drills up to ⅜″ in diameter.

Using the Hand Drill

1. Mark the locations for the holes with a scratch awl or sharp-pointed nail. The drill starts more easily when the location is punched.

2. Fasten the work in a vise so that you can drill either vertically (up and down) or horizontally. Figs. 20-3 and 20-4.

3. Grasp the shell of the chuck in your left hand. Turn the crank counterclockwise (opposite of clockwise) until the shank of the drill will slip in. Then turn the crank in the other direction to tighten. Make sure the drill is in the chuck straight so that it doesn't wobble.

4. If holes of a certain depth are needed (holes for screws, for example), make a *depth gauge* from scrap wood. Fig. 20-5.

5. Place the point of the drill where you want the hole. Turn the crank evenly as you apply light pressure to the handle. Press straight down or ahead. *Be careful not to tip the hand drill after it is started.* This will break the drill.

6. Continue to turn the handle in the same direction as you pull the drill from the hole.

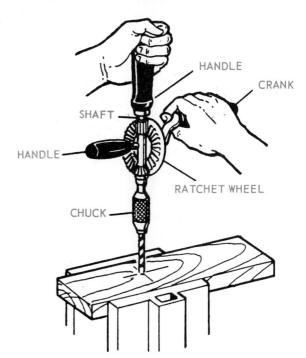

20-3. Drilling with the hand drill held in a vertical position.

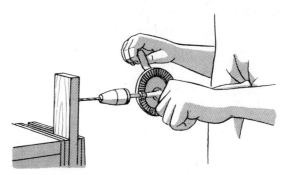

20-4. Drilling a horizontal hole with a hand drill.

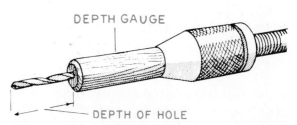

20-5. A depth gauge made from a piece of dowel rod covering a part of the drill like a sleeve. Cut the piece until the drill sticks out the right amount.

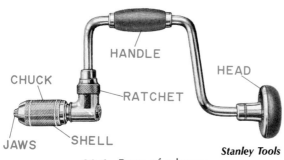

Stanley Tools

20-6. Parts of a brace.

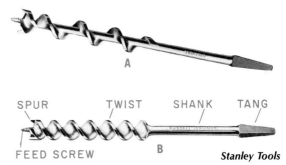

Stanley Tools

20-7. (A) A single-twist auger bit. (B) Parts of a double-twist auger bit.

7. Always return the drill to the correct holder.

Boring Holes

TOOLS

A *brace* holds the auger bit when the holes are bored. Fig. 20-6. The auger bit goes into the wood as you turn the handle of the brace. The two most common braces are the *plain*, or *common*, and the *ratchet*. The plain brace is used when you can make a full swing of the handle. If you must bore in a corner or in close quarters, you need a ratchet brace. To use it, turn the ratchet control to the right (clockwise). The brace can then turn the bit to the right. The ratchet slips when the brace is rotated to the left. In this way a half turn or less at a time will bore the hole. If the ratchet is turned to the left, the bit can be rotated out of the hole. The ratchet brace can be used as a plain brace. To do this, set the ratchet in the center position.

The *auger bit* is the most common cutting tool for boring holes. Fig. 20-7. It ranges in size from ¼″ (No. 4) to 1″ (No. 16), by sixteenths of an inch. A number stamped on the shank of the bit tells the size in sixteenths. For example, size 8 is 8⁄16″, or ½″, while a size

9 bores a 9⁄16″ hole. The screw on the end of the bit pulls the bit into the wood.

A *depth gauge (bit gauge)* is a device that is attached to the auger bit to limit the depth of the hole. You can make a depth gauge by boring a hole through a piece of dowel rod. Then cut the rod until the correct bit length is exposed. See Fig. 20-5. Two commercial bit gauges are shown in Fig. 20-8.

Stanley Tools

20-8. Bit or depth gauges: (left) Solid type; (right) Spring type.

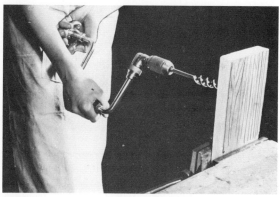

20-9. Horizontal boring. Remember to keep the auger bit at right angles to the work.

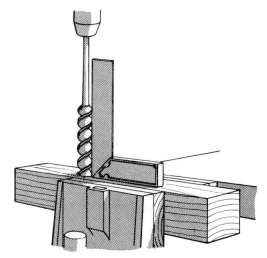

20-11. Checking to make sure the auger bit is square with the work.

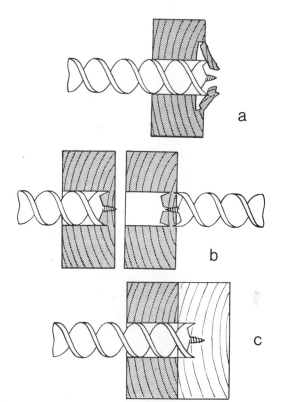

20-10. (A). This shows what happens when you continue to bore from one side. (B) Boring from one side until the screw appears and then reversing the auger bit. (C) Using a piece of scrap stock to bore directly through the work.

HORIZONTAL (FLAT OR LEVEL) BORING

1. Choose the correct size bit. For example, if the drawing calls for a ¾″ hole, choose a No. 12 bit (¹²⁄₁₆″ equals ¾″).

2. Insert the bit in the brace. Grasp the shell firmly in one hand. Rotate the handle to the left until the jaws open enough to receive the shank. Then turn the handle to the right to tighten the bit.

3. Mark the location of the hole with two intersecting (crossing) lines. Center punch with a scratch awl or the point of a nail.

4. Fasten the work in a vise with the punch mark near the top or side of the vise jaw.

5. Guide the bit with your left hand until the screw point is exactly on the punch mark. Hold the head in your left hand braced against your stomach. Grasp the handle in your right hand. (If left-handed, reverse these positions.)

6. Now you should ask a friend to help you "sight" the tool so that the hole will be square with the wood surface. You sight it right and left. Have your friend sight it up and down.

7. Turn the handle steadily. Fig. 20-9. In softwood, little pressure is needed because

the screw easily draws the point into the wood. For hardwood, press a little harder on the head.

8. Watch carefully for the feed screw to start coming out the opposite side. Stop. Turn the handle in the opposite direction to remove the bit. If you don't stop, the wood will split out. Fig. 20-10.

9. Turn the work around and finish the hole by boring from the other side.

10. You can bore the hole completely through from one side if you place a piece of scrap stock on the back of your work.

VERTICAL BORING

1. Mark the hole. Clamp the work with the marked surface up.

2. Start the auger bit by turning it clockwise.

3. Use a square or a block of wood to make sure the bit enters the wood straight. Fig. 20-11.

4. Continue the boring as described in the section on the horizontal boring.

STOP BORING, OR BORING TO DEPTH

1. Attach a depth or bit gauge to the bit, with the right length of the cutting tool showing.

2. Bore the hole until the gauge touches the surface.

USING AN EXPANSION BIT

An *expansion (expansive) bit* is used to bore a hole larger than 1". Most expansion bits have two cutters, each a different size. Thus, a wide range of hole sizes can be bored. Fig. 20-12.

1. Choose a cutter of the correct size and slip it into the bit. Adjust the cutter until the distance from the spur to the feed screw equals the radius of the hole. The *radius* is

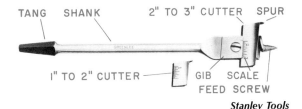

TANG   SHANK   2" TO 3" CUTTER   SPUR

1" TO 2" CUTTER   GIB   SCALE
                        FEED SCREW

Stanley Tools

20-12. Parts of an expansion bit.

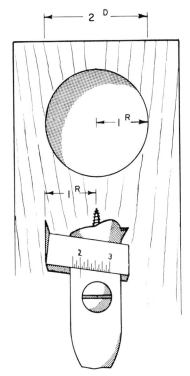

20-13. Notice that the expansion bit is set to "2" on the cutter graduations in line with the index mark. This will cut a 2" hole.

one-half the diameter. A scale on the cutter helps set it. This scale shows the hole diameter. Fig. 20-13. On some types there is an adjusting screw for moving the cutter. Lock the cutter by tightening the lock screw.

2. Fasten the bit in a brace.

3. Clamp a piece of scrap stock in the vise

or to the bench top and make a test cut. Is the hole size correct?

4. Mark the location of the hole on the workpiece.

5. *It is very important to have the work held tightly.* Since the bit has only one cutter, it will twist the work if it isn't clamped. It's a good idea to put a piece of scrap stock behind the work. Thin wood tends to crack or split.

6. As you rotate the tool, use just enough pressure to make it cut.

7. When the spur shows through, reverse the work and cut from the other side.

REVIEW QUESTIONS

1. Describe the parts of a hand drill.

2. Tell how to fasten a twist drill in a hand drill.

3. Describe an auger bit.

4. Name the two kinds of braces.

5. How is the size of an auger bit shown?

6. What size hole will a No. 7 bit cut?

7. For what is a bit or depth gauge used?

8. Tell how to install a bit in a brace.

9. Why should you have someone help you sight the tool when boring a hole?

10. How do you keep the auger bit square with the work surface?

11. What is the purpose of an expansion bit?

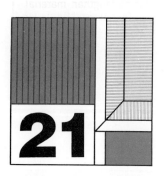

Joints and Their Uses

Furniture, houses, and the items you make in the shop are all assembled with *joints*. There are over one hundred different kinds of joints. Most of them are somewhat alike. Only eight are really different from each other. You will use the simpler ones when you build the projects shown in this book. The more difficult joints are found in fine furniture. They are usually made with machines. When you take an advanced course in woodworking, you will have a chance to make some of these. Table 21-A.

Making Joints Stronger

Joints are held together with glue or with glue plus nails or screws. Sometimes a joint is

Table 21-A. Common Wood Joints

Kinds	Uses	How Made	Similar Kinds
Edge	For tops of tables, chairs, desks, and other furniture needing large surfaces.	Plane a square edge on both pieces. Add dowels or spline for strength. Glue.	Dowel, tongue-and-groove, or rabbet.
Butt	For simple boxes, cases, cheap drawers, frames, and chairs.	Cut corners square in a miter box. Fasten with nails or screws and/or glue. Use doweling jig for corner dowel joint.	Glued and blocked or doweled corner for greater strength.
Rabbet	For corners of modern furniture, simple drawer construction, and boxes.	Cut rabbet with backsaw. Glue, nail, or fasten with long screws.	Dado and rabbet for good drawer corners.
Dado	For shelves, steps, drawers, and bookcases.	Cut with backsaw and trim out with router plane or chisel. Fit second piece into dado. Glue.	Blind dado (gain) for front edge that doesn't show joint.
Miter	For frames of pictures, boxes, molding around doors or furniture.	Cut with miter box. Fit corners carefully. Fasten with glue, nails, or corrugated fasteners.	Dowel or spline for greater strength.
Cross-Lap	For legs of furniture, doors, frames, and braces.	Make like two dadoes. Assemble with glue.	Half-lap to lengthen material. End-lap for frames. Middle-lap for doors.
Mortise-and-tenon	For best chair, table, and chest construction.	Cut tenon with backsaw. Drill out mortise on drill press. Trim out with chisel.	Open mortise-and-tenon for frames. Haunched mortise-and-tenon for panel construction.
Dovetail	For best drawer and box construction. Furniture corners.	Cut dovetail with jigsaw. Glue.	Blind dovetail for quality furniture.

made stronger by adding dowels or a spline. A *spline* is a thin piece of wood inserted in a groove between the two parts of a joint. Fig. 21-1.

A *dowel* is a peg or pin of wood or plastic that fits into two matching holes to strengthen a joint. Fig. 21-2. Dowels are also used for decoration or as parts of projects.

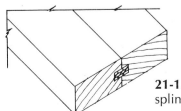

21-1. An edge joint can be strengthened with a spline.

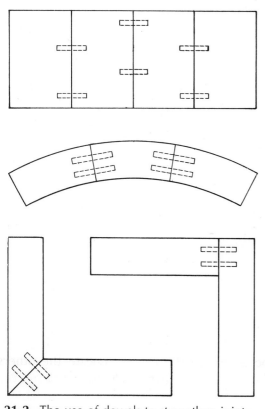

21-2. The use of dowels to strengthen joints.

21-3. A dowel pin with a spiral groove.

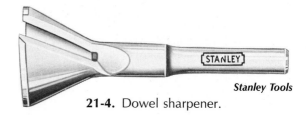

Stanley Tools

21-4. Dowel sharpener.

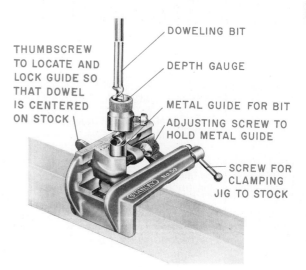

THUMBSCREW TO LOCATE AND LOCK GUIDE SO THAT DOWEL IS CENTERED ON STOCK

DOWELING BIT

DEPTH GAUGE

METAL GUIDE FOR BIT

ADJUSTING SCREW TO HOLD METAL GUIDE

SCREW FOR CLAMPING JIG TO STOCK

Stanley Tools

21-5. Doweling jig.

Tools and Materials

Dowel rod is usually made of birch in 36″ lengths. The common diameters range from ⅛″ to 1″, in intervals of 1/16″. Sometimes a groove is cut along the dowel so that glue holds better. Small *dowel pins* are made with a spiral groove and chamfered ends. The spiral helps the piece go in more easily. It also helps the glue flow. Fig. 21-3.

A *dowel sharpener* points the ends of dowels. Fig. 21-4.

A *doweling jig* will help locate the position of the holes and guide the auger bit for boring. This jig comes with several metal guides in sizes of 3/16″, ¼″, 5/16″, ⅜″, 7/16″, and ½″. Fig. 21-5.

Dowel centers are small metal pins used for marking the location of holes on two parts of a joint. They come in sizes of ¼″, 5/16″, ⅜″, and ½″. Fig. 21-6.

Dowel bits are auger bits for boring dowel holes. These bits are shorter than regular

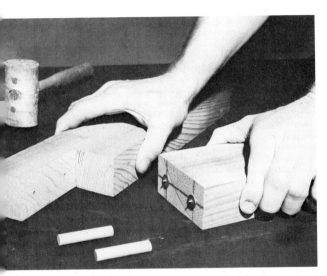

21-6. The location of the dowels has been marked on one piece. Dowel centers have been fastened in place. Hold the two pieces together and tap them with a mallet. The dowel centers will mark the location of the holes in the second piece.

auger bits. Fig. 21-7. Other tools for making dowel joints include a marking gauge, try square, rule, and pencil.

Making a Dowel Edge Joint

1. Square up the pieces to be joined.
2. Place the pieces on the bench side by side. Arrange them with their grain running in the same direction and their growth rings turned in opposite directions. Fig. 21-8. This will help to prevent warping.
3. Mark the face surface with matching numbers at each joint: 1-1, 2-2, etc.
4. Check the edges to be joined. They should be:
• Square with the face surface.
• Straight along the length. Use a large framing or carpenter's square to test them.

Stanley Tools

21-7. Bits for doweling. These bits are shorter than the standard auger bit.

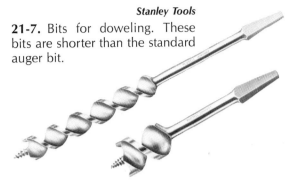

• Planed with a slight opening in the center and the ends fitting tightly.
5. Clamp the first two pieces in a vise with the face surfaces out.
6. Mark lines for the position of dowels across the edges. There should be a dowel every 12″ to 18″. If three dowels are used, locate one in the center. Locate the others about 2″ or 3″ in from each end. These are the

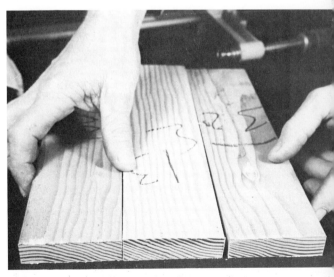

21-8. Turn the pieces so that the growth rings on the ends face in opposite directions.

only layout lines needed if a doweling jig is used.

7. If a doweling jig isn't used, mark centers for the holes. Use a marking gauge set at half the thickness of the stock. Mark from the face surfaces. Fig. 21-9.

8. Choose a dowel rod equal in diameter to about half the thickness of the stock.

9. If a doweling jig is used, proceed as follows:

(a) After you choose the dowel rod, select a metal guide of the same size for the doweling jig. Suppose the rod is ¼". Select a guide this size and slip it into the clamp of the jig. Adjust the guide so that it is centered on the thickness of stock.

(b) Clamp the jig over the stock so that it is lined up with the cross line.

(c) Place the jig with the solid side against the face surface. Clamp a stop to the bit for the correct depth of hole.

10. Choose an auger bit equal to the size of

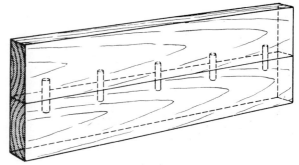

21-10. Edge joint with the dowels installed.

the dowel. Attach a bit gauge so that the depth of holes will be 1½" to 2".

11. Use a square to line up the bit. Bore the holes to the correct depth. Make sure the holes are bored squarely and on center. If they aren't, the two parts of the joint won't fit together right.

12. Bore all the holes on both parts of the joint. Countersink the holes so that the dowels will start easily.

13. Cut the dowels about ⅛" to ¼" shorter than the combined depth of the two holes. Chamfer or point the ends.

14. Insert the dowels in one edge. Then assemble the joint to check if it fits. Fig. 21-10.

15. Take the assembly apart. Remove the dowels. Dip the dowels one-third of the way into glue. Drive them into one edge with a mallet.

16. Apply glue to this edge and to the exposed dowels.

17. Put the two edges together and clamp them. (Clamping is discussed in Unit 22.)

Making a Rabbet Joint

A *rabbet* is a slot cut at the end or edge of a board. The end or edge of another piece is

21-9. Mark the location of the dowel holes with a marking gauge.

made to fit into this slot to make a rabbet joint. Fig. 21-11. This joint is one of the simplest.

TOOLS AND MATERIALS

You will need a marking gauge, try square, backsaw, pencil or knife, vise, hammer, nail set, screwdriver, nails, screws, or dowels, and glue.

Four steps are required in all *joinery* (joint making): layout, cutting, fitting, and assembling.

LAYOUT

1. Square up stock to the correct dimensions: thickness, width, and length.

2. Mark the shape of the rabbet on the end or edge of one piece.

• One way to do this is to measure from the end or edge a distance equal to the thickness of stock. This is the shoulder line. Mark a line across the stock with a try square and a pencil or knife.

• Another method is to place one piece of stock over the other as shown in Fig. 21-12. Mark a line across. Square the lines across both edges of the first piece.

3. Adjust a marking gauge for depth of ½"

21-12. Lay out the width of the rabbet or dado by holding one piece over the other. Mark the width with a pencil or knife.

to ⅔" the thickness of the stock. Mark a line across the edges and end to outline the rabbet.

CUTTING

1. Fasten the marked piece in a vise, or clamp it to the top of the bench.

2. Make the shoulder cut to correct depth with a backsaw. It might be a good idea to use a *guide board* for this. Fig. 21-13.

3. Clamp the work vertically in a vise. Make a second cut to form the rabbet.

FITTING

1. Place the end of the second piece in the rabbet and see if it fits tightly. The end of the first piece and the surface of the second piece should be flush.

2. Trim with a sharp chisel until the pieces fit snugly.

ASSEMBLING

1. The rabbet joint is assembled with nails

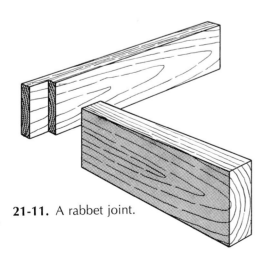

21-11. A rabbet joint.

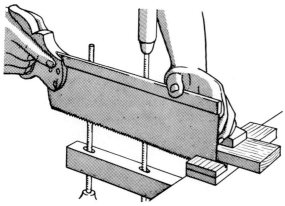

21-13. Making the shoulder cut. Notice that a guide board is clamped next to the layout line. Carefully cut the shoulder with a backsaw. The saw kerf must be in the waste stock.

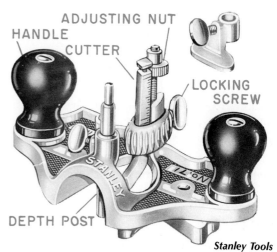

Stanley Tools

21-15. Parts of a router plane.

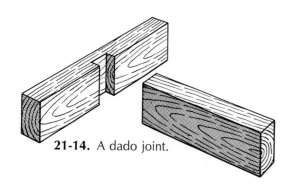

21-14. A dado joint.

and glue or screws and glue. Apply glue to the rabbet. Fit the second piece in the rabbet and hold or clamp it securely.

2. Install several nails or screws to fasten the two pieces permanently.

3. Rabbet joints can also be fastened with dowels and glue.

Making a Dado Joint

A *dado* is a slot cut **across** the grain of the wood. Fig. 21-14. By contrast, a *groove* is a slot cut **with** the grain.

Dado joints are strong. Bookcase shelves are often assembled with dado joints. Because one piece fits into a slot in another piece, the dado joint is strong enough even for stair steps.

TOOLS

A *router plane* is a cutting tool made for surfacing the bottom of grooves and dadoes. Fig. 21-15. It consists of a bed with two handles. There are three cutters: two straight cutters (¼″ and ½″) and one V cutter. The cutters can be adjusted to different depths.

Other tools needed include the try square, pencil or knife, backsaw, chisel, marking gauge, and hand clamps.

LAYOUT

1. Square up the stock. The end not exposed can be cut to length.

2. To locate one side of the dado, mark a line across one piece with a try square and a pencil or knife.

3. Place the end of the second piece across the first at this line.

4. Mark the width of the dado with a pencil or knife. See Fig. 21-12.

5. Continue the lines down the edges of the first piece. Fig. 21-16.

6. Adjust the marking gauge to the depth of the dado. Usually the dado is cut half the thickness of the stock.

7. Draw lines along the edges to show the depth.

CUTTING

1. Fasten the wood in a vise or to the bench top.

2. With a backsaw, make cuts just inside the layout line in the waste stock. Fig. 21-17. If you cut outside the line, the joint will be poor. You can do a better job with a guide board.

3. Now make several more saw cuts in the waste stock to the correct depth.

4. Remove the waste stock with a chisel. Chisel from both sides to the center. Fig. 21-18. Another method is to remove the waste stock with a router plane. Fasten the stock securely to the top of the bench with a good clamp. Select the widest cutter that will fit into the dado. Adjust for a light cut. Hold the

plane in both hands. Work across the stock with short, jerky strokes. Fig. 21-19. Don't try to make the cut too deep at one time. Adjust

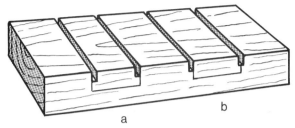

21-17. (A) The correct way to make the cuts. The saw kerfs are inside the layout line, in the waste stock. (B) The incorrect way. The saw kerfs are on or outside the layout line.

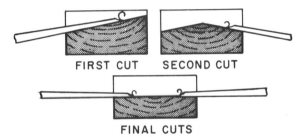

21-18. Steps in trimming a dado. Work first from one side and then the other.

21-16. Marking lines down the edges of the stock.

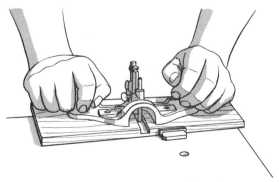

21-19. Removing the waste stock with a router plane. The work is clamped between the bench stop and the vise dog.

the plane each time to a slightly deeper cut until the correct depth is reached. Trim out the corners with a chisel.

5. Check the depth of the dado with a combination square. (See Unit 12.)

FITTING

1. Hold the second piece over the dado and press the end in. Fig. 21-20. It should go in with hand pressure.

2. If it is too tight, plane a little off the sides of the second piece until it fits snugly.

ASSEMBLING

Use glue alone or glue and screws or nails. In a fine piece of furniture, only glue is needed. Sometimes screws are added for extra strength. In carpentry, such as for building steps, the joint can be nailed.

MAKING A LAP JOINT

The *cross-lap joint* is made when two pieces of wood must cross. You find it on frames, table legs, and some kinds of chairs (especially outdoor furniture). The carpenter often uses it to strengthen the frame of a house. The pieces may cross at any angle. Other common kinds are the *half-lap*, the *middle-lap*, and the *end-lap*. Lap joints are made in the same way as rabbet or dado joints.

Making a Miter Joint

A *miter joint* is an angle joint made by cutting the end of two pieces of stock at equal slants. The most common miter joint is made by cutting each piece at an angle of 45°. When put together, the two pieces make a right angle. Fig. 21-21. A miter joint is used where no end grain should show. For example, it is used for making picture frames, box corners,

bulletin boards, and trim for cabinets. A miter joint is found at the upper corners of the trim around the doors and windows in some homes. A plain miter joint is not strong. However, it can be reinforced with a spline, key, or dowel. Fig. 21-22.

21-20. Fitting a dado joint. The piece should slip in with slight pressure.

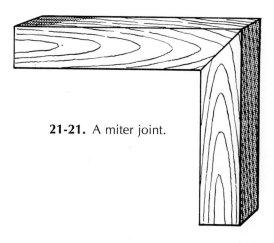

21-21. A miter joint.

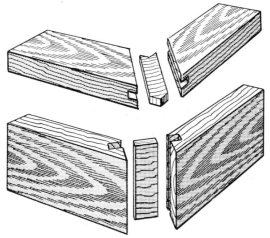

21-22. Miter joints can be strengthened with splines. A spline is a thin piece of wood, plywood, hardboard, or metal. It is inserted in a slot between two parts of a joint.

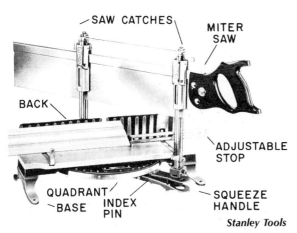

Stanley Tools

21-23. Parts of a metal miter box.

TOOLS

Most shops have a *metal miter box* for cutting angles. Fig. 21-23. The *miter saw* is a large backsaw. The base and frame of the miter box hold the saw in position. You don't have to guide the saw as you move it back and forth. The quadrant is divided in degrees. An

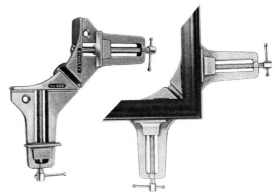

21-24. This miter-and-corner clamp is good for making picture frames. It holds the corners firmly in place as they are fastened together.

index pin drops into a hole for sawing at angles of 12°, 22½°, 30°, 36°, and 45°. To cut a four-piece frame, use the saw with the angle set at 45°. If a frame has eight sides, the miters are cut at 22½°.

A *handmade miter box* is good to have in a home workshop for making a square or 45° cut. To make a miter box, choose three pieces of wood about ¾″ × 4″ × 6″. Fasten them together to make a trough (a U shape). Make one cut at right angles to the sides and two 45° angle cuts, one in each direction. The distance between the 45° angle cuts on the outside must equal the width of the box. These cuts can be made on a metal miter box if one is available.

A *miter-and-corner clamp* is ideal for assembling frames. This clamp allows you to fasten the corner with the two pieces held firmly in place. Fig. 21-24. If the joint is glued, you can wipe away extra glue easily. If the joint isn't quite perfect, you can true it up with a backsaw. A four-corner miter-frame clamp holds all four corners at the same time. Fig. 21-25.

Other tools needed for making miter joints

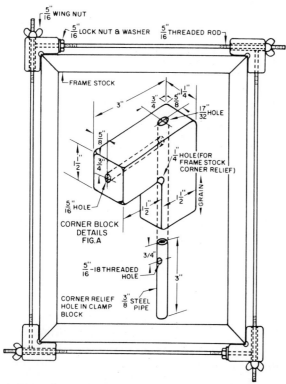

21-25. This miter-frame clamp can be made in the shop. The four clamp blocks are made of hardwoods such as maple, birch, hickory, or oak. The sides are $^5/_{17}$" threaded rod. A $^3/_8$" steel pipe acts as a bushing. It allows the rods to be easily moved for adjustments.

twice this measurement to the length of the glass or board. Fig. 21-26.

(c) Mark the length of all pieces on the back edge.

(d) If the frame is rectangular in shape, remember to measure the two sides and then the two ends. Make sure both matching pieces are the same length.

3. If no miter box is used, mark the angle of the joint with a combination square.

CUTTING

1. Hold the stock in the miter box. The back edge of the work should be against the back of the saw. Turn the saw 45° to the left and cut the right end. Fig. 21-27. Cut the right end of all pieces. When using a metal miter box, put a piece of scrap stock under the work. This will keep the saw from marring the base. Hold the saw firmly. Then release the catches that hold the saw up. Lower the saw slowly until the blade is just outside the layout line. Hold the stock firmly against the back with one hand. Saw with uniform strokes.

2. Shift the stock. Turn the saw 45° to the right and cut the left end. Remember, *reverse the saw, not the material.* Cut all pieces.

are the backsaw, combination square, and pencil.

LAYOUT

1. Mark the length of the stock along the edge away from you (the back edge).

2. If you are using picture-framing material with a rabbet edge, make the layout as follows:

(a) Measure the overall size of the glass or the board that will go inside the frame.

(b) Measure the width of the framing material from the rabbet edge to the outside. Add

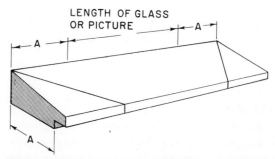

21-26. Laying out a picture frame. The length marked on the outside of the frame is equal to the length of the glass plus twice the width of the stock measured from the rabbet to the outside edge.

21-27. Using a homemade miter box to cut a 45° angle. Notice that a handsaw with fine teeth is being used. A backsaw could also be used. This is very satisfactory for doing small jobs around the home.

FITTING

1. Place the parts of the frame on a flat bench.

2. Check across the corners with a try square to see that they fit properly.

3. Measure with a rule across the diagonals. Both measurements must be the same.

4. If the corner is slightly off, clamp the two pieces in a miter or corner clamp. Then saw through the joint with a very fine backsaw.

5. Another method is to plane or sand any high spots to make the corner fit snugly.

ASSEMBLING

1. There are several ways of fastening a miter joint. The simplest is to nail the corner. Drive a nail into the first piece until the point just comes through the wood. Clamp the second piece in a vertical position in a vise. Hold the first piece with the corner slightly over the edge of the second piece. Drive the nail. The second piece will slip into place as the nail is set.

2. Clamp the two pieces in a miter-and-corner clamp. Nail or glue them.

3. Drill or bore a hole at right angles to each miter cut. Fit a dowel across the corners.

4. The joint can also be strengthened by adding a key or spline.

5. For rough work, the joint can be fastened with corrugated fasteners (wiggle nails) across each corner.

Making a Mortise-and-Tenon Joint

The *mortise-and-tenon joint* is one of the strongest. It is found on better-quality chairs, tables, and benches. Fig. 21-28. The *mortise* is the rectangular opening. The *tenon* is the part that fits into the opening. Mortise-and-tenon joints take a lot of time and experience when made by hand. With power tools they can be made quickly.

Making a Dovetail Joint

The dovetail joint is used on the corners of the best drawers and boxes. Fig. 21-29. Look

21-28. Two types of mortise-and-tenon joints are shown here. A blind mortise-and-tenon joint is shown on the left. It is used to fasten rails to legs on tables and chairs. An open mortise-and-tenon joint is shown on the right.

21-29. The dovetail joint is found in fine box and drawer construction. The most difficult joint to make, it is found only in furniture of the highest quality.

REVIEW QUESTIONS

1. How can joints be strengthened?
2. What is a rabbet?
3. Name the principal use for the dado joint.
4. At what angle is the corner of a miter joint usually cut?
5. Where are lap joints used?
6. What kind of joint is found in better-quality chairs and tables?
7. What is a mortise?
8. What is a tenon?
9. Where are dovetail joints usually found in furniture?

at a drawer on a well-made chest or cabinet. The front and sides almost always have dovetail joints. This joint is very difficult to make by hand. Today, power tools are used.

‖‖‖‖‖‖‖‖‖‖‖‖‖‖‖‖‖‖‖‖‖‖‖‖‖‖‖‖‖ *KEY IDEA* ‖‖‖‖‖‖‖‖‖‖‖‖‖‖‖‖‖‖‖‖‖‖‖

DEVELOPING LEADERSHIP

Do you have a favorite quarterback in professional football? Do you know the captain of one of your school's sports teams?

These people must be leaders, people who take charge. A leader is a person who gets other people to perform efficiently without resentment. A good leader also helps others to work together. There are many opportunities for you to develop leadership abilities. You can develop leadership skills by working in the shop. You also can develop them by joining in the mass production of a project. Club membership also will help develop leadership.

Everyday activities in the school shop can help develop leadership skills. For example, you may be asked to serve as the safety officer. You may also be placed in charge of the toolroom. Both of these jobs require a sense of responsibility. Responsibility helps develop leadership.

Perhaps your class has decided to mass-produce a product. To do this, it may want to set up a company. You may be elected one of the company's officers. This will give you an opportunity to develop your leadership skills. Leadership is important in setting up an assembly line for mass production. In such an activity, you can practice many different leadership skills. For example, you may be in charge of planning the assembly line. Here, you would need to direct those who assemble the product. You might also be in charge of the sales program. In this job, you would need to instruct those selling the product. You also would need to manage the advertising for the product. You also could be placed in charge of the shipping department. In this job, you would need to make sure that the products were properly packed and delivered.

As you can see, in any job, there are important responsibilities. Some responsibilities may not seem important. Mass production, however, is a team effort. And, in any team effort, organization is important. Proper leadership helps organize a work effort.

One of the easiest ways to develop leadership skills is by joining a club. In most

VICA

Fig. A. This machine shop student is competing for an award in a VICA contest.

schools, there are a variety of clubs. Each club brings together people with an interest in one activity. For example, there are stamp clubs, music clubs, and speech clubs. There also are industrial arts and vocational education clubs. Many of these clubs are part of a national organization. There are two national organizations of such clubs. These two organizations are the American Industrial Arts Student Association (AIASA) and the Voca-

VICA

Fig. B. This student was the winner of the first prize in a VICA contest.

AIASA and VICA
Fig. C. The emblems of AIASA and VICA.

tional Industrial Clubs of America (VICA). These organizations have similar goals. They seek to develop contacts with people in industry. They also seek to develop an understanding of our technology.

The development of good leadership skills will help you throughout your life. Such skills will be valuable to you in any career you choose. The development of leadership skills will help you:

- To improve consumer understanding.
- To develop productive use of leisure time.

- To recognize high standards of achievement, scholarship, leadership, and safety practices.

By taking part in the activities of a club, you can develop your leadership skills. In most clubs, you will be able to take part in the following activities. You will learn:
- To conduct a meeting using parliamentary procedure.
- To do fund raising.
- To plan an open house for the community.
- To be an officer in the organization.
- To develop technical skills.
- To participate in regional, state, and national contests.

Taking part in any group activity will help you develop your social skills. It is these skills that help you get along with others. All of the following skills are important in everyday life. They also are important in developing leadership. It is important to be able:
- To speak on your feet and communicate clearly with other people.
- To write clearly and express your ideas.
- To do the best job possible.
- To adapt your behavior to a variety of situations and individuals.
- To react positively under unusual pressures.
- To complete a job with or without direction.
- To work safely in all situations.

The development of leadership skills is important. While in school, you should try to develop these skills as fully as possible.

Clamping and Gluing Up Stock

If a project is small or made of plywood, you probably won't need clamps and glue until you assemble it. However, for larger projects, you will have to glue pieces together as you go. For example, you might have to glue stock edge-to-edge to make the top for a table or chair. Stock may have to be glued face-to-face to make legs. Parts must also be glued in final assembly.

Tools and Materials

Clamps hold pieces together. They are used:
- To find out how they fit.
- To hold them as the glue dries.
- For installing nails or screws.
- To do chiseling or planing on them.

Hand screws are used for gluing face-to-

22-1. Using hand screws in assembling a project.

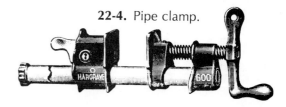

22-2. C-clamp.

22-4. Pipe clamp.

22-3. Bar clamp.

face, for clamping small parts, and for holding work as it is cut or formed. This clamp can be used on finished surfaces without clamp blocks. The best size has a jaw length of 8″ to 12″. Fig. 22-1.

The *C-clamp* is used for clamping face-to-face, for repair work, and for holding parts

22-5. Spring clamps are useful when making repairs.

together. The 6″ to 10″ size is for general use. Fig. 22-2.

The *bar clamp* is used for large work such as gluing stock edge-to-edge or assembling projects. The common lengths are 3′ to 5′. Fig. 22-3.

The *pipe clamp* is similar to the bar clamp. The clamping devices attach to steel pipe.

This tool can be made as long as needed by using different lengths of pipe. Fig. 22-4.

Spring clamps can be applied quickly without turning a handle. Some spring clamps have plastic tips to protect the wood from the metal. Fig. 22-5.

Three-way edging clamps apply "right-angle" pressure to the edge or side of work. Fig. 22-6.

A *rubber* or *wooden mallet* is used to strike the wood when assembling projects.

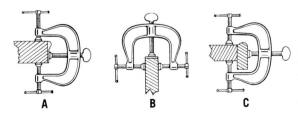

A   B   C

22-6. Three ways of using three-way edging clamps: (A) With the right-angle screw off-center. (B) With the right-angle screw centered. (C) Clamping around an edge.

	Liquid Hide Glue	White (Polyvinyl) Liquid Resin Glue	Resorcinol	Powdered Resin	Powdered Casein	Flake Animal
Especially good for:	First choice for furniture work and wherever a tough, lasting wood-to-wood bond is needed. A favorite for cabinet-work and general wood gluing.	A fine all-around household glue for mending and furniture making and repair. Excellent for model work, paper, leather, and small assemblies.	This is the glue for any work that may be exposed to soaking: outdoor furniture, boats, wooden sinks.	Use it for wood-working and general gluing where considerable mois-ture resistance is wanted.	Will do most woodworking jobs and is especially desirable with oily woods: teak, lemon, yew.	Good for quantity woodworking jobs that justify the time and trouble of mixing and heating the glue.
Not so good for:	Because it is not waterproof, do not use it for outdoor furniture or for boat building.	Not sufficiently moisture-resistant for anything to be exposed to weather. Not so strong and lasting as liquid hide glue for fine furniture work.	Not good for work that must be done at tempera-tures below 70°F. Because of dark color and mixing, not often used unless waterproof quality is needed.	Do not use with oily woods or with joints that are not closely fitted and tightly clamped. Must be mixed for each use.	Not moisture-resis-tant enough for outdoor furniture. Will stain acid woods such as redwood. Must be mixed for each use.	Too much trouble to use for small jobs or most home shop work. Not waterproof.
Advantag-es:	Very strong because it is rawhide-tough and does not become brittle. It is easy to use, light in color, resists heat and mold. It has good filling qualities, so gives strength even in poorly fitted joints.	Always ready to use at any temperature. Nonstaining, clean, and white. Quick-setting qualities recommend it for work where good clamping is not possible.	Very strong, as well as water-proof. It works better with poor joints than many glues do.	Very strong, although brittle if joint fits poorly. Light-colored, almost waterproof.	Strong, fairly water-resistant, works in cool locations, fills poor joints well.	Same advantages as liquid hide glue but must be mixed, heated, kept hot, used at high temperatures.
Source:	From animal hides and bones.	From chemicals.	From chemicals.	From chemicals.	From milk curd.	From animal hides and bones.

Table 22-B. Fastening Wood with All Types of Glue

Glue Type	Room Temperature	How to Prepare	How to Apply	70°F Clamping Time	
				Hardwood	Softwood
Liquid Hide	Sets best above 70°F. Can be used in colder room if glue is warmer.	Ready to use.	Apply thin coat on both surfaces; let get tacky before joining.	2 hours	3 hours
White Liquid Resin	Any temperature above 60°F, but the warmer the better.	Ready to use.	Spread on and clamp at once.	1 hour	1½ hours
Resorcinol	Must be 70°F or warmer. Will set faster at 90°F.	Mix 3 parts powder to 4 parts liquid catalyst.	Apply thin coat to both surfaces. Use within 8 hours after mixing.	16 hours	16 hours
Powdered Resin	Must be 70°F or warmer. Will set faster at 90°F.	Mix 2 parts powder with ½ to 1 part water.	Apply thin coat to both surfaces. Use within 4 hours after mixing.	16 hours	16 hours
Powdered Casein	Any temperature above freezing, but the warmer the better.	Stir together equal parts by volume glue and water. Wait 10–15 minutes and stir again.	Apply thin coat to both surfaces. Use within 8 hours after mixing.	2 hours	3 hours
Flaked or Powdered Animal	Must be 70°F or warmer. Keep work warm.	For each ounce glue add 1½ ounces water (softwood) or 2 ounces water (hardwood).	Apply heavy coat at 140°F to both surfaces. Assemble rapidly.	1 hour	1½ hours

Glues are used to fasten pieces permanently. Table 22-A lists the best kinds of glue for various jobs. Table 22-B lists the common types of glue. Liquid resin is a very good all-purpose glue. It comes in tubes, squeeze bottles, and cans. The squeeze bottle is best for most projects. It is neat and there is little waste. This glue dries fast.

Clamp blocks are small pieces of scrap wood. They are used with bar, pipe, and

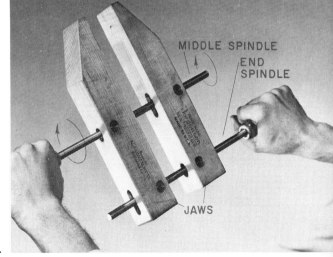

22-7. Parts of a hand screw.

C-clamps to protect the finished parts of a project.

Clamping

USING HAND SCREWS

The parts of a hand screw are shown in Fig. 22-7. To adjust a hand screw, grasp the handle of the middle spindle in one hand. Grasp the handle of the end spindle in the other. Revolve the spindles at the same time. Revolve them in one direction to open and in the other to close. If the jaws aren't parallel, adjust one spindle until they are. Always tighten the middle spindle first. Then tighten the end spindle. Reverse to remove.

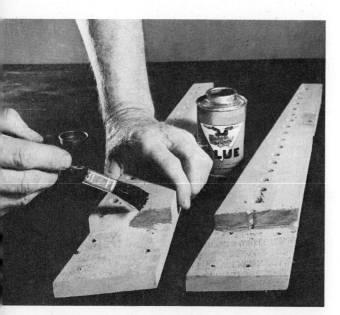

22-8. When gluing end grain, apply a thin coat of glue first. The end grain will absorb the glue. When applying glue to the rest of the joint, apply a second coat to the end grain. Notice that a brush is used to apply the liquid glue.

TIPS ON CLAMPING
• Dry-clamp all pieces before gluing. Then you will know if the joints fit properly and if you have enough clamps for the job.
• For easy and accurate assembly, mark all pieces before gluing.
• Use small pieces of scrap wood or plastic to protect the wood from metal clamp jaws.
• Don't apply too much pressure. This will force the glue from the joints, causing a weak, "starved" joint.

Gluing

MIXING POWDERED RESIN OR CASEIN GLUES

1. Follow directions on the can carefully. Never mix more glue than you can use at one time.
2. Many powdered glues are mixed with an equal amount of water.
3. Stir the glue briskly. Then allow it to stand about 10 to 15 minutes.
4. Mix again for about 1 minute. The glue should be about as thick as whipping cream.
5. Apply the glue with a brush or stick.

MIXING RESORCINOL GLUE

1. This glue comes in two separate cans. One contains the liquid resin and the other the powdered catalyst. The catalyst makes the glue hold better and helps it to harden.
2. Mix the liquid and the powder in the exact amounts stated on the label. Never mix more than you need for one job.

APPLYING GLUE

Follow these tips in applying all glues:
• Work at correct temperature.
• Apply two coats of glue to end grain. End grain tends to soak up glue. Fig. 22-8.

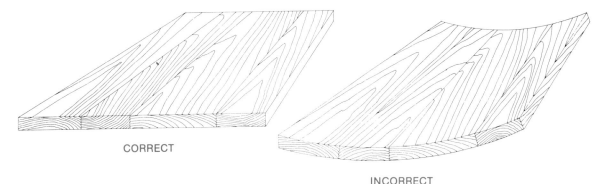

CORRECT

INCORRECT

22-9. Correct and incorrect way to assemble stock edge-to-edge. If assembled with growth rings in same direction, the piece is more likely to warp.

• Find the most convenient way to apply the glue (tube, squeeze bottle, etc.).
• Cover surfaces evenly.

GLUING STOCK EDGE TO EDGE

1. Choose the number of pieces needed to make the larger surface. Use pieces not more than 5″ to 6″ wide.

2. Square up each piece.

3. Arrange the pieces so that:
• The grain matches.
• The grain runs in the same direction.
• The growth rings at the ends of boards are in opposite directions. Fig. 22-9.

4. Mark the matching joints 1-2, 2-2, etc.

5. Test the edge joints to make sure the ends are tight. On long pieces the edges are planed so that there is a little opening (about the thickness of paper) near the center.

6. Add dowels or splines if you want a stronger joint.

7. Choose at least three bar clamps to hold the parts together. There should be a clamp every 10″ to 12″ along the assembly.

8. If the outer edges must be protected, use clamp blocks.

9. If the assembly is wide, put cleats across the ends to keep the surface level.

10. Make a trial assembly to see that everything is all right. Open the bar clamps slightly wider than the assembly. Alternate the clamps —one above, the next below. Fig. 22-10. Tighten the clamps with moderate pressure.

22-10. Note that the clamps are fastened from opposite sides.

Check to make sure the surface is level and the joints are closed.

11. Take the assembly apart.

12. Apply glue to the edges and dowels or splines. Cover the edges, but do not put on so much glue that it will squeeze out.

13. Put the joints together quickly.

14. Tighten the clamps a little at a time. If necessary, force the parts together with a rubber mallet.

15. If necessary, put cleats across the ends. Wax paper under the cleats will keep them from sticking.

GLUING STOCK FACE-TO-FACE

1. Choose pieces to make the correct thickness. For most furniture legs, two pieces glued together are enough.

2. Square up the stock to rough size. This is done so that you can see the grain and know how to match the parts.

3. Assemble with the growth rings in opposite directions. Check to make sure the grain matches. Don't put a very light and a very dark piece side by side.

4. Use glue blocks and C-clamps or hand screws to hold the parts together. Fig. 22-11.

5. Apply the glue evenly over the surfaces. Clamp together.

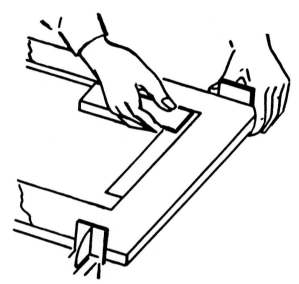

22-12. Checking the project for squareness.

22-11. When gluing face-to-face with C-clamps, always use clamp blocks.

22-13. Checking the project for levelness.

Assembling a Project

The steps in gluing up a project depend on how difficult it is. For a simple project of two or three pieces, all the gluing is done at the same time. For a more advanced project, such as a small table, the assembling is done in the following steps:

1. Get all the parts together. Check to see that everything is complete.

2. Decide on how the project is to be assembled. Some projects have four legs and four rails. The best way is to glue the ends together first and then the complete project.

3. Cut clamp blocks to protect the finished wood surface.

4. Select the correct kind and number of clamps.

5. Clamp the parts together to see if they fit. Make sure the parts are square and level. Figs. 22-12 and 22-13. Then take the project apart.

6. Mix the correct kind and amount of glue.

7. Apply the glue with a brush or squeeze bottle. Don't put on too much. Put a little extra glue on end grain.

8. Assemble the first part of the project. Clamp lightly. Then recheck to make sure the parts are square and level. Sometimes you have to shift a clamp or strike a joint with a rubber mallet to bring it into place.

9. Remove excess glue before it dries.

10. Allow the first section to dry.

11. Follow these steps for each section. Then assemble the complete project.

REVIEW QUESTIONS

1. Name five kinds of clamps.
2. Which glues are waterproof?
3. What three things must you check for when gluing stock edge-to-edge?
4. What can be used on the edge of stock to make a stronger joint?
5. Should a small table be glued up all at once? Explain.

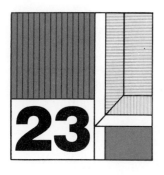

Using Nails

Nails are used to hold wood pieces together. Nailing is one of the most common ways of assembling projects. Although it seems very simple, nailing takes a good deal of skill. Just watch an experienced carpenter or cabinetmaker drive nails and you'll appreciate this skill.

Tools and Materials

The *claw hammer* has a wood, metal, or fiberglass handle. Fig. 23-1. Some workers like the metal handle. Others prefer the wood or fiberglass because these don't vibrate so much. Hammer size is shown by weight and varies from 7 to 28 ounces. A 16-ounce hammer is good for average work.

There are many kinds of nails. The four used the most are the common, box, casing, and finishing. Most nails are made of mild steel or aluminum. Aluminum nails have the advantage of not rusting when used out-of-doors.

Common nails are for rough construction such as home building. Fig. 23-2(12). *Box nails* are somewhat smaller. Fig. 23-2(1). They are used where the common nails might split the wood, such as in building boxes or crates. *Casing nails* have a smaller head. Fig. 23-2(6).

They are used in interior trim in houses and in cabinetmaking. *Finishing nails* have small heads. Fig. 23-2(2). They are ideal for project making, cabinetwork, and finish carpentry.

There are also many special nails used in construction. Fig. 23-2. These are available with different kinds of shanks, heads, points, and finishes or coatings. For special nailing problems, your building supply dealer can suggest the correct nails to use.

Nail size is given by the term *penny*, which is shown by the letter *d*. No one knows exactly where this term came from. Some people think it meant the cost of nails in pence (English money). Others think it meant the weight per thousand. In either case, the term

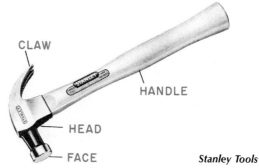

CLAW

HANDLE

HEAD

FACE

Stanley Tools

23-1. Parts of a claw hammer. The handle is hickory.

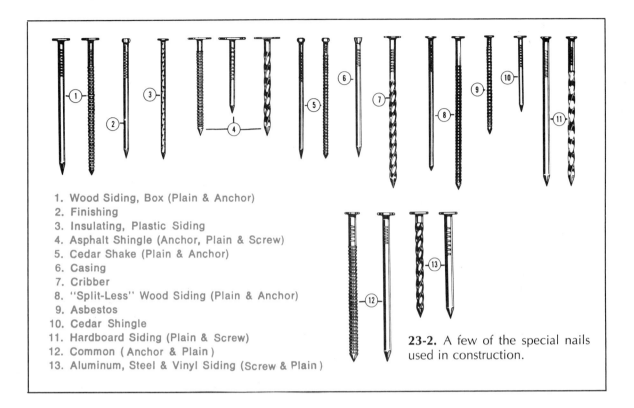

1. Wood Siding, Box (Plain & Anchor)
2. Finishing
3. Insulating, Plastic Siding
4. Asphalt Shingle (Anchor, Plain & Screw)
5. Cedar Shake (Plain & Anchor)
6. Casing
7. Cribber
8. "Split-Less" Wood Siding (Plain & Anchor)
9. Asbestos
10. Cedar Shingle
11. Hardboard Siding (Plain & Screw)
12. Common (Anchor & Plain)
13. Aluminum, Steel & Vinyl Siding (Screw & Plain)

23-2. A few of the special nails used in construction.

is still used. For example, a 3d nail is 1¼″ long; a 6d nail is 2″ long. A 6d common and a 6d finishing nail are both 2″ long. However, the common nail is larger in diameter. That is because the nails are made from different gauge wire—11½ gauge for common, 13 gauge for finishing. (The higher the gauge number of the nail, the smaller its diameter.) Table 23-A.

Escutcheon pins and wire brads are small nails. They are used in making novelties and small articles. *Escutcheon pins* are small brass nails with round heads. They come in lengths from ¼″ to 1¼″ and in diameters from 20 gauge to 16 gauge. *Wire brads* are small, flatheaded, mild steel nails with sharp points. They come in lengths from ½″ to 1½″ and in

gauge numbers from 20 to 14. You can get these fasteners at a given length in several gauges.

A *nail set* is a small metal punch with a cupped end. The cupped end prevents it from slipping off the head of the nail. The tool is used to sink the heads of casing or finishing nails below the wood surface. Fig. 23-3.

Driving Nails

1. Decide on the size and kind of nails you need. Choose the smallest diameter that will do the job. A nail too large will split the wood. Nails should be a little shorter than the thickness of the pieces being nailed. In some cases

Table 23-A. Nail Sizes

Size	Length in Inches	American Steel Wire Gauge Number		
		Common	Box and Casing	Finishing
2d	1	15*	15½	16½
3d	1¼	14	14½	15½
4d	1½	12½	14	15
5d	1¾	12½	14	15
6d	2	11½	12½	13
7d	2¼	11½	12½	13
8d	2½	10¼	11½	12½
9d	2¾	10¼	11½	12½
10d	3	9	10½	11½
12d	3¼	9	10½	11½
16d	3½	8	10	11
20d	4	6	9	10
30d	4½	5	9	
40d	5	4	8	

*Note: The decimal inch equivalent of common gauge numbers is:

15 = 0.072	12 = 0.106	9 = 0.148	6 = 0.192
14 = 0.080	11 = 0.121	8 = 0.162	5 = 0.207
13 = 0.092	10 = 0.135	7 = 0.177	4 = 0.225

movement. Strike the nail with a few good blows, keeping your eye on the nail.

5. If the nail bends, don't try to straighten it by striking it on the side. Remove the nail and use a new one. Nails driven at an angle have better holding power. When nailing into end grain, drive the first nail in straight and the other nails at an angle.

6. If the nail is a casing or finishing nail, drive it until the head still shows. Then use a nail set with a point slightly smaller than the

23-3. Drive the head of the nail about 1⁄16″ below the surface.

23-4. Using a piece of scrap wood under the head of the hammer to increase leverage.

nails are driven through and their points stick out the other side. Then the points are *clinched* (bent over) with the grain.

2. Decide on the number and location of the nails. The nails should be evenly spaced but *staggered* (not in a straight line). Putting several nails along the same grain line will split the wood. When nailing hardwood, put a little wax or soap on the point of the nail. This will make it go in more easily. If there is danger of splitting the wood, first drill a hole that is about three-fourths the diameter of the nail.

3. Hold the nail between your thumb and forefinger. Grasp the hammer handle near its end. Tap the nail lightly to start it. Take your hand away from the nail.

4. Drive the nail by swinging the hammer and your arm as a unit. Use just a little wrist

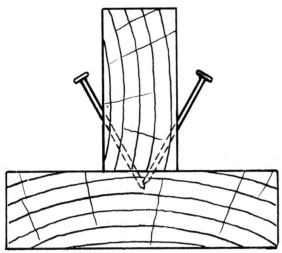

23-5. The correct method of toenailing.

head of the nail. Place the point of the nail set over the head of the nail, guiding it with your fingers. Drive the head about ¹⁄₁₆″ below the surface.

Removing Nails

1. To remove nails from a board, use the claw of the hammerhead. Slip the claw under the nailhead and pull the handle down.

2. On finished surfaces, place a thin board or piece of plywood under the claw to protect the surface. If the nail is quite long, put a thick block under the claw after the nail is partway out. This helps to keep the nail straight. It also gives you better leverage. Fig. 23-4.

Toenailing

Toenailing is a way of fastening the end of one board to the edge or face of another. The nails are driven at an angle from both sides of

the first board. This helps to hold the boards tightly together. Fig. 23-5.

Using Corrugated Fasteners

Corrugated fasteners are a wiggle nail used in general construction and repair work. They are often used, for example, to hold the corners of window screens together. These fasteners hold best when placed at an angle to the grain. However, this is not always possible. Fig. 23-6.

REVIEW QUESTIONS
1. Name the parts of a claw hammer.
2. Name the four kinds of nails used most often.
3. Describe an escutcheon pin.
4. Why should nails be staggered?
5. How is a nail set used?
6. Describe the way to start nailing.
7. How do you remove a nail?
8. What is toenailing?

23-6. Using a corrugated fastener to reinforce a miter joint. This fastener has greater strength than an ordinary nail.

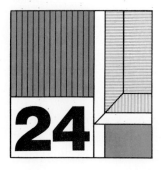

Installing Screws

A *screw* is a fastener with a groove twisting around part of its length. It is one of the best wood fasteners. A screw is strong. It does not come out easily. It can be tightened and later loosened to take an article apart.

Tools and Materials

Wood screws are made of mild steel, brass, aluminum, or copper. Brass screws are used for boats, water skis, or other items used around water. The most common head shapes are *round*, *flat*, and *oval*. Fig. 24-1. Round-head screws of mild steel are made with a blue finish. Flathead screws of mild steel have a bright finish. Ovalhead screws are usually plated with cadmium or chromium. They are used most often to install hinges, hooks, and other hardware. Most screws have a plain *slotted* head. However, the *recessed* (Phillips) head is becoming more popular.

Screws come in different lengths from ¼" to 6". They also come in different gauge sizes from 0 to 24. The gauge tells the diameter. The larger the gauge number, the greater the diameter of the screw. Screws of the same length come in different gauge sizes. For example, a No. 6 screw, 1½" long, is a very slim screw. A No. 14 screw, 1½" long, is a fat

PHILLIPS OVAL HEAD WOOD SCREW

PHILLIPS ROUND HEAD WOOD SCREW

PHILLIPS FLAT HEAD WOOD SCREW

SLOTTED OVAL HEAD WOOD SCREW

SLOTTED FLAT HEAD WOOD SCREW

SLOTTED ROUND HEAD WOOD SCREW

24-1. Common head shapes and types of slots.

TIP   BLADE   HANDLE

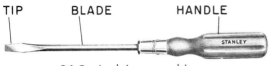

24-2. A plain screwdriver.

Stanley Tools

24-3. Phillips-head screwdriver.

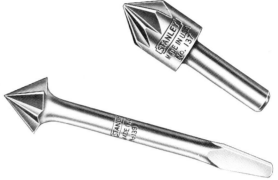

Stanley Tools

24-4. A countersink for a brace (left) and for a hand drill or drill press (right).

Stanley Tools

24-5. Screwdriver bit to be used in a brace.

screw. Generally, screws with lower gauge numbers are used for thin wood. Those with higher gauge numbers are used for heavy wood.

Screws are sold by the dozen or by the hundred in hardware stores. They are packed in factories by the pound.

The five most common sizes of flathead screws are:

- No. 7: ¾" long.
- No. 8: 1" long.
- No. 8: 1¼" long.
- No. 10: 1¼" long.
- No. 12: 1½" long.

There are two types of screwdrivers. The *plain* screwdriver is used to install slotted-head screws. The size depends on the length and diameter of the blade. Fig. 24-2. The *Phillips-head* screwdriver is also made in different diameters and lengths. It is used to install Phillips-head screws. Fig. 24-3. Its tip cannot be reshaped.

An *82° countersink* is needed for flathead screws that must be flush with the surface.

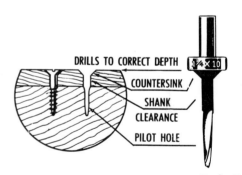

DRILLS TO CORRECT DEPTH

COUNTERSINK

SHANK CLEARANCE

PILOT HOLE

Stanley Tools

24-6. A screw-mate drill and countersink to use with flathead screws.

This tool makes a cone-shaped hole for the head of the screw. Fig. 24-4.

A *screwdriver bit* can be used in a brace for setting screws. Fig. 24-5.

A *screw-mate drill and countersink* is a tool for installing flathead screws. Fig. 24-6. It will do all of the following operations at one time:

- Drill the hole to correct depth.
- Countersink.
- Make the correct shank clearance.
- Make the correct pilot hole.

This tool is stamped with the length and gauge number. For example, a ¾" × #6 is used for a flathead screw ¾" long with a No. 6 gauge size.

A *counterbore* will do all the operations performed by the screw mate. It also will drill plug holes for wooden plugs. Fig. 24-7.

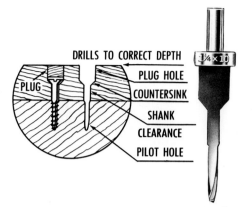

DRILLS TO CORRECT DEPTH
PLUG HOLE
COUNTERSINK
SHANK
CLEARANCE
PILOT HOLE
PLUG

Stanley Tools

24-7. A screw-mate counterbore that does five things at once. A wood plug can be used to cover the screwhead.

Installing Screws

1. Choose a screw long enough to go two-thirds its length into the second piece of wood. Another rule to follow is to make sure that all the threaded part of the screw will go into the second piece. The diameter of the screw should be chosen according to the thickness of the wood.

2. Mark the location of the screw hole in the first piece of wood. Make a punch mark with a center punch or scratch awl.

3. Select a drill that will be equal in diameter to the shank of the screw. Drill a shank

hole in the first piece. Table 24-A shows the correct drill size. You can also hold the drill behind the screw shank and sight for size.

4. Place the first piece of wood over the second. Mark the location of the screw hole in the second piece.

5. Drill a pilot hole (anchor hole) to the depth the screw will go. If the wood is very soft, this hole may not be needed. The drill for the pilot hole must be about equal to the

Table 24-A. Drill Sizes for Wood Screws

Screw Gauge No.	0	1	2	3	4	5	6	7	8	9	10	11	12	14	16	18	20
Shank Hole Hard & Soft Wood	¹⁄₁₆	⁵⁄₆₄	³⁄₃₂	⁷⁄₆₄	⁷⁄₆₄	⅛	⁹⁄₆₄	⁵⁄₃₂	¹¹⁄₆₄	³⁄₁₆	³⁄₁₆	¹³⁄₆₄	⁷⁄₃₂	¼	¹⁷⁄₆₄	¹⁹⁄₆₄	²¹⁄₆₄
Pilot Hole Soft Wood	¹⁄₆₄	¹⁄₃₂	¹⁄₃₂	³⁄₆₄	³⁄₆₄	¹⁄₁₆	¹⁄₁₆	¹⁄₁₆	⁵⁄₆₄	⁵⁄₆₄	³⁄₃₂	³⁄₃₂	⁷⁄₆₄	⁷⁄₆₄	⁹⁄₆₄	⁹⁄₆₄	¹¹⁄₆₄
Pilot Hole Hard Wood	¹⁄₃₂	¹⁄₃₂	³⁄₆₄	¹⁄₁₆	¹⁄₁₆	⁵⁄₆₄	⁵⁄₆₄	³⁄₃₂	³⁄₃₂	⁷⁄₆₄	⁷⁄₆₄	⅛	⅛	⁹⁄₆₄	⁵⁄₃₂	³⁄₁₆	¹³⁄₆₄
Auger Bit Sizes For Plug Hole			3	4	4	4	5	5	6	6	6	7	7	8	9	10	11

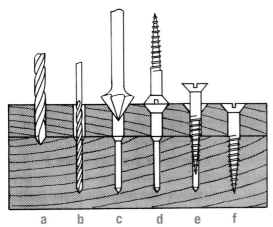

24-8. Steps in installing a flathead screw: (A) Drill the shank hole. (B) Drill the pilot, or anchor, hole. (C) Countersink. (D) Check the amount of countersink with the screwhead. (E) Install the flathead screw. (F) Screw properly installed.

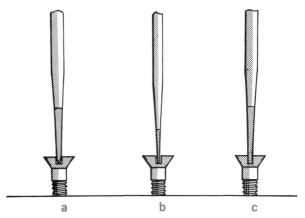

24-9. Incorrect and correct way of grinding a screwdriver for slotted-head screws: (A) Tip rounded. (B) Tip too thin. (C) Tip properly fitted.

smallest diameter of the threaded part of the screw. Here again you can use a chart or sight for size. Use a depth or bit gauge if several screws must be installed.

6. When using flathead screws, cut a conical (cone-shaped) hole with a countersink. This hole will allow the head of the screw to be flush with the surface. To check, turn the screw upside down and see if the hole is just right. Fig. 24-8. If you are installing many screws of the same size, put a depth or bit gauge on the countersink.

7. The blade of a plain screwdriver should be equal to the width of the screwhead. A screwdriver that is too small will slip. It will make a *burr* (a rough edge) on the screwhead. A screwdriver that is too large will mar the wood as you finish tightening the screw. The tool should be ground so that it has a straight, square blade. Fig. 24-9.

8. Hold the screw between your thumb and forefinger. Hold the handle of the screwdriver lightly in your other hand. Start the

screw. Then slip the hand holding the screw up behind the tip of the screwdriver to guide the tool as you tighten the screw. Fig. 24-10.

9. Don't tighten the screw too much. You may break the screw or strip the threads in the wood. Then the fastener won't hold. You must

24-10. Starting to drive a screw. Note that the screwdriver is guided with the thumb and forefinger.

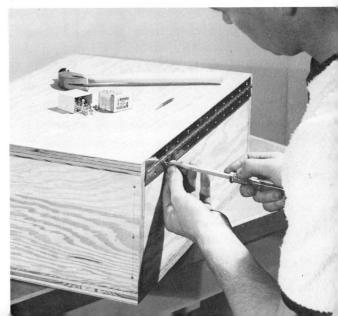

be especially careful with aluminum or brass screws.

10. If several screws are used to fasten two parts together, it is a good idea first to drill all the shank holes (and countersink). Then drill one pilot hole. Install the screw before drilling the other pilot holes. This makes it easier to line up the parts to be put together.

11. In driving a large number of screws, a screwdriver bit may be used in a brace to speed the work.

Concealing the Screwhead

On some projects you don't want the screwhead to show. As a first step, bore a shallow hole with an auger bit that is the same diameter as the screwhead. Then, after the screw is set, you can cover the screw with plastic wood or a plug. Fig. 24-11. A plain plug or button (small wood covering) can be cut on the drill press, or a decorative plug can be bought. Fig. 24-12.

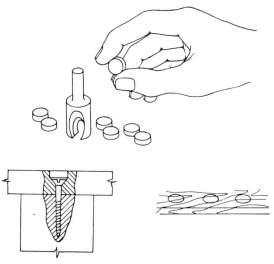

24-12. If you make a project where screws are countersunk or counterbored, it will pay to use a plug cutter. This tool cuts perfect plugs from the same stock used for the project. Plug cutters are made in sizes 6, 8, 10, and 12 to match the commonly used screw sizes. The plugs are a snug fit in the counterbored holes.

Plates

Repair and mending plates come in many sizes and shapes. Fig. 24-13. *Mending plates* are used to strengthen a butt or lap joint. The *flat corner* iron is used to strengthen corners of frames such as a screen door or window frames. The *bent corner* iron can be applied to shelves and the inside corners of tables, chairs, and cabinets. It can also be used to hang cabinets and shelves. *T plates* are used to strengthen the center rail of a frame. Many other metal devices, such as tabletop fasteners and chair braces are also available.

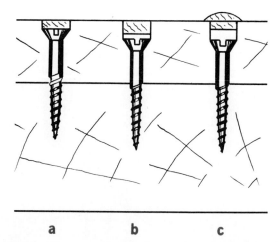

                a   b   c

24-11. Three methods of covering the heads of screws: (A) Plastic wood. (B) A plain wood plug. (C) A fancy wood plug.

Household Screw Devices

Figure 24-14 shows some of the common household screw devices. Common sizes of

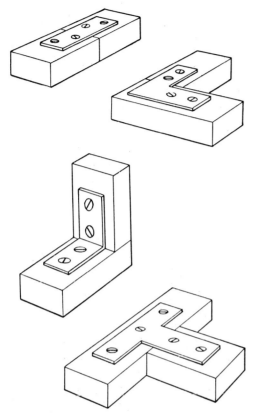

24-13. Four types of repair plates: mending, flat corner, bent corner, and T plate.

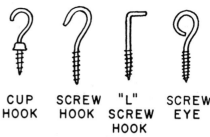

CUP   SCREW   "L"   SCREW
HOOK   HOOK   SCREW   EYE
HOOK

24-14. These devices are often used around the home. For example, cup hooks are installed under kitchen cabinet shelves to hold cups.

2¼". *Screw eyes* are made with either small or medium eyes in many different sizes.

cup hooks (usually made of brass) are ½", ⅝", ¾", 1", 1¼", and 1½". *Screw hooks* are made in lengths from 1¼" to 2½". *"L" (square-bent) screw hooks* are available in lengths from 1" to

REVIEW QUESTIONS

1. Why is a screw better than a nail?
2. Name three of the materials from which screws are made.
3. What are the three most common head shapes?
4. Which is larger in diameter, a No. 4 or a No. 10 screw?
5. Name the five most common sizes of flathead screws.
6. When is an 82° countersink needed?
7. How do you choose the correct size screw?
8. What is a shank hole?
9. Tell how to install a screw.
10. How can you hide the heads of screws?

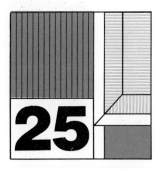

Sanding and Preparing for Finishing

25

Sanding

Sanding is a way of smoothing the surface of stock with an *abrasive*. An abrasive is a hard, sharp material that wears away a softer surface. Abrasive grains are found on sandpaper and in grinding wheels. They are used also as a powder.

Sanding is done (1) on each part after it is cut to final shape and (2) on the whole project after it is put together. Sanding should never be done in place of cutting. Only a poor or careless worker would try to make abrasive paper (sandpaper) do what a plane or chisel should do.

Never use sharp tools on a surface after it has been sanded. The fine abrasive grains left by the sandpaper would dull the tools.

TOOLS AND MATERIALS

Sandpaper is a strong paper with abrasive grains glued on it. The abrasives used most often in the wood shop are:

● *Flint*, which is made of quartz. The paper is light tan on the abrasive side. It is used for hand sanding. It is cheap but does not last long.

● *Garnet* is a reddish brown, hard mineral that is excellent for hand sanding. It is also used on power sanders. It will last much longer than flint but costs more.

● *Aluminum oxide* is a synthetic abrasive with a brown color. It is used for both hand and power sanding on hardwoods.

Abrasive coarseness is shown in one of two ways. A mesh number, such at 100, shows the size of screen through which the abrasive particles can pass. The larger the mesh number, the finer the abrasive. The older method

Table 25-A. Grades and Uses of Abrasive Paper

	Grit No.	O Grade	Uses
VERY FINE	400 360 320 280 240 220	10/0 – 9/0 8/0 7/0 6/0	For polishing and finishing after stain, varnish, etc., has been applied.
FINE	180 150 120	5/0 4/0 3/0	For finish sanding just before staining or sealing.
MEDIUM	100 80 60	2/0 1/0 ½	For sanding to remove final rough texture.
COARSE	50 40 36	1 1½ 2	For sanding after very rough texture is removed.
VERY COARSE	30 24 20 16	2½ 3 3½ 4	For very rough, unfinished wood surfaces.

uses a numbering system. For example, 2/0 is the same as 100. Table 25-A.

The following common sizes of garnet paper are used:

- 1 or 1½ (40 to 50) for sanding parts with deep tool marks.
- ½ (60) for all general sanding.
- 1/10 (80) for sanding after the project is assembled.
- 2/0 or 3/0 (100 to 120) for sanding before applying a finish.
- 4/0 to 6/0 (150 to 220) for sanding finishes.

A *sandpaper block* is very helpful. A rectangular block is a good one. A piece of leather or heavy felt glued to the base makes a good backing. Putting the sandpaper right over the block is not good. If a sliver of wood gets between the paper and the block, the hard spot can tear the paper or make the sanding uneven.

CUTTING OR TEARING SANDPAPER

Sandpaper can be bought in sizes to fit sandpaper holders and power sanders. You

25-1. Sand end grain in one direction. Notice the guide boards clamped over the end to keep the sanding square with the face surface. A commercial sandpaper holder is being used.

can also get larger sheets and cut or tear them to the size you need. To cut or tear the paper:

1. Grasp the opposite corners of the paper with the paper side down. Soften the paper by drawing it across the edge of the bench.

2. Fold the paper, abrasive side in. Then hold the folded edge over the corner of a bench and tear with a quick jerk.

3. To cut sandpaper, place the paper with the abrasive side down on a bench. Place the cutting edge of a saw on the paper and tear.

4. Always use a piece of sandpaper as small as possible to do the job.

GENERAL SUGGESTIONS

- Make sure that all cutting is finished before you start sanding. Sanding is done to finish the surface, not to shape it.
- Always sand *with the grain*—never across it.
- When sanding end grain, always sand in one direction. Fig. 25-1.
- Apply just enough pressure to make the sandpaper cut. Don't press so hard that it makes scratches.
- Clean off the sandpaper and the surface often with a brush.
- Don't sand surfaces that are to be glued.
- Don't try to sand off pencil or knife marks. Remove them with a plane or scraper.
- Always brush off the surface after sanding.
- When you have finished sanding, use a *tack cloth* to remove dust before going on to the next step. A tack cloth is a rag lightly moistened with varnish and turpentine.

SANDING A SURFACE

1. Clamp the stock to the bench or hold it firmly with one hand.

2. Place the sandpaper on a block.

3. Take long strokes, sanding with the grain. Sand evenly from one side to the other.

Always hold the block flat on the surface, especially as you near the end.

SANDING AN EDGE

1. Clamp the stock in a vise.
2. Hold the block as shown in Fig. 25-2. Guide the block with your fingers and keep it from rocking. Remember that you must sand surfaces square. Unless you are careful, you will tend to round all edges.
3. "Break" all edges slightly to prevent splintering. This is done by holding a piece of fine sandpaper in your hand and going over all the sharp edges lightly.

25-4. Sanding an inside edge.

25-2. Sanding an edge. Notice how the sandpaper block is held.

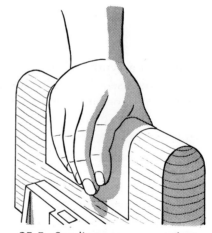

25-5. Sanding a convex surface.

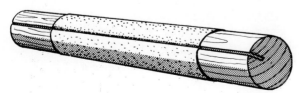

25-3. A dowel rod with sandpaper attached.

SANDING CURVED SURFACES

1. To sand a concave (inside) curve, wrap a piece of sandpaper around a piece of large dowel rod or a round file. Fig. 25-3. Twist the tool a little as you sand the surface. Fig. 25-4.
2. For convex (outside) curves, hold a piece of sandpaper in the palm of your hand. Fig. 25-5. Another method is shown in Fig. 25-6.

Preparing for Finishing

Before applying a finish, make sure your project is really ready for it. A finish will not cover up mistakes. In fact, it tends to show them up! Time spent in preparing the project for finishing is well worth it.

TOOLS AND MATERIALS

Shellac sticks are hard, colored pieces of shellac that become soft when heated. They come in these colors: oak tones of natural, light, medium, golden, and dark; walnut tones of light and dark; mahogany tones of light, medium, and dark. Other colors are transparent (clear), old ivory, white, and cedar. Shellac sticks are used to repair cracks and dents.

Plastic wood is a wood paste. It comes in light mahogany, oak, walnut, mahogany, and neutral. It is used to fill holes and cracks.

Wood patch is a synthetic (artificial) wood that also can be used for filling holes and cracks. It comes in cedar, walnut, pine, mahogany, fir, and oak, as well as a neutral color.

Wood sawdust mixed with powdered resin glue makes a good crack filler. Don't use sawdust from the power sander. It contains abrasive grains that would darken the mixture. Use sawdust from white pine or basswood for lighter wood filler. Mix the sawdust half and half with glue. Then add water to make a thick paste.

A *hand* or *cabinet scraper* is sometimes used on open-grained wood to get a fine finish.

Oxalic acid crystals for bleaching can be purchased in any drugstore.

Commercial acid bleaches come from paint or hardware stores.

You will also need a putty knife, Bunsen or alcohol burner, chisel, and scraper.

REPAIRING DENTS, CRACKS, AND HOLES

1. If there is a small dent in the wood, cover it with a wet cloth for several hours. This will raise the grain. Then sand the surface.

2. For deeper dents, put a heavy, wet cloth over the dent. Apply a hot soldering copper or iron to the cloth.

3. Fill all cracks, dents, and nail and screw holes with plastic wood, wood patch, or stick shellac. Fig. 25-7. Clean out the crack or hole carefully. Make sure the wood is dry. To use stick shellac, heat the end over a Bunsen or alcohol burner until it is soft. Also heat the blade of a putty knife. Then press the shellac into the dent or crack with the knife.

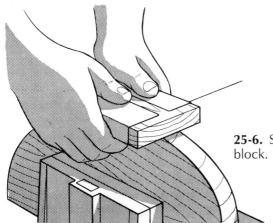

25-6. Sanding an outside curve with a sanding block.

25-7. Filling a crack with stick shellac. The alcohol burner is used to heat the end of the stick shellac and the blade of the putty knife. This is a good way to repair dents. It is easy to match the color of the wood.

Apply enough filler to make it slightly higher than the surface. Sand off when dry until it is smooth and level.

SCRAPING AND/OR SANDING THE SURFACE

1. Use a chisel to remove excess glue that has squeezed out around joints. This must be done because glue will not take stain.

2. On a large piece of furniture made of open-grained wood, scrape the surface with a hand or cabinet scraper. Fig. 25-8. This must be done before any sanding.

3. Finish-sand your project with 3/0 to 6/0 garnet paper. The finer the grit you finish up with, the more prominent will be the grain pattern and the glossier the final finish. Check for rough areas that may need further sanding. Do this by running a nylon stocking over the wood. If it snags, you must sand some more. Soften all sharp edges and corners by lightly sanding them.

4. Remove most of the sawdust from the project with a bench brush or shop vacuum. Then give it a thorough rubdown with a tack cloth. This will remove any dirt, dust, or

abrasive particles and leave a perfectly clean, smooth surface.

REVIEW QUESTIONS

1. Can sanding be done in place of cutting?
2. Should you use a chisel on a piece of wood after it has been sanded? Explain.
3. Name three kinds of sandpaper or abrasives.
4. What grade of sandpaper would you use for general sanding?
5. How do you cut a piece of sandpaper into equal parts?
6. Describe the way to make a good sanding block.
7. Should you sand across grain? Why or why not?
8. What must you watch for when sanding an edge?
9. How do you sand an inside curve?
10. How can you raise a small dent in wood?
11. How should you remove excess glue around joints?

25-8. Scraping the surface of the wood with a hand scraper. This is usually done on open-grained woods such as oak, mahogany, or walnut. Hold the scraper with both hands at an angle of 50° to 60° to the surface. Turn the blade a little toward the direction of the stroke. Then push or pull the blade.

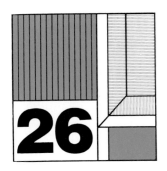

Drill Press, Scroll Saw, and Band Saw

The first three power tools you are likely to use are the drill press, the scroll saw (also called the jigsaw), and the band saw. Each is easy and safe to use when you follow directions.

Drill Press

A *drill press* is a machine for drilling and boring holes. (Holes ¼" or less in diameter are said to be drilled. Holes larger than ¼" are bored.) The drill press can also be used for sanding, planing, shaping, and many other operations.

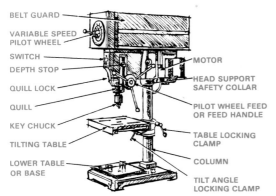

BELT GUARD

VARIABLE SPEED
PILOT WHEEL

SWITCH

DEPTH STOP

QUILL LOCK

QUILL

KEY CHUCK

TILTING TABLE

LOWER TABLE
OR BASE

MOTOR

HEAD SUPPORT
SAFETY COLLAR

PILOT WHEEL FEED
OR FEED HANDLE

TABLE LOCKING
CLAMP

COLUMN

TILT ANGLE
LOCKING CLAMP

26-1. Parts of a drill press.

Tools

A *bench-type drill press* is the most common. Fig. 26-1. The size is shown by the diameter of the largest workpiece that can be drilled on center. For example, a 15" drill press will bore a hole through the center of a round tabletop 15" in diameter. A key chuck holds the cutting tools.

A *drill-press vise* holds small pieces of work. Fig. 26-2. Larger pieces can be held in the hand or clamped to the table.

Machine and power *auger bits* have a straight shank and a brad point. Fig. 26-3. Never try to use hand auger bits in the drill press. Only a straight shank will fit into the chuck. *Spade bits* work well in a drill press or electric hand drill. Machine *Foerstner bits* are also available. Fig. 26-4.

Twist drills like those used in a hand drill are best for drilling small holes.

DRILLING OR BORING HOLES

1. Select the correct cutting tool and fasten it in the chuck. Rotate the drill by hand to make sure it runs straight. *Always remember to remove the chuck key.* Never try to fasten a square shank in a chuck.

2. Place the work on the table over a piece of scrap stock. Adjust the table up or down

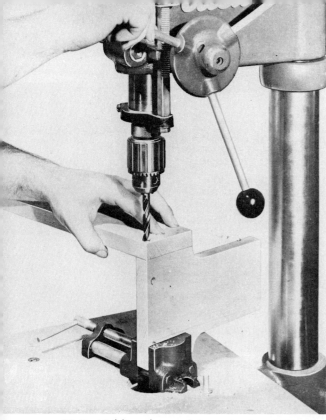

26-2. Holding the work in a vise for drilling.

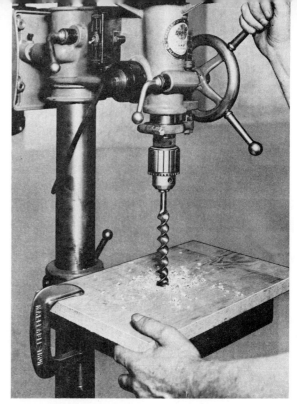

26-3. Using a machine auger bit to bore a hole. The work is clamped to the table with a C-clamp.

until the work just clears under the cutting tool.

3. Adjust the speed according to the cutting tool size and the kind of wood. Speed adjustment is of two types—the variable speed drive and the step pulley. Adjust the speed of the variable speed drill press *with the machine running.* Adjust the speed on the step pulley machine *with the switch off.* To obtain the fastest speed, use the *largest* pulley on the motor and the *smallest* pulley on the drill. Fast speed is for small-diameter cutting tools and softwoods. Speeds should be slow for large bits and hardwoods.

4. Turn on the power. Hold the work firmly with your left hand. If the piece is small or the bit large, clamp the work in a vise or to the table with hand screws or C-clamps.

5. Apply light pressure on the feed handle to cut the hole. Fig. 26-3.

6. Release the pressure slightly as the tool cuts through the bottom of the work.

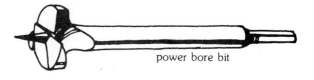

power bore bit

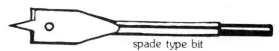

spade type bit

26-4. Two of the bits that can be used in a drill press.

7. A *sanding disk* can be fastened to the spindle to sand the ends and edges of the wood.

Scroll Saw (Jigsaw)

The *scroll saw (jigsaw)* has a narrow blade held in a frame. The blade cuts by moving up and down. The scroll saw is used to cut inside and outside curves and irregular shapes. It is a simple, safe power tool.

TOOLS

The *belt-driven scroll saw* has a belt and pulley arrangement that controls its speed. Fig. 26-5. Scroll saw size is determined by the distance from the blade to the inside of the frame. A 15″ saw, for example, will cut to the center of a 30″ circle.

Power scroll saw blades are made with a blank end for larger machines. Blades are 3″,

5″, or 6″ long and have from seven to twenty teeth per inch. The thinner the work to be sawed, the more teeth the blade should have. A good rule to follow is to make sure that three teeth touch the work at all times. *Jeweler's piercing-saw blades* can be used in power scroll saws to cut metal. These come in widths from very fine (6/0 is about ¹⁄₁₆″ wide) to rather wide blades (about ³⁄₁₆″).

INSTALLING A BLADE IN A BELT-DRIVEN SCROLL SAW

1. Remove the insert (throat plate) from the table.

2. Loosen the knob that tilts the table. Pull the right side of the table up. Turn the belt until the lower chuck is at the highest point.

3. Loosen the jaws in the lower chuck. Either a thumbscrew or an Allen wrench placed in the setscrew is used to do this.

4. Fasten a blade of the correct size in the lower chuck. *The teeth must point down.*

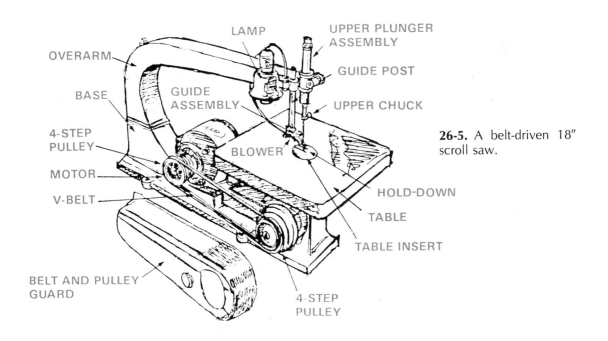

26-5. A belt-driven 18″ scroll saw.

5. Loosen the screw that releases the tension sleeve and lower it.

6. Fasten the other end of the blade in the upper chuck.

7. Now lift up on the tension sleeve about 1" to get the correct tension (tightness). Tighten the screw.

8. Adjust the blade guide until the blade just clears on the side and the roller just touches the back of the blade.

9. Replace the throat plate. Level the table and tighten it.

10. Place the work on the table. Lower the guide until the hold-down holds the work firmly on the table.

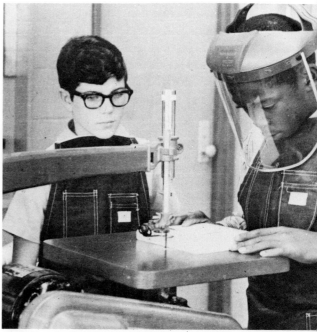

26-7. Cutting with the scroll saw. It is important to cut slowly and follow the layout line carefully. Avoid "crowding" the work into the blade, especially on sharp curves.

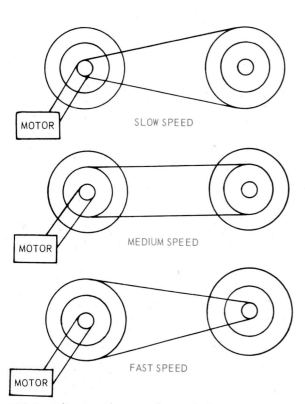

26-6. Adjusting the speed on a belt-driven scroll saw.

11. Turn the saw over by hand once to see if it runs freely.

12. Adjust the speed. For the fastest speed, place the belt on the largest motor pulley and the smallest machine pulley. Use this speed with a very fine blade and thin material. Set the machine to a slower speed for a wider blade and thicker stock. Fig. 26-6.

CUTTING WITH A SCROLL SAW·

1. Stand directly in front of the saw so that you can guide the work with both hands.

2. Apply forward pressure with your thumbs. Guide the work with your fingers.

3. Start in the waste stock and cut up to the layout line.

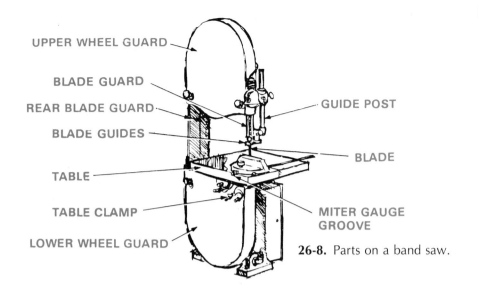

UPPER WHEEL GUARD

BLADE GUARD

REAR BLADE GUARD

BLADE GUIDES

TABLE

TABLE CLAMP

LOWER WHEEL GUARD

GUIDE POST

BLADE

MITER GAUGE GROOVE

26-8. Parts on a band saw.

4. Carefully guide the work so that the saw stays just outside the line. Never force the work into the blade. Fig. 26-7.

5. At sharp corners turn the work slowly without pressing forward. If you turn the work too fast, the blade will break. Never twist the blade.

6. For inside cutting, first drill or bore a hole in the waste stock. Loosen the upper end of the blade and slip it through the hole. Fasten the upper end again in the chuck. Cut from the waste stock up to the layout line.

Then cut around the line to make the opening or design.

7. For angle sawing, the table on many machines can be tilted as much as 45°.

8. When cutting a complicated part, first make relief cuts up to the layout line. Then start in the waste stock and come up to the layout line at a slight angle. As the cut is made, each piece of scrap stock falls away.

Band Saw

The band saw is used mainly for cutting exterior curved edges. It can do straight cutting. However, it cannot do internal cutting as the scroll saw does, nor will it cut so sharp a curve. The size of the machine is determined by the diameter of the wheels. Fig. 26-8. The most common of the small machines is the 14″ band saw. The blade lengths are made to fit the particular size machine. They come in widths from ⅛″ to ½″. Sharp curves are more easily cut with narrow blades than with wide blades. Fig. 26-9.

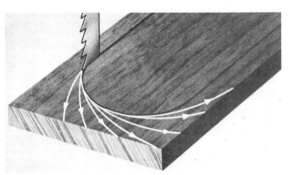

26-9. Cutting a curve. If the blade is too wide, make a series of cuts as shown.

Follow these guidelines when using the band saw:

• Maintain proper belt tension. Keep the belt just tight enough to prevent slipping.

• Use the correct blade. Choose the largest blade with the coarsest teeth that will cut the stock cleanly. The blade also should be able to follow the sharpest curve in the pattern.

• Always move the blade guide close to the work. This helps insure accurate cutting and prevents the blade from twisting.

• Before operating the saw, check the blade for proper tension and proper mounting. The teeth should point down on the downward stroke.

• Before sawing, examine the stock carefully to make sure it is free of nails.

• Feed the stock evenly and slowly. This will help prevent twisting the blade or crowding it beyond its cutting capacity. Fig. 26-10.

• Clean sawdust from the table frequently.

• Be sure the wheels turn clockwise as viewed from the front of the saw. The arrow on the motor pulley indicates the direction of rotation.

• Make sure the blade is sharp and in good condition. A clicking noise may indicate a crack in the blade.

USING THE BAND SAW

1. Choosing the proper blade for each job is of great importance. Always use the widest blade possible to cut the sharpest contours of your pattern. A ⅜″ blade should cut a circle 3″ in diameter; a ¼″ blade, a 2″ circle; a ³⁄₁₆″ blade, a 1″ circle; and a ⅛″ blade, a ½″ circle. For all straight and general cutting, a ⅜″ blade is recommended.

2. Adjust the top blade guide so that it clears the work by about ¼″.

3. Start the machine and allow it to come to full speed. Stand to one side, not directly in front of the blade.

4. Feed the stock slowly through the blade.

5. Cut to the outside of the layout line in the waste stock. "Back out" only as a last resort, drawing the work very slowly away from the saw blade and making sure the blade

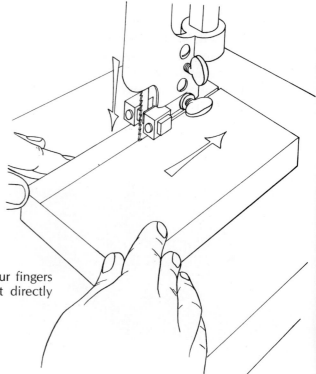

26-10. Cutting a straight line. Keep your fingers on either side of the cutting line, not directly behind the saw blade.

26-11(A). Make short cuts first.

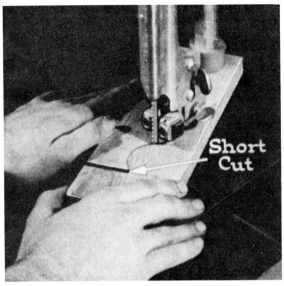

26-11(B). Then make the long cuts.

follows the saw cut. Failure to do this may force the blade off the wheels.

6. Make short cuts before long ones. Fig. 26-11.

7. The pattern to be cut may have a number of sharp curves. In this case, it is best to make a series of saw kerfs in the waste stock opposite each curve before starting the cut.

8. A miter gauge attachment which slides in the table slot can be used to hold the work when doing straight cutting. The work should be held firmly against the gauge.

REVIEW QUESTIONS

1. What operations can be done on a drill press?
2. What kind of shank must bits for a drill press have?
3. How do you adjust the speed on a drill press?
4. What kinds of cuts can you make with a scroll saw?
5. How do you choose the correct blade for a scroll saw?
6. What kind of blade should you use to saw metal on the scroll saw?
7. Describe the way to install a blade in a belt-driven scroll saw.
8. What are the common causes of blade breakage on the scroll saw?
9. Tell how to cut an inside opening with a scroll saw.
10. Name the parts of the band saw.
11. How is the size of the band saw determined?
12. How can a sharp curve be cut on the band saw?

|||||||||||||||||||||||||||||||||||||||||||||||| **KEY IDEA** ||||||||||||||||||||||||||||||||||||||||||||||||

BEING A WISE CONSUMER

Careful judgment in the buying of products and services is known as *consumerism*. This word is based on the word *consumer*. A consumer is a person who buys products and services. The word consumerism is somewhat new. The idea, however, is not. Always, people have wanted to get the best value for their money. This is a natural human desire. Careful buying can help you save dollars. A buyer who gets the most value for the dollar will have more dollars to spend.

Recently, consumerism has suggested consumer watchfulness. This means that those who buy products are concerned with what they are getting for their money. In fact, the dollars consumers spend can help control the quality of the goods and services offered. For example, a poor product will not be purchased. Since it is not purchased, its manufacturer would withdraw it from the market. Consumers have made it known that they expect to be satisfied with the quality of a product.

To be a wise consumer, you must be a careful shopper. Before buying any product, ask yourself the following two questions.

What, exactly, do I need? You should have a firm idea of how often you will use the product. It would not be a good idea, for example, to buy a complete set of carpenter's tools if you only plan to fix a screen door. On the other hand, you would not want to buy just a hammer if you planned to build a garage. By identifying your needs, you will have a better idea of the best way to spend your money.

In buying any product, you must know what you want the product to do. This prac-

tice will help you get the best value for your dollar.

How much money can I afford to spend? The answer to this question is important. You may not be able to afford to spend enough to buy a product of the best quality. You may have to buy a product of lesser quality. You should remember, though, that some cheap products can have the same usefulness as expensive products. This is especially true of products such as watches and cars. The basic purpose of a watch is to give the time. The purpose of a car is to transport a person from one point to another. The fact that a watch is made of gold does not affect its capability of telling time. The fact that a car has leather seats and wire wheels does not affect its capability of transporting people. In these cases, the gold in the watch and the leather seats and wire wheels on the car are not needed.

After you have answered these two questions, you will need to do some *comparison shopping*. In comparison shopping, you check the prices and the quality of several items that you are thinking of buying. For example, you may be thinking of buying a bicycle. In comparison shopping, you would check the quality of the bicycles in the price range you can afford. Remember, comparison shopping takes time. Because it takes a lot of time, many people use comparison shopping only for expensive items. One easy way to comparison shop is to check product prices by telephone. Of course, you would still need to check the product for quality.

Before buying any product, you should check its quality. Look at the product careful-

Georgia-Pacific

Fig. A. In buying lumber, check that the boards are of good quality. They should be straight and free of knots.

ly. It should have the properties you expect to find in such a product. In checking product quality, keep the price of the product in mind. A product of better quality might be available, but such a product might cost more. If you cannot afford the better product, you will have to buy the product of lesser quality. Always, though, you should try to get for your dollar the best product you can afford.

In checking the quality of a product, you will need to consider its use. For example, a shovel that is intended to be a child's toy would have different qualities than one intended for factory use.

If you are dissatisfied with a product, you should return it. If you have a sound complaint, the seller should give you a refund or replace the product.

Careful shopping will make you a wise consumer. This has several advantages. One advantage is that your dollar goes farther. This gives you more money to spend or to save. Another advantage is that you will be more satisfied with the products you buy.

Other Machine (Power) Tools

27

Have you enjoyed working with the drill press, scroll saw, and band saw? If so, you will want to find out what other machines are used by woodworkers. So far, most of your projects have been built with hand tools plus a few simple machines. For example, you have had a chance to see how much easier it is to cut out a shape with a scroll saw than with a coping saw. You have found that drilling is simple on the drill press.

In more advanced woodwork, however, much of the cutting and shaping of wood is done with power tools which eliminate much of the hard handwork. In industry, machines process lumber. They are used for cutting down the trees and making the finished products. Using these machines requires different skills from those needed when using hand tools. Yet even if you learn to handle these woodworking machines, you must still be able to use hand tools skillfully.

Power tools can be very dangerous, especially if they are used by an inexperienced or careless person. Anyone who uses them incor-

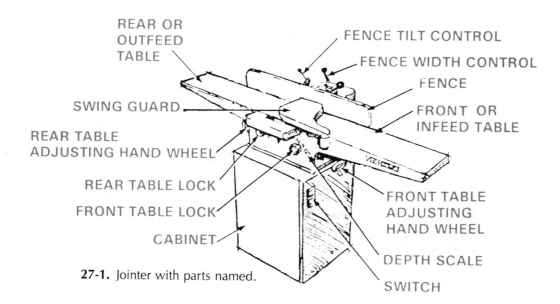

27-1. Jointer with parts named.

rectly usually gets hurt. That is why your instructor will not allow you to use even the simplest power tool without safety instruction.

Jointer

The jointer is a machine that does the work of a hand plane, except that the cutting is done by revolving cutterheads with three or more knives. Fig. 27-1. The size is determined by the widest cut that can be made. There is a table in front and in back of the cutterhead. The front, or infeed, table can be adjusted up and down to vary the depth of cut. The rear, or outfeed, table is adjusted to the height of the cutterhead.

JOINTING AN EDGE

Check the stock to determine grain direction. (Always plane with the grain.) Adjust the infeed table to cut about ¹⁄₁₆″ for rough cuts and about ¹⁄₃₂″ for finish cuts. The kind of wood helps to determine the depth of the cut. For example, you can take a deeper cut on pine or basswood than you can on harder woods such as walnut or birch.

Check the fence with a square to make sure it is at right angles to the table. Make sure the guard is in place. Turn on the machine. Apply uniform pressure to the work to hold it securely against the fence and table. Feed the stock at a uniform speed. Fig 27-2.

FACE PLANING

Place the stock flat on the front table. Turn on the power. Start the planing by first holding the work with both hands over the front table. Place your left hand on the front portion of the stock over the outfeed (rear) table as soon as it rests solidly on this table. As your right hand approaches the cutterhead, use a

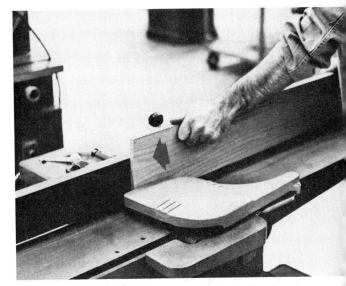

27-2(A). In starting a cut, as the stock advances and your left hand nears the cutterhead, stop pushing. Use your right hand to hold the stock down. Shift your left hand back to its original position, and shove the stock ahead again.

27-2(B). Continue moving the stock forward until the end of the board is on the infeed (front) table. Then place your left hand on the stock on the other side of the revolving knives. Keep your hands out of the area just over the cutterhead.

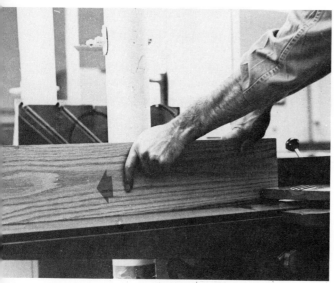

27-2(C). To complete the cut, shift your right hand to the other side and push the stock the rest of the way over the cutterhead.

27-3. Using a push block to complete the surfacing.

27-4. Feeding stock into a planer.

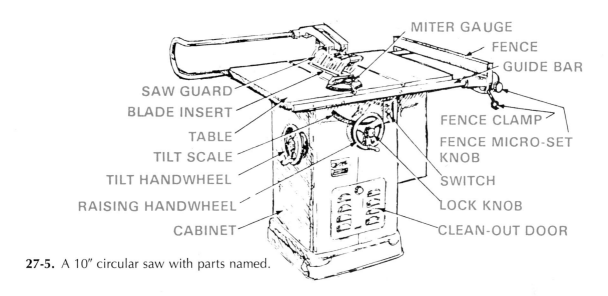

MITER GAUGE
FENCE
GUIDE BAR
SAW GUARD
BLADE INSERT
TABLE
TILT SCALE
TILT HANDWHEEL
RAISING HANDWHEEL
CABINET
FENCE CLAMP
FENCE MICRO-SET KNOB
SWITCH
LOCK KNOB
CLEAN-OUT DOOR

27-5. A 10″ circular saw with parts named.

push block to feed the stock past the blades. Fig. 27-3. *Never allow your hands to move above the revolving blades.*

Planer

The planer, or surfacer, is used to plane the surface of stock and to bring it to proper thickness. Most of the wood you will use has been surfaced at the lumber mill. However, if the stock is rough, you or your instructor will run it through a planer. Fig. 27-4. Wood that comes from the surfacer or planer has small mill or knife marks made by the rotating cutter. These must be removed with a hand plane.

Circular Saw

The circular saw is used for making all types of straight cuts. It is used for ripping, crosscut-

ting, mitering, and beveling. The size of the saw is determined by the size of blade used, usually from 8″ to 10″. Fig. 27-5.

The principal blades are shown in Fig. 27-6.
● The *crosscut* blade is for cutting across the grain. This blade is used for sawing all types of wood.
● The teeth of the *combination* blade are designed for both crosscutting and ripping. This blade is ideal for general use.
● The *ripsaw* blade has specially designed hook-type teeth for sawing with the grain of the wood. This saw blade runs free of sawdust accumulation.
● The *chisel combination* blade has a new tooth design made for both crosscutting and ripping. It is adaptable for sawing all types of wood.
● The *fine-tooth crosscut* blade is designed to produce a minimum amount of tearing when sawing fiberboard, plywood, and similar materials.

A fence is needed for all types of ripping

CROSS CUT TOOTH

STANDARD
COMBINATION TOOTH

RIP TOOTH

CHISEL
COMBINATION TOOTH

EXTRA FINE
TOOTH CROSS CUT

27-6. Kinds of saw blades.

operations. A miter gauge is needed for cross-cutting. The fence is a metal guide clamped parallel with the saw blade. The miter gauge slides in the grooves of the table. To keep the operator from getting his or her fingers too near the blade, a guard is used. Circular saws are responsible for a large number of accidents in woodworking shops, so be careful.

CROSSCUTTING

Crosscutting is sawing across the grain. Follow these steps:

1. Adjust the height of the blade so that it will just cut through the stock. Several teeth should be above the stock. This will permit the blade to free itself of sawdust.

2. Place the stock on the table and against the miter gauge. Line up the cutoff mark with the saw blade. Make sure the guard is in place.

3. Turn on the machine.

4. Hold the stock firmly against the gauge with both hands. Push the miter gauge along the groove, feeding it slowly into the saw. Fig. 27-7. Stand behind and to the left side of the miter gauge, not in line with the blade.

5. After the cut is completed, do not attempt to remove the scrap stock with your fingers.

6. Turn off the machine. Wait for the blade to stop. Push the scrap stock out of the way with a push stick.

RIPPING

Ripping is sawing in the direction of the grain. Follow these steps:

1. Remove the miter gauge. Place the fence in the correct position. Do this by measuring the desired distance from the right edge of the blade to the fence. This is the amount that will be cut off.

2. Place the guard in position.

3. Start the machine.

4. Hold the board firmly against the fence and push it slowly into the blade. When three-fourths of the cutting is completed, finish the cutting with a push stick. Push the

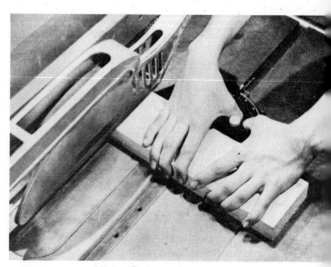
27-7. Crosscutting.

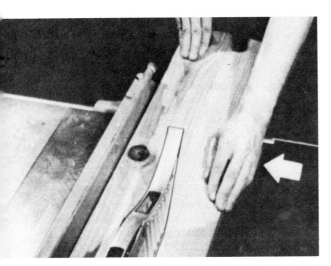

27-8. Starting a ripping cut. With your left hand, hold the work firmly against the table and fence. Place your left hand near the left edge of the board and as far as possible from the blade.

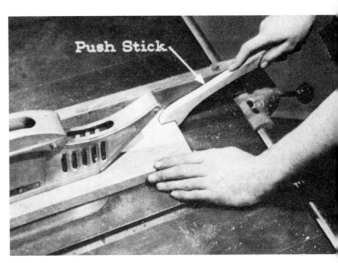

27-9. Completing a ripping cut. Use a push stick to complete the cut. This makes it unnecessary to place your hand between the blade and the fence.

board completely past the blades. Figs. 27-8 and 27-9.

5. Turn off the machine. Do not pick up any of the pieces until the blade has stopped completely.

Radial-Arm Saw

The radial-arm saw is an upside-down saw that can be used for the same kind of cutting as the circular saw. Fig. 27-10. This machine is popular with carpenters when building houses because the cutting action is more easily seen. Fig. 27-11.

Wood Lathe

The wood lathe is used to shape round and cylindrical parts such as turned chair and table

legs, lamp bases, and bowls. Fig. 27-12. The size of the wood lathe is indicated by the swing (the largest diameter that can be turned) and the distance between centers. When the work is mounted between centers, the operation is called *spindle turning*. When the work is mounted on a faceplate, it is called *faceplate turning*.

While few wood lathes are used in industry, many craftspeople make use of this machine. It is fascinating to watch a piece of wood take shape under the capable hands of a woodcrafter. Many people find that woodturning is a fascinating hobby.

Sanders

The most common sanding machine is a combination belt and disk sander. These may also be separate machines. Figs. 27-13 and 27-14 (page 222).

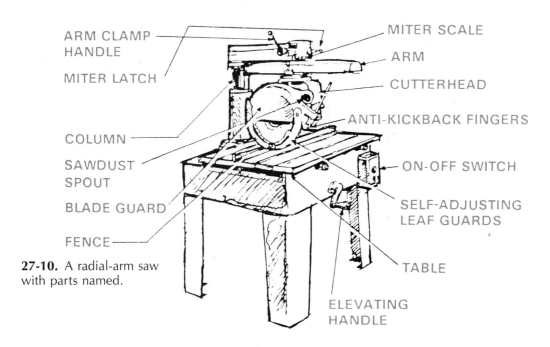

ARM CLAMP HANDLE

MITER LATCH

COLUMN

SAWDUST SPOUT

BLADE GUARD

FENCE

MITER SCALE

ARM

CUTTERHEAD

ANTI-KICKBACK FINGERS

ON-OFF SWITCH

SELF-ADJUSTING LEAF GUARDS

TABLE

ELEVATING HANDLE

27-10. A radial-arm saw with parts named.

27-11. You can easily watch the cutting action of a radial-arm saw.

DISK SANDER

The disk sander is used primarily for edging operations, and, except for squaring and chamfering, such work is done freehand. The work should be held lightly against the disk. The work should then be moved smoothly back and forth across the half of the disk revolving downward. The sanding disk should rotate counterclockwise. On the downstroke, the friction of the disk helps you hold the stock against the table. Fig. 27-15. *Caution: Keep the work moving.* If it is held in one spot, the wood will be burned and the abrasive ruined.

For angle and chamfer sanding, tilt the disk table to the desired angle. The table tilts to 45° below the horizontal position. A miter-gauge attachment, which slides in the table

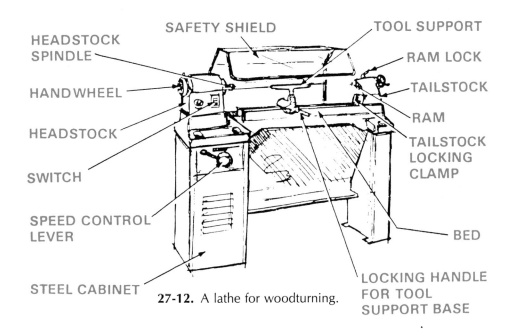

HEADSTOCK SPINDLE

SAFETY SHIELD

TOOL SUPPORT

RAM LOCK

HANDWHEEL

TAILSTOCK

RAM

HEADSTOCK

TAILSTOCK LOCKING CLAMP

SWITCH

SPEED CONTROL LEVER

BED

STEEL CABINET

LOCKING HANDLE FOR TOOL SUPPORT BASE

27-12. A lathe for woodturning.

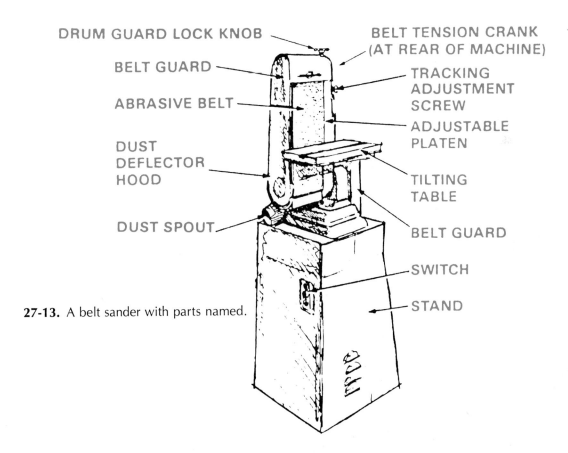

DRUM GUARD LOCK KNOB

BELT TENSION CRANK (AT REAR OF MACHINE)

BELT GUARD

TRACKING ADJUSTMENT SCREW

ABRASIVE BELT

ADJUSTABLE PLATEN

DUST DEFLECTOR HOOD

TILTING TABLE

DUST SPOUT

BELT GUARD

SWITCH

STAND

27-13. A belt sander with parts named.

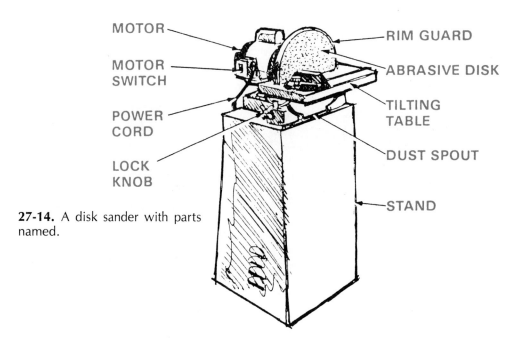

MOTOR

MOTOR
SWITCH

POWER
CORD

LOCK
KNOB

RIM GUARD

ABRASIVE DISK

TILTING
TABLE

DUST SPOUT

STAND

27-14. A disk sander with parts named.

slot, should be used to hold the work when squaring, burring, or chamfering the ends of stock.

The abrasive used on the disk sander depends upon the type of work to be sanded. Garnet is used for wood and plastics. Aluminum oxide and silicon carbide abrasives are used for wood and metal. Since the disk sander is usually used for edge work, the abrasive can be more coarse than for surfacing. When sanding wood, a ½ or 1/0 abrasive can be used for fast cutting. A 2/0 or 3/0 abrasive can be used for finish sanding.

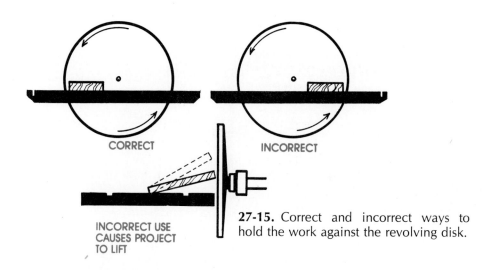

CORRECT

INCORRECT

INCORRECT USE
CAUSES PROJECT
TO LIFT

27-15. Correct and incorrect ways to hold the work against the revolving disk.

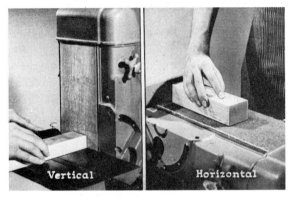

27-16. The belt sander can be used either in a vertical or horizontal position.

To remove old abrasive from the disk, soak it in hot water. Remove the loose abrasive with a putty knife. Be sure the disk is dry before mounting the new abrasive. It can be glued to the disk with water glass or a heavy grade of rubber cement. Hold the abrasive in place with a flat piece of wood and clamps to prevent wrinkles.

BELT SANDER

The belt sander is used mainly for surface sanding. It is usually operated in a horizontal position. Fig. 27-16. The work should be pressed slightly but firmly against the belt. Excessive pressure should be avoided. Short stock should be held against the stop fence.

Remove the stop fence for sanding pieces that are longer than the table. To sand wide boards, remove the sanding disk (if it is a combination machine), the guard, and the belt-sander stop fence. Feed the work diagonally, using a small angle and fine belt. These will minimize the effects of cross-grain sanding.

By using the belt sander in a vertical position and mounting the disk-sanding table to the stop fence, all kinds of angle, edge, or end

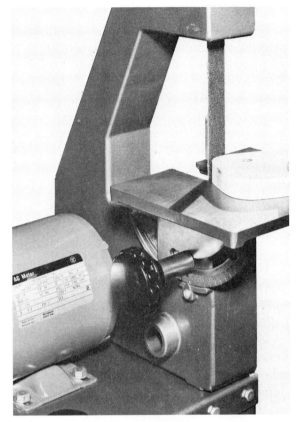

27-17. This type of belt sander can be used for many kinds of sanding operations.

work can be done. A miter gauge should be used for edging or beveling.

Inside curves are sanded on the end drum. The sanding-belt guard must be removed for this operation.

For beveling or angle sanding of long pieces, the belt sander fence attachment is needed. The fence can be tilted from 0° to 45°, left or right.

Another type of belt sander has a narrow belt that runs over three wheels. It is very useful for sanding recesses and other hard-to-reach places. Fig. 27-17. Some narrow belt sanders also have a small disk sander.

REVIEW QUESTIONS

1. Describe a jointer and tell what it can do.
2. What are the safety rules for operating a jointer?
3. How can the jointer be used for face planing?
4. What is the purpose of the planer?
5. Name four uses of a circular saw.
6. Name three types of circular saw blades.
7. State the safety rules to observe when using a circular saw.
8. Describe the crosscutting operation.
9. Should a push stick be used for ripping? Explain how ripping is done.
10. What advantage does the radial-arm saw have over the circular saw? What kind of cutting can the radial-arm saw do?
11. How is the size of a wood lathe indicated?
12. Name and describe the two kinds of turning.
13. Make a list of the safety precautions needed for using a wood lathe.
14. What is the most common sander?

28 Portable Power Tools

Portable power tools make woodworking jobs go faster. They also allow greater accuracy. They are the ideal tools for work around the home. In a well-equipped shop these tools are used when stationary power machines are less convenient. The three most-used portable tools are the electric drill, the router, and the finishing sander. Other common tools are the belt sander, saber saw, and portable circular saw.

A power tool should have a symbol that indicates it meets the standards of an independent testing agency, such as Underwriters'

Laboratories. The tool should protect you from electrical shock by either of two safety systems:

• A tool with *external grounding* has a wire that runs from the housing through the power cord to a third prong on the power plug. When this prong is connected to a grounded three-hole electrical outlet, the grounding wire will carry any current that leaks past the electrical insulation of the tool.

• A *double-insulated* tool has an extra layer of electrical insulation. This eliminates the need for a three-prong plug and grounded outlet.

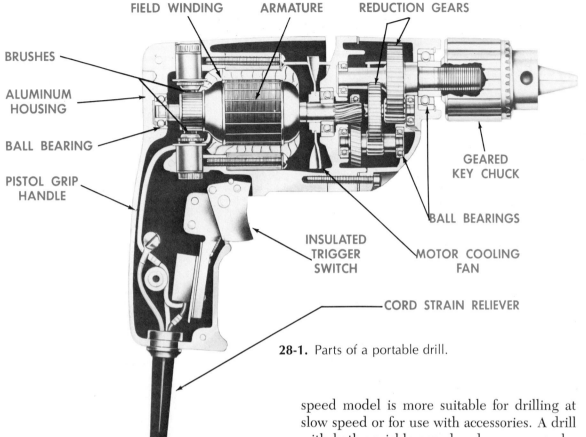

FIELD WINDING   ARMATURE   REDUCTION GEARS

BRUSHES

ALUMINUM HOUSING

BALL BEARING

PISTOL GRIP HANDLE

GEARED KEY CHUCK

INSULATED TRIGGER SWITCH

BALL BEARINGS

MOTOR COOLING FAN

CORD STRAIN RELIEVER

28-1. Parts of a portable drill.

Portable Electric Drill

The portable electric drill is an excellent tool for drilling and boring holes. It also has other uses. Fig. 28-1. It consists of a housing with a handle, a motor, and a chuck. The size of the electric drill is stated as the maximum size of bit the drill will hold. Most portable electric drills have a key-type chuck. The chuck will hold drill bits up to ¼" or up to ½".

For most jobs, a single-speed drill is adequate. However, a two-speed or variable-speed model is more suitable for drilling at slow speed or for use with accessories. A drill with both variable speed and reverse can be used to drive and remove screws.

Most drills have a pistol-grip handle. Some models also have a side handle. With this the drill can be held with both hands for heavy work or for drilling in an unusual position. A trigger switch on the pistol-grip handle starts the drill. On variable-speed drills you can change the speed by varying the pressure on the trigger. The harder you press, the faster the speed.

To put a twist drill or a bit in the electric drill, first unplug the drill. Open the chuck and insert the shank of the twist drill or bit. Turn the outside of the chuck clockwise until the jaws close on the shank. Make sure the drill or bit is centered in the chuck. Then use

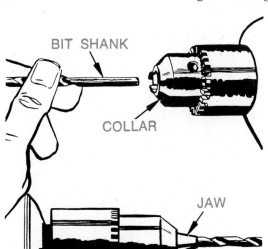

28-2. Installing a twist drill in the chuck. Make sure the shank of the twist drill is in the jaws straight before tightening with the key.

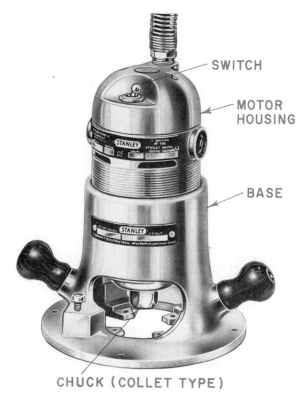

28-4. Portable router.

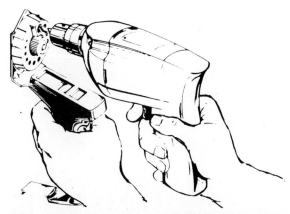

28-3. Using a drill guide. Mark the location of the hole. Rotate the dial to the correct drill size. The guide will hold the drill straight. Thus, the hole is drilled accurately.

a chuck key to tighten the jaws. *Be sure to remove the chuck key before starting the drill.* Fig. 28-2.

USING AN ELECTRIC HAND DRILL

1. Mark the location of the hole with an awl or center punch.

2. Hold the point of the drill over the place you want the hole.

3. Guide the drill with one hand on the housing or side handle. You can also use a drill guide. Fig. 28-3. Apply pressure with the other hand. The drill cuts a hole quickly. Be careful that it doesn't go in too far. If the revolving chuck touches the wood surface, it will mar the wood.

4. It is easy to break small bits in an electric

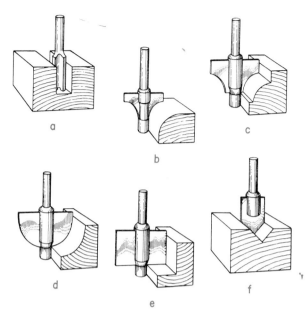

28-5. A few of the common router bits: (A) Straight. (B) Rounding-over. (C) Beading. (D) Cove. (E) Rabbeting. (F) V-grooving.

28-6. Freehand routing. The router is moved and controlled by the operator.

28-7. Using a guide attachment for cutting a dado.

hand drill. Hold the drill steady. Do not force it into the wood.

Portable Router

The portable router can do many cutting and shaping jobs. Fig. 28-4. It consists of a powerful motor mounted in an adjustable base. There is a collet chuck at the end of the motor shaft. This chuck can hold many different kinds of cutting tools. Some of the common router bits and cutters are shown in Fig. 28-5. To adjust for depth of cut, the router base is raised or lowered. In some routers the base screws onto the motor housing. In others it slides up and down.

The bit turns clockwise. Therefore, when cutting straight edges, move the router from left to right. When making circular cuts, move the router counterclockwise. Routing can be done freehand or with a guide. Fig. 28-6. A guide is used for making straight cuts, such as dadoes and grooves. Fig. 28-7. The width of the cut is determined by the bit. A wide cut can be made with a narrow bit by making two or more passes.

USING A PORTABLE ROUTER

Shaping an Edge

By using a bit with a pilot on the end, the edge of stock can be shaped. The pilot extends from the bottom of the bit and guides it along the edge of the stock. Fig. 28-8.

1. Select the correct bit to match the shape of the edge you want.

2. To install the bit, unplug the router and lock the shaft. Loosen the nut or nuts. Insert the bit and tighten the chuck.

3. Adjust the depth of cut. Allow some stock to remain on the edge to serve as a guide for the pilot tip. Try the cutter on a scrap piece of wood of the same thickness as the finished piece.

4. Securely clamp the work to be routed.

5. Start the motor. Hold the router firmly. Place the router base on the wood. Move the router into the stock until the pilot edge touches the stock. Start the cut at one corner and work from left to right. Make the end grain cuts first. Feed the router slowly along each edge.

6. The speed with which the router is moved will depend on the kind of wood, its hardness, and the depth of cut. Cutting too fast will cause a rough edge and burned surfaces.

General Suggestions

• Never work with stock less than 6″ wide without using safety devices. These include a push stick and board to hold stock against the fence.

• Be sure the work is free of splits, checks, and knots. The fast-spinning router bit could hurl a knot quite a distance. This can be dangerous, and the workpiece may be ruined.

• When you turn the router upside down in the shaper table, the rotation of the tool is reversed. The work now should be fed from right to left so that you work against the rotation of the cutter.

• When you feed work into the shaper, the cutter blade is hidden by the workpiece. Never permit your fingers to come within 3″ of the cutter. Use a push stick for moving narrow work past the cutter.

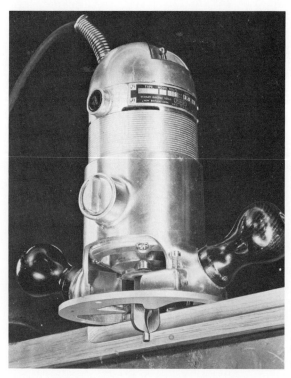

28-8. The pilot on the end of the cutter controls the amount of cut. It rides on the edge and does no cutting.

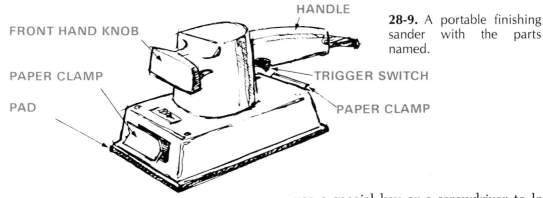

28-9. A portable finishing sander with the parts named.

HANDLE

FRONT HAND KNOB

PAPER CLAMP

PAD

TRIGGER SWITCH

PAPER CLAMP

Finishing Sander

Sanding wood before applying a finish is easier and faster when you use a power sander. Fig. 28-9. The size of the sanding pad and the speed and length of the sanding strokes tell the work capacity of a sander. You can find these specifications on the sander. Some finishing sanders have a self-contained dust collection bag.

To replace a worn abrasive sheet, you must operate a special mechanism. On some models a lever opens and closes clamps at the front and back of the sanding pad. On others you use a special key or a screwdriver to loosen and tighten pad clamps. Still others have spring-loaded clamps. These must be held open while an abrasive sheet is inserted. Fig. 28-10.

USING A FINISHING SANDER

1. Clip a sheet of abrasive paper to the pad. The sander should be unplugged while you do this.

2. Clamp the workpiece securely.

3. Turn on the power and let the sander reach full speed. Lower the pad onto the workpiece. Move the sander back and forth slowly. Sand with the grain. Do not press down on the sander. The tool's weight and movement will do the work.

4. When you are finished, lift the sander off the workpiece before turning off the power. Wait for the sander to come to a full stop before setting it down.

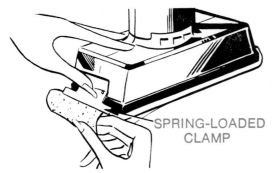

SPRING-LOADED CLAMP

28-10. Some finishing sanders have spring-loaded clamps to hold the abrasive paper on the sander.

28-11. A belt sander with dust bag.

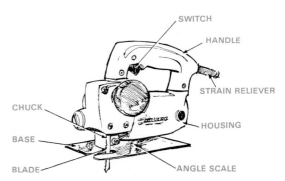

28-12. A saber saw with the parts named.

Portable Belt Sander

Portable belt sanders are excellent for sanding assembled pieces. Fig. 28-11. The size of the machine is determined by the width and length of the belt. The most common sizes are 2″ × 21″, 3″ × 24″, 3″ × 27″, 4″ × 22″, and 4½″ × 26″. The belt should be installed so that the splice runs off the work. An arrow stamped on the back of each belt indicates the direction the belt should run. It is a simple job to replace a belt on most machines. Usually a clamp opens to release the tension on the belt. After a new belt is installed, it can be centered on the pulleys by turning the belt-tracking adjustment. The belt should never rub against the side of the machine. If the belt is thick and soft, there must be extra clearance between the pulleys and the housing.

USING A PORTABLE BELT SANDER

1. Place the cord over your right shoulder out of the way. Hold the machine firmly with both hands. Turn on the power.

2. Lower the sander so that the heel touches the work first. Then move the sander back and forth in a straight line with the wood grain. Sanding is actually done *on the pull stroke.*

3. Never apply pressure to this machine, since it cuts very rapidly. Do not allow the sander to stand in one place for any length of time. If it does, it will cut deep grooves in the wood. It is especially important to watch this when sanding plywood. Always machine slowly and evenly.

4. Cross sanding is sometimes done first to obtain a level surface. On woods such as fir, with both hard and soft grain, cross sanding should be done as much as possible.

5. To sand the edges of boards, allow the belt to extend beyond the edge a little. Be careful that the sander doesn't tilt. If it does, you will round the edges.

6. Always lift the sander from the surface before turning off the power. Let the sander

come to a complete stop before setting it down.

Saber Saw

The saber (bayonet) saw has a long, slender blade. It is used to cut curved shapes in flat materials. Fig. 28-12. It cannot make long straight cuts as accurately and quickly as a circular saw. The simplest measure of the saw's work capacity is its maximum depth of cut in different materials.

Common uses of the saber saw are shown in Fig. 28-13. The shoe (bottom part of the tool) consists of a base (skid), a cutting-angle adjustment, and a place to attach rip or circle guides. The base, or skid, provides stable support. It should extend at least ¼" in front of the blade. It prevents the saw from tipping forward as you guide it through the work. A rip fence for keeping the saw blade parallel with the edge of the work can be quickly attached, adjusted, or removed by turning screws. Fig. 28-14. Some designs can also be used as circle guides.

The cutting-angle adjustment is a large, scaled hinge between the skid and the housing that allows precision angle cuts up to 45°. The hinge is loosened by a lever, wing nut, screws, or small hex key. Then the base is tilted to the desired angle and the hinge is tightened.

The screws that hold a saw blade are loosened or tightened by a screwdriver or a small hex key. The type of blade to use depends on the material being cut and kind of cutting. Woodcutting blades have 6 to 12 teeth per inch. Choose wide blades for straight cuts and narrow blades for curves. Fig. 28-15.

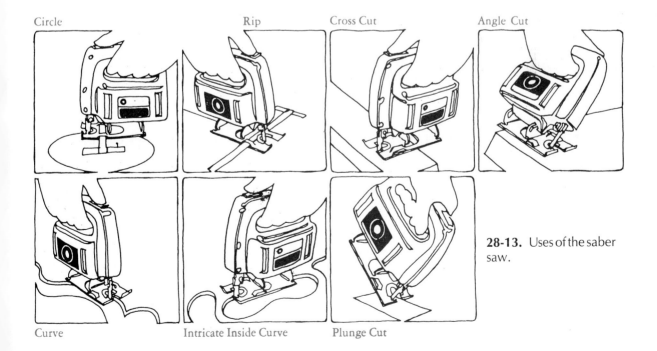

Circle   Rip   Cross Cut   Angle Cut

Curve   Intricate Inside Curve   Plunge Cut

28-13. Uses of the saber saw.

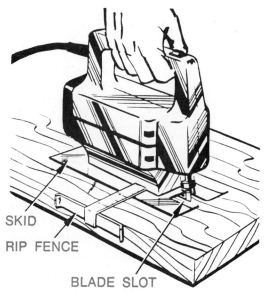

28-14. Note the use of the rip fence to control the width of cut.

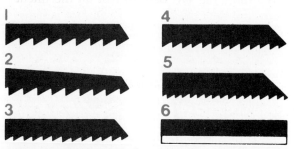

28-15. Saber saw blades: (1) A 7-tooth blade for fast, rough cuts in wood. (2) An extra-long rough-cut blade for thick boards. (3) A 10-tooth blade for hardwood, plastics, etc. (4) A 10-tooth taper-ground blade for smooth cuts in plywood and veneers. (5) A 24-tooth hacksaw for metal. (6) A knife blade for rubber, leather, paper, and cardboard.

USING A SABER SAW

1. Install the blade with the teeth facing *forward* and pointing *upward*. The cutting is done on the upstroke.

2. Clamp the work rigidly. If it vibrates, it will break the expensive blade. When clamping, be sure to leave space beneath the cutting line.

3. Start the motor and allow it to come up to full speed. Hold the saw firmly on the work. Then move it along slowly. Do not force the cutting. Use only enough pressure to keep the saw moving at all times.

Portable Circular Saw

To cut wooden building materials easily and quickly, you need a portable circular saw. Fig. 28-16. This saw is especially useful for cutting large panel stock.

The blades are similar to the ones used in the stationary circular saw. Some saws have a slip clutch or special washers where the blade fastens to the drive shaft. These are designed to prevent motor burnout if the saw blade sticks. They may also reduce the likelihood of kickback and loss of control.

The housing encloses the motor, electrical parts, and gears. It also includes blade guards, a base, and cutting-depth and cutting-angle

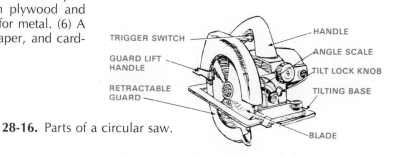

28-16. Parts of a circular saw.

adjustments. Some models also have a rip guide. Fig. 28-17.

The blade guards include a stationary upper guard that covers the front, top, and back of the saw blade. There also is a movable lower guard that covers the blade bottom when the saw is not in use. As you push a running saw into the work, this guard moves backwards and upwards into or outside the upper guard.

The base rests on the workpiece and holds the saw upright when it is operating.

The depth adjustment moves the base up and down. The angle adjustment tilts the base as much as 45°. The scale numbers should be easy to read. The adjustment tilt lock knob should be easy to grasp and turn and should tighten securely.

A circular saw has a contoured handle at the top. Some models have a second handle at the side. The tool should be comfortable to hold. It should provide a clear view of the blade when the saw is in operating position.

USING A PORTABLE CIRCULAR SAW

1. Clamp the stock to a bench or put it over sawhorses. The good side of the stock should be facing *down*. Make sure the layout line is clear of obstructions. For example, make sure you won't cut into the bench top. If you cut across a sawhorse, place a piece of scrap wood under the workpiece so that you don't cut the support.

2. Place the base of the saw on the stock with the blade in line with the layout line. The blade must not touch the stock.

3. Turn on the saw and allow it to come to full speed.

4. Slowly but steadily move the blade up to

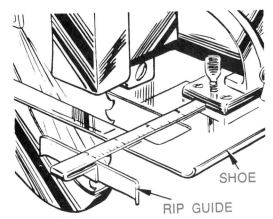

28-17. The rip guide controls the width of cut. Without this guide, it is very difficult to make a straight cut with the circular saw.

and then along the layout line until the cut is complete.

5. Allow the saw base to rest on the uncut stock and turn off the power. Do not remove the saw until the blade has come to a complete stop.

REVIEW QUESTIONS

1. How is the size of a portable electric drill indicated?
2. What part of the drill holds the twist drill or bit?
3. Describe how to shape an edge with a portable router.
4. On a belt sander, what does the arrow on the back of the belt indicate?
5. How should you determine what kind of blade to use in a saber saw?
6. Describe the two kinds of blade guards used on the portable circular saw.

Wood Finishing

Finishes are applied to wood to protect and beautify the surface. It is important to choose a finish that will suit the project and be easy to apply. Table 29-A lists some clear finishes that bring out the natural beauty of wood.

How to Select a Finish

1. For simple outdoor items such as birdhouses and rabbit hutches, apply exterior paint or enamel.
2. For outdoor sports items such as gun stocks, baseball stands, and other game equipment, use a simple penetrating finish. Such a finish soaks into the wood.
3. For indoor novelties, use a simple transparent finish or interior paint or enamel.
4. For furniture and accessories, apply a penetrating finish for simpler pieces. Apply a standard finish for larger furniture.
5. For kitchen items that come in contact with foods, use an oil that will not become rancid (spoiled). Light mineral oil is a good choice.

Simple Finishes

WAX FINISH

Repair any cracks, dents, or holes. Sand the surface of the project. Then apply one of the finishes described here.

1. Apply a coat of shellac to the surface.
2. Rub down with fine steel wool.
3. Apply a coat of paste wax. Let it dry about 10 minutes. Rub in with a soft wool rag.

NATURAL FINISH

1. Apply a thin coat of oil mixture (one part boiled linseed oil, one part solvent, and one part varnish). Use a rag to apply. Allow to dry for 15 minutes. Wipe with a clean, dry cloth.
2. Brush on a coat of thin white shellac (two parts shellac and one part alcohol). Allow the surface to dry about 24 hours. Rub down with fine steel wool.
3. Apply a second coat of shellac.
4. After the shellac is dry, cover the surface with paste wax.

Standard Finish

While the finishing material may vary, all finishing is done in about the same way. These are the major steps:

1. *Staining.* Staining adds the desired color to wood or improves the natural color. For a completely natural finish, staining may not be required.
2. *Sealing.* It is usually a good idea to seal

Table 29-A. Transparent (See-Through) Finishes

Finish (solvent)	Application	Drying Time	Durability	Color	Appearance	Notes
Wax (none)	Hand rub with soft cloth.	30 minutes	Good moisture resistance.	Tends to yellow with age.	Soft sheen	Paste wax can be used for sealer.
Shellac (alcohol)	Wide brush or hand wipe.	30 to 60 minutes	Poor. Water turns shellac white. No outdoor use.	Orange shellac dries honey-colored. White shellac dries clear.	Sheen to gloss	Good as a liquid wood filler on some woods. Better as a sealer.
Oil: Boiled linseed (turpentine or mineral spirits)	Rub with soft cloth.	Indefinite	Won't peel or crack.	Darkens quickly.	Soft sheen	Driers can be added to increase hardness.
Oils: Sealacell®, Watco, tung (mineral spirits)	Rub with soft cloth.	2 days	Won't peel or crack. Better moisture resistance.	Dull, but shines to satin luster when steel wool is used between coats.	Soft sheen	Finish is more durable than boiled linseed oil.
Varnish (turpentine or mineral spirits)	Bristle brush or foam poly-brush.	1 to 1½ days	Good weather and wear resistance.	Spar varnish tends to darken.	Sheen to gloss	Avoid shaking varnish. Apply several thin coats. Finish in dust-free place.
Lacquer brushing (lacquer thinner)	Brush (sable or camel).	4 hours	Fair moisture resistance, good durability.	Won't discolor wood.	High gloss	Foam polybrush can be used.

the stain to prevent bleeding of the stain into the top coat. A *wash coat* (one part shellac to seven parts alcohol) is good for most stains. If the top coat will be lacquer, apply a lacquer sealer.

3. *Filling.* Paste filler is used on open-grain woods. A liquid filler is used on other woods.

4. *Sealing.* A sealer should again be applied over the filler. It should be a commercial sealer, a wash coat of shellac, or a lacquer sealer.

5. *Applying a standard finish.* A shellac, varnish, or lacquer top coat is applied after sealing. Usually two or more coats are required. Always sand the surface with 5/0 sandpaper after each coat is dry. To give a rubbed finish to varnish, rub on pumice or rottenstone after the second and third coats. After the second and the final coat, all finishes can be made smoother. Rub first with pumice in oil and then with rottenstone in oil, using a felt pad. Always apply a coat of paste wax to protect the final finish.

There are also many wax and penetrating

finishes that you can use. These can be bought at hardware stores and home improvement centers.

Penetrating and Wipe-on Finishes

Many modern commercial finishes can be used in the shop. These include finishes that soak into the wood (penetrating and wipe-on finishes). Fig. 29-1. Most can be applied with a small cloth or pad. Thus, there is no need for spray equipment or brushes. These finishes also do away with the dust problem that is so bothersome when using varnish. Penetrating and wipe-on finishes are synthetic, chemical materials.

SEALACELL®

Applying Sealacell® is a three-step process. It involves three different materials to complete the finish. Each can be applied with a rag or cloth. The materials are as follows:

1. *Sealacell®* is a moisture-repellent, penetrating wood sealer that is applied over the raw wood. Ground-in-oil pigments can be mixed with the Sealacell® to serve as a stain. Stain and filler can be applied in one step by mixing paste filler into the Sealacell.® Ground-in-oil pigment is then added to get the desired color. Apply Sealacell® very liberally with a cloth. The depth of penetration depends upon the amount applied. Let dry overnight. Buff lightly with fine steel wool.

2. *Varno wax®* is a blend of gums and waxes. To apply, make a small cloth pad about 1″ × 2″. Coat the wood with wax, rubbing first with a circular motion. Then wipe with the grain. Buff lightly with 3/0 steel wool.

3. *Royal finish®* is the final coat. It is applied in the same way as the Varno wax®. Two or more applications of Royal finish®

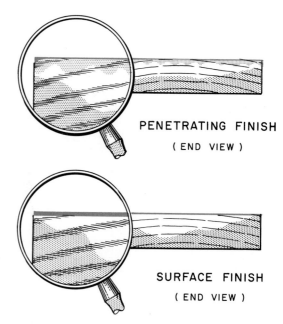

PENETRATING FINISH
(END VIEW)

SURFACE FINISH
(END VIEW)

29-1. Here you see the difference between a penetrating finish and a surface finish.

increase the depth and luster. A soft, eggshell (slightly glossy) finish can be obtained by buffing with fine steel wool.

MINWAX®

Minwax® is a penetrating wood seal and wax that is applied directly to raw wood. Two coats will complete the job. The natural beauty of the wood is preserved because this finish penetrates and seals. The finish is *in* the wood, with very little on the surface. Minwax® is available natural and in colors. It dries rapidly. This makes it possible to apply more than one coat in a day. You do not need to rub this finish after each coat. However, rubbing with 4/0 steel wool will give a very fine finish.

DEFT®

Deft® is a semigloss, clear, interior wood finish. It is easy to use and requires no thinning. It will not show brush marks and will not darken. This material seals, primes, and finishes the wood. It dries in 30 minutes. Three coats are recommended. The first coat seals the wood. The second coat adds depth. The third coat results in a mirror-smooth, fine finish. The third coat can be sanded with 6/0 wet-or-dry sandpaper. It also can be rubbed mirror-smooth with pumice and rottenstone. All three coats can be applied in a few hours. Deft® can also be applied from a spray can.

DANISH OIL FINISH

Penetrating oil finishes like linseed oil have long been used. For example, they are used to beautify and preserve gun stocks and other fine woods. To produce a Danish oil finish, penetrating resin-oil is needed. This finish actually improves the wood. It does not require hours of hand rubbing. Danish oil is long lasting. It seldom needs replenishing. It never needs resanding. One of its big advantages is that a surface that has become marred from hard usage is fairly easy to refinish.

Danish oil finish is applied as follows:

1. After sanding, apply a quick-dry alcohol or water-base wood stain with a clean cloth or brush.

2. Let dry for about 45 minutes.

3. Apply liberal amounts of the penetrating resin-oil finish.

4. Allow the oil to soak into the wood for about 30 minutes or until penetration stops. Keep the surface uniformly wet with the finish.

5. Wipe the surface completely dry with a soft, absorbent cloth.

6. For more luster, let the surface dry for 4 hours.

7. Wet-sand lightly with a small amount of resin-oil finish.

8. Dry the wood thoroughly with a clean cloth.

9. Polish briskly with another cloth.

REVIEW QUESTIONS

1. What finish should you choose for a birdhouse?
2. What should be chosen for projects to be used in the kitchen?
3. Describe the way to apply a wax finish.
4. Tell how to apply a natural finish using boiled linseed oil.
5. Describe the steps for applying a standard finish.
6. How many steps are needed to apply a Sealacell® finish?
7. How many coats are usually needed for a Minwax® finish?
8. How long does it take for Deft® to dry?
9. Describe how to apply a Danish oil finish.

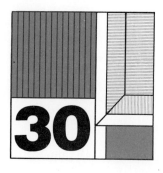

Lumbering

30

Lumber is one of the most useful products of the tree. The terms *forest products* and *lumber* mean the same thing to most people. If you ask anyone to name a tree product or something that means the same as wood, the answer is usually "lumber."

About 60 percent of the nation's lumber comes from privately owned forest lands. The forest products industry supplies another 12 percent. Public lands—mostly national forests —give us the other 28 percent. Fig. 30-1.

How Timber is Harvested

The harvesting of trees for lumber is called *logging*. Like any other industry, logging has its own language. You don't *cut* a tree, you *fell* it. And then you probably will *buck* it to log lengths. You'll go to work in a *crummy*, a small bus usually painted orange and almost always scarred inside and out by rough use.

MARKING THE TREES
Which trees are to be cut in a timber harvest is not decided by the people who cut them down. Trained foresters do this, and they supervise the harvest. Foresters mark the trees with a spray of white paint. They are careful to leave seed trees and young growing stock for future crops.

FELLING THE TREES
Trees selected for harvest are cut down by people called *fallers*. These people notch the tree on the side toward which it is to fall. They then use power saws to cut down the tree close to the ground. All limbs are removed. The main stem is cut into equal lengths suitable for lumber. The fallers know just how to get the most from each tree.

In recent years, advanced equipment has been introduced to reduce time, labor, and waste. For example, the feller-buncher is a huge mobile machine big enough to grasp a tree up to a foot in diameter in its mechanical hands. It cuts the tree near the base, leaving a 6″ stump. The feller-buncher then removes the limbs. Some models cut the stem into log lengths. They may even store the logs briefly in a holding rack.

Other machines actually do partial manufacturing right in the woods. Whole trees go in one end of the machine. Precision-cut wood chips come out the other and are blown into waiting trucks. The chips are used to make pulp for papermaking.

TRANSPORTING THE LOGS TO THE MILL
Years ago, logs were moved to the nearest river or stream and left there through the winter. In spring, as the water rose, the logs

Forest Regions of the United States

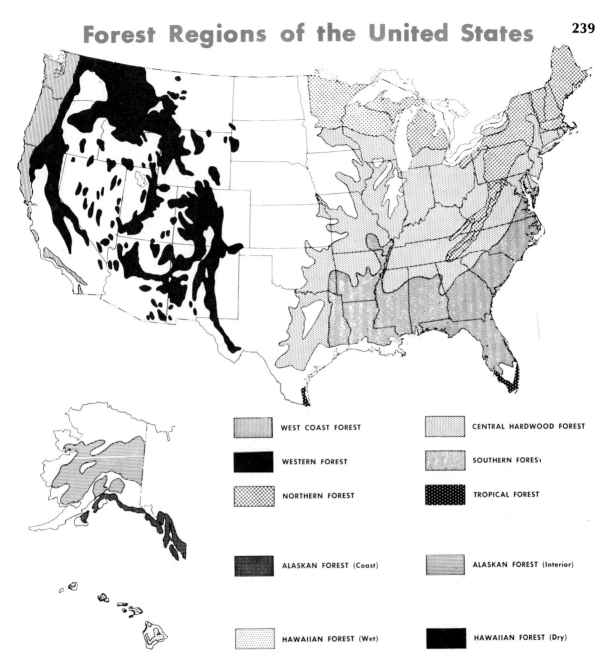

WEST COAST FOREST		CENTRAL HARDWOOD FOREST	
WESTERN FOREST		SOUTHERN FOREST	
NORTHERN FOREST		TROPICAL FOREST	
ALASKAN FOREST (Coast)		ALASKAN FOREST (Interior)	
HAWAIIAN FOREST (Wet)		HAWAIIAN FOREST (Dry)	

30-1. This map shows areas of renewable natural wealth. The West Coast or Pacific forests are primarily Douglas fir. However, they also have western red cedar, spruce, and hemlock. The western forests include much of our softwood timber, primarily pine, although there are some hardwoods. The northern forests have such trees as hemlock, red spruce, white pine, and several kinds of hardwoods. The central hardwood forests include oak, cherry, birch, and many other kinds of hardwoods. In the southern forests are such softwoods as pine and cypress and many kinds of hardwoods. The tropical forests have ebony and palm trees. The coast regions of Alaska have primarily western hemlock and spruce. The interior forests are heavy with white spruce and white birch. The Hawaiian forests include many softwoods and some unusual types such as monkey pod and koa.

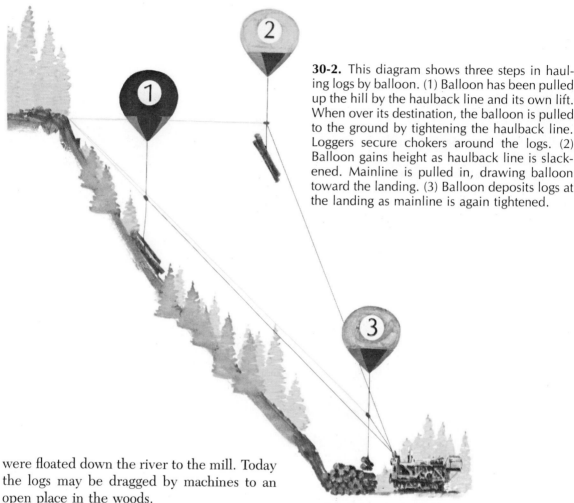

30-2. This diagram shows three steps in hauling logs by balloon. (1) Balloon has been pulled up the hill by the haulback line and its own lift. When over its destination, the balloon is pulled to the ground by tightening the haulback line. Loggers secure chokers around the logs. (2) Balloon gains height as haulback line is slackened. Mainline is pulled in, drawing balloon toward the landing. (3) Balloon deposits logs at the landing as mainline is again tightened.

were floated down the river to the mill. Today the logs may be dragged by machines to an open place in the woods.

In areas too rugged for this kind of machinery, and where trees grow larger, different logging approaches are used. In the Pacific Northwest and the Rocky Mountain states, cable yarding is the primary method.

In all cable systems, logs are dragged or carried by wire to a landing area or roadside. Some systems use stationary towers more than 100′ tall. Others rely on smaller towers or cranes mounted on mobile, self-powered platforms. The reach of the cable can range from a few hundred feet to almost a mile, depending on the system.

Sometimes helicopters or giant helium-filled balloons are used to carry the logs to a roadside, river, or railway. Fig. 30-2. There they are loaded onto trucks, boats, or railroad cars. These take them to the mill.

How Logs are Processed

A modern lumber mill is a very complex factory. It has a control room in which computers keep track of all of the operations.

When logs first arrive at the mill, they are *scaled* to check the species and quality as well as to estimate the amount of lumber that each log will produce. The logs are then stacked in a *log deck area* to await processing.

When the logs enter the mill, they go first to the *barking center*. There, the bark, dirt, and rocks are stripped from the logs. The waste wood is used as chips. The logs are then moved to the computerized *bucking station* where they are cut into the best lengths for use. From there the logs go to the *head rig* where large band saws cut them into big pieces of lumber.

The *chipper-canter*, controlled by the computer, makes sure that the maximum amount of lumber is obtained from the log. These operations are monitored at the *control console*. Then the lumber is *resawn* into desired sizes. The *chipper-edger* removes rough edges from the lumber. At the *trimming/ sorting center* the lumber is cut to exact lengths. From here the lumber goes to large kilns where it is *dried*. The lumber is then *planed* to standard sizes. It is *graded* and *stored* to await *shipment*. The lumber is moved by truck, railroad, and ship all over the world. It is used for building houses and furniture and for thousands of other uses.

REVIEW QUESTIONS

1. Who selects the trees to be cut?
2. What do fallers do?
3. How are logs taken to the mill?
4. What are the main steps in processing logs?

Thinking about a Career

CABINETMAKER

Since he was fourteen, Patrick has known what job he wanted as a career. "When I started junior high school, I decided I wanted to be a cabinetmaker," Patrick said. "My father was a carpenter. I had watched him work and thought I would enjoy working with wood. At home, the only power woodworking tool we had was a table saw. With this saw, and with my dad's hand tools, I was able to construct many projects."

Pat's junior high school did not offer woodworking courses. All of the woodworking Pat did, he did at home. In eighth grade, he constructed a small model of a covered wagon. He made the model in his small basement workshop. Entering the model in a statewide contest, he won third place.

By the time he entered high school, Pat had good woodworking skills. In high school, he took all of the woodworking courses offered. He also joined the local chapter of AIASA. Pat is enthusiastic about the support he received from being a member of that club.

Since Pat knew that his career would be in woodworking, he knew that he would need other training, as well. To develop a good sense of design, he took an art course. He also took a course in drafting. This gave him the ability to sketch out working drawings and read blueprints.

While in high school, Pat realized that he would need to gain more experience in woodworking. There were no cabinetmakers in his small Illinois town. But a cabinetmaker in a nearby city was willing to employ him part-time. "He was a master craftsman," said Pat. "He was in his seventies at the time, so I was able to benefit from the woodworking knowledge he had gained over a lifetime." Those Saturdays spent working in the cabinetmaker's shop helped Pat develop his cabinetmaking skills.

Right after graduation, Pat began work as an independent cabinetmaker. "I knew that I had a natural ability to work with wood," Pat explains. "I wanted to develop these abilities as fully as I could. I thought then that cabinetmaking would be a good career for me. I've never looked back. I've enjoyed every day I've spent working with wood."

Working out of the basement of his house, Pat designed and built a variety of projects. It was not the first time he had sold any of his projects. "When I was in high school, I made and sold a gun cabinet," he said. "I also made and sold lathe turnings."

Starting his own cabinetmaking business was a struggle. In the beginning, he worked alone. The workspace was cramped. To construct large projects, he had to rearrange the workshop. But he did good work. Soon, he had more jobs than he could handle. He knew then that it was time to find a larger workspace. He also knew that he could not continue to work alone. He would need to hire employees.

In the next five years, his business grew quickly. He moved his workshop twice—each time to a larger building. He hired more employees and bought more machinery.

Today, at twenty-six, Pat is the owner and president of his own cabinetmaking company. He has fifteen employees and a wide variety of power woodworking equipment. Several of his employees were AIASA club award winners in high school. Pat's wife, who has helped him throughout, is in charge of the bookkeeping.

In buying tools, Pat tries to buy the best. "But I now know that the best is not always the most expensive," he says. He notes that he has bought only two of his power tools new. "If you can judge machinery well, you can find some good buys in power tools," he explains.

Pat's large shop is clean and well-organized. The wood is neatly sorted and binned at the back of the shop, next to the loading dock. The power machines are arranged to ensure a smooth work flow. The floor is uncluttered.

Pat and his employees work in fine hardwoods to create a range of wood products. "We make bookcases, countertops, grandfather clock cases, and desks. In fact, we make every type of cabinet. We also make staircases." Staircases have a particular appeal for Pat. He sees the design of each one as a challenge. He likes to make staircases of laminated wood. The staircases are unusual, with smooth airy curves. He has designed such staircases for commercial buildings, as well as for private homes.

Pat foresees further growth for his business. "There is a real need for skilled workers in this field," says Pat. "Even now, I need more help. In fact, I'm hiring a new employee next week."

Pat has never advertised. All of his business has come from word of mouth. "If one customer likes what I have done, they are likely to tell someone about it. Then, that person keeps me in mind when he or she has some cabinetwork to be done. In cabinetmaking, care and precision are important. It really does take a special skill. I've always know that your reputation is important in cabinetmaking. If you do an excellent job—not merely a good job—you will definitely get work."

244

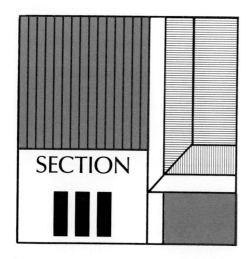

Metalworking
Technology

Reynolds Aluminum

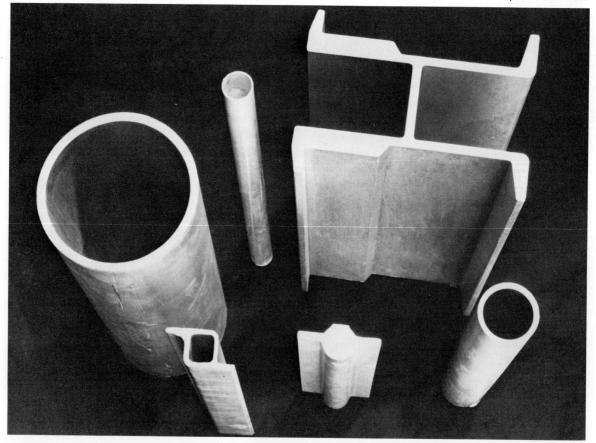

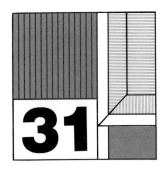

Metal Materials

Many kinds of metals are used in industry to make the hundreds of different metal products we use. Fig. 31-1. Metalworkers must know the properties of these different metals. In this unit, only the most common shop metals are discussed.

Types of Metals

There are two major types of metals, ferrous and nonferrous. Metals with a high iron content are called *ferrous* metals. These are metals such as galvanized iron, tin plate, iron sheet, and iron bars. Metals containing little or no iron are called *nonferrous* metals. These include copper and its alloys, aluminum, pewter, and nickelsilver.

Metals for projects must be chosen carefully. Each metal is different in color, properties, and ease of working. Metal properties are very important. These are shown in Table 31-A. For example, copper is *ductile*, or can be hammered thin. It also is *malleable*, which means it can be stretched easily. However, as it is worked it becomes very brittle. It must be annealed (softened), or it will crack. Copper is annealed by heating it red hot and dipping it in water to cool it. Table 31-B will help you choose the correct metal for a project. Common metal shapes are shown in Fig. 31-2.

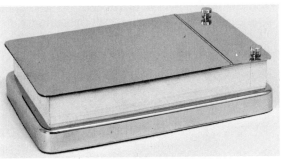

Smokador

31-1. This attractive note-pad holder is made of metal.

Table 31-A. Common Metal Properties

Property	Meaning
Ductility	Metal easily drawn or stretched into wires.
Malleability	Metal easily stretched or formed into different shapes.
Brittleness	Metal hard to work, cracks easily.
Conductivity	Heat and electricity move easily through metal.
Hardness	Metal not easily scratched or nicked.

245

Table 31-B. Nonferrous Metals

Metal	Color	Properties	Characteristics	Uses
Aluminum	Bluish-white	Ductile, malleable, easily worked, good conductor of heat and electricity.	Work-hardens easily, must be annealed, difficult to solder, light-weight.	Cooking utensils, electrical parts, drink cans, craft projects.
Brass	Yellow-gold	Brittle, hard, can be worked much as copper.	Alloy of copper (90 percent) and zinc (10 percent), work-hardens very easily, must be annealed often or it will crack, easily soldered, heavy in weight.	Plumbing fixtures, electrical parts, craft projects.
Bronze	Reddish-yellow	Brittle, hard, wear-resistant, can be worked much as brass, corrosion-resistant.	Alloy of copper (90 percent) and tin (10 percent), easily soldered, heavy in weight.	Machine bearings, plumbing parts, cast parts.
Copper	Reddish-brown	Ductile, malleable, good conduction of heat and electricity, corrosion resistant.	Work-hardens easily, must be annealed, easily soldered, heavy in weight.	Electric wire and parts, cooking utensils, plumbing pipe, craft projects.
Nickel silver or German silver	Silver-white	Brittle, hard, hard to work.	Alloy of copper (64 percent), nickel (18 percent), and zinc (18 percent).	Jewelry, tableware, craft projects.
Pewter	Silver-gray	Malleable, easily worked, very soft.	Alloy of copper (10 percent), and tin (90 percent), does not work-harden easily, heavy in weight, difficult to solder.	Bowls and vases, craft projects.

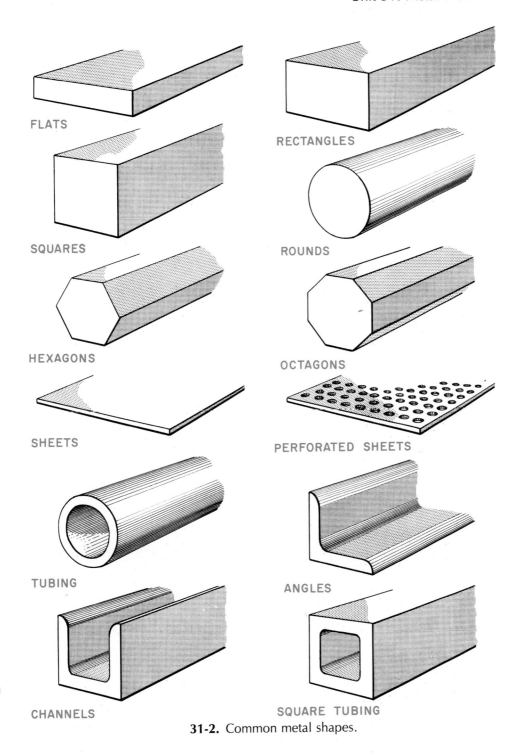

FLATS

RECTANGLES

SQUARES

ROUNDS

HEXAGONS

OCTAGONS

SHEETS

PERFORATED SHEETS

TUBING

ANGLES

CHANNELS

SQUARE TUBING

31-2. Common metal shapes.

Table 31-C. Common Metal Thicknesses

Millimeters	Inch	Approximate Gauge	
		Steel	Copper
1.20	0.0472	18	16
1.00	0.0394	20	18
0.80	0.0315	22	20
0.60	0.0236	24	22
0.50	0.0197	26	24
0.40	0.0157	28	26
0.30	0.0118	30	28
0.25	0.0098	32	30
0.20	0.0079	34	32
0.16	0.0063	36	34

Measuring Metals

Metal shapes, such as bars and tubing, are sold by the foot of length. Metal sheets are sold by the square foot. The thickness of sheet metals is measured by a gauge* size. Table 31-C. In the metric system, millimeter thicknesses replace the gauge sizes. Note that the gauge sizes for ferrous and nonferrous sizes are different.

*Gauge sometimes is spelled *gage*. Both spellings are correct.

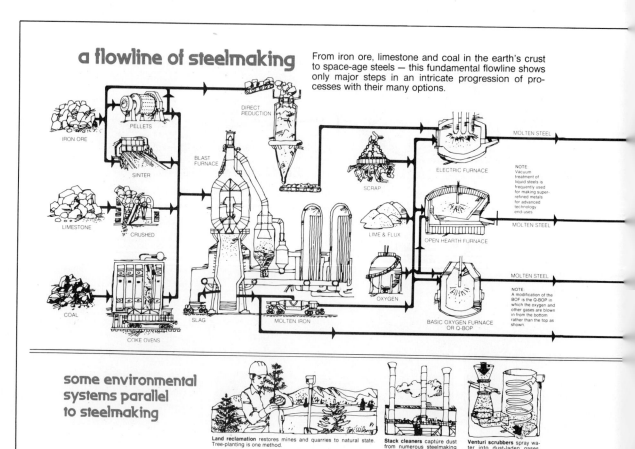

a flowline of steelmaking

From iron ore, limestone and coal in the earth's crust to space-age steels — this fundamental flowline shows only major steps in an intricate progression of processes with their many options.

IRON ORE
PELLETS
SINTER
LIMESTONE
CRUSHED
COAL
COKE OVENS
DIRECT REDUCTION
BLAST FURNACE
SLAG
MOLTEN IRON
SCRAP
LIME & FLUX
OXYGEN
ELECTRIC FURNACE
OPEN HEARTH FURNACE
BASIC OXYGEN FURNACE OR Q-BOP
MOLTEN STEEL
MOLTEN STEEL
MOLTEN STEEL

NOTE
Vacuum treatment of liquid steels is frequently used for making super-refined metals for advanced technology end-uses

NOTE
A modification of the BOF is the Q-BOP in which the oxygen and other gases are blown in from the bottom rather than the top as shown.

some environmental systems parallel to steelmaking

Land reclamation restores mines and quarries to natural state. Tree-planting is one method.

Stack cleaners capture dust from numerous steelmaking processes, keeping it out of the atmosphere.

Venturi scrubbers spray water into dust-laden gases. Recovered solid particles may often be recycled.

Mining Metals

Metals are found in ores that are mined from the earth. These ores are refined and worked into many shapes and sizes. The mining and refining industries are important. They supply the materials for metal products.

Steel comes from iron ore, copper from copper ore, and aluminum from an ore called bauxite. Figure 31-3 shows how iron ore is made into steel, which is then formed into sheets and bars. All metal ores are processed in much the same way.

REVIEW QUESTIONS

1. Of what metals are the following alloys made: brass, bronze, pewter, nickel-silver?
2. What is an alloy?
3. What is ductility?
4. What is malleability?
5. List some of the precautions the steel industry takes to protect the air and the land.

31-3. How steel is made.

Inland Steel

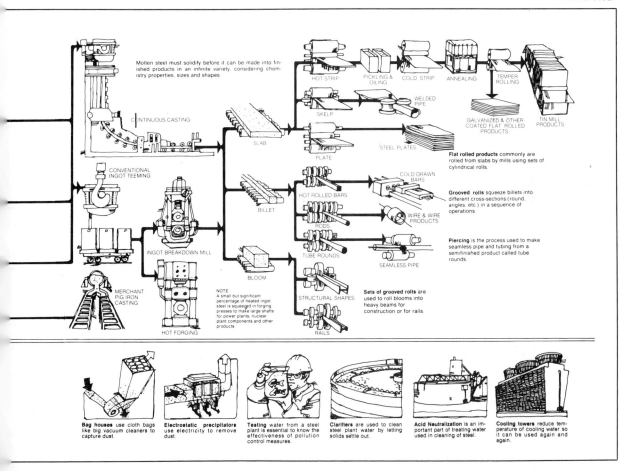

||||||||||||||||||||||||||||||||||||||||||| **KEY IDEA** |||||||||||||||||||||||||||||||||||||||||||||

PROBLEM SOLVING

One of the many skills a metalcrafter must learn is how to fasten or join sheetmetal workpieces. Let's examine some of the more common joining methods.

The stitch-fold is made with a special tool that pierces the metal sheet and results in a permanent joint. Fig. A. The clinch also requires a special tool. It is a permanent joint. It differs from the stitch-fold in that the metal is not pierced. Here a press-lock joint is produced. Spot welding also produces a permanent joint. It requires special equipment.

Several common joining methods are shown in Fig. B.

The adhesive, solder, and rivet joints are all permanent. They can be made with tools commonly found in the metal shop.

The bolt and nut, sheetmetal screw, and press nut are nonpermanent joints. They permit easy disassembly of parts. The press nut, however, requires special installation tools.

The craft skills necessary to produce each of these joints can be learned. You will learn many of them in your metalworking classes.

However, *problem-solving skills* are needed to learn when and where to use the many fastening methods. Let's look at a metal fastening problem to learn how it was solved.

The problem is to join automotive metal hood or deck (trunk) panels to metal frames. Any of the methods would work. Some, however, would work better than others. The following must be considered.

1. Automobile manufacturing is a mass-

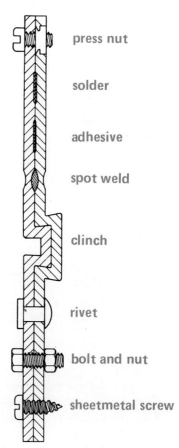

press nut

solder

adhesive

spot weld

clinch

rivet

bolt and nut

sheetmetal screw

Fig. A. The stitch-folding technique.

STITCH-FOLDING

Fig. B. Various metal-joining techniques.

Table A. Possible Joining Methods

JOINT	Automatic assembly	Smooth finish	Permanent	Reliable
		Requirements		
Pressnut	Yes	No	No	Yes
Solder	No*	Yes	Yes	No*
Adhesive	Yes	Yes	Yes	Yes
Spot weld	Yes	No	Yes	Yes
Clinch	Yes	No	Yes	Yes
Rivet	Yes	No	Yes	Yes
Bolt and nut	No	No	No	No**
Sheetmetal screw	Yes	No	No	No**
Stitch fold	Yes	No	Yes	Yes

* Soldering requires absolutely clean metal and carefully controlled heat. It is difficult to obtain these on some production lines. This would result in a nonreliable joint.

** Threaded fasteners may loosen after an automobile trunk lid has been opened and shut hundreds of times.

production job. The metal-joining method used must lend itself to automation.

2. The panels must not be dented or left with holes or fastenings that would show. The completed automobile must have a smooth, painted finish.

3. The joint must be permanent.

4. The joint must be reliable and not come apart or loosen through rough use.

Now you know the problem. You also know the requirements. The information in the problem should be organized as shown in Table A. Such a table will help you reach a decision.

Study the table. What would your choice be? If your answer is "adhesive" you are correct. It is the only method that is easily

automated. It does not damage the metal. It is permanent and reliable. In fact, most hood and deck panels are fastened in this way. If you visit an automobile plant, you will see a robot programmed to squirt a ribbon of adhesive on the metal frame. Another robot will lift a panel onto the frame and press it into place. There the adhesive will "cure." It will create a permanent bond between the frame and the panel.

This same problem-solving logic is used in any other metal-joining job. For example, a metal crafter will use sheetmetal screws to hold sheetmetal furnace ducts (pipes) together. This makes installation easier. It also permits the ducts to be separated for any necessary repairs.

Where appearance is not a problem, spot welding, stitch-folding, clinching, or screws could be used. They may also be used if the joint is redesigned, so that these fastenings would be hidden.

In solving such problems, you must first know what the problem is. You must then know what the requirements or restrictions are. You must know what equipment is available. Before solving a problem, you must gather all of the necessary information.

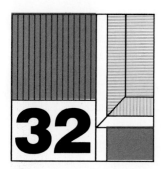

Measurement and Layout

The first step in making any metal project is to get the correct size and kind of material or stock. Knowing how to measure and mark stock is very important.

Measuring and Layout Tools

The tools discussed here are used to mark or lay out metal. Learn to use them correctly.

RULES

The most important layout tool is the *metal rule*. The most common customary rules are 6″ and 12″ long. They are marked in inches and fractions of an inch: halves, quarters, eighths, sixteenths, thirty-seconds, and in some cases sixty-fourths. Common metric sizes are 150- and 300-mm rules, marked in single millimetres with a bolder mark at each 5- and 10-mm position. Fig. 32-1.

The *circumference rule* is a very thin steel rule, usually 36″ long. With it you can find the circumference of a cylinder simply by measuring the cylinder's diameter (*Circumference* is the distance around a cylinder. *Diameter* is the distance through the middle.)

SCRIBER

A *scriber* is a very thin steel tool sharpened to a point. Fig. 32-2. A scriber is used to scratch lines and measurements on metal. It is

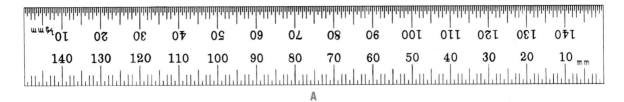

32-1. Metalworking rules. (A) 150-mm metric; (B) 6″; and (C) circumference.

32-2. The scriber is the metalworker's pencil.

often called the metalworker's "pencil." On soft metal, an ordinary lead pencil is best for layout lines.

PRICK PUNCH

A *prick punch* has a point sharpened at an angle of about 30°. Fig. 32-3. It is used in

sheet metal layout work to locate the center of an arc or hole. Then, when a dividers is used, its leg can be placed in the center mark to prevent slipping. In transferring a design from paper patterns to sheet metal surfaces, the prick punch is used to make indentations (small, round dents).

CENTER PUNCH

A *center punch* looks like the prick punch except that it has a blunter point ground at an angle of 90°. The center punch is used to mark holes to be drilled. The dent is made by striking the tool a sharp blow with a hammer.

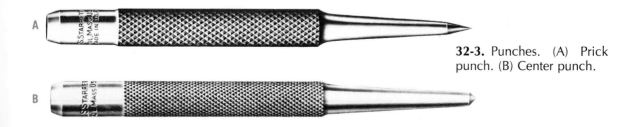

32-3. Punches. (A) Prick punch. (B) Center punch.

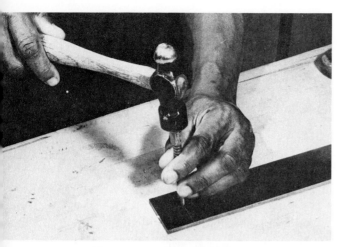

32-4. The proper way to hold the center punch. A ball-peen hammer is being used.

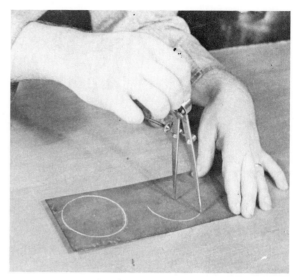

32-5. Using a dividers. The tool is held between the thumb and forefinger so that a complete circle can be scribed.

HAMMERS

Metalworking hammers have many uses. They are made in a variety of shapes, sizes, and weights. The common weights of these hammers are from 5 ounces to 2 pounds. For layout work, a 10-ounce hammer is used. Fig. 32-4.

DIVIDERS

A *dividers* has two pointed steel legs attached at the top with a spring adjustment. It is used for measuring between points. It is used also for transferring measurements directly from the rule, and scribing arcs and circles. In scribing an arc or circle, set the dividers to the correct radius with a rule. The method used to scribe arcs and circles is shown in Fig. 32-5.

COMBINATION SQUARE

The *combination square* has a blade with a groove cut along one side. It has a head that can slide along this blade to be locked in any position. Fig. 32-6. One side of the square

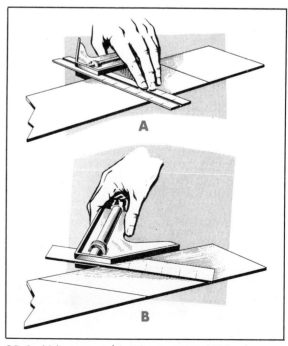

32-6. Using a combination square. (A) Laying out a right angle. (B) Laying out a 45° angle.

head makes a 90° angle with the blade. The other makes a 45° angle. This is a very useful tool for squaring up stock and checking layout lines. Center heads are available for locating the centers of round stock. Protractor heads are used for marking angles.

WIRE AND SHEET METAL GAUGES

Thin sheet stock is measured with a thickness gauge. These gauges are metal disks with slots around the outside. Before using the gauge, make sure that any burr on the edge of the metal stock is removed. Then insert the stock into the slots in the disk until you find the one that fits exactly. Fig. 32-7. The number stamped next to the opening indicates the gauge size of the stock.

Patterns

TRANSFERRING PATTERNS

After you have chosen the proper size and kind of sheet metal, a pattern or design must be transferred to it. Sometimes the layout can

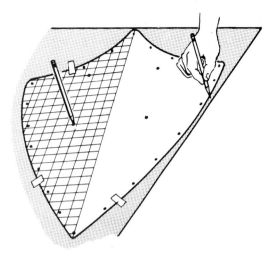

32-8. Tracing a paper pattern on metal before cutting out the design.

32-7. Using a gauge for measuring the thickness of material. Remember to remove any burrs before measuring the metal.

be made directly on the metal using layout fluids or metal marking pens. For more difficult pieces, it may be necessary to draw the pattern on paper first. It must then be transferred or traced onto the metal. Fig. 32-8. The method depends on the kind of project and the amount of detail.

DEVELOPING PATTERNS

There are four basic methods of developing *geometric* patterns such as cones, cylinders, pyramids, and rectangular boxes. These methods are described below and shown in Fig. 32-9.

In making a pattern, you must allow extra metal for hems and seams. Fig. 32-10. *Hems* are folded edges on metal. They make a piece more attractive, more rigid, and safer because the sharp edge is turned over. *Seams* are used for joining metal. These are discussed in Unit 42.

Angular (Straight-Line) Development

The layout for a letter holder is outlined below, as an example. Fig. 32-11. It is an

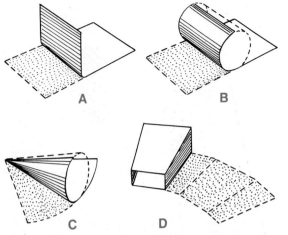

32-9. Four methods of pattern development: (The shaded areas show how each shape would look if it were unfolded. The shaded area is called the "stretchout.") (A) Angular, for boxes. (B) Cylindrical, for cylinders. (C) Conical, for cones. (D) Transition-piece (triangulation), for pieces that have a different shape at each end.

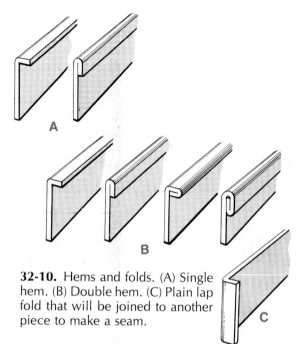

32-10. Hems and folds. (A) Single hem. (B) Double hem. (C) Plain lap fold that will be joined to another piece to make a seam.

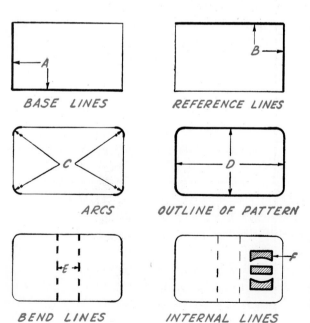

BASE LINES

REFERENCE LINES

ARCS

OUTLINE OF PATTERN

BEND LINES

INTERNAL LINES

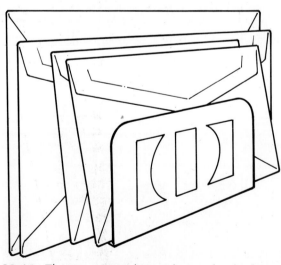

32-11. The steps in making a layout for the letter holder. This is an example of angular development.

example of angular (straight-line) development. This method is used for such projects as boxes and trays.

1. Get a piece of metal slightly larger than the plans call for. Be sure to measure the metal carefully.

2. Square two edges of the material as shown in Fig. 32-11A. These squared edges are called *base* lines.

3. Using the base lines as guides, lightly lay out all the necessary vertical and horizontal outside lines. These are called *reference* lines, or construction lines. Fig. 32-11B.

4. The letter holder will have rounded edges, so the arcs must be drawn. Fig. 32-11C.

5. Connect the rounded corners with outlines. Fig. 32-11D.

6. Locate and mark the lines at which the metal is to be bent. Fig. 32-11E.

7. Draw any internal details. In this case, the letter holder will have a design cut into it later. Fig. 32-11F.

Cylindrical (Parallel Line) Development

Cylindrical (parallel line) development is used for making pipes, tubes, scoops, watering cans, and other cylindrical objects. The stretchout (or flat pattern) of a cylinder is a rectangle.

To make a pattern for a scoop follow these directions:

1. Use a compass to draw a circle the diameter of the scoop you wish to make. This will be the *top* view.

2. Divide the top view in half vertically and then horizontally. Use these divisions as base lines for your protractor. Mark off divisions at 30° and 60°, until the circle has been equally divided all the way around. In Fig. 32-12

there are twenty-four divisions. The more divisions, the more accurate the layout. Number these points.

3. Next, draw the *side* view. Lightly sketch a base line the same length as the diameter of the top view. In Fig. 32-12 this is 2″. Starting at the numbered points in the top view, draw light, vertical construction lines down from the top view into the side view. Measure off the correct length of the scoop. In Fig. 32-12, this is 3″.

4. Draw the curve with the help of a drawing instrument called the *irregular curve*.

5. Next, draw the *stretchout*. This is the scoop as it would look stretched out on a flat surface. Extend light reference lines from the top and bottom of the side view.

6. Set a dividers or compass for the distance from points 1 to 2 on the top view. Transfer this distance to the extended lines of the stretchout to measure off divisions 0 through 23. Number them. This will be the circumference. Draw light vertical lines at each of the divisions. (You may double-check your measure by multiplying the diameter of the cylinder times 3.1416, or *pi*.)

7. Find point A as shown on the side view in Fig. 32-12. To reproduce the curve already drawn in the side view, extend a light, straight line from point A until it meets line 2 on the stretchout. Where the construction lines meet a marking point is formed (B). Do this for each of the other points. Draw the lines all the way across the stretchout to carry through with the curve on the opposite side (point C) to lines 14 through 23. Connect the intersecting points with the irregular curve.

8. Remember to allow for a seam at each end of the stretchout. The seam halves will be bent in opposite directions.

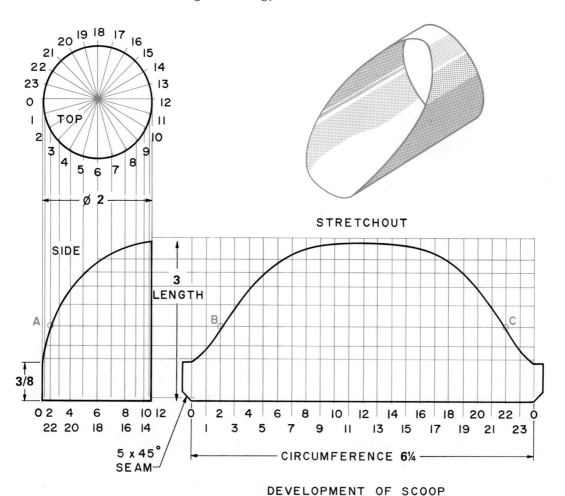

STRETCHOUT

3/8

5 x 45°
SEAM

CIRCUMFERENCE 6¼

DEVELOPMENT OF SCOOP

32-12. Parallel line development is used to lay out a scoop.

REVIEW QUESTIONS

1. How is the circumference rule used?
2. What is the difference between the prick punch and the center punch?
3. List the different heads used with the combination square. What is each head used for?
4. What is the purpose of a hem? What is the purpose of a seam?
5. List the four methods of pattern development.

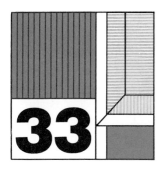

Cutting Heavy Metal

To cut thick metal in the school shop, or in the home workshop, one of the following tools is used:

- Hacksaw.
- Metal-cutting band saw.
- Throatless shears.
- Slitting shears.

Hacksaw

A hacksaw is a thin, narrow blade with small teeth along one edge, mounted in a U-shaped frame. Fig. 33-1. Follow these directions when using the hacksaw:

1. *Select the correct blade.* Blades are made of low-carbon or low-tungsten steel, or tougher alloy steel. Common blade lengths are 10″ and 12″.

When selecting the correct tooth size for the material to be cut, remember that at least two teeth should be engaged in cutting at all times. Soft or heavy metals require a coarse-tooth blade (fourteen or eighteen teeth per inch). Thin wall sections, such as tubing, require one with fine teeth (twenty-four or thirty-two teeth per inch).

The teeth are set or staggered to form the cutting edge to prevent binding the blade in the workpiece.

2. *Position the blade.* Adjust the frame for the correct length of blade. Make sure that the teeth point *forward*, or *away from* the handle. Fig. 33-2. Insert the blade. Tighten it just enough to hold it rigid at all times. A loose blade will not cut straight. After a blade has been used for a while it will tend to loosen. It should then be retightened. Fasten the work in the vise. Use soft vise jaws of wood, copper, or aluminum when clamping soft metals or stock with a fine finish.

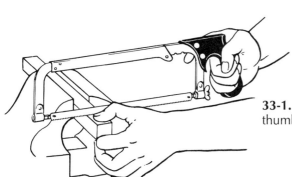

33-1. The hacksaw. To start the cut, use your thumb as a guide. Begin with slow, careful strokes.

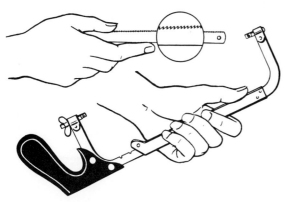

33-2. Adjust the hacksaw frame for the blade to be used. Hold blade with teeth pointing away from handle. Place front hold over pin on front stretcher. Then place second hold over pin at back. Tighten the blade by turning the wing nut.

Rockwell

33-3. This metal cutting bandsaw can be used in either a horizontal or vertical position. The teacher and student are checking the squareness of a piece just cut.

3. *Start the cut.* The best way to start a cut in hard metals is to file a notch. A cut should always be started at a shallow angle off the edge of the workpiece. Guide the blade with your thumb. Begin with light pressure and a steady forward stroke. When the cut is started, use both hands to hold the frame. Apply steady pressure on the forward stroke. Then release the pressure on the return stroke, and bring the saw back to starting position. Without proper pressure the teeth will dull rapidly because of the rubbing action. Remember to use the *total length* of the hacksaw blade in cutting. When the cut is nearly complete, hold the end to be cut off in your left hand. Make the last few strokes with the saw in the right hand only.

Metal-cutting Band Saws

The metal-cutting band saw cuts continuously. Since it uses a thin blade, it removes little material. Some types of band saws can also be used in either a horizontal or vertical position. Fig. 33-3. The blades have from four to fourteen teeth per inch. They should be selected so that at least two teeth are engaged at all times. Fine-tooth blades are used for cutting thin metal and light tubing. Coarser blades are used for larger diameter stock.

Here are some directions that should be followed when using this saw:

• Be sure that the blade has enough tension to keep it from weaving and making a crooked cut.

• The feed pressure should vary according to the size and kind of material being cut. A slow speed and a steady, gentle feed pressure will cause blades to last longer. Heavy pressure will dull the blade. A light feed will cause the blade to slip over the work and wear the

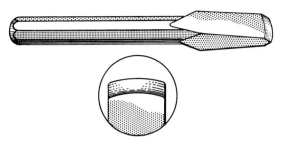

33-4. A flat cold chisel that has been properly ground.

blade. Use a light feed on thin materials. Use a heavier feed on thicker ones. A sliding weight is used for the feeder control. Move the weight away from the motor end to increase the feed.

• Check the fixed jaw to make sure that it is at right angles to the saw blade for cut-off work. Jaws can also be adjusted up to 45° for angle cutting. Open the jaws so that the material will just slip in. Then release the catch and lower the blade so it lines up with your length mark on the stock. Tighten the vise. Turn on the power. Release the catch, and slowly lower the saw to the work. After this point the cutting will be automatic. On some machines the power is automatically turned off after the cut is complete. Power hacksaws with heavy blades (like hand-hacksaw blades) are also used.

Cold Chisels

The cold chisel is used for both shearing and cutting stock. The cutting edge of the cold chisel should be ground to an angle of 60° to 70° with a slightly rounded cutting edge. Fig. 33-4. The cutting can be done by placing the stock over a soft metal or wooden surface to protect the cutting edge of the chisel. Hold a

cold chisel at a slight angle. Tap it with a hammer to start the cut. After you have traced the area to be cut, strike the cold chisel with firm, careful blows to cut through the metal. Fig. 33-5. The cold chisel can also be used for shearing metal in a vise, or for shearing rivet heads. Fix the metal in a vise with the cutting line just above the top of the jaws. Hold the cold chisel at an angle of about 30° or 35°. Strike it with a hammer to shear off the metal.

Throatless Shears

A pair of throatless shears is an all-purpose tool for making curved cuts in light and heavy metals. Because of the curved blade design, the work can be turned in any position during the cut. To use, open the shears as wide as possible. Insert the stock under the blades with the cutting line in line with the top blade. Fig. 33-6. Pull the handle down a little at a

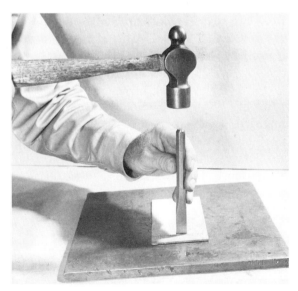

33-5. Cutting metal over a flat plate. Hold the chisel at a slight angle.

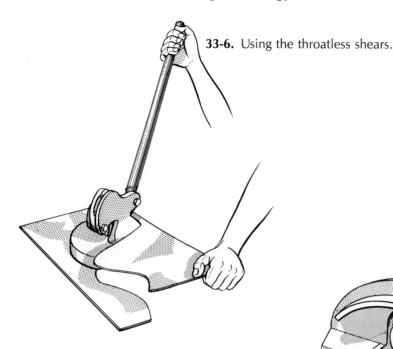

33-6. Using the throatless shears.

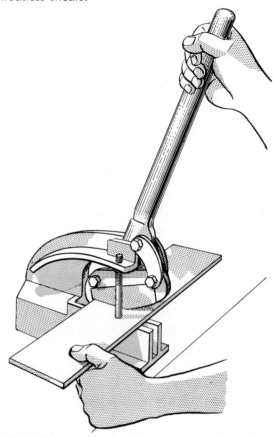

time. Then reopen the blades and slip the metal in further. The capacity of the tool depends upon its size. For example, small throatless shears will cut ⅛" thick mild steel.

Slitting Shears

Slitting shears are straight-blade, bench-mounted shears used to cut off stock. Fig. 33-7. They can be used for cutting band iron and heavier gauges of sheet metal. The cut-off line is marked on the stock. The material is inserted under the blades.

33-7. When using the slitting shears, always keep the metal flat on the bed of the shear. Start the cut at the heel of the blades, since this is the point of greatest power.

REVIEW QUESTIONS

1. What kind of blade should be used when hacksawing brass tubing?

2. How do you position the piece in the horizontal band saw to cut it to the proper length?

3. Why should you place your work over a soft surface when cutting with the cold chisel?

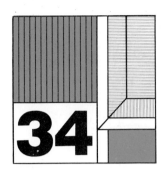

Cutting Sheet Metal

Thin metal sheets can be cut with tools such as tin snips, squaring shears, jeweler's saws, and hand punches.

Tin Snips

Tin snips are strong short-lipped hand shears generally used to cut sheet metal of 20 gauge or lighter. They come in three common types. Fig. 34-1.

- *Straight snips* are used for cutting straight lines or outside circles. Fig. 34-2.
- *Hawk-bill snips* are used for circular cutting in tight places. For example, they are used for cutting inside circles. Fig. 34-3.
- *Aviation snips* are used for straight and curved cuts. Some are especially designed for cutting to the left. Others are designed for cutting to the right. Still others are for straight or irregular cutting. Fig. 34-4.

USING HAND SNIPS
- Don't cut wire or very heavy materials with snips.
- Keep your fingers away from sharp metal edges. Never leave a jagged edge of sheet metal after cutting the piece that you need. File the edge smooth.
- Hold the snips so that you do not pinch yourself when cutting. To make a straight cut,

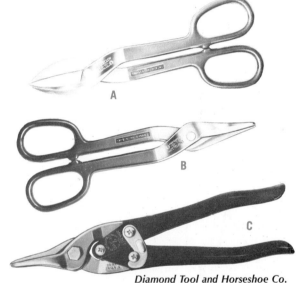

Diamond Tool and Horseshoe Co.

34-1. Tin snips. (A) Straight. (B) Hawk-bill. (C) Aviation.

34-2. Cutting metal with straight snips. Notice how the metal is held, with the cutting line easily followed.

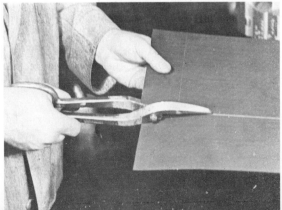

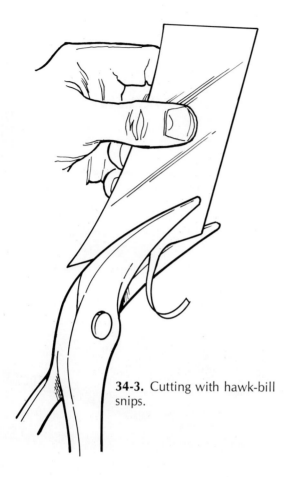

34-3. Cutting with hawk-bill snips.

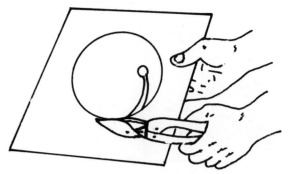

34-4. Cutting on inside opening with aviation snips.

cut to the line. The waste material will curl away.

Squaring Shears

Squaring shears may be either of the *bench* or *floor* type. The size of the shears is shown by the width of stock they can cut. A common size will cut 18″-width stock with a thickness of 20 gauge. Never use them to cut metal wire or bars. This will damage the blade. Fig. 34-5. Squaring shears have stops (or gauges) on the front, back and side of the bed of the shears. These can be adjusted to cut different metal sizes and angles.

When cutting, stock should be held firmly against the left side gauge. Squaring shears have a safety guard to keep the fingers away from the cutting edge.

Jeweler's Saws

Cutting metal from the inside of a design with a jeweler's saw is called *piercing*. Fig. 34-6. This is done mainly in art metal and jewelry work.

start with the jaws open as wide as is comfortable for your grip. Keep the blade at right angles to the work. Cut the sheet by closing the blades just short of full length. Be careful to keep the blades on line as you finish the cut.
• To cut an outside circle, first cut off the metal at the corners so that is is easier to handle. Then begin the cut, turning the metal slightly as the cut is made. Whenever possible, remove the waste material in one piece.
• To make an inside cut, use hawk-bill or aviation snips. To start the cut, punch a hole so the tool can get started. Make a rough cut to within about ⅛″ of the line. Then make a finish

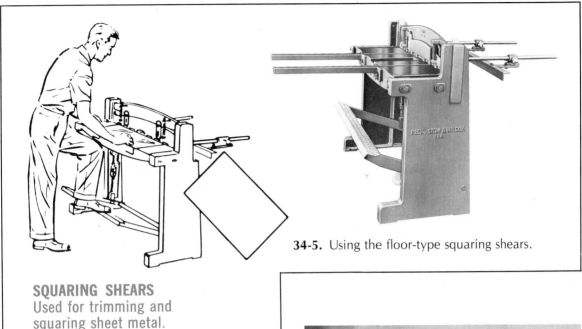

SQUARING SHEARS
Used for trimming and
squaring sheet metal.

34-5. Using the floor-type squaring shears.

The size of the jeweler's saw *frame* is measured by the *depth* of the frame. Common sizes are 2½″ deep and 5″ deep. Jeweler's saw blades come in sizes from 8/0 (smallest) to 14 (largest). The No. 0 or No. 1 size is used for most work.

To use the saw, first draw the design on the metal. Then mark the areas to be removed. Drill a small hole in one of the metal waste areas. Insert the blade through this hole. Then clamp the blade in the saw frame. A V-block should be used to hold the workpiece. The area to be cut is placed over the V, which allows the blade to move freely. When using the V-block, the saw blade should be clamped with the teeth pointing *toward* the handle. Hold the work on the V-block that is clamped in a vise. Cut by moving the saw up and down with a steady, even stroke. You can lubricate

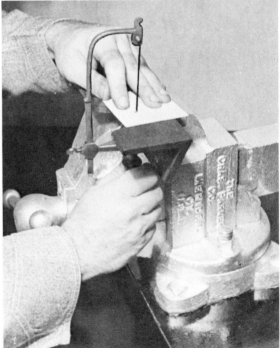

34-6. Cutting metal with a jeweler's saw. Notice that the workpiece is held firmly on the V-block. The saw is moved with the other hand.

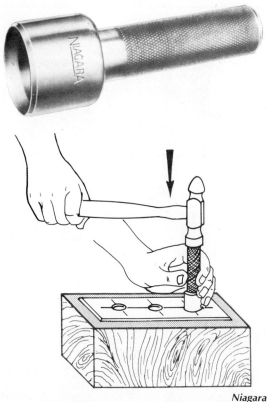

Niagara

34-7. The hollow punch. To use this tool, place the sheet metal over an end-grain hardwood block. Strike the punch firmly with a hammer.

the saw blade with beeswax or soap. Move the saw slowly, especially when you are turning a sharp corner. Otherwise you may break the blade.

PUNCHES

The hollow punch is used to cut holes in sheet metal. This tool is a hardened steel tube with sharpened edges. It has the same inside diameter as the hole to be cut in the stock. Fig. 34-7. These punches come in sizes from ¼" to 3". Industry uses punch presses. These will cut holes of various shapes and in sizes as large as 4" in diameter. These power presses can punch holes rapidly. They are used in the mass production of metal parts.

REVIEW QUESTIONS

1. List three kinds of tin snips and describe their uses.
2. What tool is used in piercing metal?
3. In what direction should the teeth of the blade point when using the jeweler's saw and a V-block?
4. What do you use to lubricate the blade of the jeweler's saw?

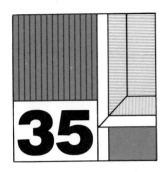

Bending Heavy Metal

Heavy metal, such as flats, rounds and tubing, can be easily bent into angular and circular shapes. Little special equipment is needed. Most metal projects made of heavy stock include these bends. Metal up to ¼" thick can be bent cold.

Most angular bends can be made with a good metal vise and a ball-peen hammer. A wrench is also helpful in making bends greater than 90°. Pieces of pipe, rod, or wood form blocks may be used for circular bends. Pliers are often needed to hold heavy metal during bending.

Making Right-angle Bends

1. Lay out the bends on the metal. Mark them with chalk or a marking pencil. Fig. 35-1. An allowance equal to half the thickness of the metal should be added to the total length for each bend you will make.

2. Place the metal in a vise. The bend line

should be even with the upper jaws. The allowance end should show above the vise. Fig. 35-2. Hold it with the left hand and push on it. At the same time strike the metal near

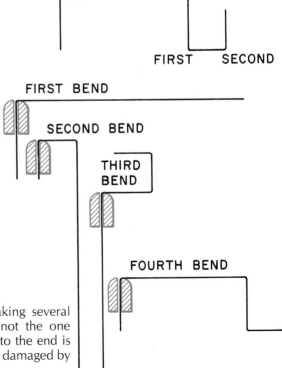

35-1. The steps to follow when making several bends. Note that the first bend is not the one closest to the end. The bend closest to the end is put in second to prevent it from being damaged by the vise.

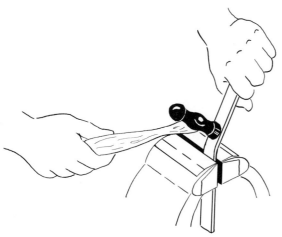

35-2. Bending strap iron in a vise. Apply pressure with one hand. Strike the metal near the vise jaws with a hammer.

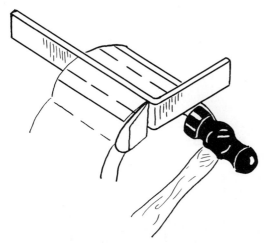

35-3. Squaring off a bend. The vise jaw serves as a metal form in shaping a right-angle bend.

the bend line with a hammer. The metal will bend evenly.

3. To finish the bend, place the metal in a vise with one edge level with the top. Fig. 35-3. Use one corner of a vise jaw as a form. Then strike the metal near the bend. This will make the bend sharp and clean.

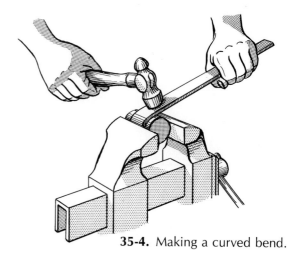

35-4. Making a curved bend.

Making Curved Bends

1. Select a piece of pipe or rod with the same diameter as the bend you want to make. Place the pipe in the vise.

2. Clamp the end of the metal between one jaw of the vise and the cylinder. Grasp the end of the metal with one hand. Pull it over the pipe to begin the curve. Continue to move the stock a little at a time, pulling it over the pipe. Then use a ball-peen hammer to form the curve. Fig. 35-4.

Making Scroll Bends

A scroll adds beauty and interest to many band iron projects. It is especially attractive if the curves are smooth and graceful. With the right tools and care a perfect scroll can be formed.

BENDING FORKS

A bending fork is used to form a scroll. A simple fork can be made from a square metal block in which holes are drilled at varying

35-5. Starting a scroll with a bending fork. Notice that only a small amount of metal is bent at once.

distances. Two steel pins are made to fit easily into these holes. These pins can be moved to allow for different metal thicknesses and types of scrolls. Fig. 35-5.

MAKING THE PATTERN

Before the scroll can be formed, a full-size pattern of the curve must be laid out on paper. Use this pattern to find the length of metal needed. Use it also to test the accuracy of the finished scroll. To find the length of metal, shape a piece of soft wire, such as wire solder, over the full-size pattern as shown in Fig. 35-6. Straightened out, this soft wire will be the correct length for the scroll.

35-6. Using a piece of wire solder to measure the length of the scroll on a full-size pattern. After the solder is bent to fit the pattern, it can be straightened out. It can then be used to measure the length of stock needed.

MAKING THE BEND

1. Flare, flatten, or decorate the end of the stock. This can be done by flattening or tapering the ends with a ball-peen hammer.

2. When starting the curve, allow the metal to extend over the edge of an anvil or bench plate. With a ball-peen hammer, strike the metal with light blows as you move it slowly forward, until the curve begins to form.

3. Adjust the steel pins in the bending fork. Place the curved end in the bending device. With your left hand hold one end of the metal and apply some pressure. Use your right hand to control the amount of bend. See Fig. 35-5. As the curve forms, move the metal through the fork a little at a time. Do not make sharp, short bends. Try instead to form a slow, even curve.

4. Check the scroll by holding it over the full-size pattern. Fig. 35-7. If the metal is bent too far, open the curve slightly. Rebend it to

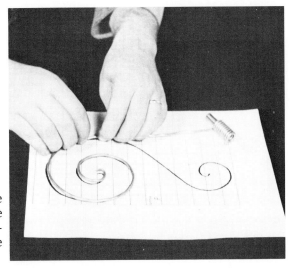

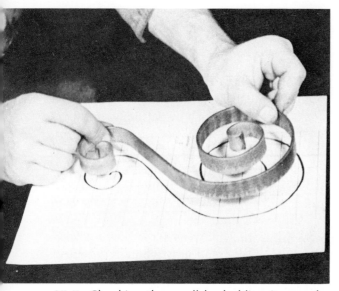

follow the pattern. As the direction of the curve changes, reverse the direction of pressure on the metal.

5. After the scroll has been formed, place it on edge between the jaws of a vise. Tap the scroll on one side or the other to align it. It should then lie flat on the bench top.

Twisting Metal

Metal can be twisted to form a spiral. This strengthens the metal. It also is a good decorative idea for tall, narrow projects.

1. Twisting shortens metal, so it is hard to know the exact length needed. You can check the "shrinkage" by making a single twist on a piece of scrap metal. Multiply this twist by the number of twists in the finished piece. Then choose the correct length of stock.

35-7. Checking the scroll by holding it over the full-size pattern. This shows whether the scroll needs to be opened or closed to match the pattern.

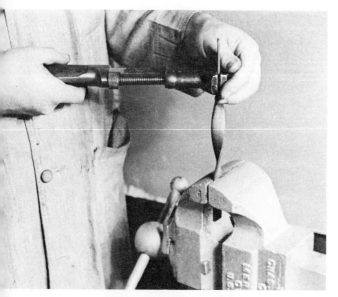

35-8. Making a short twist in metal. For a twist, the metal should be placed in a vise in a vertical position.

35-9. Bending machines are convenient and accurate for making bends in metal.

2. Place the metal vertically in a vise, with the area to be twisted above the top of the vise jaws.

3. Slip a crescent or monkey wrench over the metal at the upper limit of the area to be twisted. Tighten the jaws.

4. Guide the wrench and the metal with your left hand. At the same time, turn the handle of the wrench until the desired number of twists is formed. Apply even pressure to get an even twist. Fig. 35-8.

Using the Bending Machine

Metal can be bent more easily and accurately by machine than by hand. Bending machines are used by industry. They also are found in school shops. One such bender, accurately forms round and flat bar stock, as well as tubing. Fig. 35-9. Several accessories are used with this machine to form angles, scrolls, circles, and curves. Fig. 35-10. They can be purchased or made in the shop.

REVIEW QUESTIONS
1. Describe methods of bending and twisting metals.
2. What is a bending fork?
3. What is a bending machine?

35-10. Scrolls and other curved shapes can be formed by using the bender. The collar should have the same shape as the piece to be formed.

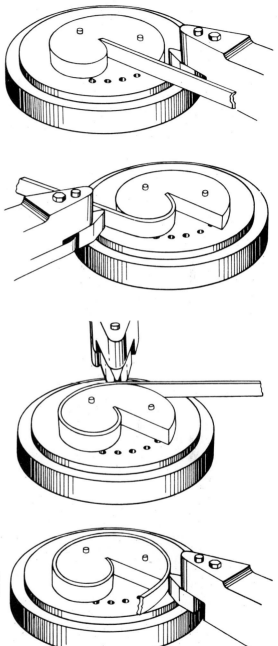

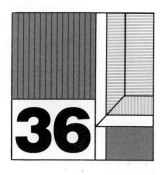

Bending Sheet Metal

Metal sheets can be bent with hand tools or with special machines. Industry uses large power equipment to form metal products. Fig. 36-1. Some of the more common tools and machines are explained in this chapter.

Equipment and Tools

Sheet-metal stakes are useful for bending sheet metals. Fig. 36-2. They can be used for bending sharp angles, cylindrical shapes, and cones. Stakes are held in a *bench plate*.

However, you do not have to have these stakes. Pieces of rod, pipe, angle iron, or rectangular bar stock can be used. The edge of a bench or a wooden form block can serve the same purpose.

A wooden, hard-rubber, plastic, or rawhide mallet should always be used for work on thin metal. A metal hammer will dent and mark the workpiece. Fig. 36-3. If metal is held in a

36-1. This motorcycle is made of many bent metal parts.
Moto Guzzi

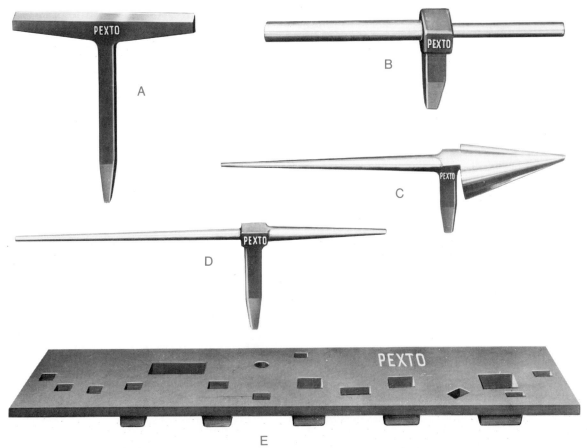

36-2. Bench plate and sheet metal stakes: (A) Hatchet. (B) Conductor. (C) Blowhorn. (D) Candle-mold. (E) Bench plate.

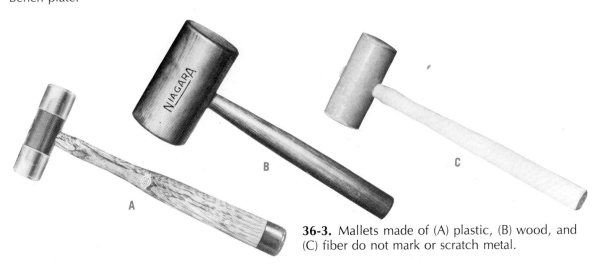

36-3. Mallets made of (A) plastic, (B) wood, and (C) fiber do not mark or scratch metal.

36-4. Making a curved bend in metal sheet by sandwiching the metal between boards clamped in vise. Start bend by hand over shaped block. If necessary, assist bending by hammering with rubber mallet.

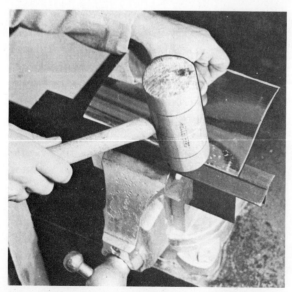

36-5. Bending metal between angle-iron jaws held in a vise. The metal is held on the edges close to the vise jaws and forced over. Finish the job with a mallet.

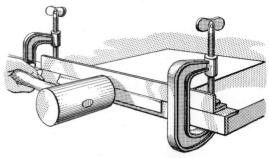

36-6. Bend-clamping method for forming a hem. The bend line and bench edge must be parallel.

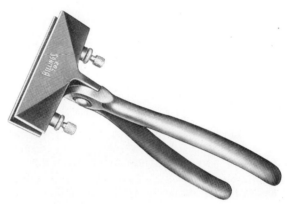

36-7. The hand seamer can be used to bend hems.

vise when it is bent, the jaws should be covered with soft metal such as copper sheet.

Some typical bending methods are shown in Figs. 36-4 and 36-5. The sheet metal hem is a narrow bend in the metal edge to stiffen the metal. A way of doing this is shown in Fig. 36-6. A hand seamer can also be used. Fig. 36-7.

SHEET METAL BENDING MACHINES

The machines usually found in the school shop are the bar folder, the brake, and forming machine.

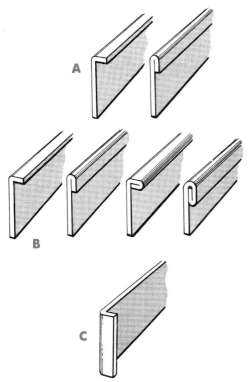

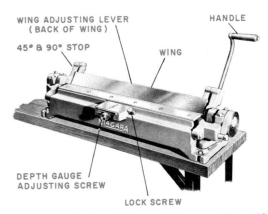

36-9. Using the bar folder or folding machine. The folding machine is used extensively for edging sheet metal or forming locks or angles.

36-8. The common bends made with the bar folder. (A) Single hem. (B) Double hem. (C) Plain lap seam fold.

The *bar folding* machine is used to fold (bend) edges of metal. It will form open and closed bends from ⅛" to 1" wide. Figure 36-8 shows some of these bends. Metal as heavy as 22 gauge can be bent on this machine. Fig. 36-9. There are two adjustments:
● The depth-gauge adjusting screw is for setting the depth of the fold.
● The wing-adjustment lever is for setting the sharpness or roundness of the bend.

The machine also has a stop bar which can be quickly set for 45° or 90° bends.

Using the Bar Folder
1. Turn the adjusting screw for the proper depth of fold. Tighten the lock screw. Set the wing adjustment lever for the desired sharpness of bend. Set 45° or 90° stops if necessary. Make a trial bend in a piece of scrap metal.

2. Insert the metal in the folder jaws. Hold it in place with your left hand.

3. Pull the handle with your right hand until the bend is completed. Release it gently. Don't let it snap back.

Single hems may be closed on the bar folder. To do this, place the metal on the flat bed of the folder. Make sure the hem is up. Pull the handle sharply to close the hem.

The *brake* is a machine for making bends and folded edges on larger and heavier pieces of metal than are worked on the bar folder.

The *cornice brake* is a very large heavy-duty machine. The *box and pan brake* is smaller and is generally used in school shops. Fig. 36-10. They are simple to operate.

1. Lift the clamping bar handle and insert the metal. The bending line must be directly under the front edge of the clamping bar.

2. Tighten the clamping bar by pulling the handle.

3. Lift the bending wing lever until you have the proper bend angle. Bend a few

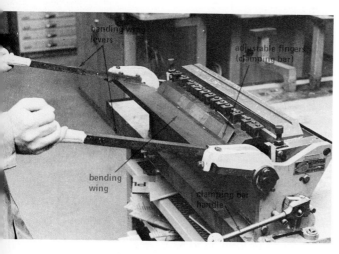

36-10. Using the box and pan brake.

degrees beyond this angle because the metal will spring back slightly.

4. Boxes can be formed by adjusting the fingers on the clamping bar to the inside width of the box. The cornice brake has no such fingers.

The *forming machine* bends cylinders and cones quickly. Such machines are also called *forming rolls*. Metal as thick as 22 gauge and 36″ wide can be formed on the machine. Fig. 36-11. This machine has three rolls. The lower roll is set to the thickness of the metal against the top roll. Use the front adjustment screws for this setting. The back, or *idler*, roll does the actual forming of the metal. This is set with the back adjustment screws. One end of the top roll can be released to remove a

cylinder after rolling. Use the release handle for this adjustment. Some machines have grooves in the rolls when pieces of metal with wired edges are to be formed. This machine is used as follows:

1. Lock the top roll-release handle. Set the lower roll to the thickness of the metal. Be sure that it it parallel to the top roll.

2. Set the back roll to form the cylinder. It should also be parallel to the top roll.

3. Insert the sheet between the top and

36-11. Using the forming rolls or forming machine.

bottom rolls. As the rolls catch it, raise it slightly. This will start the forming. Then lower the sheet so the back roll will catch it.

4. Continue turning the handle until the cylinder is formed. If the diameter is not correct, set the back roll in closer and roll the cylinder again. Release the top roll to remove the cylinder.

To form cone shapes, hold onto one corner of the metal so that the other edge goes through faster.

1. What is a hand seamer? How is it used?
2. List four sheet-metal stakes.
3. What is the purpose of a hem in metal-work?
4. What adjustments must be made on the bar folder? The slip roll forming machine?
5. How are cones formed on the slip roll former?
6. What is the purpose of the grooves on the forming machine?

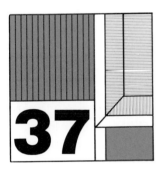

Drilling

A common but very important operation in metalworking is the drilling or cutting of round holes.

Drilling is the first step in installing the screws, bolts, and rivets needed to fasten parts together.

Drilling Machines and Equipment

A bench or floor type *drill press* is the most common machine for drilling operations. Fig.

37-1. The largest workpiece a drill press can handle is determined by measuring the distance from the drill chuck and bit to the support column.

A chuck holds straight-shank twist drills. The shank is the end that fits into the chuck, or holder. On larger drill presses, a taper-shank drill fits directly into the spindle or is held by a sleeve or socket.

The *electric hand drill* has a pistol-grip handle on which the on-off switch is located. Fig. 37-2. Light electric hand drills take

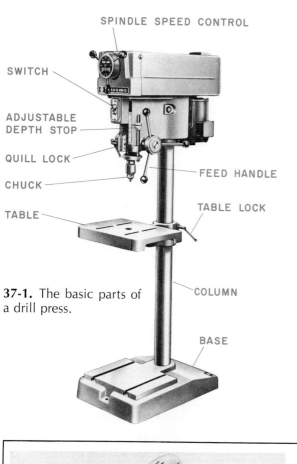

SPINDLE SPEED CONTROL

SWITCH

ADJUSTABLE
DEPTH STOP

QUILL LOCK

CHUCK

TABLE

FEED HANDLE

TABLE LOCK

COLUMN

BASE

37-1. The basic parts of a drill press.

straight-shank drills up to ¼" in diameter. Heavier ones may take twist drills up to ½". The manual hand drill is used much the same as the electric hand drill. Fig. 37-2. Hand drills usually found in school shops can take drills up to ⅜".

A *drill press vise* is used to hold workpieces. Fig. 37-3. Other clamping and holding devices such as wrenches, pliers, and C-clamps are also useful for safely holding work to be drilled. A V-block is used when drilling round stock.

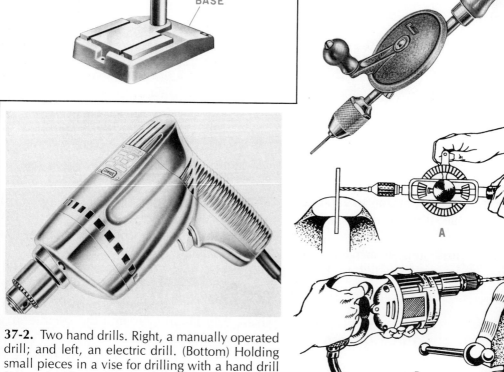

A

B

37-2. Two hand drills. Right, a manually operated drill; and left, an electric drill. (Bottom) Holding small pieces in a vise for drilling with a hand drill (A), and with an electric drill (B).

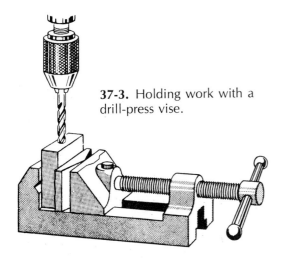

37-3. Holding work with a drill-press vise.

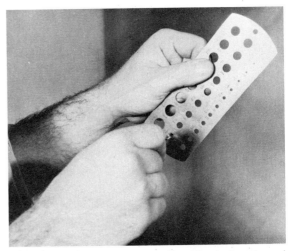

37-5. The drill gauge is used to check the size of twist drills.

Twist drills are made of high-speed steel. Fig. 37-4. They are marked HS or HSS. Straight shanks fit into a chuck. Taper-shank drills are used on larger drilling machines and lathes.

Customary drill sizes are shown by *number*, *letter*, and *fraction*. Number (wire gauge) sizes range in diameter from the smallest, No. 80 to the largest, No. 1. Letter sizes range from the smallest, A, to the largest, Z. Fractional sizes range from 1/64″ upwards by 64ths. Fractional drills are used for most work. Sometimes number and letter drills are needed for accurate tapping or reaming.

Common metric sets of twist drills range in size from 1 mm to 12 mm.

DRILLING WITH THE DRILL PRESS

1. Select the correct drill for the hole to be made. Fasten the drill in the chuck. A drill gauge may be used to check the size of a drill. Fig. 37-5. Be certain that the drill is placed straight in the chuck jaws before you tighten them. Otherwise the drill will wobble and not run true.

2. Locate the hole to be drilled by drawing two short, intersecting lines. Use a center punch to make a small dent where they meet.

3. Fasten the work securely on the table of the drill press. If it is a small piece, clamp it in

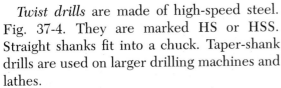

37-4. Twist drills. (A) Tapered-shank twist drill. (B) Straight shank twist drill.

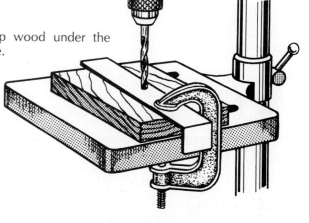

37-6. Place a piece of scrap wood under the workpiece to protect the table.

a vise. Hold a larger piece with a C-clamp. For small, thin sheet metal, hold the stock with pliers. Be sure that the drill is directly over the hole in the table of the drill press. A piece of scrap wood placed beneath the drill will protect the table. Fig. 37-6.

4. Adjust the speed according to the drill size and the material. For a fast speed, use the largest pulley on the motor and the smallest pulley on the drill. Use fast speeds for small-diameter drills and soft metals. Use slower speeds for larger drills and harder metals. Many machines have a variable speed control. Turn the handle to the desired speed as shown on the dial face.

5. Turn on the power. Apply even pressure on the feed handle to cut the hole. Use cutting oil as needed.

6. As the point of the drill begins to cut through, reduce the pressure to ease the drill through the hole. This is especially important in drilling sheet metal. If it is not done, the drill may dig in too deeply. Then metal will spin dangerously or the drill will break off.

7. In drilling large holes, first use a small drill to make a *pilot hole*. Then use a larger drill to complete the hole.

COUNTERSINKING

Countersinking enlarges one end of a drilled hole to a cone shape. It is used for installing a countersunk rivet, a flathead machine screw, or a bolt. Fig. 37-7. It is also done when getting stock ready to turn on a lathe. The most common countersink has an 82° cutting surface. Use a slow speed and a light feed. Make sure the work is held tightly so the tool does not chatter. Enlarge the diameter of the hole so that the head of the fastener will be flush with the surface of the metal.

REVIEW QUESTIONS

1. What are the three ways in which customary twist drill sizes are shown?
2. What is the drill press used for?
3. What holds the twist drill on a drill press?

37-7. A countersink.

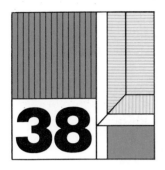

Filing and Grinding

Files and grinders are used to remove metal from a workpiece that has been shaped by some other tool, such as a chisel or hacksaw. Abrasives are used to smooth and polish metal. They will all be discussed in this unit.

Files

Files vary in length, shape, type of cut, and coarseness of cut.

- *Length.* Regular files range in length from 3″ to 20″. The 10″ file is best for general use.
- *Shape.* Common shapes of files are rectangular, square, round, half-round, and triangular.
- *Type of Cut.* The type of cut indicates the way teeth are formed on the file face. Fig. 38-1. A *single-cut* file has the teeth cut in one direction. This file is good for finishing work. A *double-cut* file has two rows of teeth cut in opposite directions. This file is used to remove large amounts of metal quickly. A *curved-tooth* file is used on soft metal, such as aluminum and copper, because its teeth do not clog easily. A *rasp* has separate, shaped teeth. It is used on wood and very soft metals.
- *Coarseness.* Coarseness indicates the number of teeth on the file in relation to its length. The six common grades of coarseness are rough, coarse, bastard, second cut, smooth, and dead smooth.

38-1. The cut of the file means the way the teeth are formed on the file face. Four file cuts are shown here. (A) Single cut. (B) Double cut. (C) Rasp cut. (D) Curved cut.

A   B   C   D

KINDS OF FILES

Of the several hundred kinds and sizes of files, only a few are needed by most metalworkers. The following, shown in Figs. 38-2 and 38-3, are commonly used.

• The *mill file* (A) is used for drawfiling, finish filing, shaping, and tool sharpening.

• The *triangular file* (B) is double cut. It is used for forming grooves, squaring holes, and filing in sharp corners.

• The *hand file* (C) is double cut. One edge has no teeth, to allow filing in corners when one surface should not be filed.

• The *half-round file* (D) is double cut. It has a flat side used for filing on flat and convex (curved outward) surfaces. The rounded back is good for filing concave (curved inward) surfaces.

• The *round file* (E) is used for dressing the inside of holes and curves.

• The *curved-tooth file* (F) is used on copper, brass, and aluminum. The teeth are not easily clogged.

• The *needle,* or *jeweler's, file* is for very fine filing. Fig. 38-3. It is made in a wide variety of shapes, sizes, and degrees of coarseness.

USING FILES

Follow these suggestions when using files.

• Be sure to have a handle on the file, for safety. Fig. 38-4.

• Keep the file clean with a file card or brush. This will keep the file from gouging and scratching the workpiece.

• Whenever possible, mount the workpiece in a vise. This makes filing easy, safer, and

38-2. Files commonly used in the shop. (A) Mill. (B) Triangular. (C) Hand. (D) Half round. (E) Round. (F) Curved tooth.

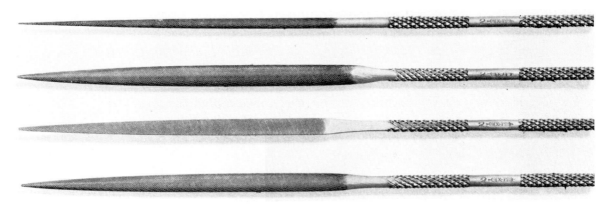

38-3. Needle, or jeweler's, files.

38-4. Before using a file, be sure that it has a tightly fitting handle. The handle will prevent injury from the sharp tang. To put a handle on the file, first select a handle large enough for the tang. Then insert the tang in the hole in the handle. Tap the butt end of the handle on the bench to drive the file into place.

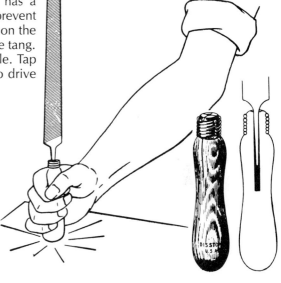

38-5. In straight-filing the file is held at both ends. This setup is being used to form the cutting edge of a letter opener.

more accurate. For straight-filing, hold the file as shown in Fig. 38-5. Apply pressure on the forward stroke only.

● *Drawfiling* can be used to give a very smooth surface. This filing is done with a single-cut file. Fig. 38-6.

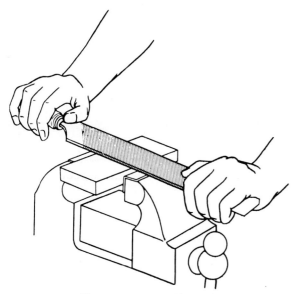

38-6. Drawfiling gives small surfaces smooth square edges or accurately finishes flat surfaces. When drawfiling, hold the file at right angles to the work. Push the file back and forth parallel to the metal surface. Keep the file in contact with the work at all times.

Abrasives

An *abrasive* is a hard substance used to wear away a softer material. Abrasives are crushed into small grains having sharp cutting edges. Each grain of abrasive is actually a cutting tool like a saw or chisel. These abrasive grains are used to make grinding wheels. They are also glued to belts, discs, and sheets to form a metal-cutting "sandpaper." These are called *coated abrasives*.

KINDS OF ABRASIVES

Emery is a natural, black abrasive that is seldom used today. More commonly, aluminum oxide (gray-brown) and silicon carbide (shiny-black) manufactured abrasives are used. They are sharp, tough, and durable. Aluminum oxide is used for most grinding wheels and abrasives for steel. Silicon carbide is used on softer metals. Abrasives are graded according to the grit numbers given in Table 38-A. Abrasives are graded into grit sizes by sifting them through screens. Each screen is of a certain size.

Grinding

GRINDER SAFETY

• Make sure that the grinder has protective shields. Always keep these shields in place. For added safety, wear goggles or a protective face mask. The fine particles of abrasive and

Table 38-A. Comparative Grit Numbers

	Very Coarse	Coarse	Medium	Fine	Very Fine
Aluminum Oxide Silicon Carbide	12 16 20 24 30	36 40	50 60 80 100	120 150 180	220 240 280 320 360 400 500 600
Emery		3 2½	2 1½ 1 ½	0 2/0 3/0	

NOTE: Emery grit number 1 is directly under grit number 80 for aluminum oxide and silicon carbide. This indicates that the coarseness of these abrasives is the same. Similarly, grit number 3 (emery) is between 30 and 36 because it is finer than 30 but more coarse than 36.

38-7. Using a star wheel dresser.

metal that fly from the wheel can cause eye injuries.

• Adjust the tool rest edge so that it is from $\frac{1}{16}''$ to $\frac{1}{8}''$ from the face of the wheel. It is dangerous to have too great a space between the wheel and the tool rest. Pieces of metal can become wedged between the revolving wheel and the rest, causing damage to the grinder and injury to the worker.

• Always grind with the face of the wheel, not the side. Heavy pressure on the side of the wheel may break it.

• Keep the water pot on the grinder full. When grinding or sharpening a tool, dip it in the water to keep it cool. It is important to keep the cutting edges of tools cool when grinding. If the cutting edge becomes overheated, it will lose its hardness.

• Dress the grinding wheel to keep it true, even, and clean. Fig. 38-7.

USING THE GRINDER

Hand grinding includes the rough shaping of metal pieces and the sharpening of small tools. The hand grinding of steel parts of tools is usually done on a bench or floor grinder. In many shops there are two machines. These machines are a small bench grinder for tool

grinding only and a larger, floor-type grinder for general pupose work. Fig. 38-8.

To use the grinder, hold the metal firmly against the tool rest. Then press the metal against the revolving wheel. Fig. 38-9. Move it back and forth across the wheel face so that the grinding is done evenly. To round an end, hold the metal on the tool rest. Move the back of the metal in an arc while keeping the end to be rounded in contact with the wheel.

When grinding points and edges of tools, check frequently to be sure they hold the right shape. Use a gauge to check this. Correct shapes of common tools are shown in this book. When sharpening chisels, remember to grind the "mushroom" heads.

38-8. A floor grinder for general grinding and tool sharpening.

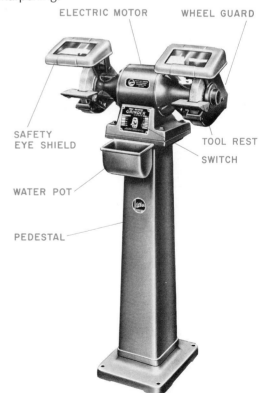

38-9. Grinding a rounded end on a metal work-piece.

Polishing and Buffing

Polishing and buffing improve the appearance of a project.

Polishing is fine grinding in which metal surfaces are smoothed by coated abrasive belts or wheels covered with abrasive materials. When finishing kitchen utensils and machine tools, polishing is often the final step. If the item is to be buffed, this is done after polishing.

Buffing further smooths a metal surface and brings out a high luster.

SAFETY IN POLISHING AND BUFFING
• Wear safety goggles.
• Never polish or buff small parts without clamping them in a holder.
• Hold the work firmly against the wheel or belt. When necessary, wear gloves to protect your hands.
• Hold the work below the center of the wheel so the sharp edges and corners will not catch. Always buff or polish *over* an edge, never to an edge. Fig. 38-10.
• Never attempt to polish or buff sharp articles such as knives. They may catch in the wheel and cause a serious accident.
• Never wear loose clothing when polishing and buffing.

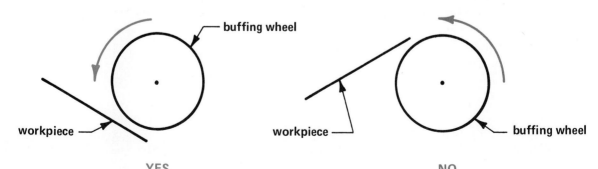

YES   NO

38-10. In polishing and buffing a workpiece, hold it as shown. If the workpiece is held incorrectly, it may catch on the buffing wheel.

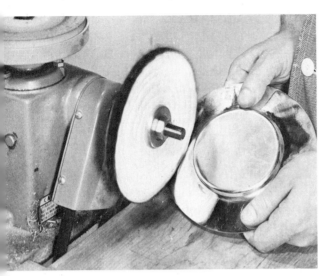

38-11. Buffing a copper dish. Make sure you wear safety glasses. Hold the work firmly against the surface of the wheel.

● Never stand near a revolving buffer unless you are working with it.

POLISHING AND BUFFING OPERATIONS

Polishing is done on a belt or disc sanding machine. Be sure that the machine is set up for polishing metal, and not for sanding wood. Number 40 (coarse), No. 80 (medium), or No. 120 (fine) grit abrasives are generally used. When using the polishing machine, wear goggles. Touch the workpiece gently to the belt or disc. Do not overheat the metal. Hand polishing can also be done with abrasive paper.

Buffing is done by holding the work against a flexible wheel. Fine abrasive materials have been applied to the wheel, using glue or some other material as a binder. Plated objects and nonferrous metals are often buffed.

A *buffing machine* is shown in Fig. 38-11. Buffing wheels are made of stitched pieces of cotton, muslin, chamois, or flannel. *Buffing compounds* are bars of emery, tripoli, rouge, pumice, rottenstone, and whiting.

Apply the compound to the wheel as it is rotating. Press the bar or stick of compound lightly on the wheel until the entire edge is treated. Hold the article to be buffed in a slanting position. Press it lightly against the wheel. Move it back and forth and up and down until the desired finish is obtained.

REVIEW QUESTIONS

1. What are the four ways in which files are classified?
2. Why should a file be cleaned before being used?
3. What type of cut do the teeth on a mill file have?
4. List some safety rules to follow when grinding, polishing, and buffing.
5. List and describe three kinds of abrasives.

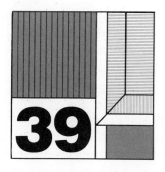

Riveting

Riveting is placing a metal pin into a hole and clinching it so there is a head at each end. These metal pins, or rivets, are permanent fasteners. They are used to fasten together two or more sheets or pieces of metal.

A head is formed on one end when the rivet is manufactured. To join two metal pieces, the shank (body) of the rivet is placed in a hole that extends through both pieces. Then the tip is pounded to form the second head.

In automobile manufacturing, riveting has been largely replaced by welding, special glues, and sheet metal screws. However, rivets are still commonly used in many industries, such as building construction. Heavy metal beams that make up the skeletons of office buildings, bridges, and similar structures are riveted. It is a cheap and quick assembly method. Aircraft and space industries use rivets in assembly because such materials as aluminum and magnesium are hard to weld. In a jet airliner thousands of rivets hold the parts together.

Kinds of Rivets

Rivets vary as to the *kind of metal*, *kind of head*, *diameter* (or *shank size*), and *length*. In ordering rivets, it is necessary to give this information completely. The following order

is complete: blackiron rivets, rounded, 1/8", 1/2" long.

Rivets are made of aluminum, copper, brass, and mild steel (blackiron). The three common head shapes are round, flat, and countersunk. Fig. 39-1.

Tinner's rivets are made for use on sheet metal. They are mild steel rivets with a flat head. They are coated with black oxide, tin, copper, or zinc. The customary size of the rivet is indicated by its weight per thousand. (A thousand of the smallest size weigh 6 ounces.) Common sizes are 10 ounce, 1 pound, 2 pound, and 2½ pound. For No. 26-gauge metal, for example, use a 1-pound rivet.

Equipment

The riveting equipment needed includes a ball-peen or riveting hammer, a rivet set, and a punch or drill. For all types of riveting

39-1. Rivet head types. (A) Flat. (B) Round. (C) Countersunk.

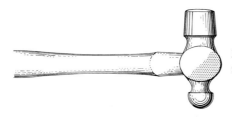

39-2. To protect the rivet head, place it in the rivet set, and peen gently.

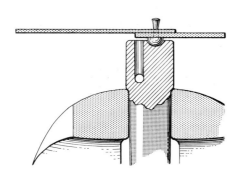

except for tinner's rivets, select a ball-peen hammer heavy enough to form a head. The rivet set has a clearance hole on one side and a concave opening next to it. The rivet set is used to squeeze two pieces of metal together before riveting. It also forms the rivet head. Select a rivet set with a hole large enough for the rivet shank to slip into easily.

The hand punch is used in joining lighter gauges of metal. Its punch should have the same diameter as the shank of the rivet. Use a drill on heavier gauges of metal.

Methods of Riveting

HEAVY METALS

1. Lay out the location of the rivet holes. The rivets should be located at least two shank diameters from the edge of the joint and at least three diameters from other rivets. Select a drill of the same diameter as the rivet shank. Drill the holes at the proper locations. It is good practice to drill all the rivet holes in one

piece first. Then drill one hole in the second piece. After one rivet has been installed, the other holes can be drilled accurately, using the top piece as a guide.

2. If countersunk rivets are used, countersink *both* pieces. Even when roundhead or flathead rivets are used, the second piece is often countersunk. Thus, the rivet can be flattened and filed off to form a flush surface. It is a good idea to countersink all holes slightly to remove the burr formed by drilling.

3. Insert the rivets in the holes. The shank should extend beyond the metal about one and one-half times the shank's diameter. If the back surface is to be countersunk and the shank flattened, about three-fourths of the shank's diameter is needed.

4. When using roundhead rivets, protect the head by placing it over a rivet block or set. Fig. 39-2. To form the second head, strike the shank squarely with the ball-peen end of the hammer. This will round off the shank. Be careful not to bend it.

RIVETING SHEET METAL

1. Lay out the locations for the rivets and then punch or drill the holes. When using the hand punch, place the metal over a block of wood. Fig. 39-3.

2. Insert a rivet in a hole. Place the workpiece over a solid metal surface.

3. With a rivet set, draw the seams together. Fig. 39-4.

4. Strike the rivet with the hammer to set the rivet enough to hold the pieces together. Fig. 39-5.

39-3. Punching holes in metal with a hand punch. The metal is placed over the end grain of a piece of hardwood.

5. Place the concave portion of the rivet set over the rivet and head it. One or two blows will usually be enough.

RIVETING WITH A POP RIVETER

The easiest and fastest method of riveting is to use a tool called a *pop riveter*. This tool eliminates the need for setting and flattening rivets by hand. With the pop riveter, rivets can be installed in holes where there is not enough space to use regular riveting tools.

Unlike hand-installed rivets, pop rivets are hollow. They have a flange that grips the work on one end and a pin, or mandrel, which is set in the riveter. The body of the rivet is placed in the hole. By squeezing the handles of the riveter, the mandrel is pulled out of the rivet body until it breaks away from the ball-like head. By this time the head is firmly imbedded in the rivet body and the rivet is securely installed.

Always use pop rivets of the same metal as the metal in the product to be joined. Rivets

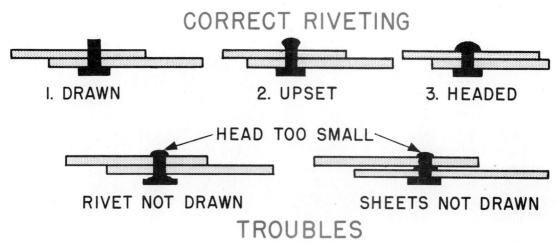

CORRECT RIVETING

1. DRAWN   2. UPSET   3. HEADED

HEAD TOO SMALL

RIVET NOT DRAWN   SHEETS NOT DRAWN

TROUBLES

39-4. Correct and incorrect riveting.

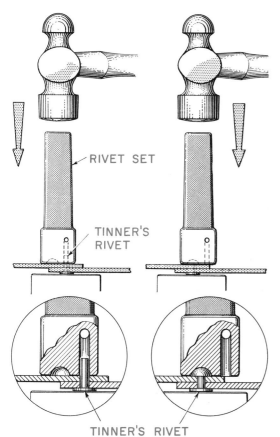

39-5. Using the rivet set to draw and head a tinner's rivet.

are available in diameters of ³⁄₃₂″, ⅛″, ⁵⁄₃₂″, ³⁄₁₆″, and ¼″. They are made of aluminum, steel, copper, and stainless steel.

USING THE POP RIVETER

Drill a hole in the two parts to be joined using the correct size drill. Insert the pointed end of the rivet mandrel into the rivet tool. Fig. 39-6. Place the rivet in the drilled hole. As you operate the tool, the mandrel head is pulled into the rivet body. This expands it into a blind rivet and securely clamps the materials to be joined. Fig. 39-7. The mandrel is separated from the body and ejected. The tool is now ready for the next rivet.

REVIEW QUESTIONS

1. What metals are commonly used to make rivets?
2. How do you protect the round heads of rivets when riveting?
3. Make a sketch of the three common rivet head shapes.

39-6. Using a pop riveter to install rivets in a sheet metal box.

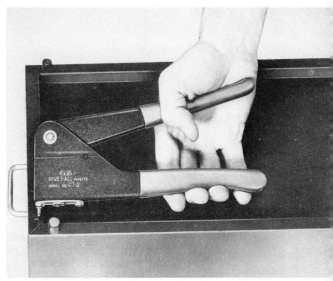

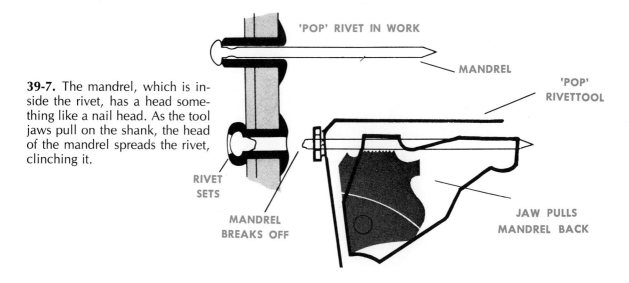

'POP' RIVET IN WORK

MANDREL

'POP'
RIVETTOOL

39-7. The mandrel, which is inside the rivet, has a head something like a nail head. As the tool jaws pull on the shank, the head of the mandrel spreads the rivet, clinching it.

RIVET
SETS

MANDREL
BREAKS OFF

JAW PULLS
MANDREL BACK

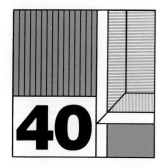

Threads and Fasteners

If you look closely at a piece of machinery, you will find that many of its parts are joined by bolts, nuts, and other threaded fasteners. Industry uses threaded fasteners for the following three reasons:

1. With threaded fasteners, the machinery can be taken apart for repairs, and reassembled without damaging any of the parts.

2. Threaded parts can be used for fine adjustments such as controlling the lens of a camera.

3. Threads can exert force through movement. The screw on a clamp is a good example of this.

Common Threaded Fasteners

Threaded fasteners are made in hundreds of different shapes and in inch and metric sizes. The most common head styles are shown in Fig. 40-1. Threaded fasteners are made of

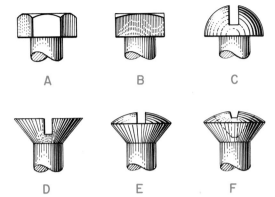

40-1. Common head styles for threaded fasteners. (A) Hexagon. (B) Square. (C) Round. (D) Flat. (E) Oval. (F) Phillips.

many different metals and platings (metal coatings). For example, fasteners used in home appliances often are chrome plated for appearance.

For assembling with many types of bolts and screws, washers and nuts are needed. Fig. 40-2. Nuts come in many sizes and shapes. Washers are *plain*, which protects the surfaces of metal pieces. They also are of the *lock type*, which prevents a fastener from becoming loose.

You will be using many fasteners in your metalworking classes. Let's look at a few of the more common ones.

● *Machine bolts and nuts* are made in diameters from ¼″ to 1″ and in lengths from ½″ to over 30″. They are used to fasten metal parts together. The bolt head can be held with a wrench as the nut is tightened.

● *Cap screws* are not used with nuts. They are used to hold together two pieces of machinery. The screw is passed through an unthreaded hole in one piece. It is screwed into a tapped hole in the second piece.

● *Machine screws* are smaller than nuts and bolts. They are used to assemble small mechanical and electrical parts.

● *Setscrews* hold two parts together to prevent one part from moving or turning. For example, they are used to hold a pulley on a shaft. They come in a variety of head and point shapes.

● A *stud* is a headless fastener that is threaded on both ends. The threaded parts may have different diameters. The wheel on an automobile is held on by nuts tightened onto studs.

● *Self-tapping screws* are made of hard steel. They are designed to cut their own threads in softer metals, such as galvanized sheet and

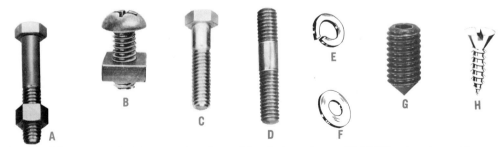

40-2. Threaded fasteners. (A) Hexagon-head machine bolt and nut. (B) Phillips-head machine screw and nut. (C) Hexagon-head cap screw. (D) Stud. (E) Lock washer. (F) Plain flat washer. (G) Cone-point socket setscrew. (H) Flathead self-tapping screw.

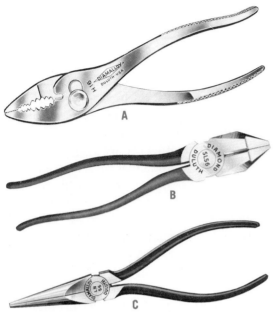

40-3. Pliers. (A) Slip joint. (B) Side cutting. (C) Long nose.

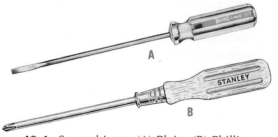

40-4. Screwdrivers. (A) Plain. (B) Phillips.

40-5. Wrenches. (A) Monkey. (B) Adjustable. (C) Pipe. (D) Open. (E) Box.

aluminum or in plastics. They have many styles of heads and points.

Tools for Threaded Fasteners

PLIERS

Pliers are ideal for holding and turning round pieces. Fig. 40-3. They *should not* be used on the heads of bolts and nuts because they will damage the head shape. The following are some common types of pliers.

- *Slip joint.* General purpose tool with good gripping power.
- *Side cutting.* For use in electrical work or whenever wire must be cut.
- *Long nose,* or *needle.* For holding very small parts, or for working in tight places.

SCREWDRIVERS

There are two types of screwdrivers.

BOLT   NUT

40-6. External threads are shown on the bolt. The cutaway view of the nut shows its internal threads.

- *Plain.* For use on slotted-head screws.
- *Phillips head.* For use on recessed-head screws. Fig. 40-4.

The screwdriver is made to tighten and loosen screws. It should not be used as a chisel, punch, or prybar.

WRENCHES

Wrenches are used to tighten nuts and bolts. They are also used to hold metal parts. Some common types of wrenches are shown in Fig. 40-5.

Cutting Threads

Threading is the cutting of a spiral groove around the outside of a bolt or shaft or on the inside of a nut or of a hole in metal. Fig. 40-6. A *tap* is the tool used to cut internal or inside threads. A *die* is used for cutting external or outside threads.

Many kinds of threads are used in industry. The most common series are National Coarse (NC) and National Fine (NF). Table 40-A. For the same diameter bolt or nut, the National Fine has more threads per inch than the National Coarse.

For example, a ¼″ diameter National Coarse has twenty threads per inch, while a ¼″ National Fine has twenty-eight threads. Below the ¼″ size, machine-screw thread sizes

are used. For example, an 8-32 machine screw is made from No. 8 wire as measured by the American screw wire gauge. It has thirty-two threads per inch. Metric threads are also used. Most threaded fasteners on automobiles are metric.

The coarse thread is the most common metric series. These are shown in Table 40-B. Metric fine threads have special uses. They are used on the tiny screws on eyeglasses and telescopes. The proper way to write the description (or specification) of a thread is shown in Fig. 40-7.

The diameter of a thread is measured with a drill gauge, hole gauge, or micrometer. The reading will be in inches or millimetres, depending upon the instrument used.

To measure the pitch of customary threads, place an inch rule along the threads. Count the number of grooves or threads in one inch. This will give the number of threads per inch, or the pitch. Thread gauges are also used. Fig. 40-8. Metric pitch is the distance between threads.

Table 40-A. Common Thread and Tap Drill Sizes

National Fine		National Coarse	
Size and Thread	Tap Drill	Size and Thread	Tap Drill
4–48	#42 (0.094)	4–40	#43 (0.089)
5–44	37 (0.104)	5–40	38 (0.102)
6–40	33 (0.113)	6–32	36 (0.107)
8–36	29 (0.136)	8–32	29 (0.136)
10–32	21 (0.159)	10–24	25 (0.150)
¼–28	3 (0.213)	¼–20	7 (0.201)
⁵⁄₁₆–24	"I" (0.272)	⁵⁄₁₆–18	"F" (0.257)
⅜–24	"Q" (0.332)	⅜–16	⁵⁄₁₆ (0.313)
⁷⁄₁₆–20	²⁵⁄₆₄ (0.391)	⁷⁄₁₆–14	"U" (0.368)
½–20	²⁹⁄₆₄ (0.453)	½–13	²⁷⁄₆₄ (0.422)

Diameter mm	Pitch mm	Tap Drill* mm	Diameter mm	Pitch mm	Tap Drill* mm
M1.6	0.35	1.25	M20	2.5	17.50
M2	0.40	1.60	M24	3.0	21.00
M2.5	0.45	2.05	M30	3.5	26.50
M3	0.50	2.50	M36	4.0	32.00
M3.5	0.60	2.90	M42	4.5	37.50
M4	0.70	3.30	M48	5.0	43.00
M5	0.80	4.20	M56	5.5	50.50
M6	1.00	5.00	M64	6.0	58.00
M8	1.25	6.75	M72	6.0	66.00
M10	1.50	8.50	M80	6.0	74.00
M12	1.75	10.25	M90	6.0	84.00
M14	2.00	12.00	M100	6.0	94.00
M16	2.00	14.00			

Table 40-B.
Metric Thread Sizes

* To get the tap drill size, subtract the pitch from the diameter.

COMPARISON OF COMMON THREAD SIZES

ISO METRIC THREAD   UNIFIED NATIONAL

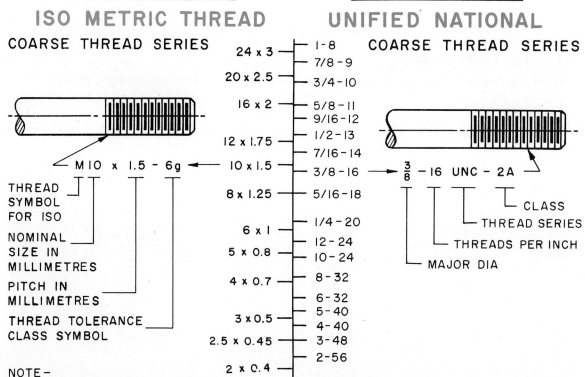

NOTE—
THE METRIC THREAD ILLUSTRATED IS A LITTLE LARGER IN DIAMETER THAN 3/8"
AND HAS ALMOST 17 THREADS PER INCH. (NOT TO SCALE)

40-7. Note how the descriptions of each kind of thread are written. The class of fit usually is omitted.

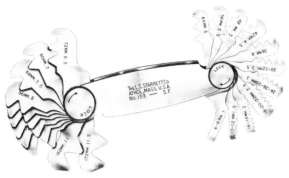

40-8. A thread gauge.

Thread-Cutting

Tools for cutting threads are shown in Fig. 40-9.

Hand taps, for cutting internal threads, are made as *taper*, *plug*, or *bottoming* taps. For a hole extending through a piece of metal, a taper tap is used. When cutting threads to the bottom of a closed hole, a taper tap is used first. Then a plug tap and, finally, a bottoming tap are used. Taps are held in a tap wrench.

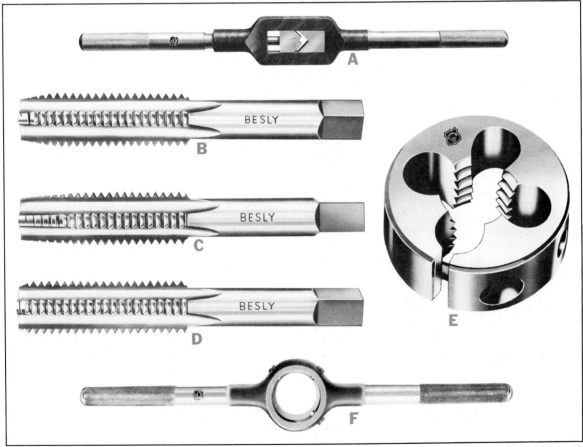

40-9. Tools for cutting threads. (A) Tap wrench. (B) Plug tap. (C) Taper tap. (D) Bottoming tap. (E) Die. (F) Die stock. Remember to use a cutting oil when cutting threads. This makes threading easier and prevents tap and die breakage.

Dies are used for cutting external threads. Dies are held in a *diestock*. A complete set of the common taps and dies in a wooden carrying case is called a *screwplate*. The size of the tap is stamped on the shank. The die size is shown on the face side.

TAPPING

In tapping, follow these steps.

1. Select the correct size of tap. Insert it in a tap wrench.

2. Select the correct tap drill.

3. Lay out and drill the hole for tapping.

4. Hold the tap square with the work. Fig. 40-10. Turn the tap until the thread catches. Then apply steady pressure and give the tap one more turn. Apply a few drops of cutting oil near the point of the tap. Only steady, even pressure should be applied because the thread pulls the tap into the hole.

5. When the threads have been cut, back the tap off and clean out the hole. Test the threaded hole by inserting a screw or threaded rod.

CUTTING EXTERNAL THREADS

1. Grind or file a *chamfer* (slanted surface across part of an edge) at the end of the stock. This helps to protect the finished thread and aids in starting the die.

2. Fit the proper die in the diestock, with the tapered portion of the die toward the guide collar.

3. Fasten the piece to be threaded in a vise. Apply a few drops of oil.

4. With one hand, hold the die over the workpiece. Turn the die to get it started. After the thread has started, apply even pressure to both handles. Turn the die about one complete turn. Fig. 40-11. Then back it off slightly.

5. Continue to cut the threads until the

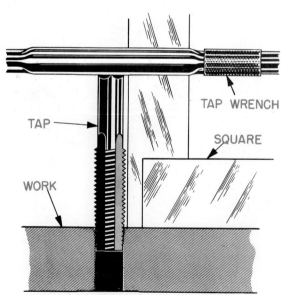

40-10. Make sure that the tap is square with the workpiece.

40-11. Cutting external threads with a die. Apply even pressure on both sides of the diestock.

desired length is reached. Remove the die and carefully clear away the chips. Test the piece in the threaded hole.

REVIEW QUESTIONS

1. Tell the special use for each of the following fasteners: (a) machine screws, (b) cap screws, (c) machine bolts, and (d) set screws.

2. Why should you not use pliers to tighten nuts and bolts?
3. For what is the tap used?
4. What tool is used for cutting external threads?
5. What is the correct tap drill to use for cutting a ¼-20 thread?

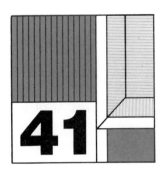

Soldering, Brazing, and Welding

Soldering, brazing, and welding are three common ways of fastening metal parts together using heat.

Soldering

Soldering is joining metal parts with a filler metal, called *solder*, at temperatures below 800°F. Soldering differs from welding in that the metals joined are not actually melted. Because of this, the melting point of the solder must be lower than that of the metal workpieces.

Soldering is not difficult if a few simple rules are followed. First, the metal to be soldered must be clean. Second, a *flux* must be used. This will prevent oxidation and help the flow of the solder. Third, enough heat must be applied to melt the solder. Fourth, the correct solder must be used for the job.

SOLDERING EQUIPMENT

The following tools to provide heat for soldering are commonly found in the shop:

• The *soldering copper* is heated in a gas furnace. Fig. 41-1.

• An *electric soldering copper* is convenient to use. Fig. 41-2. These coppers range from 50 to 300 watts. The 200-watt copper is a good

41-1. A gas furnace and soldering coppers.

41-3. A propane gas soldering torch.

size for most sheet-metal soldering. Small electric soldering guns are also used for electrical work.

• A *propane torch* is used for soldering copper tubing and general sheet-metal work. Fig. 41-3.

Soft solders for most metals, such as galvanized iron, tin plate, and copper, are made from a combination of tin and lead. They are available in bar and wire forms. A good solder to use is fifty-fifty, or half-and-half, solder which melts at about 414°F. Fluxes are used to keep the metal clean while soldering. They also help the solder spread evenly. Acid flux and rosin paste fluxes are generally used. Rosin fluxes must be used in electrical work to stop the parts from corroding. Some solder wire has a hollow core filled with flux.

TINNING A SOLDERING COPPER

A soldering copper must be tinned (coated with solder) if it is to do its job properly. This is done by filing the point clean, and then heating the copper. Rub the point of the heated copper on a cake of sal ammoniac. Then apply a few drops of solder until the tip is coated. The copper is now ready for use.

41-2. An electric soldering copper.

SOLDERING A JOINT

1. Place the pieces to be soldered over a bench that has a heat-resistant top.

2. Heat the soldering copper. A copper is hot enough if it makes a "frying" sound when rubbed on the sal ammoniac block. Never allow a copper to become red hot.

3. Apply the correct flux.

4. Press the copper to one end of the seam until its heat melts the solder it touches. This is called *tacking*. Don't let the solder melt on the soldering copper.

5. Tack the seam at both ends. Then start at one end and hold the copper flat against the seam until the solder starts to flow freely. Apply a little solder beneath the copper and push or draw the copper slowly along the seam. Make sure that the solder melts and spreads correctly. Sometimes a tool or other piece of metal can be used to hold the pieces together while the solder is hot. Fig. 41-4.

Brazing

Brazing is a form of soldering that uses a gas torch to produce heat. The metals to be joined are not melted in brazing. Instead, another piece of metal, called a *brazing rod*, is melted onto the edges of the pieces to be joined. When this molten metal hardens, the joint is formed.

BRAZING EQUIPMENT AND MATERIALS

Brazing equipment consists of a cylinder of oxygen, a cylinder of acetylene, two regulators, two lengths of hose with fittings, and a welding torch with assorted tips. Fig. 41-5. You will also need a spark lighter to light the torch, goggles to protect your eyes, a welding table with a firebrick top, and clamps to hold the work. You should wear gloves to protect your hands.

To braze, you need a brazing rod, usually of copper alloy or silver, and a matching flux. Rods and fluxes, are available for brazing on many types of metals and at many temperatures.

LIGHTING AND ADJUSTING THE WELDING TORCH

Your teacher may prefer one way to light and shut off the welding torch. Check with your teacher before performing either of these operations. Following is one way of lighting, adjusting, and shutting off the welding torch.

1. Place the pair of welding goggles over your forehead so they will be ready for use.

41-4. While soldering, use a piece of metal to hold hot pieces of metal together.

41-5. The tanks, hoses, gauges, and torch used for brazing and welding.

2. Select and insert the correct size tip in the torch. A small tip should be used for thin metals and a large tip for thicker ones.

3. Turn out the handles on the regulators to relieve all pressure.

4. Turn the valve on top of the oxygen tank until it is wide open.

5. Open the acetylene tank with a tank wrench about one to one and one-half turns. Soon the pressure gauge on the regulator will show the amount of pressure in the tank. The reading is in pounds per square inch (psi).

6. Open the pressure-regulating screws on the two regulators until each shows about 5 psi of pressure. The exact working pressure will vary with the kind and size of tip used and the size of the workpiece. It may be necessary to increase this pressure slightly, but it usually ranges from 1 to 5 psi.

7. Pull the goggles down over your eyes. Open the acetylene valve on the torch about one-quarter turn and light the flame with a spark lighter. Fig. 41-6. Adjust the acetylene until the flame just jumps away from the tip. Then turn on the oxygen a little at a time until the flame contains equal amounts of oxygen and acetylene. This flame is called *neutral*. It has a sharp inner cone with an envelope flame of a delicate bluish color. The torch should not make a hissing noise.

8. To turn off the torch, close the acetylene valve first. Then close the oxygen valve.

9. After you have finished welding, turn off the torch. Then turn out the handles on the pressure regulators. Next, close the valves on the acetylene and oxygen tanks. Finally, open the torch valves to release all gases in the hose.

PROCEDURE FOR BRAZING

First make sure that the parts to be joined are very clean and free of dirt. With the torch, heat the metals until they are red hot. Then heat the end of the rod and dip it into the flux. Hold the rod just ahead of the flame. Apply heat until the flux melts. Avoid overheating. Do not let the flame strike the rod directly and melt it. Both of these errors will cause a weak joint.

Welding

Remember that in brazing, the metal workpieces are not melted. They are heated red hot and the bronze rod is melted to form the joint. In welding, the metal workpieces are melted together. The welding rod supplies filler metal to produce a smooth, even, strong joint. Fig. 41-7.

To begin welding, light the torch as you did when brazing. Place the two metal workpieces so that the edges to be joined are touching.

41-6. Lighting the torch. Always use the spark lighter. Never use matches.

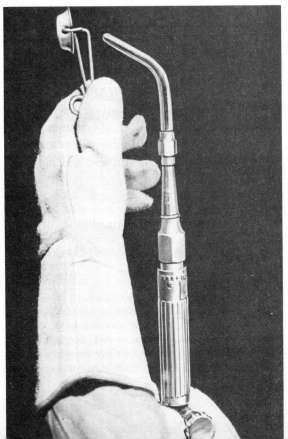

Start about ⅛″ from the end. Move the torch back and forth in a slight arc until the metal melts and tacks together. Tack the other end.

Next, start at one end. Move the torch to the other end and back with a slight zigzag motion until the metal begins to melt, forming a small puddle. Stick the welding rod into the puddle as needed. Move the torch along as fast as the metal will melt to form a smooth, even bead.

REVIEW QUESTIONS

1. What is the purpose of a flux?
2. List three kinds of heating devices for soldering.
3. What two metals are generally found in soft solders?
4. What is meant by tinning a copper? How is this done?
5. What is the difference between welding and brazing?
6. What are some safety rules to remember when welding and brazing?

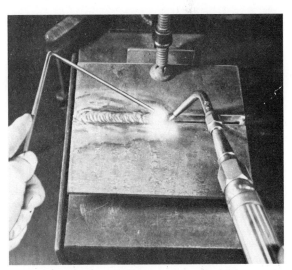

41-7. Using the welding torch and welding rod.

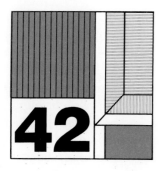

Fastening Sheet Metal

Seams

Seams join two pieces of metal. They can be made in various ways. Some common metal seams or joints are shown in Fig. 42-1. The *butt joint* is made when the seam should show as little as possible. *Lap*, *folded*, and *grooved* seams are made when extra strength is needed.

A seam can be strengthened by adding rivets or sheet metal screws.

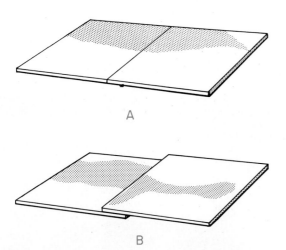

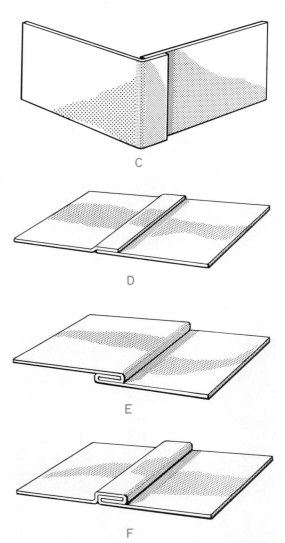

42-1. Sheet metal seams. (A) Butt. (B) Lap. (C) Corner lap. (D) Lap with joggle. (E) Folded. (F) Grooved. Seams can be strengthened with rivets, with sheet metal screws, or by soldering.

EQUIPMENT

Much of the equipment used for bending sheet metal is also used for making metal seams. See Unit 36. The only new tool is the *hand groover*. It is used for locking a grooved seam. Fig. 42-2. The size of a hand groover is determined by the width of its slot. See Table 42-A.

MAKING A BUTT SEAM

The simplest seam is made by butting together two metal edges. The metal should be cut carefully so the edges will join tightly. File both edges at the same time by moving the pieces back and forth across the face of a file locked in a vise. Most butt seams are fastened permanently by soldering or brazing. It is a good idea to file a slight V-joint or bevel on the workpiece to allow the solder to run freely along the seam. This is the weakest of the sheetmetal seams.

MAKING A LAP SEAM

In a simple lap seam, the edge of one piece overlaps the other enough to allow the seam to be riveted or sweat-soldered. Be sure that one piece of metal covers the other an equal distance all along the seam. An outside lap seam is used for corner joints.

Sometimes a *joggle* (or offset) is formed on one piece so that the surfaces of the seam will be flush. This can be done by placing a piece of metal of thickness equal to the workpiece flat on a table top. Place the metal on which

Table 42-A. Hand Groover Sizes

The small number stamped on the hand groover indicates its size.	
Number	**Size of Groove (In Inches)**
6	1/8
5	5/32
4	7/32
3	9/32
2	5/16
1	11/32
0	3/8

the joggle is to be formed directly over this piece. Let one edge extend an amount equal to the width of the lap seam plus about twice the thickness of the metal. Cover the two metal pieces with a strip of wood and clamp them to a table top. With a cross-peen or riveting hammer, form the joggle by striking the workpiece along the edge where it overlaps the bottom piece of metal. This will make the seam fit, with the surfaces flush.

MAKING A FOLDED OR GROOVED SEAM

The folded or grooved seam has three thicknesses of metal above the surface of the joint. Fig. 42-3. Allow for this by adding an amount equal to three times the width of the seam. Usually half the amount of extra stock is allowed on either side of the seam during layout. For example, if a 1/4" folded or grooved seam is made, 3/4" of extra stock must be allowed, with 3/8" added to each of the two pieces to be joined. When making a seam, bend the fold on either edge as if you were making a hem. Do not close the fold completely, however. A bar folder, if available, can be used to fold the edges.

42-2. Hand groover.

306

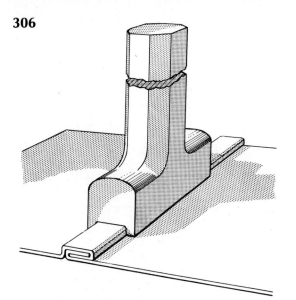

42-3. A properly made grooved joint. Notice that there are three thicknesses of metal in the joint.

When making a seam on a continuous piece, such as a cylinder, remember that the edge must be folded in the opposite way on each end. Join the two edges together, and place the seam over a solid backing. Close the joint by striking it with a wooden mallet. If a grooved seam is to be made, select a hand groover with a groove equal to the width of the seam. Place the tool directly over the

seam. Strike the tool with a hammer until the two edges are flush. Move the groover along the seam, closing the entire joint. Both folded and grooved seams can be made watertight by soldering.

Using Adhesives

Adhesives are glues and cements used to join materials. They can fasten metal to plastic, wood, leather, or another piece of metal. Industry uses them to join pieces of metal. Adhesives eliminate soldered, riveted, welded, or grooved seams in certain operations.

Contact adhesives, super glues, and industrial bonding cements can be used easily in the school shop or at home. Follow the directions on the container when using these adhesives.

REVIEW QUESTIONS

1. List three types of sheet-metal seams. Make a sketch of each.
2. How can seams be made watertight?
3. What tool is used to make a grooved seam?

|||||||||||||||||||||||||||||||||||||||||||||||||||| **KEY IDEA** ||||||||||||||||||||||||||||||||||||||||||||||||||||||||

POLLUTION AND ECOLOGY

Technology aids people in many ways. However, it also causes some problems, such as the need to train for new jobs because of computerized factories. However, there is another great problem that we face today. This problem is perhaps more serious than any other. It is the problem of pollution.

All pollution results from waste. In modern

technical societies, there is a large amount of waste. This may seem surprising at first, since efficient production would seem to eliminate waste. However, it is sometimes cheaper and more profitable to throw away a material rather than reuse it.

For example, in the United States labor costs are high. Thus, it is cheaper to throw

Fig. A. Pollution can take many forms. The smoke rising from burning trash is one form of pollution (top). The dumping of garbage beside a country road is another form of pollution (bottom). Most of us have probably seen scenes such as those shown here. Often, we are bothered only by the pollution we see. However, every type of pollution affects the environment. Pollution does not need to be visible to be harmful.

away "tin" cans than it is to recycle them. Likewise, it is easier for a beverage firm to use throw-away bottles rather than those that must be returned to the store.

In nonindustrial, developing nations, waste hardly exists. Every material is too valuable to throw away. By contrast, every year Americans discard millions of autos, tires, bottles, and cans. We also discard millions of tons of paper. Some of our factories release vast amounts of smoke and fumes into the air. Because of our carelessness, we dump tons of waste into our waterways. This pollutes the water we need for drinking, washing, transportation, and recreation.

Our society is not the first one to be concerned with pollution. Have you heard of the dense fogs that used to occur in London? You may have read of these fogs in some of the Sherlock Holmes stories. Or, you may have seen such fogs in movies set in nineteenth-century London. These fogs were heavy. They were sometimes so dense that people were unable to make their way home. The thickness of the London fogs was caused by the many coal fires in the city. However, few Londoners suspected the smoke from these fires as the cause. Remember, at this time, London was the largest city in the world. It had a population of more than 2 million people. There was no central heating as we now know it. To keep warm and to cook their food, people needed fireplaces. In London, coal was the fuel usually burned in these fireplaces. Coal-burning furnaces were also used in industry.

Since there were hundreds of thousands of these fires, a smoky haze hung over the city. The soot and ash carried up by the smoke fell back into the city. It has been estimated that in a single year more than one ton of soot and ash fell on the average city block in central London! The soot and ash were breathed in by the people. For many, they caused severe lung problems. The soot and ash also affected the vegetation. For example, the trees in some parts of London actually lost their leaves because of the large amount of soot and ash that fell on them. Simply, the leaves could not breathe. As you may remember from science class, leaves take carbon dioxide from the air. They give forth oxygen. Thus, the loss of these trees caused the quality of the London air to worsen even more.

The fogs in London are no longer as dense as they were. This is because coal is no longer burned in that city. In this century, natural gas was introduced as a source of heat and light. Gas produced a clean bright flame. There was almost no smoke. There was very little pollution. Gas is still used for heating and cooking. For lighting, however, it has been replaced by electricity.

In the last few years, you may have heard the word *ecology*. Ecology is simply the study of living things and the conditions that surround them. We now know that some things in our environment depend on other things to survive. For example, trees need sunlight and clean air to remain healthy. In London, where the air was smoky, many trees died. As mentioned, this smoke was caused by the coal fires burned in the city. These coal fires show one way in which human beings damaged their environment. You may be familiar with other ways in which our environment has been damaged.

Through cooperation, thoughtfulness, and individual effort people can solve the world's ecological problems. Ecology is everyone's business. What can you do, personally, to help solve the problem?

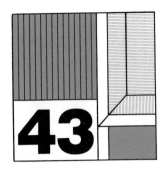

Forging and Heat Treating

Forging

Forging is heating metal and hammering or pressing it into a shape. When metal is hot enough to be shaped in this way, we say that it is *plastic*. The three major operations in forging are drawing, upsetting, and bending.

Years ago the village blacksmith forged metal by heating it in a coal forge. The blacksmith then shaped it over an anvil by pounding it with a hammer. Today, forging is still one of the major methods used by industry. It is used to shape metal parts when great strength is needed. Forging also improves metal by refining the grain structure and increasing its strength. Fig. 43-1.

Forging in the school shop is more like that done by the blacksmith. You can use forging to shape a chisel or a punch. You can use it also to bend heavy pieces of metal that would be difficult to bend cold.

43-1. Metal becomes plastic when heated. This illustration shows how metal "flows" during forging. (1) Original piece of metal. (2) First stage of forging. (3) Second stage of forging.

EQUIPMENT AND TOOLS

The *gas-fired forge* is used to heat the workpieces. It has largely replaced the coal forge used by village blacksmiths. It is much cleaner, easier to take care of, and easier to light than a coal forge.

The *blacksmith's anvil* is used as a base for the hand forging operation. Fig. 43-2.

Blacksmith's hand hammers are used. These are sledge, ball-peen, straight-peen, and cross-peen hammers. Fig. 43-3.

Blacksmith's tongs are used to pick up the

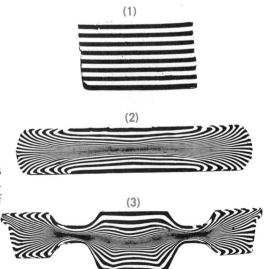

(1)

(2)

(3)

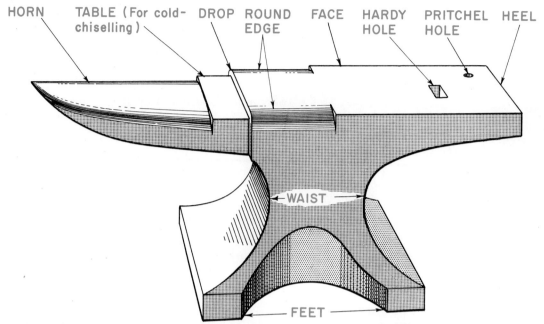

HORN   TABLE (For cold-   DROP   ROUND   FACE   HARDY   PRITCHEL   HEEL
        chiselling)   EDGE   HOLE   HOLE

WAIST

FEET

43-2. Parts of the anvil. The pritchel hole is used for bending small rods and for punching holes in metal.

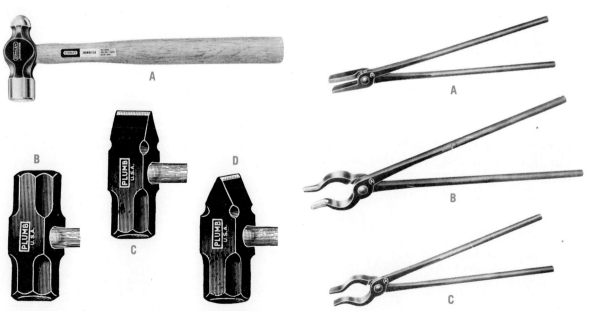

43-3. Forging hammers. (A) Ball-peen. (B) Sledge. (C) Straight-peen. (D) Cross-peen.

43-4. Blacksmith's tongs. (A) Flat lip. (B) Curved lip. (C) Pickup.

43-5. The hardy cutter is a special chisel that fits into the anvil's hardy hole.

hot metal. They are made with curved or flat lips. Fig. 43-4.

The *hardy cutter* (sometimes called the *anvil hardy*) is a hot and cold chisel made to fit into the hardy hole of the anvil. Fig. 43-5. Metal is cut by placing it over the cutter and then striking it with a hand hammer.

HEATING METAL

Before heating metal, put on your safety glasses and gloves. To light the furnace, first open the air valves slightly. Then place a piece of lighted paper near the gas valve. Open the valve slowly until the gas begins to burn. After a few minutes, turn on more air and gas. The flame should turn into a roaring blast of heat that is almost colorless.

For forging, metal must be red hot. Temperatures for forging range between 1300 and 2000°F. Low carbon or mild steel requires more heat than tool steel.

Heat the metal slowly until it is bright red. Forging should be done before the metal begins to lose its color. Use tongs to hold the metal. Reheat the metal as necessary.

THE FORGING PROCESS

Drawing

Drawing is a way of working a piece so that it increases in length, width, or both, and decreases in thickness. Hammer the metal over the flat face of the anvil. When a long piece of metal must be drawn out (increased in length and width), heat and work one section at a time. Always direct the blows toward the heavier part of the metal. Work the metal in "steps", as shown in Fig. 43-6.

Upsetting

Upsetting is the reverse of drawing. In upsetting, the length is *decreased* and the

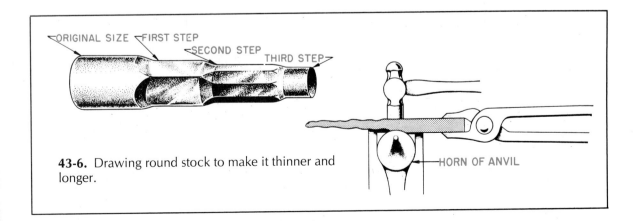

43-6. Drawing round stock to make it thinner and longer.

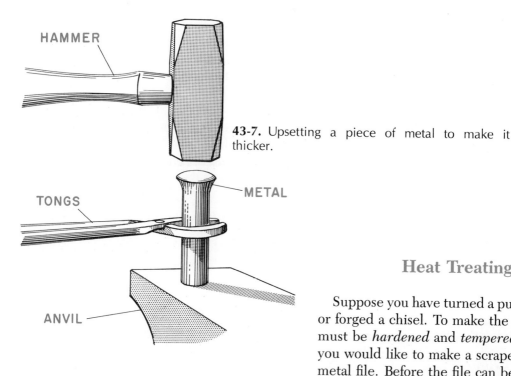

HAMMER

43-7. Upsetting a piece of metal to make it thicker.

METAL

TONGS

ANVIL

thickness is *increased*. Fig. 43-7. There are several methods used for upsetting. For short pieces, the metal can be held upright on the anvil and the end struck with a hammer. The head of a bolt is formed in this way.

Bending

Hot bending of squares and angles should be done over the face of the anvil.

Large curved bends are made over the rounded horn of the anvil. Figure 43-8 shows the steps to follow in forging a ring or a loop on a rod.

With practice you can learn to forge metal using the anvil, a vise, and the different hammers.

Heat Treating

Suppose you have turned a punch on a lathe or forged a chisel. To make the tool strong, it must be *hardened* and *tempered*. Or perhaps you would like to make a scraper from an old metal file. Before the file can be reworked, it must be softened, or *annealed*. Hardening, tempering, and annealing are *heat-treating* processes.

Heat treating is best done in a heat-treating furnace. However, it can also be done in a small soldering furnace or with a welding torch.

Here are the steps to follow in heat treating a cold chisel forged from tool steel.

First, anneal the metal by heating it until it is cherry red. Then cool it in the air. This softens the metal and relieves the strains of forging. File the metal smooth and polish it with abrasive cloth and oil.

Next, harden the metal by reheating about 1" of its tip until it is cherry red. This heats the metal to the *critical temperature*. Table 43-A. Plunge the metal quickly into water, moving it with a circular motion. Test the hardness with a file. If the file nicks the chisel, anneal and

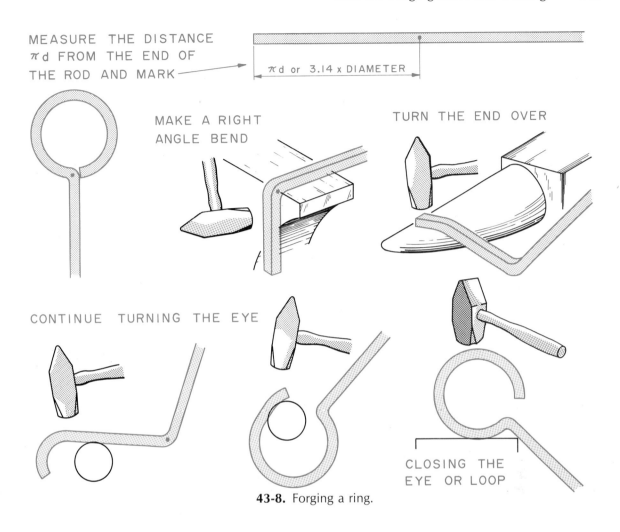

MEASURE THE DISTANCE π d FROM THE END OF THE ROD AND MARK

π d or 3.14 x DIAMETER

MAKE A RIGHT ANGLE BEND

TURN THE END OVER

CONTINUE TURNING THE EYE

CLOSING THE EYE OR LOOP

43-8. Forging a ring.

Table 43-A. Steel Temperatures

Color	Temperature (°F)
White	2200
Lemon	1825
Orange	1725
Cherry red	1325
Dark red	1175
Faint red	900
Pale blue	590

harden again. Hardness testing machines are also used.

Finally, polish the tip with abrasive cloth. Then temper the metal by applying heat about 1″ above the tip. Fig. 43-9. When the temper color—brown, in this case—reaches the tip, plunge the tool into water. Temper colors for other tools are shown in Table 43-B. Tempering reduces the brittleness of the piece.

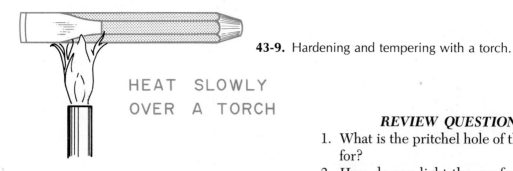

HEAT SLOWLY
OVER A TORCH

43-9. Hardening and tempering with a torch.

REVIEW QUESTIONS

1. What is the pritchel hole of the anvil used for?
2. How do you light the gas forge?
3. What are the three major operations performed in forging?
4. List some safety rules for forge work and heat treating.
5. Briefly, what is heat treatment?
6. Describe how to harden a tool.

Table 43-B. Tempering Tool Steels

Tool	Color	°F
Scribers, hammer faces	Pale yellow	445
Center punches	Full yellow	470
Cold chisels	Brown	500
Screwdrivers	Purple	530

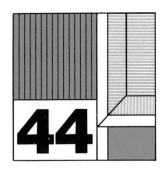

Metal Casting

Metal casting is a way of making parts by pouring molten (liquid) metal into a mold or cavity. When the metal cools, it takes the shape of the mold.

Many types of castings are used in industry. One common type of casting is *sand casting*.

Making a Casting

TOOLS AND MATERIALS

The following tools and materials are used in making a casting.
- A *pattern*, which is usually a wooden model of the part to be cast. Fig. 44-1.
- A *flask* is an open box made in two parts. The top section is the *cope*, the bottom the *drag*. Fig. 44-2.
- A *molding board* is a flat board on which the pattern is placed when ramming the drag (packing it with sand). Fig. 44-3.
- The *bottom board* or plate is a board placed on top of the drag before rolling it over to support the bottom of the mold.
- A *riddle* is used to sift the sand over the flask.
- A *rammer* is a wooden tool used to pack the mold.
- A *trowel* and a *slick* are tools used to smooth the face of the mold.

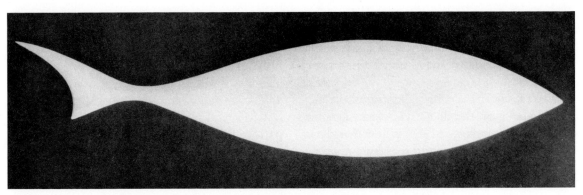

44-1. One-piece wooden pattern for a decorative fish casting.

44-2. The two parts of a metal-casting flask.

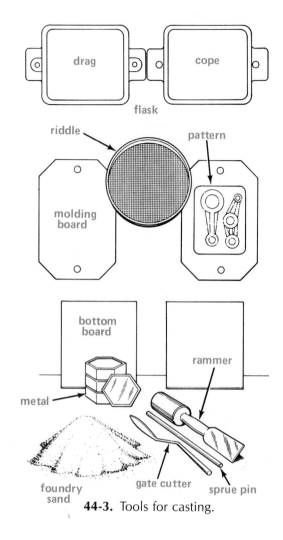

44-3. Tools for casting.

- A *sprue pin* is a tapered pin used to form the hole into which the molten metal is poured.
- A *riser pin* is a straight pin used to form an opening in the cope. This opening holds molten metal to feed the casting. This helps prevent shrinkage when the metal cools.
- A *gate cutter* is a tool used to cut *gates* and *runners* in the mold from the sprue hole to the mold itself. The metal flows from the sprue to the mold cavity through the gate.
- A *vent wire* is a straight piece of wire about ⅛" in diameter. It is long enough to go halfway through the cope or drag. It is used to make small holes in the mold to allow gases to escape.
- A *strike-off bar* is used to scrape the excess sand off the mold.
- A *bulb sponge* is used to wet the edge of the pattern and mold so that the pattern can be removed more easily.
- A *molder's bellows* is used for blowing away loose sand.
- A *shovel* is used for mixing and moving sand.

- *Molding sand* is used to make the mold. It is made by mixing silica, clay, and water. To see if the sand is moist enough, squeeze a handful and then break it. The break should be clean.
- *Parting compound* is a dry, light, powder that is water repellant. It is sprinkled on the pattern and between the mold halves to form a parting line. The compound helps the mold halves come apart easily. It also helps the pattern come out freely.
- *Casting metals* of many kinds are used. The

Metal	°F
Lead	620
Aluminum	1220
Bronze	1675
Brass	1700
Copper	1980
Iron	2200

Table 44-A. Melting Temperatures of Metals

metals and their melting temperatures are given in Table 44-A.

MAKING THE MOLD

1. Place the drag, pins down, on the molding board. Center the pattern on the molding board. Dust parting compound lightly on the pattern. Fig. 44-4.

2. Riddle a 1″ layer of sand over the pattern. Push the sand around the pattern with your fingers. Fig. 44-5.

3. Fill the drag with sand and ram it firmly. Fig. 44-6.

4. Strike off the excess sand from the top of the drag with the metal straightedge, using a shearing motion. Make about ten or twelve equally spaced vent holes around the pattern area.

5. Add some loose sand to the top of the drag. Then place the bottom board on top of it. Seat the board firmly by moving it with a circular motion.

44-4. Dust the pattern lightly with parting compound.

44-5. Riddle sand onto the pattern until it is covered.

44-6. Ramming the mold.

sprue hole in the shape of a funnel so it will make a good pouring hole or basin. Remove the riser pin.

10. Lift the cope off carefully and place it on its side on the bench. Blow any loose sand away from the pattern. Moisten the edge of the pattern with a sponge bulb. Remember, do not get it too wet as this will weaken the mold.

11. Insert a rapping pin (or a long wood screw) into the pattern. Tap the pattern lightly to loosen it. Then pull the pattern straight up. If any edges are broken away, repair them carefully, using a slick.

12. Cut a U-shaped channel (or gate) from

6. Hold the molding board and the bottom board firmly together and turn the drag over. Remove the molding board. Blow off any loose sand with the bellows. Place the cope (the top part of the flask) over the drag. Dust a little parting compound over the surface.

7. Insert the sprue and riser pins. The sprue pin should be about 2″ from the pattern. Fig. 44-7.

8. With the riddle, sift about 1″ of sand. Tuck it around the pattern and pins. Fill the cope with sand, using the same procedures as for the drag. Remember to vent the cope.

9. Carefully remove the sprue pin by moving it slightly in all directions. Round off the

44-7. Making holes in the cope for the sprue and riser.

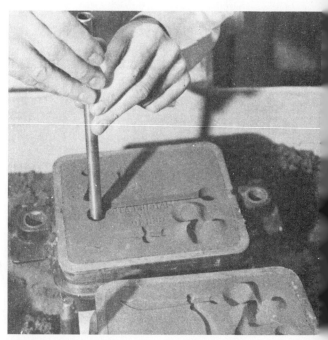

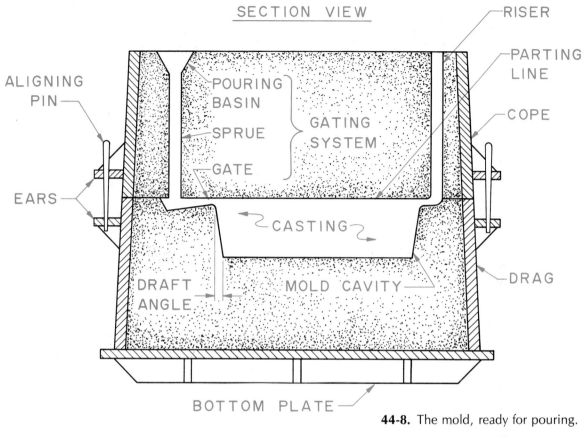

SECTION VIEW

RISER

PARTING LINE

ALIGNING PIN

POURING BASIN

SPRUE

GATE

GATING SYSTEM

COPE

EARS

CASTING

DRAG

DRAFT ANGLE

MOLD CAVITY

BOTTOM PLATE

FOR CAST IRON

44-8. The mold, ready for pouring.

the sprue to the pattern cavity. Cut another such channel from the riser to the cavity.

13. Blow off the loose sand. Carefully replace the cope. Place the whole unit on the floor, ready for pouring. Fig. 44-8.

EQUIPMENT FOR MOLDING

The following equipment is used in molding.

• A *crucible furnace*, which will provide temperatures up to 2200°F. Fig. 44-9.

• *Crucibles*, or graphite containers in which the metal is melted in the furnace.

• *Crucible tongs* to handle crucibles when removing them from the furnace and when pouring the molten metal.

• A *ladle*, to pour small amounts of metal from the crucible. A ladle with holes in it, called a *skimmer*, is used to remove impurities from the top of the molten metal.

MELT AND POUR SAFELY

In melting and pouring metal, observe the following precautions.

• Wear safety goggles, asbestos gloves, leggings, apron, and long sleeves.

• Always keep water away from molten metal. Mixing them can cause an explosion.

44-9. Removing a crucible from the furnace with tongs.

44-10. Pour the metal into the sprue hole from a crucible or a ladle.

• Follow instructions carefully when lighting the furnace. Make sure that the cover is off before lighting the furnace. Don't have your face near the furnace opening.

• Use crucible tongs and other equipment when pouring.

• Check all the details carefully, and take your time.

• Stay as far away from the molten metal as possible.

• Work with a partner. Use the "buddy" system.

MELTING AND POURING THE METAL

1. Light the furnace and allow it to come to full heat for ten or fifteen minutes. Place the crucible containing the metal scraps in the

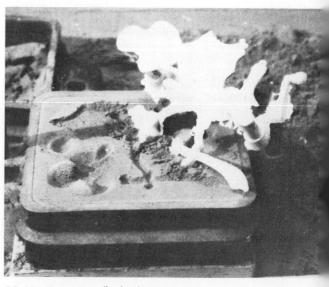

44-11. An open flask showing gates, sprue, and riser attached to casting.

furnace. Allow it to heat to the proper temperature.

2. With tongs, remove the crucible from the furnace. Fig. 44-9.

3. Pour molten metal into the sprue hole from the crucible or a ladle. Make sure that you pour evenly. Pour until the metal comes to the top of the sprue hole. Fig. 44-10.

4. Allow the casting to cool completely before removing it from the mold. Fig. 44-11.

REVIEW QUESTIONS

1. What is a pattern used for?
2. What is a mold?
3. What is the purpose of a sprue pin?
4. Describe the steps in making a mold.
5. What safety practices should be followed in melting and pouring metal?

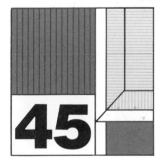

Machining

45

Machining is an important way of shaping metal. Machines or machine-operated tools are used to remove chips from the metal, giving it the desired shape or surface.

Machining is one of the four major ways of shaping metal. The others are casting, hot forming, and cold forming.

The basic machining processes are drilling, turning, milling, shaping, and grinding. Fig. 45-1. In this unit you will learn about turning metal on a lathe.

The Metal Lathe

PARTS OF THE LATHE

The metal lathe is the most useful and versatile metalworking machine. It can do straight and tapered turning. It also can cut threads, drill, bore, ream, and perform many other operations. The major parts of the lathe are shown in Fig. 45-2. Simply stated, the lathe consists of a rigid *bed*, with a fixed *headstock* on one end and a movable *tailstock*

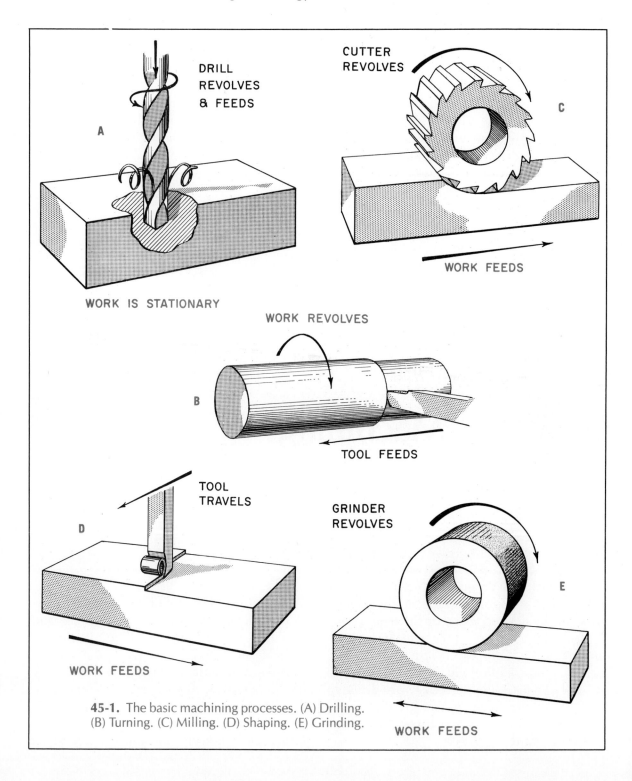

45-1. The basic machining processes. (A) Drilling. (B) Turning. (C) Milling. (D) Shaping. (E) Grinding.

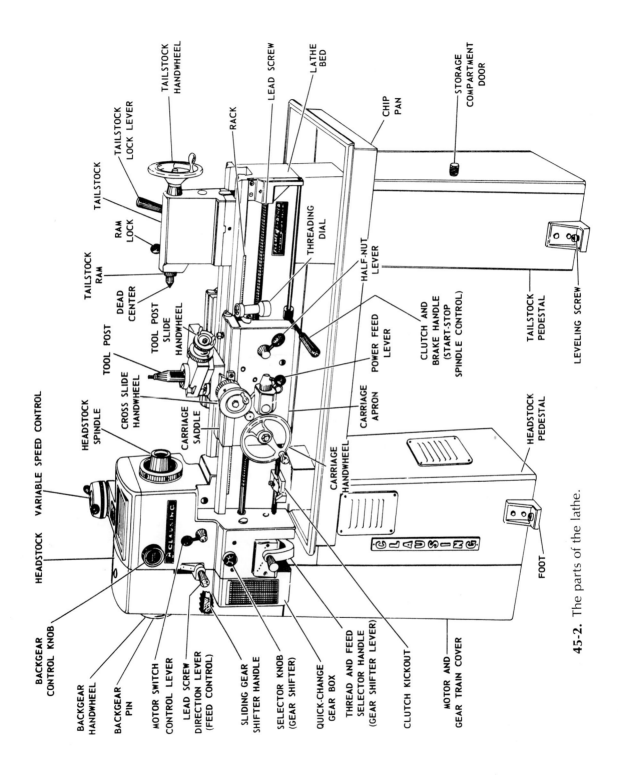

45-2. The parts of the lathe.

BACKGEAR CONTROL KNOB

BACKGEAR HANDWHEEL

BACKGEAR PIN

MOTOR SWITCH CONTROL LEVER

LEAD SCREW DIRECTION LEVER (FEED CONTROL)

SLIDING GEAR SHIFTER HANDLE

SELECTOR KNOB (GEAR SHIFTER)

QUICK-CHANGE GEAR BOX

THREAD AND FEED SELECTOR HANDLE (GEAR SHIFTER LEVER)

CLUTCH KICKOUT

MOTOR AND GEAR TRAIN COVER

HEADSTOCK

VARIABLE SPEED CONTROL

HEADSTOCK SPINDLE

TOOL POST

CROSS SLIDE HANDWHEEL

CARRIAGE SADDLE

CARRIAGE HANDWHEEL

CARRIAGE APRON

POWER FEED LEVER

CLUTCH AND BRAKE HANDLE (START-STOP SPINDLE CONTROL)

HALF-NUT LEVER

HEADSTOCK PEDESTAL

FOOT

TAILSTOCK

TAILSTOCK LOCK LEVER

TAILSTOCK HANDWHEEL

RAM LOCK

TAILSTOCK RAM

DEAD CENTER

TOOL POST SLIDE HANDWHEEL

RACK

LEAD SCREW

THREADING DIAL

LATHE BED

CHIP PAN

STORAGE COMPARTMENT DOOR

TAILSTOCK PEDESTAL

LEVELING SCREW

on the other. The *carriage* is mounted on the bed. It carries the tool post and the cutting tool.

The headstock houses the headstock spindle, the gears, and the speed-change belts or levers. When you use the lathe, you will fasten your workpiece between the headstock spindle and the tailstock. Then you will choose the cutting tool you wish to use, and mount it on the tool post. The spindle will cause the workpiece to rotate so that cutting can take place.

ACCESSORIES

There are many accessories, or pieces of special equipment, used with the lathe. These are some of the more common ones.

• *Cutting tools* or *bits*, are small, rectangular pieces of high-speed steel ground for different operations. They are used for straight turning, taper turning, thread cutting, and boring. Fig. 45-3.

• *Lathe toolholders* are straight, left-hand, and right-hand, enabling you to cut at different angles. Fig. 45-4.

• *Lathe dogs* are clamped to stock to hold it in place when turning it between centers of the lathe. One common type is the *bent tail*. See Fig. 45-6.

TURNING BETWEEN CENTERS ON THE LATHE

A workpiece can be fastened between the headstock spindle (*live center*) and the tailstock (*dead center*) of the lathe. It can then be turned against a cutting tool mounted on the post. This is called *turning between centers*. For the workpiece to be held securely by the

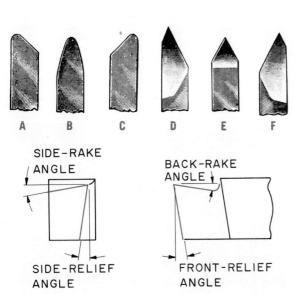

45-3. Lathe cutting tools. (A) Left-cut turning. (B) Round-nose. (C) Right-cut turning. (D) Left-cut side facing. (E) Threading. (F) Right-cut side facing.

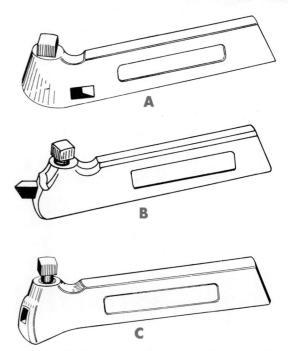

45-4. Toolholders. (A) Left. (B) Straight. (C) Right.

45-5. Drilling the center of the workpiece in a drill press.

1. File off any burr on the edge of the stock. Use a center head of a combination square set (see Unit 32) to draw two or three lines to locate the center. Prick punch the location.

2. Select a combination drill and countersink, (usually a No. 2 for small diameters). Check with your teacher to be sure you have the size you need.

3. Fasten the drill and countersink in the chuck of the drill press. Clamp the work on end in a vise so it is held securely on the table of the drill press. Drill the holes about three-quarters as deep as the countersink. Fig. 45-5.

Rough Turning

Rough turning is the first of the cutting operations performed with the stock held between centers. It is followed by finish turning, which produces a smooth finished surface.

1. Attach a lathe dog near one end of your workpiece.

2. Adjust the tailstock of the lathe until the opening between centers is slightly longer than the workpiece. Lock the tailstock in position.

3. Screw a faceplate onto the headstock spindle. Insert the tail of the lathe dog in the opening of the faceplate so the work is attached between the centers. Lubricate the dead center with a small amount of oil.

4. Turn up the tailstock handwheel until the work is held snugly, then lock it with the

centers, it must have shallow holes drilled in both ends into which the centers will fit.

Select the stock for the workpiece. The stock should be about ¾" longer than the finished size is to be. This will allow for the holes that will be drilled in both ends. After the turning has been finished, the extra length and holes may be cut away if necessary.

The stock should also be about ⅛" larger in diameter than the finished size. This will allow for the metal that will be removed by the cutting tool.

Locating and Drilling Center Holes

Although center holes can be drilled on the lathe, it is easier for a beginner to use the drill press.

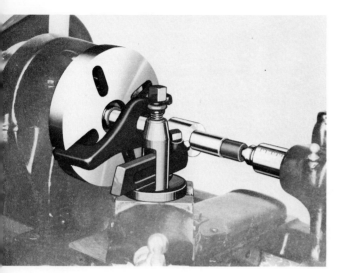

45-6. Lathe turning between centers. The work is held with a bent-tail lathe dog.

tailstock spindle lock. If it is too tight, the tailstock will heat up. If it is too loose, the lathe dog will rattle. Fig. 45-6.

5. Select the tool bit you will need for the cutting to be done. Clamp the bit in a straight toolholder. Remember there are three types of toolholders, left-hand, right-hand, and straight. Fasten the holder in the tool post. Adjust it so the cutting edge is on center and the tool turns slightly away from the direction of the headstock.

6. Adjust the lathe speed for the type of metal and size of the piece you're working on. Use high speeds for small diameters and for soft metals such as aluminum. Use slower speeds for harder stock and larger diameters.

7. Using the handwheel, move the lathe carriage back and forth, making sure that the point of the tool will clear the right end of the workpiece. When turned on, the lathe will feed automatically. Try it now to be sure the carriage moves from the tailstock to the headstock.

8. Get an outside caliper and adjust it 1/16" larger than the diameter your workpiece should be when finished.

9. Start the lathe and feed the tool into the workpiece to make sure it is cutting correctly. Move the carriage by hand a short distance from tailstock to headstock, then stop the lathe. This is called a trial cut. Check the diameter of the turned portion with the caliper. The diameter should fit the caliper. The extra 1/16" will allow enough material for finish turning.

10. When you are sure you are making the correct depth of cut, turn on the power feed lever. Allow the cutting tool to move a little over half the length of the piece of stock. When the first half has been rough turned to size, remove the work from the lathe. Reverse its position, lock it in place, and rough turn the second half. Usually, rough turning can be done in one or two cuts. Recheck often with the calipers.

Finish Turning

Adjust the lathe for a slightly higher speed and faster feed, and a shallower depth of cut. Finish turn the first half. Adjust the caliper to the diameter the work should be when finished and check the workpiece. If correct, place a soft collar of copper or brass under the lathe dog. Then reverse the workpiece, and finish turn the second half. The soft collar will protect the first half from marring.

Filing and Polishing

To file on a lathe, place the work between centers, and adjust the lathe to high speed. Use a long angle lathe file. Hold it firmly in your hands and make long, even strokes. Keep the file clean. To polish a surface, hold fine abrasive cloth on the metal. Apply a little oil for better cutting.

Other Lathe Operations

The lathe can also be used with a three-jaw chuck mounted on the headstock. A metal workpiece can be mounted in the chuck, and then turned or drilled. Thread-cutting and knurling, are also done on the lathe. Fig. 45-7.

REVIEW QUESTIONS

1. Describe the five basic machining processes.
2. What operations can be performed on the lathe?
3. Describe rough and finish turning.
4. What is a lathe dog used for?
5. How do you polish on the lathe?

45-7. In knurling, a cross-hatched pattern is cut into the surface of the metal.

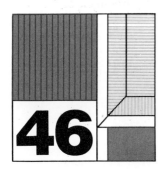

Finishing Metals

46

Metal surfaces must be protected with a finish to keep them attractive and to prevent oxidation (tarnishing). This operation is very important, since a good project can be ruined by a poor finish. All metals tarnish if exposed to air. Copper and brass discolor a great deal. Aluminum discolors very little, but it, too, should be finished. Mild steel, strap-iron stock, and galvanized iron are usually painted. Chemical finishes are also used.

There are many ways to finish metals for both protection and decoration. Some of the more common ones are discussed in this unit.

Preparing the Surface

For all metal finishing, be sure that the project is perfectly clean. Clean with lacquer thinner, or with a powder cleanser and water, and wipe dry. Also make sure that you have the type of surface you want, such as hammered, polished and buffed, or wire brushed. The surface cannot be changed after the finish has been applied. Handle the project with a clean cloth, or gloves, since dampness from the hands will discolor metals.

Applying Clear Lacquer

Lacquer flows better if the metal is warmed slightly in an oven. Be careful not to heat the metal too much, since this will make the lacquer boil and produce a rough finish. The clear lacquer should be thinned with lacquer thinner so it will flow more easily. Using a good brush, apply the lacquer to the article quickly, one section at a time. Fig. 46-1. Do not go over a section twice, since too much lacquer produces a yellowish appearance. Make sure that every part of the project is covered. When finished, the project should have a bright luster, and the lacquer should not show.

Let the project dry in a clean, warm room. Do not handle it for an hour or two. Sometimes, small articles are finished by dipping them in lacquer. Lacquers, enamels, and plastic finishes are also available in spray cans. Follow the directions on the spray can for the best results.

Apply Colored Lacquer and Paints

It is a little harder to get a good finish with colored lacquer or paints. Since metal surfaces are so smooth, it is very important to use good grades of finish and good clean brushes. These will help keep the paint or lacquer from running. Clean the metal and apply a primer coat (undercoat). Then apply a light, thin coat of paint or lacquer. Allow this to dry and add more coats until the finish is satisfactory.

Wrinkle-Finishing

Another finish for metalcraft projects is the wrinkle-finish. It is similar to the finish applied to car heaters, radiators, and toolboxes. This finish is particularly suitable for metal projects because it covers well and dries quickly. It provides a durable, scratch-resistant finish. This paint usually comes in spray cans.

Coloring Copper with Chemicals

Copper can be colored with a solution of liver of sulfur. For shades of brown to black, dissolve a small lump of liver of sulfur in 1 quart of warm water. Immediately after the

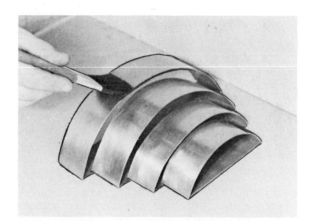

46-1. Applying clear lacquer with a brush. Use a brush of a good grade and apply a thin coat of lacquer. A coat that is too heavy will cause running.

project has been cleaned, put it in the coloring solution, or apply the solution with a brush. When the color is correct, wash the object in cold water. If the surface is to be highlighted, rub it with fine steel wool while it is still wet. After the project is dry, apply a coat of lacquer to preserve the finish.

Cold Conversion Metal Finishes

Cold conversion is a fast-acting cold chemical dip or brush-on finishing process for steel, brass, copper, bronze, or aluminum. This finish is similar to gun bluing. It is used at room temperature to produce colors from light brown to black. Follow the directions on the container for proper use according to the type of metal.

Coloring with Heat

1. Remove all dirt and grit from the project with abrasive cloth. After it is clean, handle the article with flannel gloves or a clean cloth.

2. Place the article on an asbestos pad or some other nonconductor of heat. Heat the article with a propane gas torch or welding torch. Watch the colors as they appear on the surface. Stop when the color you want appears. Apply a spray lacquer finish.

REVIEW QUESTIONS
1. What are the two reasons for finishing metal?
2. What is another word for tarnishing?
3. What metal can be colored with liver of sulphur?

Thinking about a Career

CUSTOM BICYCLE BUILDER

An Duc was born in Saigon, Republic of South Vietnam. With his father, mother, and two sisters, he emigrated to the United States in the late 1970s. The trip out of the country was difficult and dangerous. His family and their relatives left by night in a small and overloaded fishing boat. The boat was old and leaked badly. They bailed constantly to keep the boat afloat. After three days on the South China Sea, they were picked up by a freighter. An Duc was seventeen at the time.

With his family, he was placed in a camp for Vietnamese refugees. Eventually, his family made its way to the United States. They settled in Southern California. His father had run a small machine shop in Saigon. With these skills, he quickly found work. An Duc was enrolled in the local high school. Eager to learn, he was an excellent student. He had little trouble learning English.

From the moment he arrived in the United States, An Duc was determined to find a career that he liked. He wanted a challenging job, one that would develop his skills. Also, if possible, he wanted to find a job in a field that greatly appealed to him—bicycle repair.

In Saigon, the bicycle had been the principal means of transportation. There are thousands of bicycles in Saigon. After school, An Duc had worked in a small bicycle shop in Saigon. He had helped the owner repair bicycles. He had liked the work. He also learned that he had good mechanical skills. Carefully, he began to study the way in which bicycles were constructed. In his father's machine shop, he began to duplicate some of the bicycle parts. He did this because replacement parts were not available. This work helped him develop good machine shop skills.

An Duc's high school in Southern California had a fine machine shop program. Because he already had some experience, An Duc quickly developed much practice in operating the various metalworking tools. It was his skill in metalwork that suggested to him his future career. It was his after-school job in a bicycle shop that helped him along.

An Duc noticed that bicycle racing was popular in Southern California. There, the bicycle has a completely different use than it does in Vietnam. Few Americans ride a bicycle to or from work. Many, however, ride a bicycle for recreation. Some race bicycles. An Duc had never seen a racing bicycle before he came to the United States. Working at the bicycle shop, though, he saw many of them. He became very interested in their design.

He began to study the lightweight materials used to make them. He borrowed library books that discussed bicycle racing. He talked to local bicycle racers. He learned from them what they wanted most in a racing bicycle. Then, almost as an experiment, An Duc built his first racing bicycle. He was able to work after hours in the machine shop his father managed. This allowed him to make some of the parts himself. He gave careful attention to every part. He was responsible for constructing the frame from lightweight tubing. He used the best gears and sprockets he could buy. He gave particular attention to the design of the seat and handlebars.

An Duc had no trouble selling his first custom-built racing bicycle. One Saturday afternoon, as he was working on it, a customer asked if it had been sold. When he answered no, she asked the price and then said that she would take it. She then suggested a few minor changes in the bike. An Duc was easily able to make these.

The buyer of An Duc's first racing bike referred other buyers to him. Soon, An Duc had as much work as he could handle. By the time he graduated from high school, he had made and sold four custom-made racing bicy-cles. He sold the bicycles for prices ranging from $800 to $1100.

Shortly after graduation, An Duc opened his own bicycle shop. While he made some repairs on ordinary five- and ten-speed bicy-cles, he spent most of his time designing and making custom racing bicycles. He made each of the bicycles to the customer's specifications.

In the six years he has been in business, An Duc has won a reputation as a skilled builder of racing bicycles. "Most racing bicycles are built in Italy," says An Duc. "Some, however, are made by hand in England. Only a few racing bicycles are made by hand in the United States, though. I didn't know this until after I opened my shop. So, I was somewhat lucky, I guess. I was able to supply a product for which there was a steady demand. I've worked hard to do this. I usually work at least ten hours a day, including Saturdays. If you are in business for yourself, you have to want to work hard."

Recently, An Duc has hired two assistants. This will allow him to expand his bicycle repair service. It also will allow him to concentrate full time on his main interest: the design and building of racing bicycles.

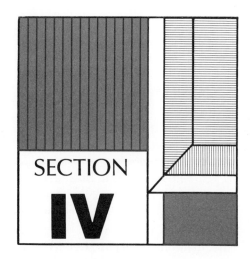

SECTION

IV

Plastics
Technology

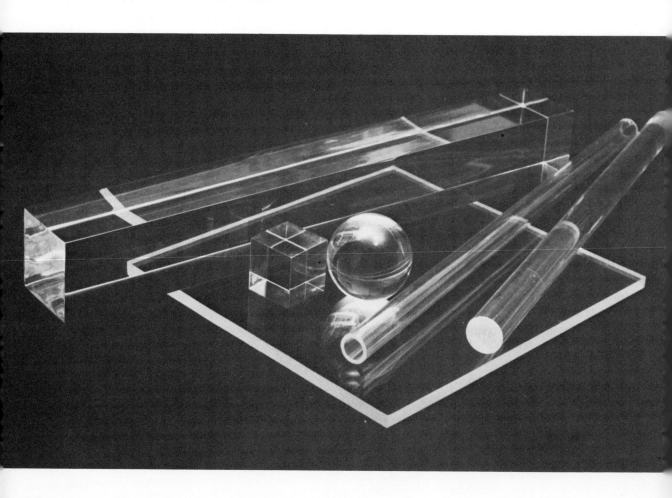

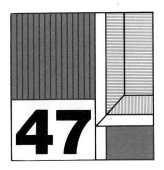

Introduction to Plastics

The Family of Plastics

Plastics are *synthetic* materials. Unlike wood and metal, they are not found in nature. Plastics are usually made from some combination of carbon, oxygen, hydrogen, and nitrogen. Other elements may also be present. The source for many of the raw materials for making plastics is oil or coal.

Plastics are a family of materials. Each branch of the family has certain characteristics. However, whatever the properties or form, all plastics fall into two groups: *thermoplastic* and *thermosetting*.

Thermoplastics soften when heated and harden when cooled. When heated, they may be shaped or molded. They can be reheated and formed a different shape.

Thermosetting plastics are cured or set into permanent shape by heat. If reheated, they soften or burn, but they cannot be reshaped. Figure 47-1 shows some common kinds of plastics and typical products made from them.

The Plastics Industry

The making and forming of plastics is one of the leading industries in the United States. Today plastics are used to make many products once made of metal or wood.

Celluloid®, developed in 1869, was the first plastic to have commercial success. It was used as a substitute for ivory in billiard balls. Motion picture film and automobile windshields were also made of Celluloid®.

The greatest development of new plastics and new uses for them has occurred since 1940. Today plastics are used in everything from automobiles to football helmets. Fig. 47-2. They are widely used by the communications industry in telephones and as insulation for power lines. They are used also for computer housings.

Plastics are widely used in the furniture industry. Much furniture—including frames, foam cushions, and chair coverings—is made of plastic. Many easy-to-clean floor coverings are also made from plastics.

Today thousands of companies in the United States manufacture plastics and form plastic products. Three types of plastic—polyethylene, vinyl, and styrene—exceed two billion pounds annual production. Research continues to develop new plastics and new ways to use them.

The plastics industry has always needed skilled people. One of the most important workers is the *mold maker*. This person must be a highly skilled machinist. Many plastic items are formed in molds. Computers also aid in the design and production of molds for

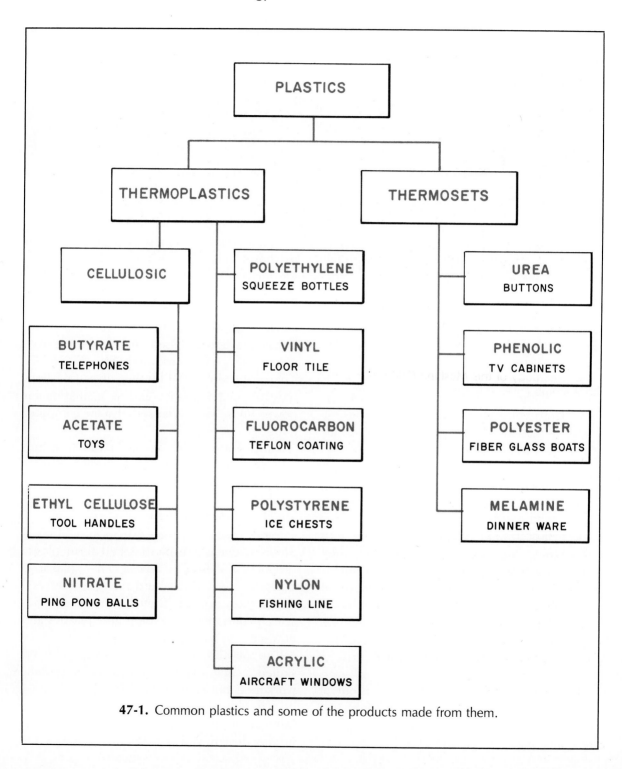

47-1. Common plastics and some of the products made from them.

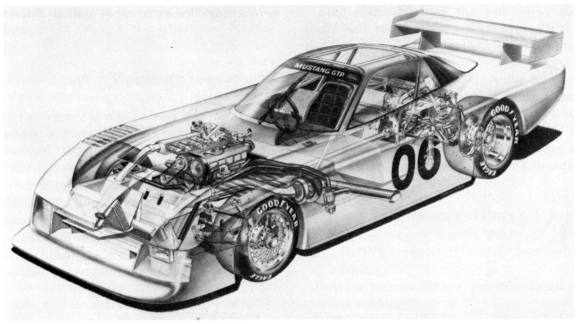

Ford Motor Company

47-2. The body of this Mustang GTP race car was computer designed. Tough and lightweight, it has a honeycomb core. This core is sandwiched between two sheets of carbon-fiber reinforced plastic.

plastic parts. These molds are shown in Unit 48.

There is now a need for a new type of worker called a *plastics* or *polymeric materials engineer*. Such a person usually has some experience in mechanical engineering and schooling in chemistry and plastics. The plastics engineer must be experienced in all aspects of plastics production, from mold making to the finishing of the final product.

Other jobs in the plastics industry are like those in other industries. These include jobs for machine operators, quality-control technicians, supervisors, and inspectors. The plastics industry will continue to grow. Thus, it will need many more workers.

REVIEW QUESTIONS

1. What was the first plastic to have commercial success? When was it developed?
2. Are plastics a synthetic or natural material?
3. What are the two groups into which plastics may be divided?
4. List some of the plastic products in your home.

|||||||||||||||||||||||||||||||||||||||||||| **KEY IDEA** ||||||||||||||||||||||||||||||||||||||||||||||

SUPERPLASTICS

In the design of new products, weight has always been important. Many products must be made as lightweight as possible. Because there is now such a demand for lightweight products, there is a high demand for plastics. Industry, of course, has used plastics for many years. The strong, tough, superplastics were developed only recently, however. These plastics were developed to meet the needs of high technology.

These plastics are heat-resistant and light. They are tougher than many metals. Here are some examples.

• An engine made of molded plastic is now being used in racing cars. It is about one-half the weight of a metal engine. Plastic engines cost less. They can be molded to a shape. Metal must be cast. It must then be machined to smooth the rough parts.

• A process called coextrusion is used to produce plastic bags. These bags are tough, flexible, and puncture proof. They are used for foods such as potato chips. The plastic is made as a five-layer sheet that blocks out light. It also prevents the loss of oxygen and flavor from the food. This plastic also can be used to seal fruit juices and milk. A special process is used. Properly sealed, these foods will keep for months without refrigeration.

• Heat-resistant plastic is available. It can be used in products normally made of metal or glass. This plastic can withstand temperatures of 300°F. It is also very strong. Such plastic is used in medical instruments, milking machines, and hair dryers.

A *composite material* is a material made of different parts. Many plastics are composite materials. These plastics are stronger and lighter than most metals. They do not corrode. They can be easily molded into complex shapes. Composites are made from fibers held by resins. Fiberglass is an example of such a composite. These fibers can be made from glass, graphite, or new synthetic fibers. One such fiber is five times as strong as steel and much lighter than fiberglass. These composites are used in the aerospace industry. They

DuPont

Fig. A. The superplastic used for this bicycle wheel is strong, yet lightweight.

are used on aircraft floors, ceilings, and doors. The Space Shuttle cargo doors are made from a graphite/epoxy resin composite. The Space Shuttle is protected from heat by plastic materials. One important example is the composite tile. This tile is made from silica fibers. Over 31,000 of these tiles are used.

They cover much of the outer surface of the Shuttle. They protect it from high heat as the Shuttle reenters Earth's atmosphere.

As technology continues to develop, plastic will find even more uses in industry. Already, it is one of the principal materials used in industry.

Industrial Plastics

The processing of plastic materials is done in several ways. Some manufacturers use only one technique. Others may use several techniques in the same plant. Some common industrial processes include:

- Extrusion molding.
- Calendering.
- Blow molding.
- Compression molding.
- Transfer molding.
- Thermoforming.
- Injection molding.
- High-pressure laminating.
- Reinforcing.
- Foaming.

Extrusion Molding

Extrusion molding is used to form thermoplastic materials into tubes, rods, shapes, and filaments. It is also used to coat wires and cables. Fig. 48-1.

Dry plastic material is loaded into a hopper. It moves through a long heating chamber. At the end of the heating chamber the molten

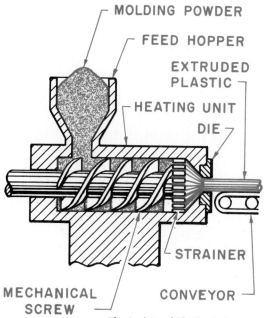

MOLDING POWDER

FEED HOPPER

EXTRUDED PLASTIC

HEATING UNIT

DIE

STRAINER

CONVEYOR

MECHANICAL SCREW

The Society of Plastics Industry, Inc.
48-1. Extrusion molding.

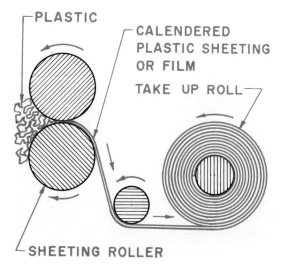

PLASTIC

CALENDERED PLASTIC SHEETING OR FILM

TAKE UP ROLL

SHEETING ROLLER

The Society of Plastics Industry, Inc.
48-2. Calendering.

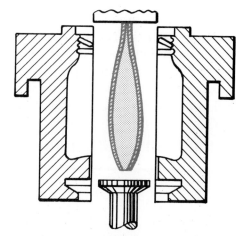

EXTRUDED PARISON-MOLD OPEN

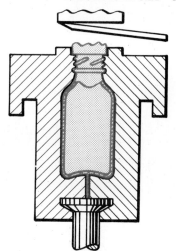

MOLD CLOSED & BOTTLE BLOWN

FINISHED BOTTLE

The Society of Plastics Industry, Inc.
48-3. Blow molding.

plastic is forced out through a *die*. A die is a small opening with the shape of the finished product. As the plastic is forced through the die, it is fed onto a conveyor belt. There it is cooled by blowers or water.

Calendering

Calendering is a process for making plastic into film and sheets. *Film* is plastic up to and including 10 mils in thickness. (A mil is ⅟₁₀₀₀″.) *Sheet* is plastic more than 10 mils thick.

In calendering, heated plastic material is squeezed between heated rollers. The space between the rollers determines the thickness of the plastic. Fig. 48-2.

Blow Molding

Blow molding stretches a thermoplastic material against a mold and then hardens it. There are two types of blow molding: *direct* and *indirect*.

In the direct method a hot, molten tube, called a *parison*, is placed into a mold. Air is blown into the plastic. The air forces the plastic against the cold sides of the mold. The plastic is then cooled and hardened. Fig. 48-3.

The indirect method uses a plastic sheet that is heated and clamped between a die and a cover. Air pressure is used to force the plastic material against the die. The plastic is then cooled and hardened.

Compression Molding

Compression molding is a common method of forming thermosetting materials. Fig. 48-4. The plastic material is squeezed into a shape

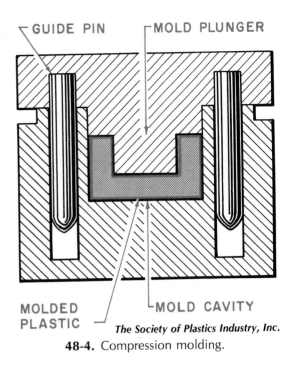

48-4. Compression molding.

The Society of Plastics Industry, Inc.

by using heat and pressure in a mold. Plastic molding powder is placed in a heated mold. The mold is closed, causing the plastic to flow into the cavity. While the mold is closed, the plastic undergoes a chemical change that permanently sets its shape. After cooling, the mold is opened and the part removed.

Transfer Molding

Transfer molding is usually used with thermosetting plastics. This method is like compression molding in that the plastic is cured in a mold under heat and pressure. It differs from compression molding in that the plastic is heated to a formable state before it reaches

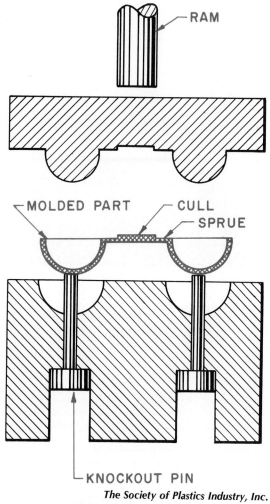

MOLDED PART — CULL — SPRUE — KNOCKOUT PIN

48-5. Transfer molding.

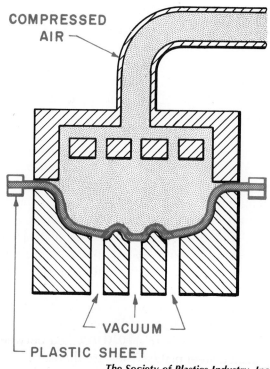

COMPRESSED AIR — VACUUM — PLASTIC SHEET

48-6. A thermoforming mold.

the mold. Also, the plastic is forced into a closed mold by a plunger. Fig. 48-5.

Thermoforming

Thermoforming consists of heating thermoplastic sheet and then using air to shape it.

There are many methods of thermoforming. One technique is vacuum forming. In this process, a plastic sheet is clamped over an airtight box. Electric heaters above the box soften the plastic. Then the air is drawn out of the box, pulling the soft plastic down on a "former" in the box. The plastic thus becomes shaped like the former. Another method uses compressed air to force the plastic into a former. Fig. 48-6.

Injection Molding

In injection molding, thermoplastic material is put into a hopper which feeds into a heating chamber. A plunger pushes the plastic through this long heating chamber, where the material is softened to a fluid state. At the end of this chamber there is a nozzle placed firmly against the opening to a cool, closed mold. The liquid plastic is forced at high pressure through this nozzle into the cold mold. As soon as the plastic cools and becomes solid, the mold opens. The finished plastic piece is then ejected from the press. Fig. 48-7.

High-pressure Laminating

Thermosetting plastics are generally used in high-pressure laminating. This is done with high heat and pressure. The plastics are used to hold together the reinforcing materials that make up the body of the finished product. The reinforcing materials may be cloth, paper, wood, or fibers of glass. These materials are soaked in a plastic solution. After drying, layers of these materials are stacked between polished steel plates. They are then subjected to heat and high pressure to bond them permanently together. Fig. 48-8.

High-pressure laminating is used to form plain flat sheets, decorative sheets (countertops, for example), rods, tubes, and formed shapes.

Reinforcing

Reinforced plastics differ from high-pressure laminates in that the plastics used require very little or no pressure in the processing. Fig. 48-9. In both methods, however, plastics are used to bind together the cloth, paper, carbon filaments, or glass fiber reinforcing material used for the body of the product. The reinforcing material may be in

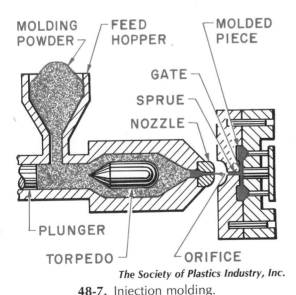

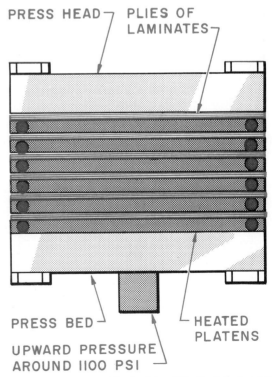

The Society of Plastics Industry, Inc.

48-7. Injection molding.

The Society of Plastics Industry, Inc.

48-8. High-pressure laminating.

REINFORCED PLASTIC MATERIAL

BACK-UP PLATES SEALING
HEAT CHANNELS

HEAT CHANNELS

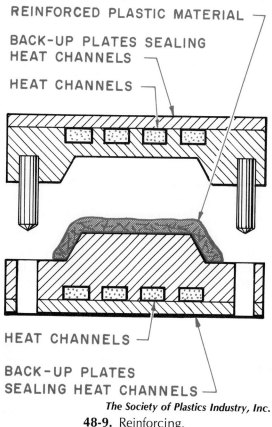

HEAT CHANNELS

BACK-UP PLATES
SEALING HEAT CHANNELS

The Society of Plastics Industry, Inc.
48-9. Reinforcing.

sheet or mat form. Reinforced plastics have very high strength, yet are lightweight. Many reinforced plastics are used in the aerospace industry. These are very light, but as strong as steel.

Foaming

Foamed or expanded plastics are made by forming gas bubbles in plastic material while it is in a liquid state. In most foamed plastics, the bubbles (cells) are separate from each other. They are connected by partitioned "walls." This makes foamed plastics very good insulating materials.

Foamed materials are made in two ways. One method uses beads of thermoplastic or thermosetting material. These beads expand when heated. The heat causes a chemical reaction within the beads and produces a gas. This gas causes the beads to expand and make the cell structure. Fig. 48-10.

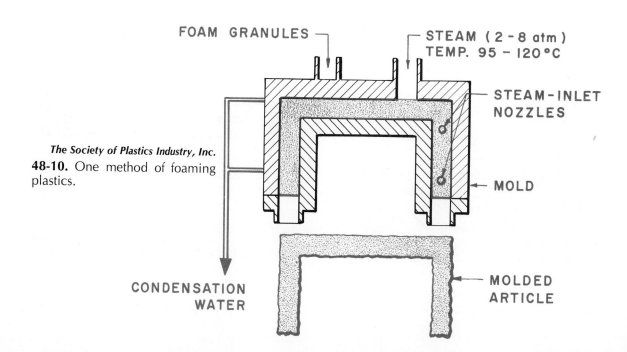

FOAM GRANULES

STEAM (2-8 atm)
TEMP. 95-120°C

STEAM-INLET
NOZZLES

MOLD

The Society of Plastics Industry, Inc.
48-10. One method of foaming plastics.

CONDENSATION
WATER

MOLDED
ARTICLE

REVIEW QUESTIONS

1. Name ten common industrial methods for processing plastics.
2. Briefly describe calendering.
3. What is the difference between a film and a sheet?
4. How does transfer molding differ from compression molding?
5. What are the two types of blow molding?

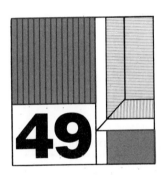

Cutting Plastics in the School Shop

49

Plastics used in the shop may be cut in several ways. The tools and methods are similar to those used in woodcutting and metalworking.

Cutting Plastics with Hand Tools

Shearing may be done on very thin sheets with scissors or tin snips. Thicker sheets, as well as rods and bars, are usually cut with a saw. The cutting tools should be sharp. *Sawing* should be done very carefully and not too fast. If you saw too fast, you will heat the plastic. This will cause the saw to stick. You may use a hacksaw, a backsaw, a jigsaw, or a band saw for cutting plastic.

A fine-tooth *hacksaw* is good for cutting rods, tubes, bars, and narrow sheets of plastic. A coping saw or jeweler's saw may be used to cut curved designs in sheet plastic. Fig. 49-1. When sawing plastic, it is best to clamp the piece in a vise.

The *jigsaw* is also used for cutting curved shapes from sheet plastic. Fig. 49-2.

Cutting Plastics with Power Tools

The *band saw* works well for cutting rods and tubing to length. It can also be used for making straight cuts on sheet plastic when a guide is used. Foam plastics are most easily cut on a band saw. Never cut them with a

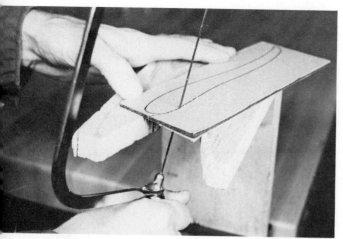

49-1. Cutting plastic with a coping saw. Hold the plastic on a V-block. Note that the protective paper has been left on the plastic.

49-2. Cutting an irregular shape on a jigsaw. A band saw may also be used.

circular saw. The saw will bind the plastic and cause a "kickback."

The *circular saw* can be used for cutting sheets of thick plastic. It is used for squaring ends and cutting grooves in sheet plastic. Cutting plastics on a circular saw should usually be done by the instructor.

Drilling Plastics

Twist drills used in woodwork or metalwork can also be used for drilling holes in plastic. Holes can be drilled with either a hand drill or a drill press. The work must be held securely. With a scriber, mark the place where you want the hole. This will keep the drill from wandering and damaging the surface of the plastic. If you are drilling holes wider than ¼″ in thick plastic, drill a ⅛″ pilot hole first. When drilling holes in plastics, use a slow or medium speed. If you drill too fast, the drill will get hot and stick to the plastic.

Sanding and Smoothing Plastics

Methods for *abrading*, or sanding, plastics are the same as for woodworking. It is important to remember that the plastic will melt if it is pressed too hard on a sanding machine.

The *shaping* and *smoothing* of plastic is done with files and other shaping tools, as in woodworking. Be careful not to bend it, as this will cause crazing or cracking.

Plastic can also be turned on a lathe. The work must be held carefully in a chuck or between centers. Too much pressure on the cutting tool can cause the plastic to break. This can be very dangerous. *Check with your instructor before attempting lathe turning.*

REVIEW QUESTIONS

1. What method is commonly used for cutting thin sheets of plastic?
2. What tool is used to cut plastic rods and bars?
3. What types of drills are used for drilling holes in plastic?
4. Why should you use slow or medium speeds when drilling plastic?
5. What tools are used to shape and smooth plastic shapes?

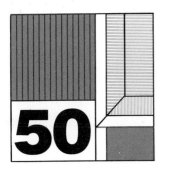

Forming Plastics in the School Shop

Many of the forming methods discussed in Unit 48 need expensive equipment. They can be done only in large factories. However, some types of plastic forming can easily be done in the school shop. Fig. 50-1. You will learn about these methods in this unit.

Bending

One of the easiest ways to form plastic is by bending. When acrylic plastics such as Lucite® or Plexiglas® are heated, they soften. Remember, they are thermoplastics. When soft, they may be made into almost any shape.

The bending of plastic requires just a few tools. You need a device to heat the plastic, such as an electric hot plate or oven. Never use an open flame on plastic. You also need a pair of cotton gloves to handle the hot plastic. If you are going to bend the plastic around a form, make the form before the plastic is heated. The form should be sanded smooth because the hot plastic will pick up any saw marks. These marks will then appear on the finished piece.

Cut a piece of plastic to the desired size. Smooth the edges. Be sure to remove all the masking paper from the plastic before heating it.

Forming in the Shop

Forming is the process of shaping a material without adding to or removing any of the material.

KINDS OF FORMING	DEFINITION	EXAMPLES
Bending (WORKPIECE, AXIS, BEND, BEND)	Forming by stretching heated plastic around a straight axis.	Letter-forming operations for signs and displays; forming heated plastic strips.
Casting (TWO-PIECE MOLD, LIQUID PLASTIC, CAVITY)	Forming by pouring liquid plastic into a hollow cavity and allowing it to harden.	Die casting and open-mold casting.
Molding (MOLD, MOLDED PART, MOLD)	Forming by squeezing heated plastic between two dies.	Compression molding, injection molding, blow forming and vacuum forming, foam molding.
Extruding (PLASTIC, SCREW, DIE, PATTERN)	Forming by forcing the heated plastic through an opening (or die), which shapes the plastic.	Plastic molding and tubing extrusion operations.

50-1. This chart shows some of the ways plastics can be formed in the school shop.

50-2. Bending plastic around a dowel form. The plastic must be heated before it can be bent.

Put the plastic on firebrick or other heat-resistant material. Place it on a hot plate, or in an oven at about 300°F. Heat until the plastic can be bent easily. Remove it from the heat. Bend to the desired shape, either by hand or on a form. Be sure to wear gloves. Fig. 50-2.

When the plastic cools, it will hold this shape. If reheated, it will go back to its original form. This is useful if you did not get

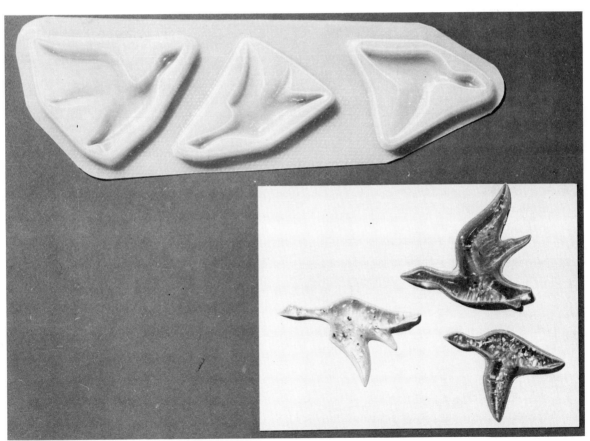

50-3. Plastic molds and finished castings. Molds may be made of wood or metal also.

the desired shape on the first try. Just reheat the piece and bend it again.

Casting

Plastic casting is done by pouring liquid polyester resin into a mold. After the plastic resin has hardened, the finished piece is removed from the mold. Industry casts lenses and jewels by this method. In the school shop, the casting resin is mixed with a catalyst or hardener before pouring. The amounts of resin and catalyst vary. Read the directions on the container.

The molds to be used must first be coated with a liquid release so that the finished piece can be removed easily. Carefully pour the resin into the mold. Wear gloves and safety goggles, and work in a well-ventilated area. Allow the resin to harden overnight. Figure 50-3 shows the plastic molds (available from the resin supplier) and the finished pieces.

Other Forming Processes

Compression and injection molding may also be done in the school shop. For each of these processes a mold or die is needed, along with the right machine. Figure 50-4 shows a student forming a part on a compression molding machine. Foam molding, and blow and vacuum forming are also done in the school shop. Not all forming machines are alike. Follow the special directions for each machine.

50-4. Student using a compression molding press.

REVIEW QUESTIONS

1. What tools are needed for bending plastics?
2. To what temperature should plastic be heated for bending?
3. What type of plastic is easily bent when heated?
4. What materials are needed for casting plastics?

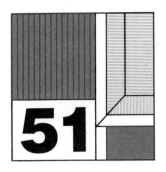

Fastening Plastics in the School Shop

Plastic materials can be joined with glues, cements, and mechanical fasteners. Permanent fastening is done with cements. Semipermanent joints are made with fasteners such as machine screws. Fig. 51-1.

Adhesion

Adhesives used for wood do not work well for gluing plastics. The two general-purpose glues for plastics are *epoxy glue* and *contact cement*. Epoxy glues come in two separate tubes. To use them, take equal amounts of material from each tube, mix the materials, and apply the mixture to the surfaces to be joined. The pieces must be held or clamped until the glue sets. Fig. 51-2. Always test a spot of epoxy on a scrap piece of plastic before joining two pieces. Some plastics will be dissolved by epoxy glue.

To fasten plastic with contact cement, coat both surfaces with the cement. Allow to dry about 20 minutes. Then bring the two surfaces together *carefully*. Once they touch, they will stick so tightly that they cannot be moved. No clamps are needed.

Model airplane cement also can be used to join plastics.

Cohesion

Plastics can be fastened together by *cohesion*, which is the fusing of two pieces of plastic. This may be done by solvent cementing or by thermal welding. The most common example of thermal welding is the heat sealing of plastic food bags. Other thermal welding methods involve friction and hot gas. (Thermal welding is not generally done in the school shop.)

In school projects, solvent cement is used to fuse plastic. This is done by the following method.

First make sure the plastic is clean, and that the joint fits well. (The use of solvent will not improve a poor joint.) Then apply the cement to all surfaces to be joined. This is usually done by soaking the plastic in the solvent or applying with a hypodermic needle. Fig. 51-3. The solvent softens the plastic. The pieces to be fastened are held together with spring clamps until the solvent evaporates. If the pieces are moved before the solvent evaporates, the joint will be broken. As a substitute for clamps, you can make a special fixture for holding the parts. Fig. 51-4. Be sure that the weights are firmly in place while the solvent evaporates.

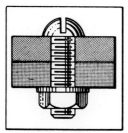

51-1. Various methods of fastening plastics.

Fastening

Fastening is the process of joining materials together permanently or semipermanently.

KIND OF FASTENING	DEFINITION	EXAMPLES
MACHINE SCREWS IN TAPPED HOLES / PLASTIC PARTS / **Mechanical Fastening**	Permanent or semipermanent fastening with special locking devices.	Fastening with screws, bolts and nuts, or drive screws.
Adhesion GLUE / PLASTIC PARTS	Permanent fastening by bonding like or unlike materials together with cements.	Epoxy cementing. Contact cementing.
SOLVENT CEMENT / **Cohesion** PLASTIC PARTS	Permanent fastening by fusing plastic pieces together with softened or liquid plastic and pressure.	Solvent cementing. Thermal welding. Sonic welding. Plastic resins.

Mechanical Fastening

Plastic parts to be joined with screws or with nuts and bolts must be carefully drilled. Otherwise the plastic will fracture and split.

The techniques used for preparing holes for screws in wood and metal should be followed for plastic. Plastic pieces can also be drilled and tapped. This way, machine screws can be used to fasten the pieces together.

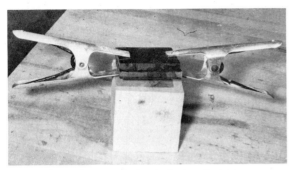

51-2. Two pieces of plastic being held by spring clamps until the cement dries.

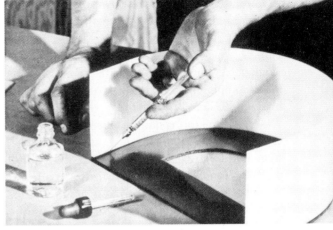

51-3. Solvent cementing can be done by soaking or by flowing cement into the joint.

Laminated Plastics

Many plastics are laminated commercially. Circuit boards in many transistor radios and television sets are laminated plastics. In the school shop plastics may be laminated in two ways. Acrylic plastics may be laminated by applying solvent cement to the surface of the pieces and then placing them together. The pieces should be clamped to keep them in close contact until the plastic hardens. Laminated pieces of different colors can be made

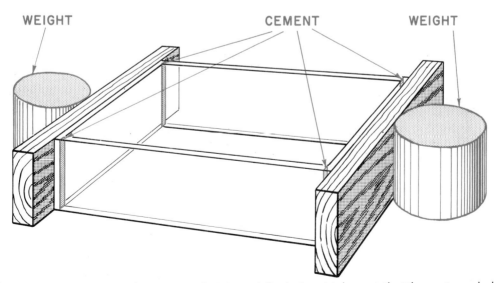

WEIGHT   CEMENT   WEIGHT

51-4. One method of holding the cemented pieces while drying. Make sure that the parts are held firmly in place.

by this process. Another common type of plastic laminate is *fiberglass*. You may be familiar with fiberglass coverings on boats. This material is made from glass fibers laminated or fastened together with special resins. The resin and a catalyst are mixed as in plastic casting. Be sure to follow the directions that come with the material. The resin mixture and fiberglass are applied to a mold in alternate layers. Fig. 51-5.

Some familiar commercial laminates are Formica® and Panelyte®. These have a hard surface and are used for tabletops and counter tops. They can be cut with ordinary woodworking tools. They are applied with contact cement. The cement is applied to the back of the laminate and to the surface to be covered. The cement is allowed to dry (about 20 minutes). Then the laminate is placed on the surface. It should be pressed down firmly. A rolling pin works well for this. A block of soft wood and a hammer may also be used.

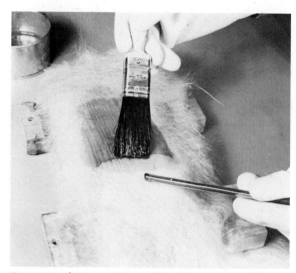

51-5. Applying resin to fiberglass material for a fruit tray. Layers of the glass material are laminated together using the liquid resin. Notice the protective gloves.

REVIEW QUESTIONS

1. What are three basic ways to join plastics?
2. What is meant by cohesion of plastics?
3. What types of mechanical fasteners may be used to join plastics?
4. How may plastics be laminated in the school shop?

Finishing Plastics in the School Shop

Among the several unique properties of plastic materials is that they do not need to be protected with a coating of finishing material. Plastic is its own finish. It is waterproof and resists many stains. Generally smooth, it needs little attention after it has been formed into a product. However, if a decorative finish is desired, it may be applied by one of two primary methods—*coloring* and *coating*. Fig. 52-1.

Before plastic is finished, it should be polished and buffed. Remove deep scratches with abrasive paper. Then buff to a high lustre on a buffing wheel. Use a light pressure on the wheel. Keep the plastic moving to prevent burning. Fig. 52-2.

Coloring

Most plastic sheet materials (acrylics) can be bought in a wide range of colors. Clear plastic can, however, be colored with special dyes. The plastic should be buffed smooth and cleaned with detergent and water. The plastic is placed in a pan or dish of dye. It is allowed to soak until colored to the desired shade. Fig. 52-3. (The dye is made from plastic coloring powders mixed with warm water.) Remove the plastic and rinse in warm water. Resins for plastic casting and fiberglass laminating can be dyed by adding the colored powder directly to the resin.

Certain plastics can be colored by applying dye to a carved design. The plastic can be carved using a high-speed cutting tool. Flower designs as well as other designs can be carved into plastic this way. The carved design may be colored by using a hypodermic needle and dye as shown in Fig. 52-4.

Coating

Some very interesting effects may be obtained by glazing a plastic surface. Crystal-glazing liquids can be purchased in a wide range of colors. They can be applied with equal success on plastic, glass, and metal. The liquid is brushed or sprayed on a clean, dry surface and allowed to dry. In drying, beautiful crystals are formed. Fig. 52-5. No further treatment is necessary, other than wiping with a clean cloth. Plastic trays, bowls, wall plaques, and containers can be glazed to add to their beauty.

REVIEW QUESTIONS
1. Why doesn't plastic need to be protected by a coating of finish?
2. How can plastics be colored?
3. How is a plastic surface glazed?

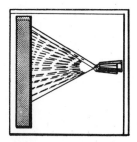

52-1. This chart illustrates the two methods of finishing plastics.

Finishing

Finishing is the process of treating the surface of a material for appearance and/or protection.

KIND OF FINISHING	DEFINITION	EXAMPLES
Coloring* DYE PENETRATES WORKPIECE	Applying penetrating dyes or chemicals to a material to change its color.	Dyeing sheet materials and liquid resins.
Coating* WORKPIECE	Applying a layer of finishing substance to the surface of a material.	Brush and spray lacquering and glazing.

*Coating could be considered a coloring process, since coating usually does change a product's color. However, it is customary to consider coating and coloring to be separate processes, as defined in the chart above.

52-2. Buffing plastic on a cloth buffing wheel. Be sure to keep the plastic moving. Always wear goggles when buffing.

52-3. Plastic being placed in a tray of dye for coloring.

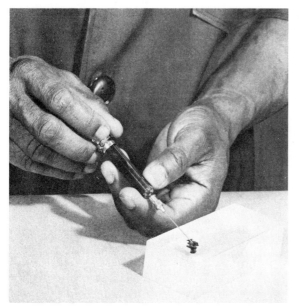

52-4. Dye being inserted into an internally carved flower.

52-5. This glazed decorative jar shows interesting crystal formations.

Thinking about a Career

PLASTICS DISTRIBUTOR

The small New England town where Bob lives has several small manufacturing plants. These factories make a variety of products. Most of the products are sold across the country. "In high school," says Bob, "I worked summers at one of the factories. They made a showcase used for displaying goods in department stores. Sheets of colored plastic were fitted into the sides of the case. These strips were for decoration only."

This factory was not the only user of plastic in Bob's city. A branch of the state university was located there. "They have a good art department," says Bob. "A friend of mine who was studying there mentioned that the school frequently ordered plastic for various art projects."

After Bob graduated from high school, he went to the local state university. He majored in business. After graduation, Bob took a job with an industrial supply firm. He worked as a salesman, traveling throughout a three-state area. He found that he was a good salesman. He also discovered that there was a strong demand for plastic in many of the factories that he visited. Industrial plastics, however, were not among the products he sold. This demand for plastics was not heavy in any single plant. However, many plants were using plastic. They ordered small quantities, but they ordered repeatedly. Bob learned from the plant managers that there were sometimes delays in shipment. The main supplier of industrial plastics was several hundred miles away. "I don't know when I first thought of selling plastics," said Bob, "but it must have been about that time."

Bob was on the road as a salesman for over five years. In that time, he married. He and his wife now have two children. "I suspect it was the need to be with my family that spurred me to look for another career," Bob says. "When I was single, I was happy as a salesman. I didn't mind spending most of the week on the road. After my marriage though, I didn't like the job at all. I needed a new career, a job that would keep me in my hometown with my family. I also needed a job that would pay me what I had been making as a salesman. Also, the new job had to offer some possibility for growth. I had made many contacts in my years as a salesman. I knew that these would be of some value if I went into the right business. In looking at the various products that I might sell, I thought again of industrial plastics.

"Finally, I decided that industrial plastics would be a good product. But I didn't just decide to sell plastic without first doing some research. I contacted the major plastic factories. I found out their prices and terms of payment. I checked on the number of nearby factories using plastic. I went back to some of the factories I had called on when I was a salesman. I asked them if their need for plastic was as strong as it had been. I tried to learn how much plastic they used in a year. All of this information gave me a better idea of whether or not I could make my business succeed. Of course, I knew that my contacts would not be enough. I also would need to offer good prices.

"I had to borrow money to start my business," Bob says. "I had some savings, but not much. I did some research on how much plastic I might be able to sell in a year. Then I went to the bank and applied for a loan. At first, the bank was not too interested in loaning me the money. Then they learned that there was no nearby supplier of industrial plastics. They then thought the loan might not be a bad risk for them. I rented a small store in an industrial park north of the city. This is my second location," says Bob, waving his hand towards his showroom of plastic samples.

In the back of Bob's building there is a small warehouse. Bob employs six people, all of them involved in cutting and making industrial plastic rods, tubes, and sheets. His business is not seasonal, but is steady year-round. He is the only distributor of industrial plastics in the city. He sells mainly to businesses. However, he sells quite a lot of plastic to people who need it for home projects. He also sells fiberglass to autobody shops. He carries a full line of plastic cements and dyes.

"Because I had done research and made some contacts, I had customers as soon as I opened the door. My prices were attractive. I could offer quick delivery and good service. I worked very hard to make the business a success. In a sense, my whole future depended on the success of the business," explained Bob.

Bob started his business over six years ago. "Plastics is a fascinating material," says Bob. "The development of the space program has created many new plastic products. The gains made in the development of industrial plastics have been remarkable in the last few years. Plastics can be used to make so many different things. In fact, two of the three local high schools are among my best customers. They offer plastics technology in their vocational programs."

Bob sees a strong future for his business. "I don't think that the need for plastics will decrease in the years ahead," he said. "In fact, it probably will grow. For me, selling plastics has been a good career."

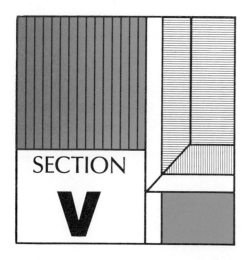

Manufacturing Technology

U.S. Department of Labor

---

53 Production Design

Designing new products, and the tooling to make them is part of designing for production. Marketing is also important in deciding whether to produce an object.

Research and Development

The new products, materials, and processes which help us to live better do not just happen accidentally. They are invented by persons who are trained in art, science, and engineering. These are the people who work in research and development. *Research and development* (or *RD* for short) is an area of industry responsible for developing and refining ideas leading to new or improved products, processes, and materials. RD is sometimes called "the industry of discovery." It is an important part of the industrial world. It requires many people of differing talents. Fig. 53-1.

Men and women have always been involved in RD work. Cave dwellers learned how to drill holes in stones. They found they could chip a stone so it would have a sharp edge. This was the primitive RD work that led to inventing the stone axe.

Throughout the ages people in all parts of the world have shown their inventiveness. Five thousand years ago the Egyptians already were using the potter's wheel. The Chinese had a workable loom before the time of Christ.

In modern research and development, corporations use the team approach. In automotive design, for example, engineers work on the engine and drive system. Artist/designers

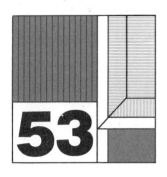

Zinc Institute, Inc.

53-1. This designer is evaluating the prototype of her product—a solar oven. She designed the oven as part of a student club activity.

deal with body styling. Similar RD teams design products such as refrigerators, motor scooters, and computers.

TYPES OF RD

As stated earlier, RD is concerned with new processes and materials as well as products. Let's take a closer look at each type.

Process RD involves experimentation with new methods of cutting, forming, fastening, and finishing the raw materials of industry. Good examples here are the development of computer-controlled machining centers and laser welding.

Materials RD uses experimental methods for creating new materials for use in industry. Think of the many plastics which have been developed in recent years. Plastics now are used for squeeze bottles, automobile bodies, and fishing rods. In the space program we have also seen many new materials such as titanium frames for electronic gear, special composite plastic airplane parts, and metal honeycomb cabin sections.

Product RD is directed toward the creation of new products for the manufacturing industries. The people who work on product development are called *industrial designers*. They are trained in art and engineering. Usually they work as teams to solve problems related to new products. Since they must design products which can be sold at a profit, they need to understand something about marketing.

Production Tooling

You may have heard the term "tooling up." This phrase is commonly used in the manufacturing industries. For example, when a company comes out with a new model automobile,

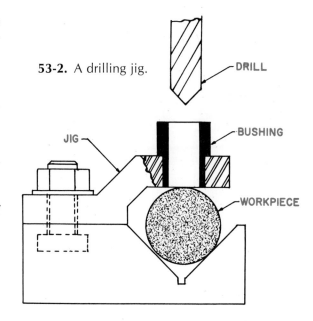

53-2. A drilling jig.

it must "tool up" for the new product. This means that special tools must be made to stamp out the newly designed bodies. The making of new bumpers, wheels, and headlights also requires new tools.

Production tooling (PT) is the element of industry concerned with these tools. Simply, it involves the assembling of all the tools, machines, and equipment necessary to make a product. If you were to make a coffee table, you would need handtools and machines to make the parts. You might need special devices to hold the pieces together while gluing them. Deciding what tools you need, and then getting or making them is all a part of "tooling up."

Production tooling, therefore, involves the following:

1. Deciding what tools are needed.
2. Ordering the tools you need but don't have.

3. Designing and making any special tools you need.

TOOLS USED IN PRODUCTION TOOLING

Jigs

A *jig* is a device that holds a workpiece securely so that a drilling or boring tool can be guided to an exact location. Study the drilling jig shown in Fig. 53-2. Note that the steel rod workpiece is held in such a position that a hole will always be drilled exactly through the diameter of the rod. This jig eliminates the task of having to locate the hole with a center punch. Then carefully clamp the piece in a vise before drilling. Jigs are valuable tools in production work. As a safety measure, small jigs are not usually fastened to the drill press table, except for holes above ¼″ in diameter. The drill bushing prevents the guide hole from enlarging.

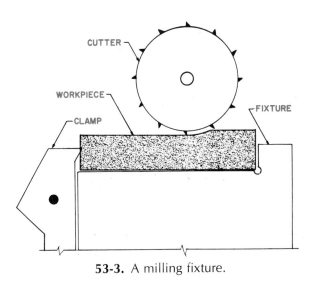

53-3. A milling fixture.

Fixtures

A *fixture* is a device that holds workpieces during machining or assembly operations. Fixtures are usually attached to a specific machine. Thus we have milling fixtures, lathe fixtures, grinding fixtures, assembly fixtures, and others. Figure 53-3 shows a fixture which clamps a workpiece securely in place during a milling operation. With fixtures, workpieces can be fastened quickly and easily. The finished pieces will always be alike.

Other Tools

While jigs and fixtures are two of the most important kinds of tools used in industry, there are many others that are also necessary. Pressing punches and dies, extrusion and drawing dies, and casting patterns are some examples. The people who make these devices are called *tool and die makers*. They are highly skilled crafters who must work and study for many years before becoming qualified.

Marketing

Marketing is the process of getting products from those who make them to those who use them. To do this, the people in marketing have certain jobs to perform. These are described in the paragraphs below.

MARKET RESEARCH

The aim of market research is to collect and study facts about customer needs and reactions to products. This is done through market or product preference surveys, test marketing, and by studying product sales. This information helps management to decide which kinds of products to make, and how products should be changed. Market research people must work closely with an RD program to ensure that the public gets the products it wants.

PRICING

Although the pricing of goods is frequently done by a separate division of a company, marketing has a part in it. Sometimes the marketing department has this as a main responsibility. Prices are set by considering all of the costs involved in making and selling a product. Raw materials, machines, tools, building rental, repayment of borrowed money, energy, employees' salaries, advertising and distrubuting—all these must be figured in the price of goods. Above all, the company must make a profit. It must be able to pay stockholders a dividend on their shares of stock. It must also invest in new equipment and in further research. In our society, profit is important to keep businesses efficient, and to keep them producing the goods we need.

PACKAGING

In industry, packaging refers to the containers used to hold products. You see and use many kinds of packages each day. The gum you chew comes in a wrapper; the shoes you buy come in a box; the soda you drink comes in a can or bottle. The purpose of these packages is to protect and identify their contents. Food wrappers keep foods clean and safe for you to eat. The wrapper also identifies the food. Of course, the package design must be attractive so that the consumer will buy the product.

ADVERTISING

The goal of advertising is to make the public aware of and interested in certain goods and services. Manufacturers advertise through television, radio, newspapers, and magazines.

They buy time or space to inform people of new products, and remind them of the value of older ones. Advertising can perform valuable services. For instance, through advertising we can learn about different brands of the same kind of product. Thus, we may select the one that suits us best. Of course, we must realize that advertisers tell us only the best things about a product. It is always best to make up our own minds about a product rather than buy it strictly because we are told it is good.

DISTRIBUTING

Distributing refers to all the activities that move a product from the manufacturer to the consumer. For most of the world's history, people used products and materials that originated in or near their own area. Many types of goods could not be transported over long distances. Those which could were very costly. Now much of what we use—food, clothes, even our homes—may have been brought from far away.

Trucks, trains, ships, and barges play an important role in distribution. Perhaps the greatest advance has come through air travel. For example, one company that makes earth-moving equipment promises delivery of replacement parts anywhere in the world within 48 hours. Without air delivery, a road construction project in a distant place could be delayed for weeks because of a defective part.

SELLING

After the product reaches the retail store or shop, someone has to sell it to the consumer. Sales personnel serve an important function for the customer in this way. They also perform other valuable services such as keeping buyers informed of new products. For example, they keep doctors up-to-date on new medicines. They make manufacturers aware of new equipment. They inform teachers about new books. Selling is the final step in the making-using cycle.

SERVICING

To service a product is to maintain and repair it when needed. Servicing is becoming increasingly important to the consumer. The reason for this is that so many of the things we use are becoming more complicated. We cannot always repair them ourselves. Electric appliances, automobiles, and power mowers need regular attention so that they will work properly. Service representatives do these jobs for us. Good service helps to sell products, because people want to know that they can get items repaired without too much trouble. As more and more of our products require regular servicing, more people are needed to service them. This is why the service industries are one of the fastest growing occupational groups.

REVIEW QUESTIONS

1. What are the three types of RD?
2. What is the job of an industrial designer?
3. What is the purpose of production tooling?
4. What is the difference between a jig and a fixture?
5. What are the seven kinds of jobs done in marketing?

|||||||||||||||||||||||||||||||||||||||||||||||| **KEY IDEA** ||||||||||||||||||||||||||||||||||||||||||||||||

THE FACTORY OF THE FUTURE

You may have heard of factories that use robots. You may have thought of these factories as "factories of the future." In fact, though, such factories exist today. The factory of the future will closely resemble these factories.

The factory of the future will be different from the factory as we now know it. In the future, factories will rely heavily on the computer. As Fig. A shows, the computer will be at the center of the future factory. All operations will be controlled by the computer. You can also see that robots will find important uses in the factory of the future. Figure A shows only one sequence of operations. A factory, of course, would probably have several such robots. Each robot would perform a different job. All of the robots would be controlled by the central computer. This computer would organize the work of the robots. It would speed the flow of workpieces through the factory.

The basic operations of the factory of the future are shown in Fig. A. These operations are explained in the following paragraphs.

1. A computer-aided design (CAD) system is used to plan the metal part. The design information is fed to the machining center (3) and the inspection station (5).

2. A parts carrier is controlled by a computer. Metal blanks are automatically loaded onto the carrier in the material storage area.

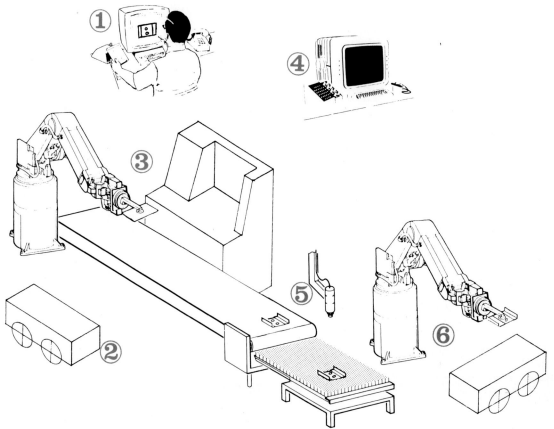

Fig. A. The basic work stations of the factory of the future: (1) computer-aided design system; (2) parts carrier; (3) robot; (4) remote computer terminal; (5) computerized inspection camera; (6) robot.

The parts carrier is guided to the production area by radio signals. These signals come from cables buried in the factory floor.

3. A robot unloads the metal blanks from the parts carrier. It places them onto the computer-controlled machining center. This machine cuts each workpiece to size. It punches holes in it and bends it to shape. The robot then unloads the shaped metal part from the machine. It places the part on the conveyor belt.

4. A remote computer terminal keeps track of the operation of the production line. It controls the number of parts being made. It also controls the speed of the line. The terminal can be used to change the type of part being made. This is called *flexible manufacturing*.

5. The finished workpieces are automatically inspected by a computerized camera. The camera compares the workpiece with the part design information in its memory. If the part fails to pass inspection, it is removed from the line. This information is then sent to the machining center (3). The computer changes the operations to correct the error.

6. A robot removes the workpiece from the conveyor. The robot places the workpiece on the parts carrier. The loaded parts carrier is then moved to an automated storage area.

The factory discussed here offers many advantages. It is more efficient than many factories today. It would also be almost accident-free. Robots could be used to per-form dangerous jobs. In a small factory of the future, there would be only a few employees. Some of these employees would operate the computer. Others would maintain and repair the robots. It is not hard to see that many jobs would be eliminated. This is one disadvantage of the factory of the future.

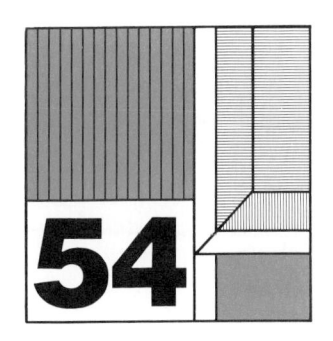

Production Planning

The planning for production must begin long before one starts to make a product. Fig. 54-1. First, the product plans and production figures (market forecast) must be studied. This information is needed to determine how many products (units) must be made. Bills of materi-

U.S. Department of Labor
54-1. In a large company, production planning can involve several people. The number of units that might be sold must be carefully estimated. Here, two members of the sales department confer with the engineer in charge of a product.

U.S. Department of Labor

54-2. Good production control is essential. Each of the steps in a production process must be carefully planned. Here, this production control specialist is checking the cost of a project.

BILL OF MATERIALS

Product: Vista Bookcase

Model Number: 2000-A   Date: Jan. 12, 19--

Drawing Number: 1100

Part Number	Description	Material	Quantity	Unit	Code
2000-A-1	Shelf, ¾ × 12 × 48	Walnut	18,000	B/Ft.	361
2000-A-2	Leg, 1 × 1 × 60	CRS Angle	20,500	L/Ft.	484
2000-A-3	Bracket, J68	CRS	4,100	Ea.	616
2000-A-4	Leg Cap, T6	ABS	4,100	Ea.	241
2000-A-5	Screws, #10 × ¾	Steel	10,000	Ea.	107

al are needed so that the proper raw materials and parts can be ordered. Fig. 54-2.

Another important activity is to estimate the cost of the product. Here one must study production costs, plus the time required for setting up the line.

54-3. Bill of materials for a bookcase. A route sheet and an assembly-line layout for the bookcase are also shown in this unit. Use these as examples when drawing up similar forms for your mass production project.

PROGRAM VISTA BOOKCASE	PART NAME SHELF				ISSUE DATE		PART NUMBER 2000-A-1		
FOR MODELS 2000-A	MATERIAL WALNUT	WT./LBS.	RGH.	FIN.	DRAWING NO. 1117				
		RELEASE					SHEET	OF	

LINE NO.	OPER. NO.	OPERATION DESCRIPTION	TOOL - MACHINE - EQUIPMENT DESCRIPTION	UNITS REQ'D.	TOOL OR B.T. NUMBER	HOURLY CAPACITY	
						GROSS	NET
1	1	CUT TO LENGTH	CUT-OFF SAW	2	1412		
2	2	SHAPE EDGES	ROUTER	3	801		
3	3	DRILL SCREW HOLES	DRILL PRESS	3	612		
4					USE DRILL		
5					JIG 1971-A-J4		
6	4	SAND SURFACES	DRUM SANDER	1	406		
7							
8							
17							
18							
19							
20							

54-4. Route sheet for the bookcase.

Production Control

If you were building a bookcase, you would not fasten the legs and brackets together until the necessary holes had been drilled. Neither would you paint the top if it had not been cut to shape and sanded. The same kind of clear thinking is necessary when making automobiles: The wheels are not put on until the frame has been completely assembled.

To make certain that a product will be made properly, the right materials must arrive at the right place, in the right amounts, and at the right time. This kind of careful planning is called *production control*, or PC. Fig. 54-3. This deals with the organization of the manufacturing processes. Its most important activities are *routing, scheduling,* and *dispatching.*

Closely related to production control is *plant layout.* The machinery and equipment must be arranged in a well-planned way within the factory. Usually this kind of layout is done by plant engineers who understand the production process.

Routing

Routing is preparing a plan of the procedures or steps needed to make something. A *route sheet* (or *plan of procedure*) is usually prepared for every kind of part to be made. For example, in making a bookcase with four shelves and four legs, you would need one route sheet for the shelves and one for the legs.

A typical route sheet is shown in Fig. 54-4. One begins this activity by analyzing or studying the product to determine how it is made. Every operational step is then listed in proper order. The route sheets are prepared from these.

Routing also involves making an *assembly-line layout* (sometimes called a *production control chart* or *process chart*). This layout gives a picture of how the materials and parts will move on the production line. A sample chart is shown in Fig. 54-5. The *process symbols* in Fig. 54-6 are used in keeping the layout up to date.

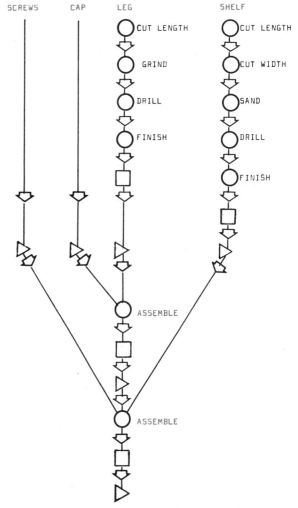

54-5. Assembly-line layout for the bookcase.

SYMBOL	MEANING
◯ OPERATION	CHANGING OR WORKING A MATERIAL
⇨ TRANSPORTATION	MOVING A PART FROM ONE PLACE TO ANOTHER
☐ INSPECTION	EXAMINING A PART FOR QUALITY
▽ STORAGE	KEEPING A PART SAFELY UNTIL NEEDED
◗ DELAY	HOLDING A PART, DUE TO UNEXPECTED EVENT

54-6. Process symbols. Study the assembly-line layout (Fig. 54-5) to see how these symbols are used.

Scheduling

Scheduling is fitting jobs or operations into a general timetable so that materials and parts enter the production line at the proper place and time. A schedule, then, is simply a method of relating facilities, orders, materials, and time.

A chart commonly used for schedules is a *Gantt chart.* One such chart is shown in Fig. 54-7. Note that it shows not only the number of planned units but also the number produced. It also shows when different production stages are to begin. It shows the dates for ordering and receiving materials, for starting production, and for sub- and final assemblies. Schedules are also called operation or progress charts.

To be useful, schedules must be based upon realistic estimates of the time needed for each operation. Time-and-motion-study technicians are responsible for this information.

Dispatching

Dispatching is issuing work orders or instructions to set the production line in motion. For example, the supervisors on the assembly line are notified when production should begin. They also are told how many units must be made each day. These orders are important. They tell when materials should be released from storage and when production should begin.

Production control is a very important activity. The smooth operation of the production line depends greatly upon the planners having done their jobs well. They must keep a constant watch on the line. All departments must report any changes or corrections in the scheduled operations. In this way the line will continue to run efficiently.

Quality Control

Products made in a factory must meet certain standards. Otherwise they will not be useful, and consumers will not buy them. The element of industry concerned with this part of production is quality control, or QC. Quality control helps prevent defective articles from being produced. In this way management tries to insure that a product will be acceptable to the consumer.

A QC program is rather broad. It begins with an inspection of incoming raw materials and parts. It also involves constant checking of the production process and the products.

It is possible to identify two main groups of quality control activities—those concerned

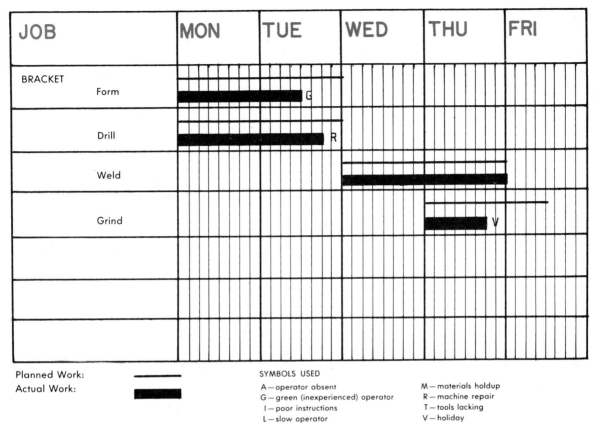

JOB		MON	TUE	WED	THU	FRI
BRACKET						
	Form		G			
	Drill			R		
	Weld					
	Grind					V

Planned Work: ————————

Actual Work: ████████

SYMBOLS USED

A — operator absent
G — green (inexperienced) operator
I — poor instructions
L — slow operator

M — materials holdup
R — machine repair
T — tools lacking
V — holiday

54-7. Example of a Gantt chart. The number of hours worked or the number of units produced can be shown on this chart. Henry L. Gantt, who developed this type of chart, was an American engineer in the 19th and early 20th centuries.

with acceptance and those concerned with prevention. *Acceptance* activities include the following:
• Inspecting raw materials and parts to be used in production.
• Designing inspection devices, gauges, and tools.
• Inspecting finished goods.
  Some typical *prevention* activities include:
• Studying defect or rejection records.
• Examining customer complaints.
• Training inspectors.
• Holding quality circle meetings with em-

ployees. At these meetings, the people who make the product discuss better ways of making the product.
• Employee morale meetings.
  When interchangeability of parts is important, there is one other very important function. This is to assure that the parts will fit together in the final assembly. This is done by setting rigid controls on the sizes of the parts. For example, a company might have to make 10,000 gears to be used in fishing reels. If the gears are just a tiny bit too large or too small, they will not fit in with the other parts of the

reel. Quality control assures that any one of those gears can be used in making any one of the 10,000 reels. This is interchangeability.

There are three steps in a quality control program: specifications, tooling, and inspection.

Specifications are detailed descriptions of the requirements for a product. Some requirements might be size, material, roundness, squareness, or flatness. For example, you might specify that a cutting board must be ¾" thick, 7" wide, and 12" long, and be made of basswood.

You might further state that you will accept boards that are ⅛" smaller or larger (±⅛") in any of the dimensions. This specifies the amount of error you will tolerate in each piece. It is important that the correct tolerance be allowed. Tool wear and operator error make it impossible for all the boards to be exactly the same size.

Tooling in quality control refers to the special devices required to measure the accuracy of parts. A "go/no-go" gauge is an example of such a tool. By slipping a part into this device the inspector can tell at a glance whether or not it is the right size.

Inspection of parts takes place after the specifications have been written and the special tools prepared. Inspectors must be trained to do their jobs in the production line. As stated above, this is a quality acceptance activity. All machine operators are expected to examine their own work. They are qualified to do this because they know what the part should look like. Thus, they can detect flaws early.

Inspection Methods

The kind of product being made determines the method by which it is inspected. In a good QC program, every automobile made is inspected thoroughly. However, it is not practical to examine every vitamin pill or electrical fuse. The main methods of inspection are described here.

Complete, or *100 percent, inspection* is done on items such as machines, vehicles, and appliances. Very complex products such as these need close attention. This method is highly expensive. Though it is very reliable, it is not foolproof.

Random sampling is a method by which decisions about the quality of a product are made by examining a small number of the items, taken from a larger batch. For example, from a batch of 10,000 ping pong balls, 100 are selected at random for testing. If 90 of them meet the product specifications, the whole batch is accepted. If not, the batch is rejected as scrap. Most of the product inspection is done by sampling methods. This is reliable and far less expensive than 100 percent inspection.

Destructive testing is a sampling method in which the sample is destroyed in order to test it. Electrical fuses are an example. The samples must be destroyed to see if they do, in fact, work. Chairs are also inspected this way. "Torture-tested" for strength and durability, they are destroyed in the process.

REVIEW QUESTIONS

1. What is the purpose of production control in industry?
2. What is a route sheet?
3. What is a schedule?
4. What are the two types of quality control? Explain each type.
5. What are product specifications?
6. What are the three inspection methods used in quality control?

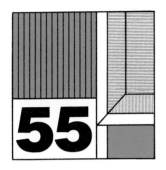

Personnel Management

Personnel management (PM) deals with the selection, hiring, training, and supervising of workers for industry. The production line cannot operate efficiently unless the right person, properly trained, is doing the right job.

Selection

Some people are recruited to fill job openings. Others are hired because they have applied for a job. In *recruiting*, members of a company's personnel department seek someone to hire. They go to schools and employment agencies. There, they talk to people who might be interested in working for their company. Those who are recruited as well as those who apply are interviewed and tested to see if they have the qualifications for the job.

Hiring

On the basis of the interview and the employment tests, the possible employee fills out an application, and has further tests and interviews with the personnel staff. These staff members are interested in learning about an applicant's education and interests. They also want to know whether he or she can get along with people. The personnel staff will explain the company benefit policies, such as sick leave, retirement, insurance, and vacations. They also describe salary and promotion opportunities.

If the interviews are satisfactory to all, the applicant or recruit will be hired. It is most important that the employee be happy with the company. The company must be satisfied that the employee can do a good job.

Training

Different jobs have different education and training requirements. Unskilled and semi-skilled workers usually can be trained *on-the-job* for their work. Some factories hold special classes for these people. For example, a janitor will be taught what is expected in keeping the shop clean and safe. He or she will be instructed about the proper use of the sanitation chemicals and cleaning compounds.

Just because these jobs require little training does not mean that they are not important. A factory that is not clean, safe, and well-maintained cannot operate.

Skilled workers come to the factory with skills they have learned in schools, in the

55-1. This personnel officer is explaining her company's benefit program to a new employee.

armed forces, or at other factories. For example, a machine operator must know how to read blueprints or plans. He or she must understand the different materials used and must know hand and machine tool skills. Still, the person must go through some training in the factory to learn how things are done there.

You can see that setting up training programs is an important task for those who work in personnel management. They must decide which person is best suited to a particular job. They must decide what additional training the person needs. A person hired as an assembler of small radios must know how to solder, use small hand tools, and test various circuits.

Supervision

After a person has been trained to do a job, supervisors from his or her own department and from PM will visit regularly to see if the work is being done properly. If the worker is making mistakes, these must be corrected. Extra training or retraining might be needed. The supervisor also identifies those workers who are doing an especially good job. Such workers are considered for promotion.

Studying Occupations

In this book you have learned about some of the kinds of jobs available in the manufacturing industries. You and many of your classmates will be working at such jobs when you leave school. What kind of job would you like? You can help yourself to prepare for a job in industry by studying some of these occupations.

Most important, you must get to know yourself. What are your likes and dislikes? What school subjects do you like the best? What kinds of hobbies do you have? What are the educational requirements for some specific occupations which interest you? In which occupations can you earn the most money? Which occupations offer the best future in

PERSONAL INVENTORY

I. Work Preferences

Check your likes with a plus (+) and your dislikes with a circle (○).
1. Work indoors.   ____
2. Work where I would sell things.   ____
3. Work involving mathematics and science.   ____
4. Work where I can be my own boss.   ____
5. Work with tools and machines.   ____
6. Work in drafting.   ____
7. Work requiring patience and accuracy.   ____
8. Work with other people.   ____
9. Work which is clean and neat.   ____
10. Work involving original thinking.   ____
11. Work directed by someone else.   ____
12. Work depending on my writing skill.   ____
13. Work which is physical.   ____
14. Work where I would meet people.   ____

II. School Subjects

Use check marks to indicate the subjects you like, and also how well you do in them.

Subject	Like it	Below Average Grades	Average Grades	Above Average Grades
1. Science				
2. Mathematics				
3. Social studies				
4. English				
5. Drafting				
6. Shop courses				
7. Business				
8. Art				
9. Physical education				
10. Others				

III. Activities

List the clubs, teams, or other groups to which you belong.

_____

_____

_____

_____

List your hobbies.

_____

_____

_____

_____

IV. Work Experience

List the jobs you have held. Check those you liked.

_____

_____

_____

_____

If you could choose anything, what kind of job would you like to have?

_____

_____

55-2. A personal inventory. The answers you give to the questions in the personal inventory can help you narrow your choice of a career. Answer the questions honestly and completely on a separate sheet of paper. (Do not write in the book.)

other ways? In which jobs do you think you will be most satisfied?

These are the questions you must answer in studying an occupation. The activities in Figures 55-1 and 55-2 will help you to gather information about a job and about yourself so that you can make an intelligent occupational choice. The most important thing you can do to prepare for an occupation is to work hard in school, and complete your high school education. The amount of education you have and your school grades are two of the first records an employer looks at. Fig. 55-3.

Safety

All workers must learn safety in their jobs in order to avoid accidents and prevent the spoilage of parts. Many factories have a *safety supervisor* who is responsible for the safety training of all workers. This person observes people at work to try to spot accidents before they happen. He or she helps instructors in the company's other training programs so that they can include safe practices as part of what they teach. Unit 9 offers more information on safety. Read it so that you can better understand the practices that must be followed to run a safe shop.

55-3. An occupational information form. By answering the questions asked here, you will be able to gather information on a job that interests you. Answers to the questions can be found through library research. A friend or neighbor might have a job similar to the one that interests you. You might interview that person. He or she should be able to give you helpful information.

REVIEW QUESTIONS
1. What are the four important activities in personnel management?
2. Why is the study of occupations important?

Occupational Information

1. What occupation interests you?
2. How much education or training is required for this job?
3. Is there now, or will there be in the future, a great demand for workers in this occupation?
4. What are the promotion possibilities?
5. Describe the salary, pension, vacation, and other benefits.
6. How many persons are now employed in this type of work?

Mass Production in the School Shop

An excellent way to learn how industries mass produce products is to plan such activities for the school shop or school student club. Fig. 56-1. In industry, divisions or departments are set up, each with certain jobs to perform. In Units 53, 54, and 55 you learned

about these tasks. If you are to mass produce an item in the shop, you will want to follow the industrial systems as far as possible. The groups and their tasks are as follows:

Research and Development
● Develops and designs a project.
● Makes detail and assembly drawings of the project.
● Constructs a pilot model (prototype).
● Works with Marketing Group.

Production Tooling
● Designs and constructs jigs and fixtures.
● Coordinates tooling work with Production Control Group.

Production Control
● Develops production flow charts.
● Keeps production records.
● Plans the work stations needed.
● Plans for the needed materials.
● Plans for the necessary tools, machines, and equipment.
● Routes and schedules tools, machines, equipment, and materials.

Quality Control
● Designs inspection gauges and systems.
● Plans inspection stations for assembly line.
● Inspects raw materials.

Personnel Management
● Sets up job descriptions.
● Selects workers.

Junior Achievement, Inc.

56-1. Manufacturing a product is just one step. The product must also be sold. This member of a student club is checking sales records.

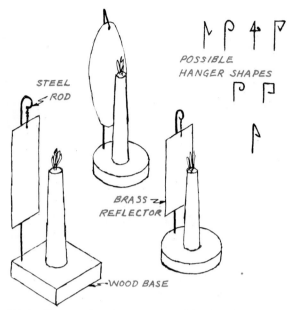

STEEL
ROD

POSSIBLE
HANGER SHAPES

BRASS
REFLECTOR

WOOD BASE

56-2. Design sketches of a candleholder. Any one of these styles may be selected for mass production. Note the possible shape for the hook at the end of the hanger.

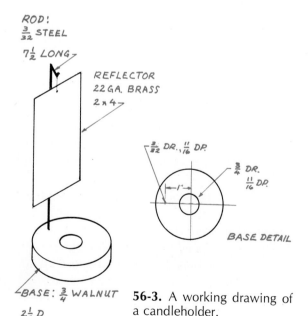

ROD:
$\frac{3}{32}$ STEEL

$7\frac{1}{2}$ LONG

REFLECTOR
22 GA. BRASS
2 x 4

$\frac{3}{32}$ DR., $\frac{11}{16}$ DP.

$\frac{3}{4}$ DR.
$\frac{11}{16}$ DP.

1"

BASE DETAIL

BASE: $\frac{3}{4}$ WALNUT

$2\frac{1}{2}$ D

56-3. A working drawing of a candleholder.

- Trains and supervises workers.
- Sets up a safety program.
- Keeps time cards of the number of hours worked.

Manufacturing
- Operates the production line.
- Coordinates work with other groups.

Marketing
- Determines the number of products (units) to be made.
- Figures the cost of each unit.
- Figures the selling price of each unit.
- Keeps sales or distribution records.
- Coordinates work with Research and Development Group. The following paragraphs discuss each of these tasks as they apply to one project. The project to be produced is a candleholder.

Research and Development

The candleholder is but one example of a project to be produced in the school shop. You may wish to select another from the project ideas shown on pages 424-440. Or, you may design something else as a class activity.

Design sketches of holder ideas are shown in Fig. 56-2. A working drawing of the selected design is shown in Fig. 56-3. The bill of materials is shown in Fig. 56-4. Note that steel, walnut, and brass have been selected as the materials. One important feature of the project is that any of a number of scrap materials can be used to keep the costs down. For example, the rod can be made of steel, bronze, or aluminum welding rod, either ⅜₂″ or ⅛″ in diameter. Small pieces of other scrap rod could be used. The base can be of any wood—walnut, mahogany, pine, cherry, or gum scraps—¾″ to 1″ in thickness. The reflec-

| No. | Size | | | Name of part | Material | Unit cost | Total cost |
	T	W	L				
1	$\frac{3}{32}''$		$7\frac{1}{2}''$	ROD	STEEL		
1	$\frac{3}{4}''$	$2\frac{1}{2}''$	$2\frac{1}{2}''$	BASE	WALNUT		
1	22 ga.	$2''$	$4''$	REFLECTOR	BRASS		

56-4. The bill of materials for the candleholder.

tor can be of any scrap metal that can be easily polished to a bright luster.

A sample, or prototype, of the project should be made to check the design and construction operations. Because of the project's simplicity, separate, detail drawings of the three parts are not needed.

The Research and Development Group must work with the Marketing Group to figure out how many of the candleholders to make. The number will depend on whether the product will be offered for sale, or whether it will be made only for class or club members.

Production Tooling

The Production Tooling Group must work closely with the Production Control Group. Both groups must study the product drawings and the prototype. They must answer the question, "What is the best way to make the candleholder?" Look at the route sheets (or plans of procedure) in Figs. 56-5, 56-6, and 56-7. Note that the only special tool you will need for the job is the rod length gauge. Fig. 56-8. You also will need a special pattern, called a base pattern. Fig. 56-9 (page 380).

PROGRAM CANDLEHOLDER		PART NAME	ROD		ISSUE DATE		PART NUMBER		
FOR MODELS		MATERIAL STEEL	WT./LBS. RGH. FIN.						
			RELEASE				SHEET OF		

LINE NO.	OPER. NO.	OPERATION DESCRIPTION	TOOL - MACHINE - EQUIPMENT DESCRIPTION	UNITS REQ'D.	TOOL OR B.T. NUMBER	HOURLY CAPACITY	
						GROSS	NET
1	1	MARK LENGTH	LENGTH GAUGE, FILE				
2	2	CUT LENGTH	NIPPERS				
3	3	DEBURR ENDS	GRINDER				
4	4	POLISH	STEEL WOOL				
5	5	BEND HOOK	VISE, PLIERS				
6	6	CLEAN	LACQUER THINNER				
7			CLEAN RAGS				
8	7	FINISH	CLEAR SPRAY LACQUER				
9							
10							
11							
12							
13							
14							
15							
16							

56-5. The route sheet for the rod.

PROGRAM CANDLEHOLDER		PART NAME	BASE		ISSUE DATE		PART NUMBER		
FOR MODELS		MATERIAL WALNUT	WT./LBS. RGH. FIN.						
			RELEASE				SHEET OF		

LINE NO.	OPER. NO.	OPERATION DESCRIPTION	TOOL - MACHINE - EQUIPMENT DESCRIPTION	UNITS REQ'D.	TOOL OR B.T. NUMBER	HOURLY CAPACITY	
						GROSS	NET
1	1	TRACE SHAPE,	BASE PATTERN,				
2		LOCATE HOLES	PENCIL, SCRIBER				
3	2	DRILL CANDLE	3/4" MACHINE SPUR				
4		HOLE	BIT, DRILL PRESS				
5	3	DRILL ROD HOLE	3/32" DRILL, DRILL				
6			PRESS				
7	4	CUT OUT	BAND SAW				
8	5	SAND EDGES	DISC SANDER				
9	6	SAND TOP	MEDIUM AND FINE				
10		AND BOTTOM	SANDPAPER				
11	7	FINISH	WIPE-ON FINISH,				
12			CLEAN RAGS				
13							
14							
15							
16							

56-6. The route sheet for the base.

PROGRAM CANDLEHOLDER		PART NAME REFLECTOR			ISSUE DATE	PART NUMBER			
FOR MODELS		MATERIAL BRASS	WT./LBS.	RGH. FIN.					
			RELEASE			SHEET OF			
LINE NO.	OPER. NO.	OPERATION DESCRIPTION	TOOL - MACHINE - EQUIPMENT DESCRIPTION		UNITS REQ'D.	TOOL OR B.T. NUMBER	HOURLY CAPACITY		
							GROSS	NET	
1	1	CUT OUT	SQUARING SHEARS						
2	2	DEBURR EDGES	SMOOTH FILE						
3	3	DRILL ROD HOLE	⅛" DRILL, DRILL PRESS						
4									
5	4	POLISH	STEEL WOOL						
6	5	CLEAN	LACQUER THINNER, CLEAN RAGS						
7									
8	6	FINISH	SPRAY LACQUER						
9									
10									
11									
12									

56-7. The route sheet for the reflector.

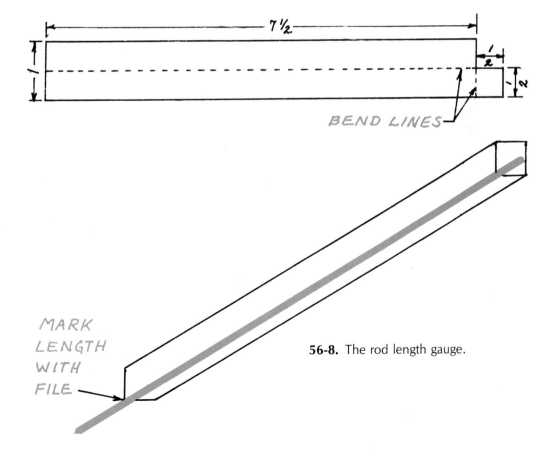

BEND LINES

MARK
LENGTH
WITH
FILE

56-8. The rod length gauge.

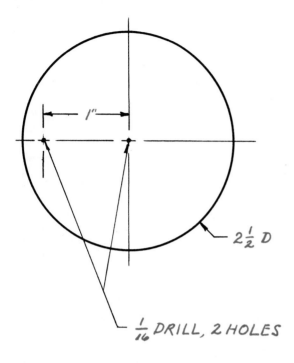

BASE PATTERN
22 GA. SHEET METAL
56-9. The base pattern.

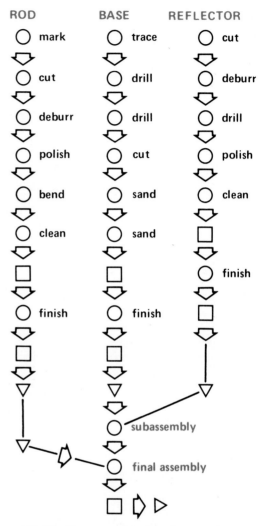

56-10. The assembly-line layout chart.

Production Control

As stated above, the tooling and control groups work closely together. Working from the route sheets, the Production Control team assembles the tools, equipment, and materials needed to make the project. From this, an assembly-line layout chart is prepared. Fig. 56-10. This will be helpful in organizing the production line so that materials move easily and efficiently to the work stations.

The following notes will be helpful in organizing the production work.

1. The rod can be cut with nippers, side-cutting pliers, or a hacksaw. Deburring (removing sharp edges) can be done with a file,

grinder, or belt sander. The hanger may have several shapes. (See Fig. 56-3.) Depending on its shape, bend the hook with hammer and vise, pliers, a metal brake, or a metal bender.

2. Trace the base pattern with the pencil. Mark the holes with a scriber. Note that the holes are drilled to within ⅛" of the base bottom. Set the drill press depth gauge for this operation. When handsanding the base,

be sure to "break" the sharp corners. Any good wipe-on oil or varnish finish can be used.

3. Set the squaring shears to cut the 2″ and 4″ dimensions for the reflector. The rod hole is drilled oversize so that the reflector can be easily moved.

Quality Control

Inspect the rod, base, and reflector prior to assembly. Look for dents, scratches, or a poor finishing job. Following the final assembly, inspect the project again. Be sure that the rod is tight in the base. If it is loose, place a drop of super-glue on the tip of the rod. Reinsert the rod in the hole. Make certain that the rod is straight in the hole, and that the reflector hangs freely.

Personnel Management

Each member of the manufacturing team must be trained to do a certain job. Short job descriptions for each task must be written before training can take place. These descriptions list the jobs that must be done to com-

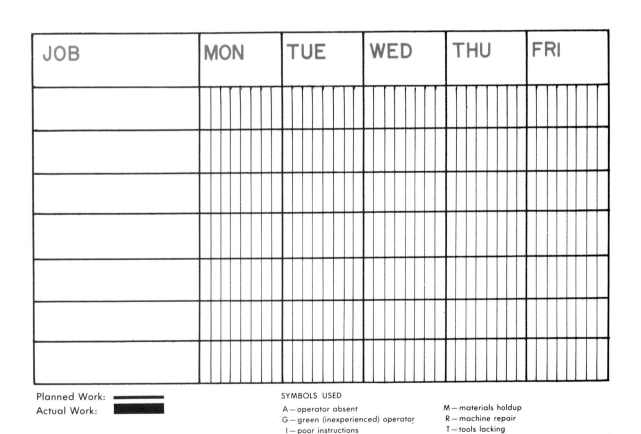

JOB	MON	TUE	WED	THU	FRI

Planned Work: ━━━━
Actual Work: ▰▰▰▰

SYMBOLS USED
A — operator absent
G — green (inexperienced) operator
I — poor instructions
L — slow operator

M — materials holdup
R — machine repair
T — tools lacking
V — holiday

56-11. The Gantt chart is used for work scheduling.

plete an operation or step. Following, for example, is a description of rod deburring.

Rod Deburring. The operator must take the rod that has been cut to length and smooth the ends of the rod on the grinder. Wear goggles while doing this operation. Roll the tip lightly against the wheel, just enough to remove any sharp burrs. Be careful not to sharpen it to a point.

When all the job descriptions have been written, the trainers must work with the class instructor to teach the operators these jobs.

Manufacturing

Manufacturing can begin when the materials are available, the tools and machines are ready, and the workers have been trained. Supervisors, working with the instructor, watch the work to be sure everything is going according to plan. A safety inspector also watches for unsafe activities. These must be corrected. The Quality Control inspectors check each piece to make sure it meets the standards of quality. Use the Gantt Chart to schedule and supervise the work. Fig. 56-11.

Marketing

As mentioned, the Marketing Group worked with the Research and Development Group to select the product and decide how many pieces must be produced. As the work proceeds, they also must decide the cost of the product. See Fig. 56-12. This cost sheet will help identify the items to be considered when calculating this cost. It will also determine how much profit should be made. If the candleholder is to be sold, the Marketing Group may wish to design a package and

---

Cost-Price Sheet – 25 Candleholders

1. Materials   Total
   a. _____
   b. _____
   c. _____   _____
2. Tools and Equipment
   a. _____
   b. _____
   c. _____
   d. _____
   e. _____
   f. _____   _____
3. Shop Rental   _____
4. Energy (gas, electricity, etc.)
   a. _____   _____
   b. _____   _____
5. Marketing (packaging, advertising)
6. Labor @ $3.75/hour. (May be omitted.)   _____
                                             _____
                        Grand Total   _____

If you produced 25 of the candleholders, how much would you have to charge for each in order to break even? $_____. How much would you have to charge to make a 25 percent profit? $_____.

56-12. A cost-price sheet. Use this sheet to figure the cost of the products. Use it also to figure the price you must charge for each candleholder to make a profit.

advertising posters. If this is to be a student club activity, salespeople may have to go out into the community and sell the holder.

REVIEW QUESTIONS

1. List some of the jobs to be done in Research and Development, Production Control, and Quality Control.
2. What is a job description?

Thinking about a Career

LAWN FURNITURE MANUFACTURER

When Tom was in high school he took all of the woodworking classes he could. In those classes, the projects he most enjoyed making were the larger projects. "Some students enjoyed making small projects, such as decorated boxes and birdhouses. I always liked making the larger projects, though. This may have been because I didn't have the patience and fine hand skills needed to make, say, a jewelry box. I always liked to work with big pieces of wood," Tom recalls. "I made a table and really enjoyed that."

In the summer before his senior year, Tom helped his father build a garage behind their house. "We bought a lot of two-by-fours," recalls Tom. "We used these to frame in the garage. Dad was not a careful estimator. So when we finished framing in the garage, we had several two-by-fours left. We could have returned them to the lumber yard for credit. However, in a magazine I had seen a photo of some yard furniture made from two-by-fours. The summer before we had laid a patio in the backyard. We had no lawn furniture for it. I thought that the furniture I planned to make would look nice there."

Making the lawn furniture was an easy job for Tom. He cut the lumber to the proper length and bolted the pieces together. He finished the wood with a weatherproof stain. In this way he made a chair, a couch, and a chaise lounge. Using some vinyl she bought at a discount store, his mother made cushions for the couches. She stuffed the cushions with foam rubber.

When his parents' friends saw the furni-

ture, they asked Tom if he could make some for them. He said he could, and named what he thought was a fair price.

"Furniture of a similar design was available at the local discount stores," said Tom. "I had seen it there and knew what it cost. I knew that my price would be attractive."

Tom found that it was not difficult to make those other chairs and couches. In fact, he found that they were easier to make than the first ones. When a few more of his parent's friends wanted lawn furniture, he went to the lumber yard and bought a good supply of two-by-fours. Then, he precut the wood to the needed lengths. By doing this, he needed only to assemble and finish the chair. "I didn't realize it then," said Tom, "but looking back, I can see that I was using one of the principles of mass production. That principle is the standardization of parts.

"After I graduated from high school, I wasn't sure what I wanted to do, but I needed an income, even though I continued to live at home. So, a few weeks after graduation, I got a job at a twenty-four hour grocery store. I stocked shelves at night. I didn't like the job and knew that I wouldn't be able to stand it very long. I needed to find another job. Then I remembered the lawn furniture I had made the previous summer. I thought that if I sold enough lawn furniture, I would be in business for myself. It was a dream—but it worked.

"I started by running a small classified ad in the local paper. This ad didn't pull very well. In fact, only one person called. I was discouraged. My mother suggested that I run a display ad on the back of the Saturday paper. I did. It cost me about $100. Mom loaned me the money. Through that ad, I sold over 40 chairs for $25.00 each. It took me almost ten days to make all of the chairs."

Today, Tom operates not out of his garage but out of a small factory. He has over twenty employees—each of them is involved in the making of wooden lawn furniture. "I started with just a power saw and an idea," says Tom. "I think that I put the most energy into my business in the beginning. It was hard then. After things got going, I found that I had talents I hadn't suspected. For example, I had never thought of myself as a salesman. However, I was able to convince several discount stores to carry my lawn furniture. My factory operates year-round, though you might think our market is somewhat seasonal. Though my factory is in the Midwest, I ship to all parts of the country.

"In high school, I never really thought of myself as being the type to head up a small manufacturing business," says Tom. "To be honest, I wasn't sure what I would do as a career. To some, it might seem that I have been lucky. But I know that it can't be all luck," says Tom. "I work hard in my business. And always, I am astonished at what resulted from an idea I had for using a few leftover two-by-fours."

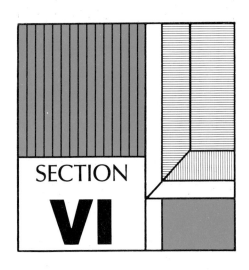

SECTION VI

Construction Technology

Georgia-Pacific

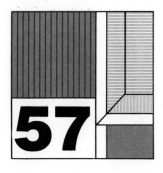

Construction—Past and Present

57

Before history was written, people lived in caves. These gave them shelter. They also protected them from wild animals and unfriendly tribes. They went out to hunt only during the day. After animals became scarce near the caves, they had to move to hunt for food. They then became wanderers. They lived in simple shelters which they built to stay in for only a few nights. Then they moved on.

It was not long before these people learned to grow their own food. This made it possible for them to live in one place and to build permanent shelter. The kinds of homes they built depended on where they lived and on the climate.

When humans first began to build, their main purpose was to protect themselves from the weather and from animals. Primitive planners made the best use of the building materials available. They also adapted their buildings to the land and the climate.

For example, thousands of years ago the Pueblo native Americans of the American Southwest dug pit homes into the ground. They also built stone houses and towers on the surface. They made cliff dwellings. Fig. 57-1. The American Indians were the first to use solar heating and cooling. The American Southwest has high daytime temperatures and very low night temperatures. Buildings there needed to be designed to delay the entry of heat into the building until late in the day, when it was needed. The Pueblo native Americans achieved this by using materials that retained heat, such as *adobe*, (a building material made of mud and straw). Often, the adobe was formed into bricks. Adobe absorbed the sun's heat during the day and released it into the dwelling at night. By building the dwelling spaces close together,

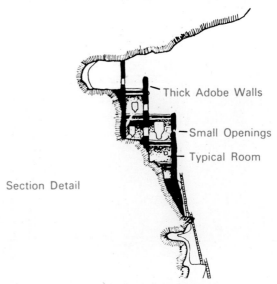

Thick Adobe Walls

Small Openings

Typical Room

Section Detail

57-1. Pueblo cliff dwellings used adobe to store the sun's heat for the cool evening hours.

57-2. The Eskimo igloo resists winds and makes use of solar heating.

the minimum surface was exposed to the outside, thus limiting the temperature change inside. Adobe homes also exist in China, Africa, and Mexico.

In rainy areas, people living in hot, damp jungle swamps built well-ventilated homes on tall poles. Thatched roofs were made of grass. Sometimes they took the shape of a great parasol.

The primitive architect adapted the shelter to the climate and the materials available. For example, the native Americans who roamed the Great Plains of North America were nomads who followed the buffalo herds. Because their housing had to be portable, they designed the tepee. This was a light structure of saplings laced to each other, tied at the top, and covered with animal skins. The tepee is an advanced form of shelter.

In other parts of the world, such as in the Mideast, a different kind of tent was used. There, the tent needed to serve as a sunshade and as a shield against sandstorms. In the far north, the Eskimo, a nomad hunter, built igloos (shelters of snow and ice). Having a dome shape, they offered the greatest resistance to high wind and exposed the least surface to its chilling effect. Fig. 57-2. These early designers had discovered the insulating value of snow. Some igloos were built of sod. Sod homes were also found in other parts of the world. Modern underground houses are adaptations of these sod houses.

As people gathered in settlements, architects began to use many materials. In Europe many kinds of stone and brick were used for building churches and commercial buildings. In early America, some of the best architects were the builders of log houses and barns. Many of the early builders studied nature to learn ways of building. For example, the bee honeycomb and the spiderweb are two examples of how nature developed structures that could be reproduced. The use of steel changed building methods in the twentieth century. Frank Lloyd Wright once said that steel is "the spider spinning." For example, the Golden Gate Bridge gains its strength from a design similar to that of a spider web.

Steel framework also made high-rise structures possible. As cities developed, high-rise buildings began to be built. Most early high-rises had a steel frame and a brick covering. Today, most high-rise buildings are constructed using a basic skeleton of steel with curtain walls of glass, ceramics, or other material. Many high rises are also constructed using cast-in-place concrete with an exterior covering of brick, stone, and glass. The modern geodesic dome, another innovation in building, is much like the Eskimo igloo. Fig. 57-3.

In the United States housing design depends on location. For example, houses in warm climates often are built of concrete block. Little wood is used. In hilly coastal areas, structures must be built over uneven ground. In cities, where privacy is important, townhouses were built.

57-3. The geodesic dome is patterned after the igloo.

The materials used in houses vary throughout the country. In the Southwest, many homes are adobe. In the Midwest, wood homes are the norm. Builders choose the materials that are plentiful, choosing the kind of wood and wood products most commonly available. Thus, many homes in California are of redwood, while cedar is used widely in the Northwest. Homes in the Midwest and South have a great deal of fir and pine. In the Sunbelt, the walls may be of concrete block or adobe. In other sections of the country, homes with brick veneer over wood frames are com-

mon. Galvanized steel and aluminum are commonly used for metal studs, trusses, and siding.

Office structures and airports are commercial buildings. They are built of steel, concrete, glass, plastics, and stone. Steel columns are set in concrete as were the stakes that were set in mud in ancient dwellings. Beams and girders are riveted to the columns just as the cross timbers of a hut were lashed together with grass rope. Glass and masonry fill the structure. Many commercial buildings have curved roofing. This roofing is a tension structure of bridge cables supported by great concrete vertical tiers.

Architecture today must meet the demands of safety, shelter, social needs, convenience, and beauty. All of these are elements of good design. In designing buildings, architects are guided by the traditions of the past.

Major Types of Construction

There are three major types of building construction.

1. *Heavy building construction*, which is primarily concerned with the erection of commercial, industrial, educational, and institutional, buildings. Materials include steel, concrete, brick, glass, and ceramics. Interiors may be of wood construction.

2. *Residential or light commercial construction*, which is concerned mainly with the building of homes, apartments, condominiums, and small commercial buildings. These often are primarily of wood frame construction.

3. *Highways and other heavy construction*, which includes railroads, earth-moving projects, pipelines, public utilities, water and sewer systems, dams, bridges, and electrical

utilities. Many different materials are used, such as gravel, earth, sand, steel, oil, wood, cement, glass, and plastic. In the units that follow, you will learn more about these three kinds of construction and the people who make the construction possible.

Careers in Construction

The construction industry offers more than two hundred different careers. They range from construction laborer to architect or engineer.

In the United States more than four million people work in the construction industry. Construction workers may work high on a skyscraper. Fig. 57-4. They also may work beneath the ground on subways and tunnels.

Some jobs in construction are available for people who do not finish high school. Other jobs require three to five years of apprenticeship. An *apprenticeship* is a method of learning "on the job" with related instruction. Construction jobs require either apprenticeship training or vocational and technical training in a vocational school and/or community college. For some jobs, a college degree is required. For example, it takes four to six years of college to become an engineer or architect.

You will learn about many of these careers by studying different kinds of construction. The following paragraphs discuss some of the major career opportunities in construction. There are three types of careers: professional careers, technical careers, and skilled-construction careers.

PROFESSIONAL CAREERS

Architects. Architects design homes, commercial buildings, bridges, and other projects.

Architects must be licensed in the state in which they work. They must graduate from an accredited college or university and then spend three years in a registered architect's office to learn details of the job. Architects plan a variety of structures ranging from homes and condominiums to churches, hospitals, and factories. An architect must work with the client and building contractor.

57-4. Many skilled construction workers must be willing and able to work in high places.

Engineers. Many kinds of engineers work in the construction trade. Two of the most important are civil and electrical engineers. *Civil engineers* design and supervise the construction of roads, airfields, tunnels, and bridges. Many civil engineers have supervisory positions. Some are site superintendents on large construction jobs. Other civil engineers do designing and planning. Others execute an entire project. *Electrical engineers* work in many different fields. They may design, manufacture, and install power plants. They also may work as supervisors of electrical or telephone systems.

TECHNICAL CAREERS

Before any structure is built, a complete set of detailed drawings that give the exact dimensions and specifications of the structure and all of its parts are drawn. The workers who draw these plans are *drafters.* Different drafters specialize in different areas of work.

After the plans are drawn, they are studied carefully to estimate what it will cost to build the structure. This estimate is used to make a bid. If the bid is accepted, the construction company or subcontractor get a contract to build. Among other things, the accuracy of that bid will determine whether the contractor makes a profit on the job.

The accurate placement of the structure upon the land is the job of the *surveyor.*

Once a bid is accepted and a contract is signed, the contractor must see to it that the proper building materials arrive on time. The person who ensures that materials arrive at the site in correct order and on time is called an *expediter.* Expediting is a support service.

The person who tests and inspects the materials used on a project is called an *inspector.* Testing and inspecting are also support services. For example, plumbing and electrical work are carefully inspected.

The *materials distributor* makes sure the contractor receives good construction materials as cheaply and quickly as possible. Materials distributors have the widest range of responsibilities and jobs of all the support services.

Many of these careers require people with two to four years of specialized training.

SKILLED CONSTRUCTION (CRAFT OCCUPATIONS) WORKERS

Craft occupations in construction fall into three major groups: structural, finishing, and mechanical.

Careers concerned with structural construction include carpenters, bricklayers, stonemasons, cement masons, iron workers, riggers, boilermakers, operating engineers, and welders.

Careers concerned with finishing include lathers, plasterers, dry wall installers, marble setters, terrazzo workers, painters, glazers, roofers, floor layers, and asbestos and insulation workers.

Careers concerned with mechanical construction include plumbers, pipe fitters, operating engineers, and elevator constructors. The largest craft groups are the carpenters, construction laborers, operating engineers, painters and paperhangers, and plumbers and pipefitters. Skilled construction workers must learn their jobs as apprentices. As an apprentice, a worker works for and with a journeyman, and takes classes in related construction. For some jobs, the worker must be a graduate of a specialized program offered by a vocational or technical school. Some of the craft occupations are discussed in the following paragraphs.

• *Carpenters* form one of the largest skilled trade groups. They build wood building frames and install exterior and interior trim. They also lay floors and build concrete forms and scaffolds. Carpenters cut, shape, and fasten wood. Carpenters usually learn their trade by completing a four-year apprenticeship course.

• *Cement masons* and *terrazzo workers* specialize in finishing the concrete surface of floors, walls, and streets. This makes them strong and watertight. Terrazzo workers are masons with certain skills.

• *Bricklayers*, *stone masons*, and *marble setters* construct walls, partitions, fireplaces, and chimneys from brick, stone, and marble. In addition to laying brick, they build structures with concrete block, cylinder blocks, structural tiles, and gypsum block.

• *Iron workers* erect, assemble, and install metal supports in the construction of industrial, commercial, and large residential buildings. *Structural iron workers* erect the steel framework of bridges, buildings, and other structures. *Reinforced iron workers* (*rod people*) set steel rods in concrete forms to reinforce concrete structures.

• *Operating engineers* operate and maintain power-driven machinery. This machinery includes cranes, bulldozers, and power shovels.

• *Plumbers* and *pipe fitters* install pipe systems. These systems carry water, steam, and other liquids or gases. Plumbers and pipe fitters are often considered to be a single trade. However, most workers in these areas specialize in one or the other. For example, water, gas, and waste disposal systems are installed by plumbers in residential and commercial buildings. Pipe fitters install pressure systems for oil refining.

• *Construction electricians* lay out, install, and test electrical fixtures, equipment, and wiring. Many electricians are self-employed, while others work for general contractors. Electricians maintain and repair equipment and wiring for homes. They also work on commercial and industrial buildings.

• *Painters* and *paperhangers* apply finishes to walls and other surfaces. A painter applies paint, varnish, stains, enamel, and lacquer to interior and exterior surfaces. A paperhanger covers inside and outside walls with wallpaper and other materials.

• *Asbestos and insulation workers* install insulation in buildings.

• *Glazers* work with glass and plastics. They cut and install the glass and plastic used in buildings.

• *Dry wall applicators* install dry walls in buildings.

• *Floor covering installers* cover floors with tile, vinyl, carpeting, and other materials.

• *Landscape gardeners* work with other craft people to complete the building's exterior design.

REVIEW QUESTIONS

1. Who were some of the first people to use solar heating and cooling?
2. What is adobe?
3. What material revolutionized building in the twentieth century?
4. Name the three major types of construction.
5. Name the three major groups of craft occupations.

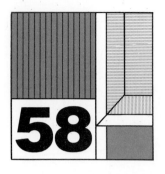

Heavy Building Construction

58

Heavy building construction is sometimes called commercial building construction. Such buildings include factories, schools, office buildings, and hospitals. Materials such as concrete, masonry (brick and stone), metal, glass, heavy timber, wood products, and ceramics are needed. The construction methods and completion techniques will vary. They depend on the size, kind, and location of each building.

Planning for Building

The exact purpose of and need for a particular building must be determined before any plans are made. A city may decide to build a new airport. A business may need a new factory. A company may decide to build a large office building. An architect is often hired to make preliminary sketches. These might be used to raise money to complete the building. Often land is already owned by the company that plans to build. Frequently, developers (people who are interested in building for profit) are used. These people look for a good location and build a specific type of building for sale or rent.

58-1. Engineers and architects are part of the management team.

Site Selection and Planning

Before construction can begin, a building site is needed. In cities, an old structure sometimes is torn down to provide the site. For factories and other industrial buildings, farm land might be purchased. Federal, state, or local governments may already own land on which to build public buildings. The site is very important. The amount of land available and the location can affect the building's design. Good transportation connections also are important. These include roads, railroads, waterways, and airports. Utilities must be available such as sewer, water, and electricity. The site must be suitable for the project. It must not interfere with any building codes.

Construction Financing

After basic plans have been made, the builder must find out if money is available to complete the structure. An industry may use its own funds to build a building. A state or local unit may issue municipal bonds to cover the cost. Developers often will go to banks and insurance companies for construction financing.

Architectural Design and Estimating

After the site has been selected and financing obtained, an architectural firm is hired to design the building. Architects work closely with the people who will own or use the facilities. Architects may specialize in a certain kind of structure. Some architects design school buildings. Others design hospitals. Still others design industrial buildings, offices, or other large structures. Architects' offices also employ engineers. They can help develop the design of the building and plan the necessary utilities. Finally, a complete set of architectural plans is prepared. At this point, an estimate of the total cost may be needed. More money may also be needed. Often, the first estimate of the building's price will have been too low.

Once the final plans are ready, they are sent out for bids to construction companies. These companies then prepare detailed drawings of the building. They need these drawings to get estimates for heating, ventilating and air conditioning, electrical, and plumbing systems. When all bids are in, the construction company will bid on the project. At this point, the company will hire a *general contractor*. The general contractor appoints a management team and hires the sub-contractors and office personnel needed to complete the project. Fig. 58-1.

In addition to engineers and architects, the management team includes other people. Expediters make sure the right building materials are delivered at the job at the right time. Site engineers and managers check the day-to-day progress of the project. Material distributors make sure that the contractor receives good construction materials as quickly and cheaply as possible. Other management team personnel include safety inspectors to oversee the construction. In addition, other inspectors may be needed. For example, concrete may need to be checked to make sure it meets specifications. At every step of the building, inspectors and testers check the material and job skills. It is far easier to correct a mistake when it is made than to correct it later.

Subcontractors must be selected to work on a specific part of the building. They may do this at one time or over a period of time. For example, the craft people who install utilities must work when the building is in its first construction stages. They also must come back at various times until the final installation of the utilities is completed.

First Steps of Construction

Before building can be started, utilities such as water, sewer, and electrical power must be available at the site. Also, the necessary roads must be constructed, particularly if the building is on raw land.

Construction managers oversee every phase of the operation. They meet with owners. They check the design of the building to make sure that it meets their needs. They also check that it is being built with the best available equipment and methods of construction. If something is wrong with the design, the construction management team must make sure that it is corrected. Construction management teams oversee the selection of subcontractors. They also develop the scheduling of the project. Once the construction is started, they coordinate the entire operation. They schedule activities, making sure that the work meets the architects' specifications. They keep a close watch on the work. This helps keep costs down and reduces scheduling problems. The most effective construction managers are well organized and budget conscious.

58-2. The 109-story Sears Tower has a steel frame.

Steps in Completing a Permanent Building

1. *Site Selection and Layout.* The site of the building must be carefully checked. Large buildings require soil that can support the structure. Site selection is also based on the use of the building. The building site is laid out by surveying the property with a builder's level. The boundaries of the site are established by markers. The location of the building itself is staked out. Batter boards are placed at each of its corners. Heavy cord is run from these boards to show the exact location of the excavation.

2. *Excavation.* The type and depth of the excavation is shown on the building blueprints. Large earth-moving equipment removes the earth for foundations and basements. Bulldozers and power shovels may be used. Operating engineers and heavy equipment operators run and maintain the equipment. Often, in building a large commercial building, excavations will go down an equivalent of two, three, or more stories. This deep excavation provides underground parking, space for utilities, and even some commercial space. Fig. 58-2.

3. *Completing the Foundation.* The foundation of the building must support the substructure as well as the building itself. For light buildings, the foundation may consist of footings and piers or foundation walls. For heavy buildings, piles, caissons, and other deep-wall foundations are needed. A *pile* is a long post of wood, steel, and/or concrete that is driven into the ground by pile drivers. These piles support the footings. A *caisson* is a shell or box filled with concrete. It is somewhat like a concrete pile but much larger. After these supports are in place, *forms* are built for footings and piers. Concrete is

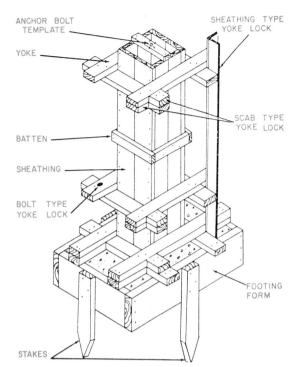

58-3. Forms for concrete columns.

poured into these forms, making them strong enough to support the rest of the building's structure.

4. *Completing the Basement Walls.* Once the foundation is hardened, forms are built for the poured concrete that will make the basement walls. The forms may be made of wood, steel, or reinforced plastic. These same kind of forms are used to build the shell of a building that is of poured concrete. Figs. 58-3 and 58-4. Once the forms are built or assembled, ironworkers called rod people place reinforced steel inside the forms before concrete is poured.

5. *Completing the Shell (Frame or Skeleton) of the Building.* There are three major methods of building the shell or skeleton.

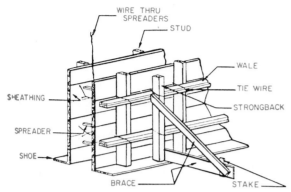

WIRE THRU SPREADERS
STUD
WALE
TIE WIRE
STRONGBACK
SHEATHING
SPREADER
SHOE
BRACE
STAKE

58-4. Forms for poured concrete walls.

• The shell may be of steel beams that are riveted or welded together.

• The shell can be of cast-in-place concrete. This kind of skeleton is assembled by building forms, installing reinforcing rod, and pouring the concrete one floor at a time. A moveable crane is placed at the center of the building. Forms are built. Rod people install steel rods for support. Liquid concrete is brought by truck. It is hoisted from ground level by the crane and poured into the forms. After each floor level is completed, the crane is raised and the next levels are poured. Skyscrapers may be built forty floors or more with this method.

• Heavy wood timbers, including laminated beams, may be used for the frame of the building. The heavy timber frame is fastened together with metal timber connectors.

6. *Installing Utilities and Other Features, such as Elevators.* This work is done as the skeleton is being constructed. All of the utilities must be roughed, including water, electricity, drainage, sewer, and elevator equipment. Other subcontractors install insulation. Heavy equipment, such as boilers and air conditioning equipment, is installed on the lower levels. Fig. 58-5.

7. *Completing the Exterior.* The roofs of many large buildings are flat. They are made of wood, steel, or reinforced concrete. Others have umbrella, dome-shaped, or gable roofs. The roof covering is made of a variety of materials. These include plastic insulation, slate, sheet metal, asbestos-cement, and built-in roofing. The exteriors of large buildings are completed in several different ways. Some are finished by installing curtain walls of masonry, stone, glass, or a combination of these. These walls are prefabricated, or built at a factory. They are lifted into place and then fastened to the outside (the skeleton, frame, or shell) of the building. Buildings of cast-in-place concrete often are finished on the exterior with brick, stone, and windows. Sometimes cast-in-place concrete exterior walls are unfinished. The only texture is the design that remains in the concrete after the forms are removed. Timber frame buildings may have an exterior of brick, stone, or wood.

8. *Completing the Interior.* The interior of the building is sprayed with insulating material before anything else is done. The interior itself may be natural, such as poured concrete walls. It may be finished with stone or plaster. The interior is divided into rooms by installing metal studs and drywall. All high-rise building plans provide openings for elevators. These may be installed or roughed in as the building is being built or after the skeleton or frame is completed.

Manufacturing companies have found that the most efficient industrial building is a one-story structure that covers a large land area. These one-story buildings usually have high ceilings to accommodate machinery.

As you can see, heavy building construction varies greatly. The type of building depends on its use and its location. By watching a large commercial building go up, you can learn a

58-5. This pipefitter is installing boiler equipment in the basement of a newly-constructed large commercial building.

great deal about the various stages of construction.

REVIEW QUESTIONS
1. What utilities must be available on the building site before construction can begin?
2. Which workers operate large earth-moving equipment?
3. What is a pile and what is it used for?
4. Name the three major ways of building the frame, shell, or skeleton of a building.
5. Which skilled craft persons install the boilers?
6. Describe a curtain wall.
7. How many stories tall is the most efficient manufacturing building?

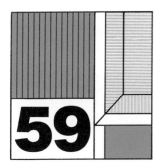

Residential Construction

59

Where do you live? Nowadays there are so many places a person can live. A person might live in a one-family house, duplex or two-family house, condominium, or apartment. They might live on a houseboat or in a mobile home. Long ago, people had to build their own homes. Today, we have trained builders. Building houses and other living units is called *residential construction* or *light construction*.

This chapter will describe the construction of a typical house.

Planning a Home

The kind of house built today depends on many things. It depends on location, the number of people who will occupy it, amount of land available, climate, building materials, skill of the workers, and cost. You can see that building a house takes careful planning.

Planning starts with an idea. The designer or architect puts this idea on paper in the form of drawings or plans called *blueprints*. These show what the house will look like and how big it will be. They also show the number of rooms, the size of each room, and what materials will be used. The blueprint in Fig. 59-1 shows a *floor plan* for the first floor. A *land (plot) plan* is also needed. It shows the boundaries of the property and the exact spot on the land where the house will be built.

Elevation plans show what the house will look like from the front, back, and each side.

Elevation plans for a one-story house are shown in Fig. 59-2.

The plans for the house also include a written list of all the materials to be used. These materials include the built-in appliances to be installed, and the care with which the work will be done. This written list is called the *specifications*, or "specs."

The Job of the Builder

The builder is like the director of a play. He or she takes the plans and makes them work. The builder figures out how much the house will cost to build and what its selling price will

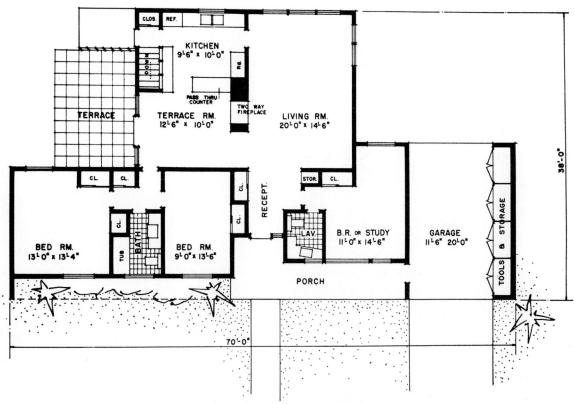

59-1. Floor plan for a house.

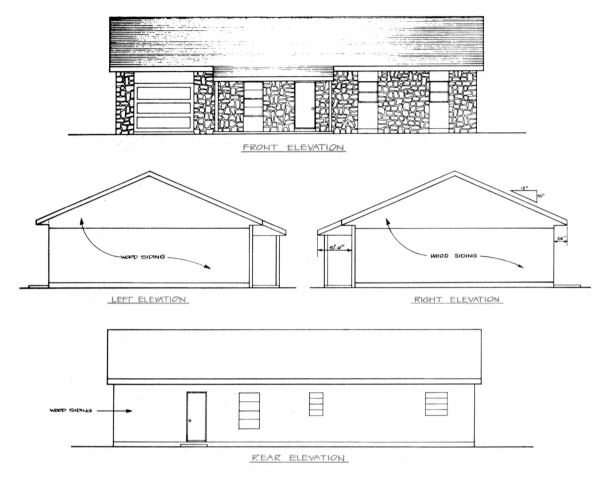

FRONT ELEVATION

WOOD SIDING

LEFT ELEVATION

WOOD SIDING

RIGHT ELEVATION

WOOD SIDING

REAR ELEVATION

59-2. The front, side, and rear elevations of a house.

be. The builder buys the best materials for the money and hires the best workers for the job. He or she makes sure that the natural environment, such as land and trees, is protected as the house is being built.

The director of the play makes sure that each actor comes on stage at the right time. In the same way, the builder makes sure that each worker is on the job at the time he or she is needed. For example, it would be a waste of time and money for the painter to be on the job before the walls are built.

Clearing the Land

First the land must be cleared with a bulldozer. This machine moves the topsoil into a big pile, which can be used after the house is built. Usually the builder makes a special effort to save trees and shrubs on the land. These can improve the value of the property.

Next, wood stakes are pounded into the earth to show where the corners of the house will be. Then the backhoe or other equipment begins to dig the basement. (Instead of a basement, some houses have concrete slab foundations which rest right on the ground.)

The cement masons build low double walls (forms) of wood that run around the inside of the hole. These forms will hold the concrete for the footings for the house. The *footings* are at the bottom part of the foundation walls. The footings are wider than the foundation walls because they must support the weight of the house. Footings are like your own foot, which must carry the weight of your body.

Concrete is cement mixed with water, sand, and gravel. The concrete arrives in huge mixer trucks ready to pour the foundation. The concrete slides down a long chute on the mixer and into the forms for the footings. When the concrete is dry, the wooden forms are removed.

The basement walls are built next. Some houses have walls of poured concrete, but the house in this example has concrete block walls. That's a job for the blocklayers. They work with *mortar*, which is a soft mixture of lime, cement, sand, and water. Mortar will harden after it is spread between the blocks and will hold them together. The blocklayers trim the blocks to fit with a bricklayer's hammer.

The cement masons will return later to fill the hole for the basement floor with gravel. They will cover it with waterproof sheeting and pour a concrete slab. They will set steel support posts in the middle of the floor. These posts will support the weight of the middle of the house.

Framework

First the carpenters put down the joists which support the floors. The *joists* are timbers placed across the foundation. Then the rough floorboards are laid down at an angle. In

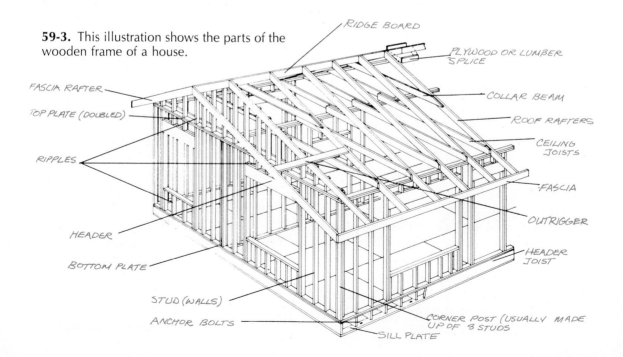

59-3. This illustration shows the parts of the wooden frame of a house.

most houses, plywood sheets are used instead of rough floorboards. These sheets or rough floorboards form the *subfloor*. Later, the regular floor will be laid on top of the rough subfloor. Two layers of flooring give the house a stronger floor.

Now the carpenters are ready to start the framework. Fig. 59-3. First they study the plans, which show what sizes to cut the wood. As the carpenters start to build the framework, it looks like a row of fence posts about 16″ apart. These posts are called *studs* or *two-by-fours*. A two-by-four is a piece of wood that actually measures 1½″ by 3½″. At each corner, the carpenters nail together three studs, called *corner posts*. After the exterior walls of the house are framed, the carpenters frame in the rooms.

Now it's time to build the roof. There are two ways to do this. The carpenters may nail joists across the top of the frame. They then put planks on top of the joists to stand on while they put up the rafters for the roof. The *rafters* are the sloped framing pieces that form the roof. Today, though, the carpenters usually use ready-made joist-and-rafter units, called *prefabricated trusses*. These look like triangles with braces.

By now the house is starting to take shape, but it's not a house yet. The builder must continue to check the blueprints.

Closing in the Structure

The next step is for the carpenters to close in the framework. They take large sheets of plywood or other sheeting material and nail them to the studs.

Up on the roof, carpenters finish closing in the roof. They cover the roof framework with large sheets of plywood.

The Roofers

The roof of a house is very important. It must keep out rain, snow, and ice. It must not leak. The roofers must make it weathertight. They put waterproof roofing felt on the roof to seal all the cracks before installing shingles or ties. They hang the gutters that catch rainwater and the leaders that direct it away from the house.

Finishing the Exterior

Homes with a furnace or fireplace must have chimneys. These are built by the masons. The plans tell them how big the chimney should be and what kind of fireplace is to be built. Everything must be built according to the "specs." The chimney must have the right amount of draft to carry smoke up through the chimney and not back into the house.

The outside of the house is finished by covering it with siding, shingles, brick, stone, or other materials.

Doors and Windows

The carpenters install the doors and windows. They drill holes in the doors for the doorknobs and the locks. Today, however, prehung doors and windows come complete from the factory with glass or screening. These are ready for the carpenters to install.

The Electrician

Now the house is ready for another member of the building team, the electrician. He or she must also check the blueprints to see where all the wires will go, how many electrical outlets and light fixtures will be needed for each room, and where the light switches go. The electrician must look for many other things, such as instructions for the doorbell and outside lights. The electrical contract for a house is a big one.

The electrician drills holes in the foundation wall where the main circuit box will be. He or she uses a drill to make holes for the main electric cables in the wooden joists and studs. The electrician strings the wires that are to be connected to the light switches and the electrical outlet boxes. He or she uses wire cutters to cut the ropelike cables that carry electricity. The electrician trims the wires so that they can be connected. These wires will carry electric power where it is needed. The electrician must take care that these wires are properly connected.

The Plumber

The plumber installs all the pipes that bring water and gas into the new house. The pipes may be copper, galvanized iron, or plastic. He or she uses wrenches, drills, hammers, saws, blowtorches, adhesives, and threading machines. The plumber connects two sets of water pipes from the main water line. One set goes to the water heater and then to the places where the washing machine, dishwasher, sinks, showers, and tubs will be connected. This is the hot water line. The other set is the cold water line. This goes directly to the places where appliances such as the washing machine will be connected. It goes also to the sinks, tubs, and toilets.

The plumber connects all the pipes from the main gas line that will go to such appliances as the stove, water heater, and clothes dryer. She or he connects the water heater and the furnace. The plumber connects the pipes that carry the waste water and sewage to the main sewer. He or she must make sure that all pipes are connected correctly, with no leaks.

The Plasterer

Next, the inside walls will be finished. First, however, the sheet metal worker must put in the air ducts that will carry warm air from the furnace and cool air from the air conditioning system. Also, the carpenter must install the insulation.

There are many ways to finish inside walls. There is the plastered wall which goes on wet and dries to a hard finish. The most popular wall, however, is *drywall*. Drywall is made of gypsum board, fiberboard, and similar sheet materials. Drywall is easily put up with nails. The joints are then smoothed over with tape and a pastelike material called *joint compound*. Once this is done, drywall can either be painted or covered with wallcovering. Drywall is solid and soundproof. These walls are not expensive to put up.

Drywall comes in large sheets 8′ long and 4′ wide. The drywall mechanic simply lines them up with the studs of the room and nails or glues them on. Then the spaces or joints between the drywall sections are covered with a special tape and joint compound. This makes the wall smooth. The joint compound hardens to make a stiff, smooth joint.

Interior Trim

Carpenters return to the job now to nail down the regular floors on top of the rough flooring. Sometimes the regular floors are of smooth hardwood. In some rooms carpets will be laid over the rough flooring. Other rooms may have vinyl, wood tile, or other floorcoverings. These jobs will be done by other workers.

Now the carpenters do all the interior trimming. They nail down the floor molding and install molding around doors, windows, and ceilings. Molding gives a neat, finished look to the places where the walls, doors, floors, and ceilings meet. This completes the work of the carpenters.

Other Jobs

The electrician must connect the appliances and add the lighting fixtures and all of the switches.

The plumber must connect many different fixtures and appliances. He or she is responsible for the things which involve water, sewer, and gas service to the house.

The painter paints the house exterior. Inside the house, she or he paints the walls, ceilings, doors, trim, and door and window frames. Painting makes the house and rooms more attractive. It also protects the surfaces it covers.

Painting is only one way to cover a wall. A wall may also be covered with paneling, tile, or wallcovering. Wallcovering may be of paper, plastic, cloth, or other materials. Putting up wallcovering is the job of the paperhanger.

The paperhanger mixes the paste and measures the walls. Then she or he cuts the wallcovering to fit the walls. The paste is spread on the back of the wallcovering. (Some wall coverings come prepasted.) The wallcovering is applied to the wall and smoothed out.

This job takes great care because the design on the wallcovering must match the design on the roll next to it.

There are a few more jobs to be done by the mason, such as outside steps, walks, or a patio. The mason builds the forms for the steps. He or she mixes the concrete, pours it into the forms and then smooths it out. The mason is skilled in using poured concrete.

The mason builds the walks and the patio. Sometimes, large smooth rocks and stones of different colors and interesting shapes are used. At other times, the mason uses poured concrete.

Next comes the driveway. This can be made of stones, gravel, concrete, or asphalt.

The carpenters, painters, paperhangers, masons, plasterers, electricians, plumbers, and all other workers have finished their work. The builder is still on the job. There is more work that needs to be done before the family can move in.

Landscaping

The landscapers must smooth the ground around the house. They must make sure that it slopes away from the house so that rain will not run under the foundation walls.

They push back the topsoil that was dug up when the land was cleared. Then they plant grass seed or lay thick strips of grass sod. The landscaping contract usually includes the planting of some trees, bushes, or flowers. These make the lot more attractive.

Learning About Carpentry

You have learned that people with many different skills are needed to complete a house or other wood building. In woodworking, your main interest will be in *carpentry*. There are many things you can build that will help you learn carpentry skills and techniques.

• Carpenters need such things as a tool box, miter box, and workbench. All of these can be built in class.

• A variety of outdoor furniture can be built using dimension lumber like that used in framing a house.

• You can build utility items such as mailboxes.

• You can make a pet house of different designs and sizes for your dog or other pet.

• A shed or lean-to to be used for tool storage, or as a playhouse, is a useful project.

• You can build a scale model of a house

following directions found in many carpentry books. The materials can be cut to scale, or a precut kit including the plans and materials can be ordered.

REVIEW QUESTIONS

1. Name some things to consider when deciding what kind of house to build.
2. Why are blueprints necessary?
3. What is the purpose of footings?
4. What is a two-by-four?
5. What materials are used to "close in" a house?
6. Name three workers who help to build the house after the carpenter has completed the exterior.

|||||||||||||||||||||||||||||||||||||||||||| *KEY IDEA* ||||||||||||||||||||||||||||||||||||||||||||||||||||

SUPPLY, DEMAND, AND PRICES

Supply and demand are important in our lives. For example, supply and demand affect the wages we are paid. These wages are really the prices we charge for performing work. Supply and demand also affect the prices of goods, services, and raw materials. They affect the "price," or interest, paid when we borrow money.

Two factors work together to determine the supply of a product or a service. The first factor is the cost of producing the product or service. The second factor is its selling price.

Suppose that buyers are willing to pay more for a product than it costs to produce. Then, a business may increase production to increase its profits. If it's large enough, this profit can

encourage new businesses to enter the field. This will create more competition among sellers. This tends to reduce prices or improve products—or both. It also means a larger supply of the product.

However, consumers may decide not to buy a product. They then are telling the supplier that the product is not worth the cost of producing it. If this continues, the product will be forced off the market. The company producing the product might then go out of business.

There is a balance between the supply of goods and services and the demand for them. Prices can affect demand. For example, when the auto model year is almost over, current

U.S. Department of Labor

Fig. A. New construction often means that there is a strong demand for housing and commercial buildings. It also means that there may be a heavy demand for construction workers.

models are often reduced in price. This is done to boost sales. For the same reason, department stores hold sales to reduce their inventories.

Food prices go up and down. The prices depend on the supply of agricultural products. However, the costs of such products are often a small part of the final price for many processed foods. For example, many farm products are used to make a loaf of bread. The cost of the farm products accounts for only about 16 percent of the bread's price. The other 84 percent of the price is for baking the bread and placing it in stores. Profit also is included.

In times past, people often obtained what they wanted by trading for it. This system was known as the *barter system*. One good or service would be exchanged for another. A piece of land, for example, might be traded for a team of oxen. Today, goods and services are not widely obtained in this way. Instead, money is used. Money is a convenient way to obtain goods and services. Also, money can be saved. In this way, it can be set aside for later use.

The buyer and the seller come together in the *marketplace*. The marketplace can be a used car lot, a supermarket, or a shoe repair shop. A marketplace is any place where money is exchanged for a product or a service. You take part in the marketplace whenever you buy or sell an item.

If you are buying an item, you may not give your money to the maker of the product. You may give it instead to a *middleman*. A middleman does not make the product. Instead, the middleman buys the product from its makers. The middleman then raises the price and sells the product to the buyer in the marketplace. One example of a middleman is a new car dealer. The dealer buys the cars from the factory and sells them to the customers.

When you buy a product, you are telling the maker that you like the product. You are telling the maker that there is a demand for the item. If the demand is great enough, the maker will make more of the product. Of course, if the maker makes too much of the product, the supply may exceed the demand. To sell the product, the maker might then have to lower the price. Or, too little of the product may have been made. Then, if there is a strong demand for the product, the price might be raised.

You can see that price, supply, and demand are related to one another. You can also see that the products you buy help decide what products will be made.

The law of supply and demand affects the price of housing and land. If you live in a city or a town, you can see the law of supply and demand in action in the housing market. There may be a house or two for sale on your block. Or, there may be a unit for rent in the apartment building in which you live. If you live in the country, a nearby farm may be for sale.

For this example, let's consider a town in which several houses are for sale. If there are several houses for sale, it might mean that there are more sellers than buyers. If there are only a few houses for sale, it might mean that there are more buyers than sellers. This, of course, is a very simple example. There are many conditions that affect the housing market.

Assume that the houses for sale are well-built. They are in good repair. They are located in neighborhoods that are quiet and well-maintained. Assume that the price asked for each house is a fair one. Still, the houses do not sell. Because there are more sellers than buyers, supply exceeds demand. For the houses to sell, they might have to be reduced in price.

The number of older houses for sale can affect the construction of new homes. If older homes are not selling, it is unlikely that new homes will be built. New homes would not be built because they might not sell. It is easy to see how the law of supply and demand affects the housing market.

Roads and Highways, Dams, and Bridges

Three other major areas of construction include highways, heavy general construction, and utilities. *Highway contractors* construct roads, airports, athletic fields, and other surface construction related to travel or recreation. *Heavy general-construction contractors* build bridges, dams, pipelines, and harbors. They also build waste disposal systems, docks, and military installations. *Utility contractors* build electrical plants and communication networks. These networks are for telephones, relay stations, and other types of communication. Much of this construction is funded by federal, state, or local agencies. Often it is paid for with tax money or other government money.

Weyerhaeuser Co.

60-1. Roads must be built to carry logs from the forest.

Roads and Highways

Roads and highways are the ways by which people move overland from one part of the country to another. Products also are moved over roads and highways. Generally, roads are of secondary importance and highways are primary travel routes. Such a ground transportation route may be a dirt road cut through a forest for log removal. Fig. 60-1. It also can be a superhighway. The United States has a 40,000-mile national system of interstate highways. These highways connect all major centers of population and industry.

MATERIALS

Roads are built of a variety of materials that will withstand weather and heavy loads. These materials include natural soil, natural gravel, and rock. Tar, asphalt, and portland cement concrete also are used. Most major highways have a final surface covering of either tar and/or asphalt or concrete.

FINANCING

The financing of public roads is done through federal and state road commissions.

Taxes on gasoline and on motor vehicles and trucks are the usual method of paying for public roads.

PLANNING

Highway planning is based on determining present and future transportation needs. Planning for a new road includes determining the type of road surface, including its width, curvature, and grades. It also includes planning for any needed bridges and tunnels. The shortest route can sometimes add expense if bridges or tunnels are needed.

Roads may be built on any kind of land—farmland, desert, or mountainous regions. Usually, civil engineers are hired to make the surveys and do the basic work. Architects who specialize in road building design the road. Once the final plans are completed, road projects are put out for bid. The contractor receives a detailed plan and specifications. There is an invitation to bid on the job. Once the bids are in, they are studied and approved.

CONSTRUCTION

Difficulty in constructing a road or highway depends largely on the land and the location. Usually, some clearing must be done. Then large earth-moving equipment must clear the highway bed and do needed excavating and filling. When necessary, temporary bridges are built across valleys and streams. With them in place, the road building can be continued beyond these points. Roadbeds are constructed by bringing in gravel, rock, and natural soil to provide a base. Also, the necessary utilities such as electrical wires are put in place alongside the roadbed. Bridges are completed after the roadbed is finished. This is also true for completing the access roads to the highway. The finished roadway is usually covered with bituminous material or concrete. Heavy paving equipment is used for this. After the roadway is completed, it is inspected by those who have financed the road. Usually, the inspectors work for state highway commissions and federal agencies. They make sure the road has been built to specification.

Dams

A dam is a large barrier placed across a stream or channel. Its main purpose is to raise the water level above the dam. The major parts of the dam include the dam itself, spillways to allow passage of floodwaters, and other outlets for regulating water. Dams have many purposes including flood control, irrigation, and power supply.

The major classifications of dams include earth-filled, rock-filled, gravity, arch, and buttress. The simplest dam is the *earth-filled dam.* This dam depends on huge mounds of earth to hold back the water. Earth dams have been used for thousands of years for flood control and irrigation.

In a *rock-filled dam*, over 50 percent of the dam's volume consists of dumped rock. This rock provides stability.

Gravity dams are built so that the weight of the material provides the stability. Today, most gravity dams are built of concrete or reinforced concrete. Fig. 60-2. Their foundations must be solid rock. Though most of these dams are straight, some dams are built to curve upstream.

The *arch dam* is one of the most important types of dam. It is often used if the dam is to be built between canyon walls. The arch shape curves upstream to give the needed stability. In an arch dam, the canyon walls absorb much of the pressure from the water behind the dam. Most of the large dams in the United States are arch dams.

Buttress dams are built with upstream sloping. There are very few buttress dams in the United States.

Designing and building dams is a highly specialized area of construction. It requires people with specific skills. Civil engineers, heavy machinery workers, cement finishers, operating engineers, ironworkers, and carpenters are needed. Dams are usually funded by the federal or state government.

60-2. The Shasta Dam in California is a gravity dam over 600' high.

American Concrete Institute

60-3. An arch bridge.

Bridges

The main purpose of a bridge is to provide a way to cross a waterway, valley, road, or other obstruction. Bridges vary from a simple rope footbridge to a superhighway or railroad bridge. All types of materials including wood, masonry, iron, steel, and reinforced concrete are needed. There are many different types of bridges including beam, truss, arch, cantilever, and suspension. A bridge may be either fixed or moveable.

TYPES OF BRIDGES

The simplest type of bridge is the *beam bridge* in which the horizontal member rests on two supports. *Truss bridges* have a rigid framework called a *truss*. In a *cantilever bridge*, the beams extend from piers toward each other. They are then joined directly or by a suspended connecting member. *Arch bridges*, built in the shape of an arc, have been used for years to span deep canyons and ravines. Fig. 60-3. Many of the early arch bridges were built of stone, but steel arcs are used today.

The most famous of all large bridges is the *suspension bridge*. A suspension bridge has a simple design. It has three major parts: towers, anchorages, and cables. Steel towers are used in most suspension bridges today. One of the most famous suspension bridges is the Brooklyn Bridge in New York. Fig. 60-4.

Pipelines

Another specialized area of construction is the building of pipelines and refineries. Oil

60-4. The Brooklyn Bridge, a suspension bridge that spans the East River between Brooklyn and Manhattan.

Zinc Institute

60-5. Here, gasoline from a tanker truck is being run into an underground storage tank. Much of the oil and gas used in the United States is moved by pipeline.

and gas are moved through pipelines. These pipelines move these energy materials from one part of the country to another or from ports on the coasts of the United States to

60-7. The underwater cable shown here was later placed at the bottom of the Hudson River. There, it carried telephone messages between several large eastern cities in the United States.

60-6. Chemical and mechanical engineers are needed to operate a refinery.

refineries. Fig. 60-5. Operating engineers, heavy equipment operators, pipe fitters, welders, and laborers are needed for building a pipeline. Refineries employ chemical and mechanical engineers. Fig. 60-6.

Utilities

Building power stations for generating electricity, including both conventional and atomic power, is another specialized part of heavy construction. To send electricity from one part of the country to another, utility lines and cables are laid underground. They also are placed in the water or stretched overhead on large towers. Fig. 60-7. Utility construction requires electrical engineers, construction electricians, and power line installers.

REVIEW QUESTIONS
1. From where does the money come for building most of our public roads and highways?
2. Name five different kinds of dams.
3. What are four major types of bridges?

Thinking about a Career

GARAGE BUILDER

In the small Texas town where Carmen grew up, every house had a garage. Since the houses were older, the garages were separate from the house. Generally, they were in the backyard. They were usually entered from the alley. They were much smaller than the garages built today. They were smaller because when the garages were built, the cars were smaller.

"Some of those garages were built for Model Ts," said Carmen. "By the time I graduated from high school, most of the garages were unused. They were too small. They had not been maintained. Many of them were about to fall down."

The garage in Carmen's back yard was just such a garage. Carmen's father and mother never parked their car in it. "We used it mostly to store junk in," says Carmen. "We also used it to store the lawnmower and the garden rakes and shovels."

Carmen never gave a thought to building a garage until she built one with her class as a construction project at the local high school. "I had taken one woodworking course my junior year," she says. "It was mostly shopwork—building small projects and turning spindles on the lathe. I liked that, but I was ready to work on a large project."

In Carmen's senior year, a construction course was offered for the first time. The project in the course was a single-car garage with space on one side for storage. The garage was to be built on school property. After being finished, it would be used to garage the tractor that was used to cut the grass on the school grounds.

"There were twenty people in the class," recalls Carmen. "Our job was to frame in the garage and finish it. We were also to hang the main garage door and the access door at the side. We were responsible for installing the three windows in the garage.

"The first few days of the course were spent in the classroom. That time was devoted to the study of the garage blueprints. The students also organized themselves into four work teams.

"We quickly realized the need for everyone to have certain responsibilities. Otherwise, it would have been confusing. Of course, we rotated jobs. By doing that, everyone gained experience in all phases of the project."

The students were not responsible for pouring the foundation. That was done by a local contractor. However, every other part of the project was their responsibility.

Carmen was a team leader for the first three weeks. These weeks were crucial to the smooth completion of the project. "Everyone was enthusiastic about the project," says Carmen. "In fact, some were too enthusiastic. I knew that if the work was not done slowly and carefully, it would not be done well."

Building the garage in class gave Carmen the idea of building a garage to replace the old garage in her backyard. She asked her dad about the idea. He said that he would pay for the materials. He also said that he would pay her $500 to build the garage. Since Carmen knew she would need help, she hired a classmate. She paid her $200. Neither Carmen nor her friend had jobs that summer. They were happy to be earning some money.

The enthusiasm that Carmen showed in building the garage brought Carmen and her friend to the attention of a local carpenter. He hired Carmen and her friend to help in his work. His direction helped them gain valuable carpentry skills. After two years working for him, Carmen and her friend had gained much experience. They had worked on a variety of projects, including several garages.

Carmen noticed that the need for new garages seemed to be fairly steady. She thought that she and her friend might go into business for themselves. They would specialize in the building of garages.

"Both of us had some savings," Carmen said. "But, we still needed to borrow some money. Both of us borrowed money from our parents. In the beginning, our office was a room in my parents' basement."

Carmen and her partner were dependable workers. Their prices for new garages were attractive. The customers were pleased with their work. After a year, Carmen and her partner decided to branch out into other towns. There, they placed ads in local papers. They advertised on the radio. Both of these approaches brought a good response. "At this point, we knew that we would need to hire help," said Carmen.

Carmen and her partner now employ over fifteen carpenters. They build garages in several Texas towns. All of the towns are in the same general area of the state. "Because our part of Texas has a relatively mild climate year-round, we have no long interruption in our building season," says Carmen.

The growth of Carmen's business changed her duties. She no longer works on the construction crew. Instead, she does the paperwork. She arranges for advertising and the purchase of materials. She also makes sales calls. Her partner is the general supervisor of the construction crews.

"I don't think that our business will decrease," says Carmen. "We have shown that we are able to do quality work at attractive prices. It seems that the need for new garages will remain fairly steady. Each year we have built more garages than in the previous year. We are now at the point where we could set up an office in several other Texas cities. But, I'm not sure that we will. We'll have to wait and see."

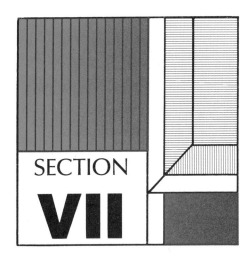

Careers

SECTION VII

U.S. Department of Labor

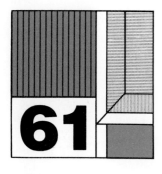

Careers

61

The economic strength of any nation depends on its workers. If the nation is to be prosperous, its workers must be skilled and competent. They must have a good understanding of their jobs. Obviously, there are many different job categories. In the world of manufacturing and construction, though, there are three basic types of workers. There are skilled workers, technicians, and engineers. All of these workers perform valuable jobs. Each of them, however, has different responsibilities. In the following pages, each of these jobs will be discussed.

Getting the Job You Want

The information presented here can help you make a career choice. To be ready for the job you want tomorrow, you should learn the facts about various occupations today. You should know what the jobs you are interested in are like. You should know how to qualify and train for them. You should know where the jobs are located. You should also learn about the employment outlook, earnings, and working conditions.

It is not too early to begin to decide on a career. Even while you are still in school, you can gather information on a job that you think might appeal to you. Of course the following guidelines apply to all jobs, not just to jobs in the fields of manufacturing and construction.

1. Refer to the *Occupational Outlook Handbook*. This book is published every two years by the U.S. Department of Labor. It provides information on over 700 occupations. It discusses the qualifications needed. It also discusses the demand for workers in a particular job. Working conditions and salaries are also covered. Sources of additional information are listed. This book is available in your local library. Your school guidance counselor should also have a copy.

2. Make the most of your school experience. Talk to your teachers or school counselor about which courses you should take. Choose those courses that broaden your general knowledge. Choose specific courses related to the occupation you're considering. For example, if you are interested in becoming a carpenter, enroll in courses in woodworking and construction.

3. Broaden your learning outside of school. If a certain job interests you, read about it at the public library. To develop your social skills, take part in volunteer activities. Try to obtain a summer job. The more you learn about life, the better will be your choice of a career.

4. Take vocational tests. These tests can alert you to your strong points. They also inform you of your weaknesses. This is valuable information. It can help you find the job for which you are best suited.

5. Learn how to fill out employment application forms properly. Filling out these forms is a necessary part of getting a job. The forms tend to be standard. Your school counselor may have some samples to show you. Obviously, you'll have a better chance for a job if your application is complete, legible, and accurate.

6. Develop job contacts. Talk to neighbors, and relatives about their jobs. Of course, you should seek advice from your school counselor. Let these people know in advance about your job interests. They can then advise and help you more effectively. Find out about job opportunities in your community. Knowledge of the local job market can help you make your own plans. The offices of union locals can offer information. You can also check with the state employment service. The newspaper classified ads can sometimes indicate the skills needed in a community.

Choosing a Career

Finding something you really like to do is one of the most important considerations in choosing a career. Here are some questions for you to ask yourself in that connection. Think carefully about your answers.

1. *Do I have the ability?* It is one thing to like a line of work—but it is another to be able to participate in it. Find out about your basic abilities by taking the courses and participating in the activities. Should you want to share in technological advance but not be able to master all the requirements for a professional career, perhaps you will want to consider becoming a technician.

2. *If I have the ability, do I also have the interest?* Ability, interest, and enthusiasm are essential if a person is to build a truly rewarding and successful career. There are many people with the necessary ability who would be miserable doing the work of an engineer. Such people will be happier—and will probably do more for themselves, for the economy and for society as a whole—if they go into some other line of work.

Skilled Workers

Skilled workers make patterns, models, tools, dies, machines, and equipment. Without these, there would be no industry. Skilled people repair the equipment used in industry. They also repair the mechanical equipment and appliances used by consumers. They also build homes, commercial and industrial buildings, and highways.

What's it like to be a skilled worker? That depends on the kind of work you are interested in. There are literally hundreds of different occupations in the classification of skilled worker. If you enjoy working with your hands, your job prospects are many and varied. You could work in transportation or communication facilities. Fig. 61-1. You could help build homes, office buildings, or factories. You could install and repair equipment. Skilled workers are needed in communications, transportation, forestry, and the building trades. They are also needed in the mining, petroleum, and electric power industries. Skilled workers are needed in the machine trades as mechanics and repair workers.

Several skilled occupations are listed below. Each of these skilled occupations has more

61-1. Telephone installers and repairpersons do much of their work outdoors. They must know the basics of electricity and electronics. They often use complex equipment to test circuits and equipment.

A.T. & T.

than a hundred thousand workers. Of these, carpenters are the largest group. They have almost one million workers. Automotive mechanics are the second largest group. They have over three-quarters of a million workers. Information about these jobs is available in the *Occupational Outlook Handbook*.

- Carpenters.
- Automotive mechanics.
- Electricians (construction and maintenance).
- Painters (construction and maintenance).
- All-around machinists.
- Plumbers and pipefitters.
- Operating engineers.
- Stationary engineers.
- Appliance servicepersons.
- Bricklayers.

- Compositors and typesetters.
- Industrial machinery repairpersons.
- Telephone and PBX installers and repairpersons.
- Tool and die makers.
- Aircraft mechanics.
- TV and radio service technicians.
- Air conditioning, refrigeration, and heating mechanics.

HOW TO PREPARE FOR A SKILLED JOB

Skilled workers must have a thorough knowledge of the processes involved in their work. They may be responsible for valuable equipment or products. Consequently, some skilled workers require considerable training to qualify for their jobs. A large proportion of skilled workers learn their trades through informal on-the-job training and experience. Many others learn their trades through apprenticeship training programs. Many acquire skills in the armed services. For others, vocational school training plays an important role.

One of the best ways to learn a skilled trade is through a formal apprenticeship program. Apprenticeship is a period of on-the-job training. There is also classroom instruction. The program is designed to teach the apprentice the materials, tools, and principles of the trade. The apprenticeship program gives the trainee a balanced knowledge of the trade. Most apprenticeship programs last four years. However, they may range from two to six years.

Apprenticeship has several advantages over less formal methods of learning a trade. An apprentice receives broader training and experience. Completion of an apprenticeship program is an advantage in finding and holding jobs. It also may increase opportunities for promotion to a supervisory-level job.

TECHNICIANS*

What's it like to be a technician? It depends on whom you ask. A metal, a plastics, a wood, or a computer technician will give very different answers. Each will have different responsibilities. Yet, there are things common to all technicians. They all help to put into action the ideas of scientists, engineers, and other professionals.

Technicians are active in areas where new technology is needed. They help in the search for new materials. They search for ways to safeguard our forests. They develop improved consumer products.

In the years ahead the need for skilled technicians will increase rapidly. The technological revolution of the past thirty years has created many career opportunities. Most of these careers require one or two years of technical education. These careers often lead

---

*Adapted courtesy of General Electric

61-2. Industrial technicians must plan the work flow within a factory. Often, they operate the equipment used to make a product.

61-3. Forestry technicians help to grow and harvest timber. They supervise production. They also help to protect the forests from fire and disease. These forestry students are getting on-the-job experience in a nursery. Thousands of hardy seedlings are grown in this nursery.

to advancement in supervisory work. The value of a technical education pays off in dollars and cents, too. A technician's salary is about double that of the average high school graduate.

Following are some examples of the kinds of opportunities open to someone who joins the fast-moving world of technicians.

Industrial technicians help develop ways of making new products. They work with automated systems such as computer-aided design and manufacturing. They may also specialize in industrial safety. Fig. 61-2.

Electrical technicians often work with the engineers in the field of power generation. They might work at massive power plants that serve large cities. They may also design new portable power systems for remote areas.

Forestry technicians may work as foresters improving our lumber supplies. Fig. 61-3. Other *wood technicians* develop new and improved wood products. Still others work in the furniture or housing industry.

Mechanical technicians help engineers design and develop machinery and other equipment. A mechanical technician may specialize and become a robot technician. He or she might also become a diesel technician or a machine and tool designer.

Metallurgical technicians are involved in the processing of metals into finished products.

Civil engineering technicians may specialize in one of several areas. They may help develop new techniques for building bridges and other structures. They may assist in highway planning or road building, or they may work in the field of automated transportation.

Architectural technicians may work in urban planning. They may help develop programs to rebuild and revitalize city areas. This work would include construction. It also would include park maintenance, traffic control, and air pollution control, as well. *Drafters* and *surveyor technicians* fall under this category. Drafters turn the ideas and sketches of engineers into working plans.

Survey technicians assist surveyors in gathering information about the physical makeup of a construction site. The survey is the first step in building highways, airfields, bridges, dams, and buildings. Survey teams also locate land boundaries and collect information for mapmaking and mining.

Computer technicians are electronics specialists. They test and inspect electronic components. They do complex assembly work. They also work in research and development. Some repair computers. Others are involved in technologies used to prepare computer circuit boards.

HOW TO PREPARE FOR A CAREER AS A TECHNICIAN

The skills necessary to help you gain a career as a technician may be obtained in a variety of ways. A year or two of technical study and training is needed after high school. This experience may be obtained at one of the following:

Technical institutes. Students receive intensive training. This qualifies them for entry-level technician jobs immediately after graduation. Practical work and laboratory work are usually emphasized.

Junior and community colleges. Programs offered are similar to those of technical institutes. There is more emphasis on theory. Courses in liberal arts (English and social sciences) are offered.

Vocational schools. The technical subjects taught are usually geared to the work available in the community area. High-school level and adult-education courses are also offered.

Many schools offer evening sessions so that high school graduates can work while they continue their education. Special examinations are offered for those who are not high school graduates. Such schools also will help a person complete a high school education.

No matter what technical career you follow, a well-rounded education in the basic high school subjects is helpful. Mathematics and science courses give you a sound background in the sources of technology. The study of English will help you express yourself clearly and accurately. History and political science stimulate your thinking. Industrial education, technology, and drafting help you recognize your aptitudes for technical work.

Ask your teachers and guidance counselor for advice about your career plans. They can best advise you on study programs. They can tell you the entrance requirements of technical institutes and community colleges.

Today is the time to plan for tomorrow. You may decide on a career in any of the fascinating areas of technology. If so, you can be sure of a good salary, responsibility, and respect.

Engineer

What is the job of an engineer? If you were to ask several engineers that question, you might receive several different answers. There are more than fifty different types of engineer.

The first people to practice engineering as we know it today were probably military leaders. Leaders of the Roman legions were usually skilled military engineers. They designed and built roads and bridges. Some of these are still in use after nearly 2000 years. They also built fortifications.

Early engineers were self-educated. There were no real engineering schools until about 1660. The graduates of these schools were called civilian engineers or civil engineers. Their job was different than that of military engineers. Even today, civil engineers are concerned chiefly with the design of public works, such as roads, bridges, and harbors.

In industry, the design for a product cannot be sent straight to the production line. It is necessary first to find out more about the materials and processes involved. This is the work of scientists and engineers. Many decisions must be made.

Have you ever seen a picture of the first typewriter? It was many times heavier than the typewriter used today. Typewriters today are lighter because they are made of improved alloys. (An alloy is a mixture of two metals or a metal and a nonmetal.) Every day some industry faces the problem of which alloy to use. Sometimes an existing alloy will work. At other times, the metallurgist must develop a new alloy.

Engineers apply science to create new products and processes. The ways they do this may be highly original and may involve research. There are many specialties in engineering. Others will emerge as technology becomes more complex. Two of the specialties that are in continuing demand in industry are mechanical and electrical engineering.

Mechanical engineers design and make machinery for all branches of industry as well as for the home. In some cases, they design new machines. In other cases, they may improve machines. In both cases, they are seeking to produce good products at a low cost. Mechanical engineers also solve problems in the operation of equipment. They help increase production by developing methods for preventive maintenance.

Electrical engineers design electric power systems for industry and for the home. Electrical engineers have helped develop the telephone, radio, television, and radar.

There are, of course, other engineering specialties. Civil engineering is the oldest branch of engineering. In industry, the civil engineer designs and constructs plant buildings and other facilities.

Petroleum engineering deals with all phases of the petroleum industry, from the location of petroleum in the ground to delivery to the user. Fig. 61-4.

The *architectural engineer* designs structures that are safe, economical, and beautiful.

The computer is a vital tool for all engineers. It is especially useful for those involved in product design and manufacturing. Engineers are closely involved with computer-aided design (CAD). They are also involved in computer-aided manufacture (CAM). The field of computer-aided design (CAD) is growing rapidly. In CAD, computers translate engineering drawings into three-dimensional

61-4. The petroleum engineer locates oil deposits. He or she also recommends methods of recovering the oil. The engineer shown here is at a drilling rig. She is discussing problems the rig operator has encountered. Drilling rigs are not always on the land. Often, they are on platforms in open water miles from land.

renderings on a video screen. The object can be looked at from all sides. It can even be looked at from inside. Using CAD, an engineer can check several designs. There is no need to build a model first.

But CAD is only the beginning. Computers that help design products are linked to computers that help manufacture products. Such manufacturing is known as computer-aided manufacturing (CAM).

CAM includes *robotics*, a vital area in manufacturing. Fig. 61-5. Robots perform demanding chores such as firing blast furnaces. They also handle repetitive jobs, allowing humans to do more complex ones. Robotics is particularly useful on assembly lines.

If you decide on engineering as a career, the field you choose will depend partly on how opportunities develop between now and the time you begin to specialize in college, partly on the course offerings available and, most important, on your own interests and aptitudes.

HOW TO PREPARE FOR A CAREER IN ENGINEERING

A career in engineering requires a broad knowledge of math and science. It also requires good communication skills. An engineer must be able to communicate clearly. If you plan to study engineering in college, you will need to study certain subjects in high school. These subjects include:

- 4 years of English.
- 4 years of mathematics.
- 3 or 4 years of history and social studies, including economics.
- 3 years of one foreign language.
- 2 or 4 years of science (1 year of chemistry and 1 year of physics are usually suggested).

Courses in technology and drafting are also helpful. Not every college requires this full program for entrance.

Everyone considers many things in selecting a college. Its reputation and location must be considered. The recommendations of friends and the availability of scholarships are important. People interested in engineering have another decision. Should such a person go to a liberal arts college or an engineering college? Or, should a person go to a university that combines both?

Some will have developed a definite professional interest by the time they are ready to enter college. For them, the choice may be obvious. However, others may not have a specific professional goal. They should remember that in many universities it is possi-

61-5. Engineers must be familiar with computer-aided design (CAD) and computer-aided manufacturing (CAM). This engineer is using a computer to check on the movements of the robot shown in the background.

obtain a higher degree. Those who obtain higher degrees will later have a broader choice of jobs. They also will have better financial opportunities. Those who decide on a career in engineering will be qualified for a number of jobs. Jobs in management as well as in research are available. Engineers are well paid. Their work is interesting and important.

REVIEW QUESTIONS

1. What government publication provides valuable information on over 700 occupations?
2. How can a vocational test benefit you?
3. What are the advantages of an apprenticeship program?
4. What high school courses will help prepare you for a career in engineering?

ble to combine liberal arts and engineering courses.

After you obtain your bachelor's degree, you may want to go on to graduate school to

422

DRAFTING PROBLEMS

Make an orthographic drawing of each of the following drafting problems. Dimension the orthographic drawing.

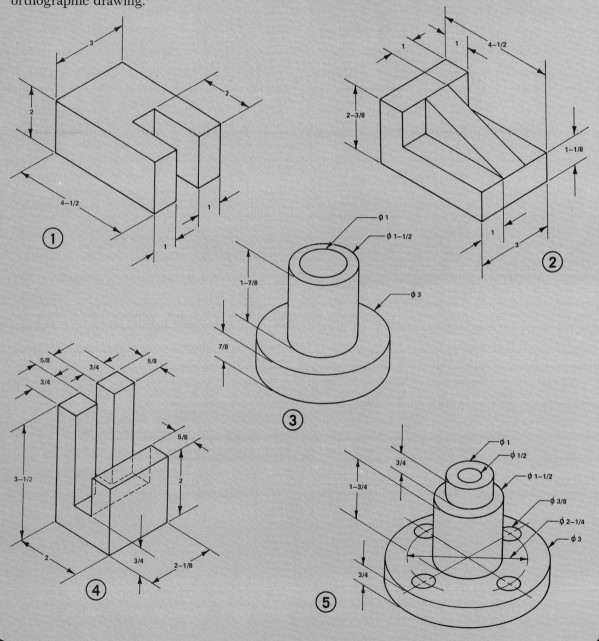

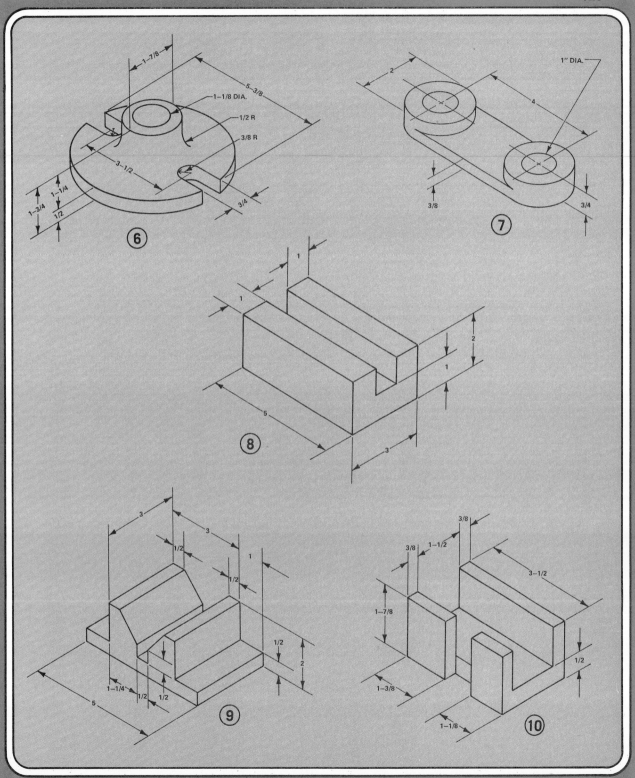

PROJECTS

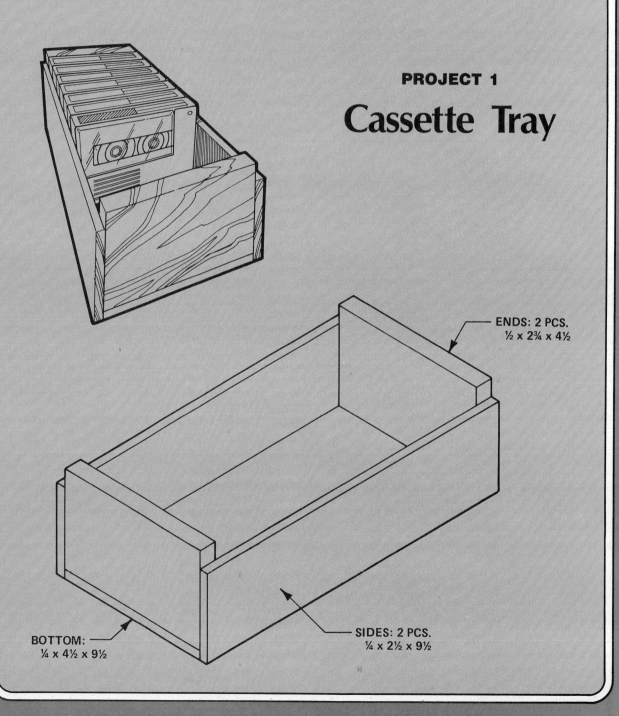

PROJECT 1

Cassette Tray

ENDS: 2 PCS.
½ x 2¾ x 4½

SIDES: 2 PCS.
¼ x 2½ x 9½

BOTTOM:
¼ x 4½ x 9½

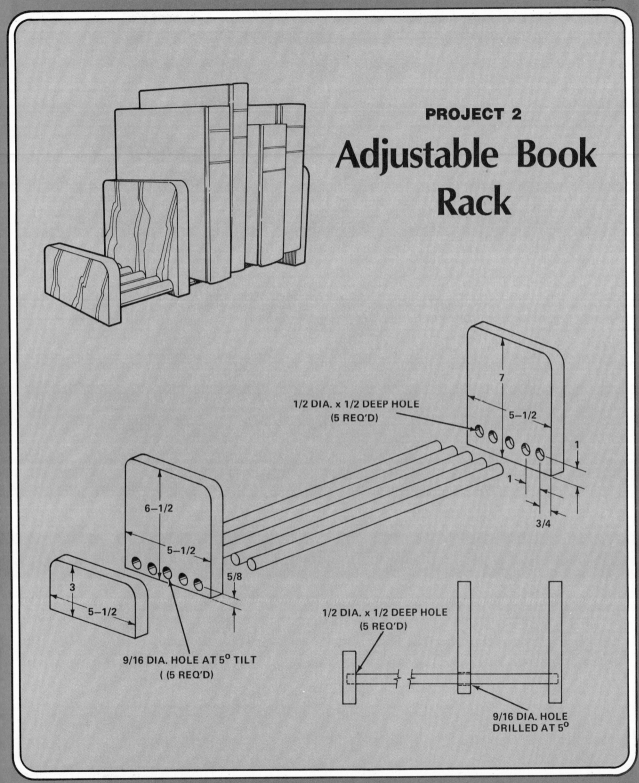

PROJECT 2

Adjustable Book Rack

1/2 DIA. x 1/2 DEEP HOLE
(5 REQ'D)

7

5–1/2

1

1

3/4

6–1/2

5–1/2

5/8

3

5–1/2

9/16 DIA. HOLE AT 5° TILT
((5 REQ'D)

1/2 DIA. x 1/2 DEEP HOLE
(5 REQ'D)

9/16 DIA. HOLE
DRILLED AT 5°

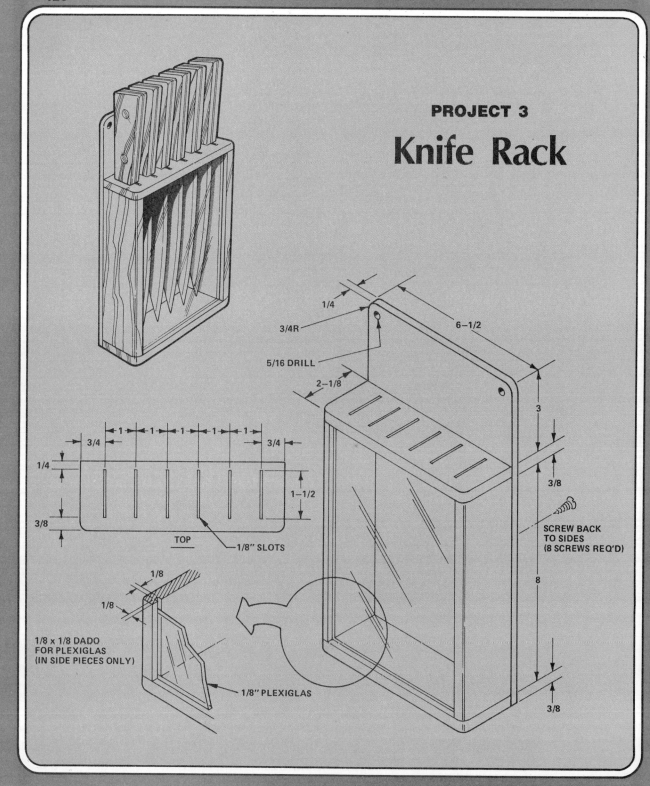

PROJECT 3
Knife Rack

1/4

3/4R

5/16 DRILL

2–1/8

6–1/2

3

3/8

SCREW BACK
TO SIDES
(8 SCREWS REQ'D)

8

3/8

3/4 — 1 — 1 — 1 — 1 — 1 — 3/4

1/4

1–1/2

3/8

TOP

1/8" SLOTS

1/8

1/8

1/8 x 1/8 DADO
FOR PLEXIGLAS
(IN SIDE PIECES ONLY)

1/8" PLEXIGLAS

PROJECT 4

Storage Cabinet

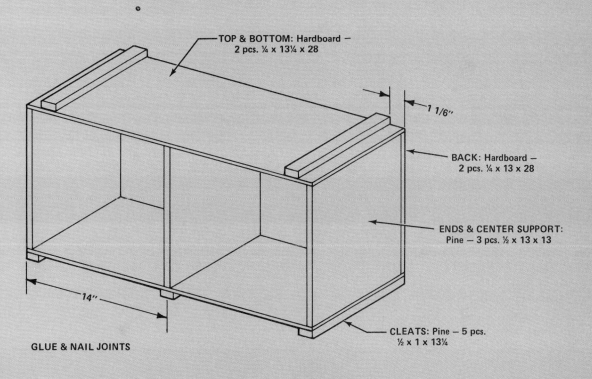

TOP & BOTTOM: Hardboard —
2 pcs. ¼ x 13¼ x 28

1 1/6''

BACK: Hardboard —
2 pcs. ¼ x 13 x 28

ENDS & CENTER SUPPORT:
Pine — 3 pcs. ½ x 13 x 13

14''

CLEATS: Pine — 5 pcs.
½ x 1 x 13¼

GLUE & NAIL JOINTS

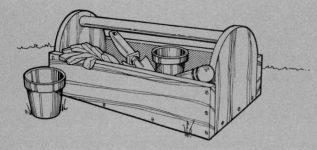

PROJECT 5
Gardener's Toolbox

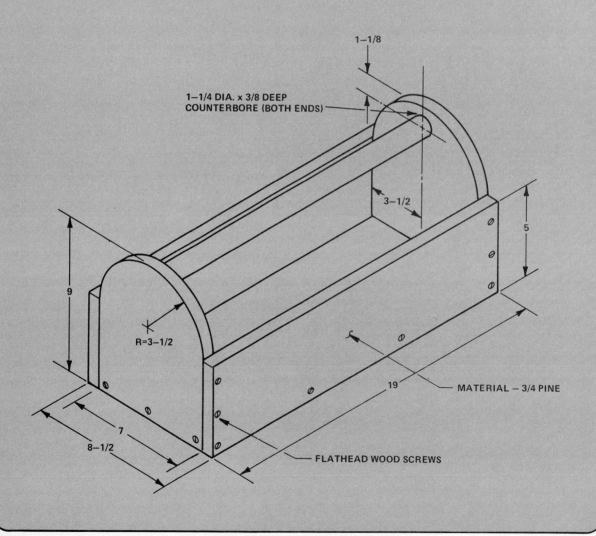

1–1/8

1–1/4 DIA. x 3/8 DEEP
COUNTERBORE (BOTH ENDS)

3–1/2

5

9

R=3–1/2

7

8–1/2

19

MATERIAL — 3/4 PINE

FLATHEAD WOOD SCREWS

PROJECT 6
Stool

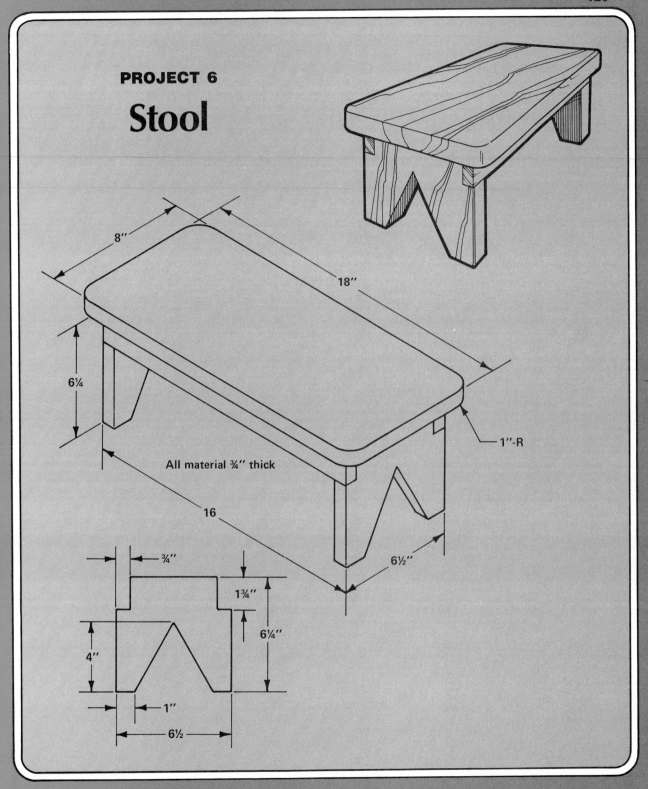

8"

18"

6¼

1"-R

All material ¾" thick

16

6½"

¾"

1¾"

6¼"

4"

1"

6½

PROJECT 7
Birdhouse

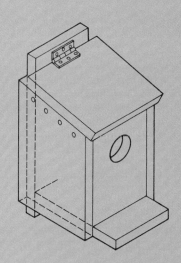

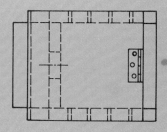

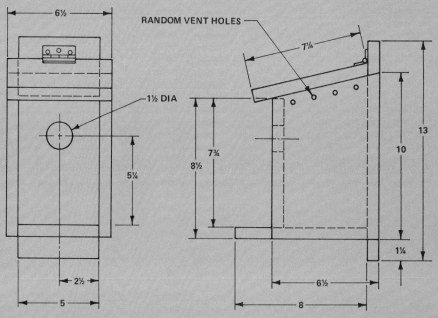

RANDOM VENT HOLES

1½ DIA

6½

5

2½

5¼

7¼

8½
7¾

6½

8

13

10

1¼

PROJECT 8

Garden Hose Holder

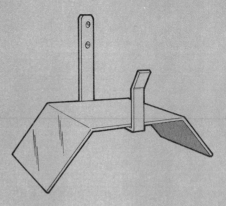

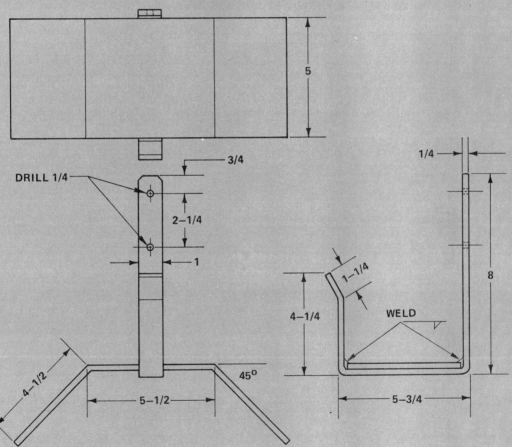

5

3/4

DRILL 1/4

2–1/4

1

4–1/2

5–1/2

45°

1/4

1–1/4

WELD

4–1/4

8

5–3/4

BRACKET 1/4 x 1 x 18 H.R.S.
APRON 5 x 14–1/2 x 11 GA. SHEET STEEL

PROJECT 9
Cold Chisel

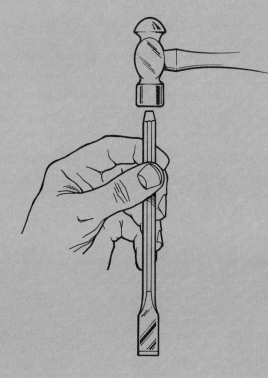

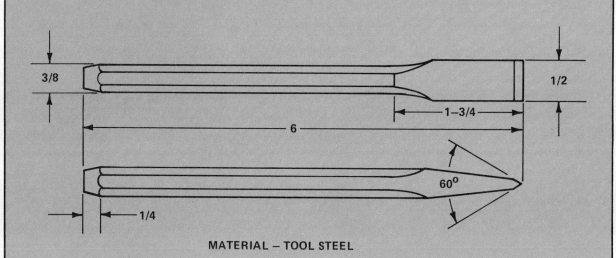

3/8

1/2

1-3/4

6

1/4

60°

MATERIAL — TOOL STEEL

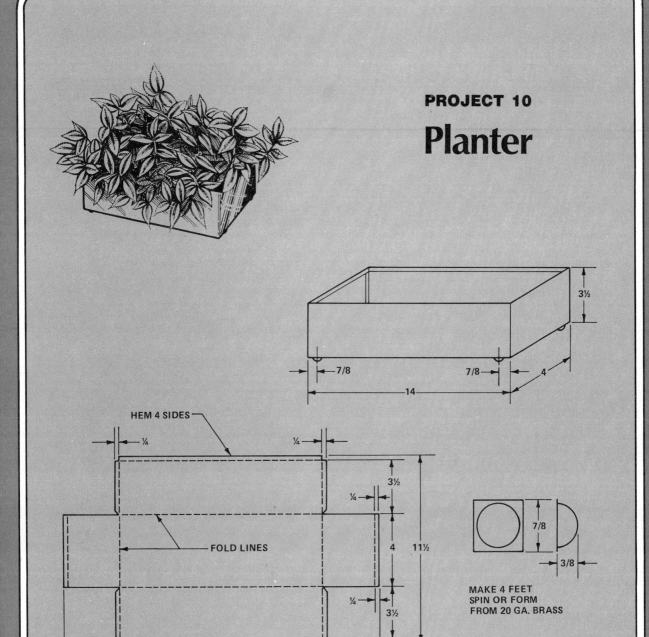

PROJECT 10
Planter

3½

7/8

7/8

4

14

HEM 4 SIDES

¼

¼

FOLD LINES

3½

¼

4

11½

¼

3½

3½

14

3½

21½

7/8

3/8

MAKE 4 FEET
SPIN OR FORM
FROM 20 GA. BRASS

PLANTER MATERIAL — 24 GA. BRASS

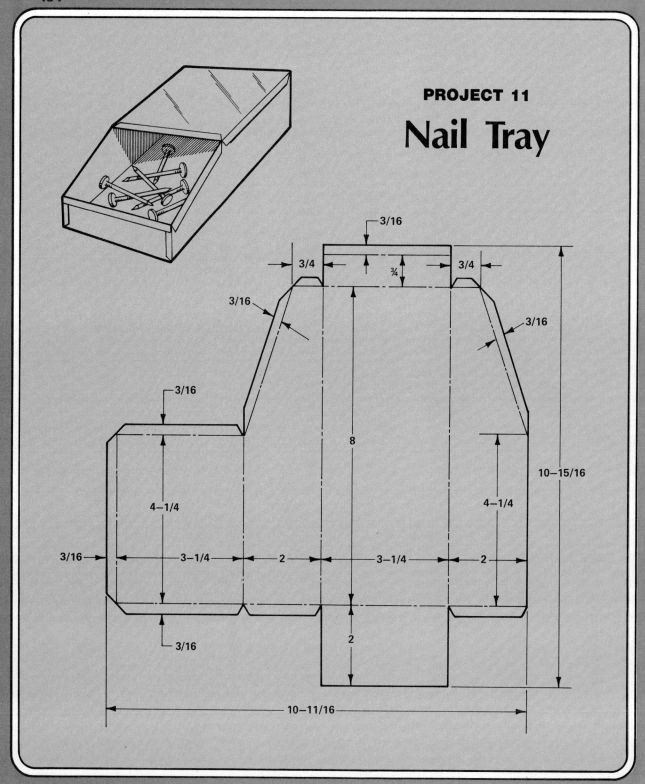

PROJECT 11
Nail Tray

PROJECT 12

Dustpan

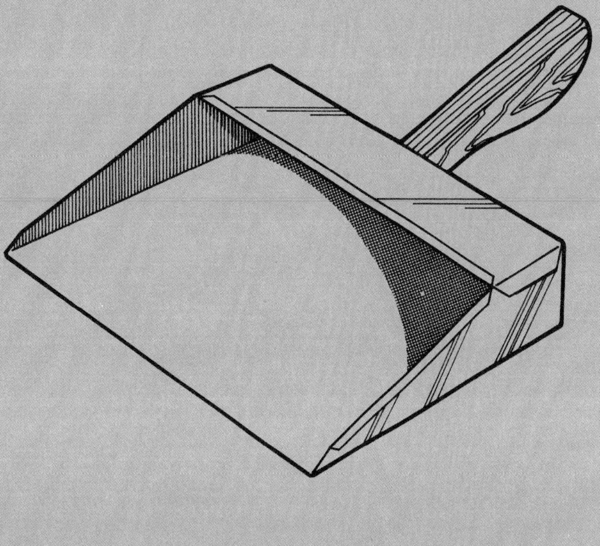

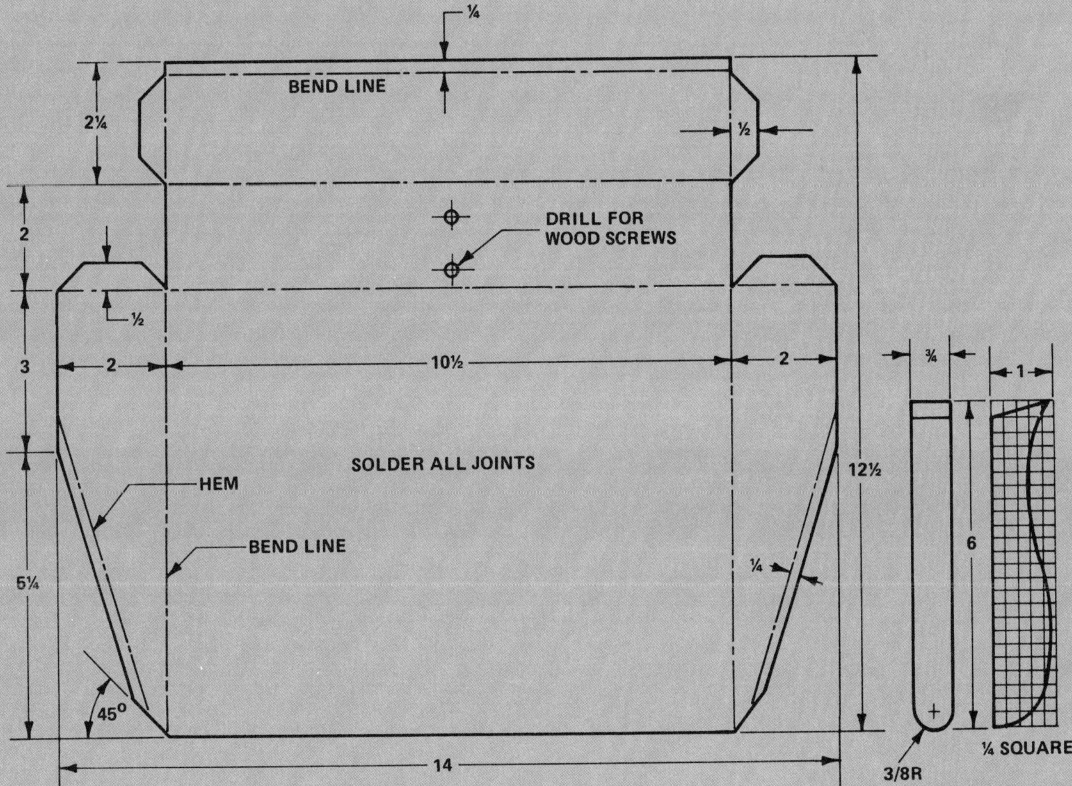

¼

BEND LINE

2¼

½

2

DRILL FOR
WOOD SCREWS

½

3

2

10½

2

12½

SOLDER ALL JOINTS

HEM

BEND LINE

¼

5¼

45°

14

MATERIAL — 28 GA. GALVANIZED SHEET METAL

¾

1

6

¼ SQUARES

3/8R

HANDLE — MAPLE

436

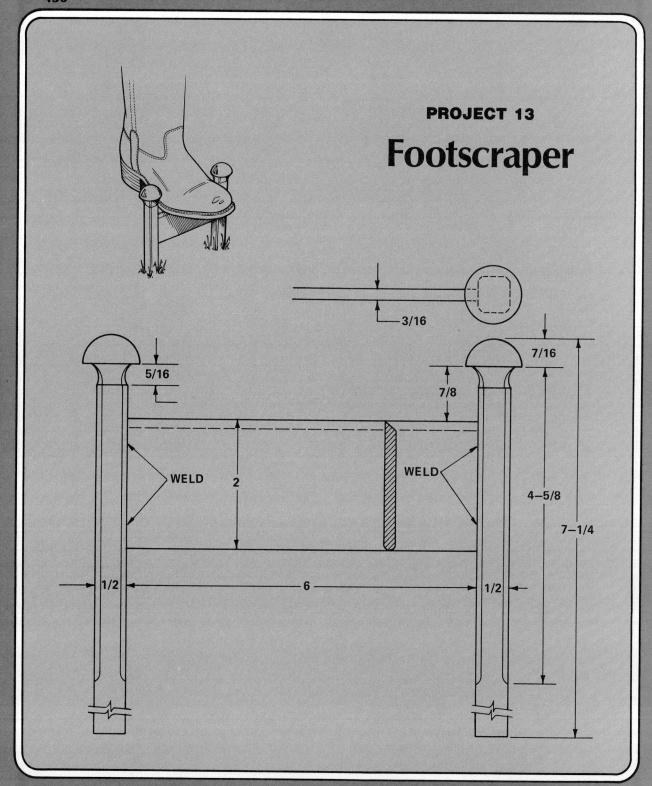

PROJECT 13

Footscraper

3/16

5/16

7/16

7/8

WELD 2 WELD

4–5/8

7–1/4

1/2 6 1/2

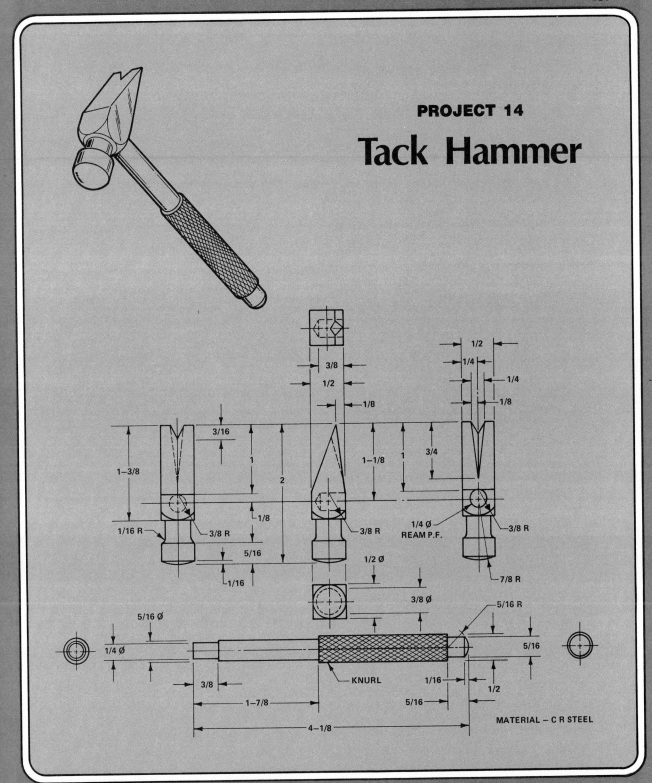

PROJECT 14
Tack Hammer

MATERIAL – C R STEEL

PROJECT 15
Letter Opener

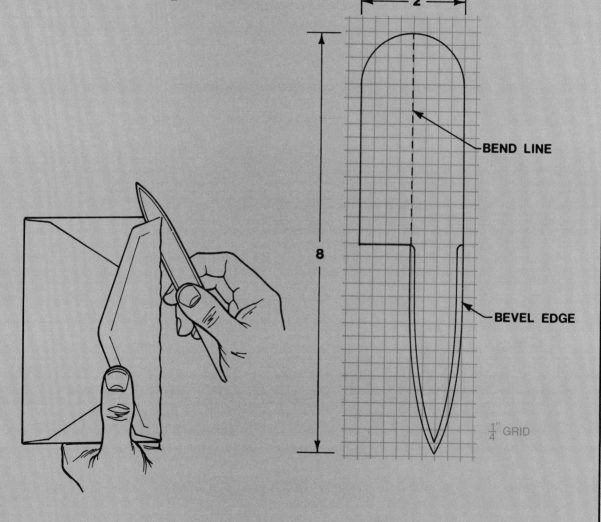

2

8

BEND LINE

BEVEL EDGE

$\frac{1"}{4}$ GRID

439

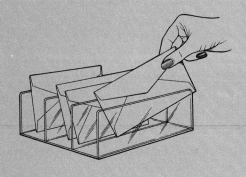

PROJECT 16
Letter File

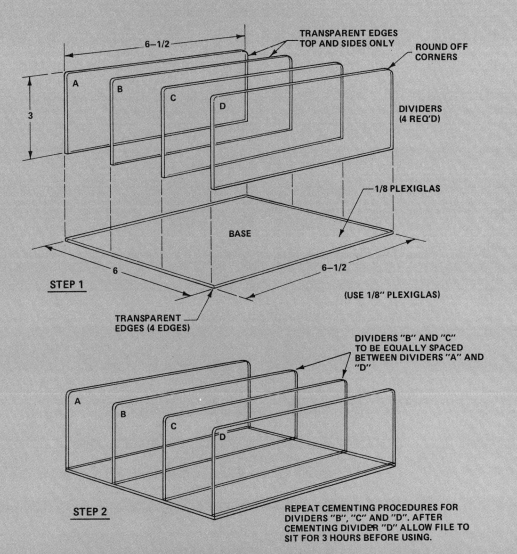

TRANSPARENT EDGES
TOP AND SIDES ONLY

ROUND OFF
CORNERS

6–1/2

A   B   C   D

3

DIVIDERS
(4 REQ'D)

1/8 PLEXIGLAS

BASE

6   6–1/2

STEP 1

TRANSPARENT
EDGES (4 EDGES)

(USE 1/8" PLEXIGLAS)

DIVIDERS "B" AND "C"
TO BE EQUALLY SPACED
BETWEEN DIVIDERS "A" AND
"D"

A   B   C   D

STEP 2

REPEAT CEMENTING PROCEDURES FOR
DIVIDERS "B", "C" AND "D". AFTER
CEMENTING DIVIDER "D" ALLOW FILE TO
SIT FOR 3 HOURS BEFORE USING.

440

PROJECT 17
Pencil and Notepad Holder

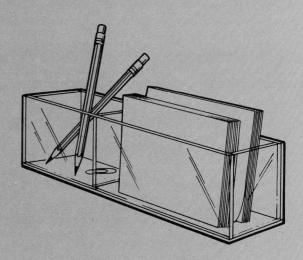

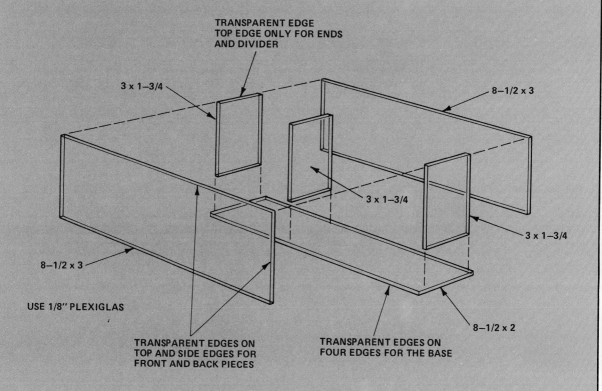

TRANSPARENT EDGE
TOP EDGE ONLY FOR ENDS
AND DIVIDER

3 x 1–3/4

8–1/2 x 3

3 x 1–3/4

8–1/2 x 3

3 x 1–3/4

8–1/2 x 2

USE 1/8" PLEXIGLAS

TRANSPARENT EDGES ON
TOP AND SIDE EDGES FOR
FRONT AND BACK PIECES

TRANSPARENT EDGES ON
FOUR EDGES FOR THE BASE

Index

61-5. Engineers must be familiar with computer-aided design (CAD) and computer-aided manufacturing (CAM). This engineer is using a computer to check on the movements of the robot shown in the background.

obtain a higher degree. Those who obtain higher degrees will later have a broader choice of jobs. They also will have better financial opportunities. Those who decide on a career in engineering will be qualified for a number of jobs. Jobs in management as well as in research are available. Engineers are well paid. Their work is interesting and important.

REVIEW QUESTIONS

1. What government publication provides valuable information on over 700 occupations?
2. How can a vocational test benefit you?
3. What are the advantages of an apprenticeship program?
4. What high school courses will help prepare you for a career in engineering?

ble to combine liberal arts and engineering courses.

After you obtain your bachelor's degree, you may want to go on to graduate school to